THE
SPECIAL EDUCATOR'S
GUIDE TO
COLLABORATION

Second Edition of *COLLABORATION: A SUCCESS STRATEGY FOR SPECIAL EDUCATORS*

THE
SPECIAL EDUCATOR'S
GUIDE TO
COLLABORATION

IMPROVING RELATIONSHIPS WITH
CO-TEACHERS, TEAMS, AND FAMILIES

Second Edition of COLLABORATION: A SUCCESS STRATEGY FOR SPECIAL EDUCATORS

SHARON F. CRAMER

CORWIN PRESS
A SAGE Publications Company
Thousand Oaks, California

For information:

Corwin Press
A Sage Publications Company
2455 Teller Road
Thousand Oaks, California 91320
www.corwinpress.com

Sage Publications Ltd.
1 Oliver's Yard
55 City Road
London EC1Y 1SP
United Kingdom

Sage Publications India Pvt. Ltd.
B-42, Panchsheel Enclave
Post Box 4109
New Delhi 110 017 India

Printed in the United States of America

Library of Congress Cataloging-in-Publication Data

Cramer, Sharon F.
The special educator's guide to collaboration: Improving relationships
with co-teachers, teams, and families / Sharon F. Cramer.— 2nd ed.
        p. cm.
Rev. ed of: Collaboration. 1997.
Includes bibliographical references and index.
ISBN 1-4129-1490-6 (cloth)—ISBN 1-4129-1491-4 (pbk.)
1. Special education teachers—Professional relationships. 2. Group work in education.
3. Teaching teams. I. Cramer, Sharon F. Collaboration. II. Title.
LC3969.C73 2006
371.9′04—dc22

                                        2006001792

This book is printed on acid-free paper.

06   07   08   09   10   9   8   7   6   5   4   3   2   1

Acquisitions Editor:	Kylee Liegl
Editorial Assistant:	Nadia Kashper
Production Editor:	Melanie Birdsall
Typesetter:	C&M Digitals (P) Ltd.
Copyeditor:	Diana Breti
Indexer:	Kathy Paparchontis
Cover Designer:	Michael Dubowe

Contents

Preface to the Second Edition

Special education teachers collaborate with adults in schools every day. Using collaboration as the basis for job pride and satisfaction, special education teachers can be roughly classified as one of two types of people at different points in their careers:

- *It's All Right With Me!* "I am so glad I took this job! I never thought I'd have such a sense of professional fulfillment so early in my career. I leave my building each night reflecting on the differences we make in the lives of our students. I love working with Jessica, Harold, and Satish. I can't wait for Monday!"
- *Working on the Chain Gang.* "Why did I ever take this job? I can't remember a day when I didn't feel disappointed, frustrated, or angry with Jessica. Harold and Satish aren't much better. Every weekend is the same—Saturday, I'm rushing around catching up on my life, Sundays are spent preparing for the week and thinking about how much I hate my job and especially Jessica. When the alarm clock goes off on Monday morning, the only good thought is 'Maybe Jessica will call in sick today.'"

The first edition of this book was written nearly a decade ago; this edition is being published 30 years after the passage of P.L. 94–142. However, the need for this book and the questions it raises still exists. Its audience remains teachers who want to improve the ways they work with others in schools who want to get off the "collaboration chain gang."

Can anything be done when essential collaborative relationships are unsatisfactory? Yes! This book was inspired by projects that master's students in special education (many of whom were already teaching) developed to answer this question.

- They learned that they did not have to suffer through the agonies of unfulfilled or difficult relationships with others in their educational settings.
- Students designed and carried out projects to change their professional interactions.
- The satisfying outcomes they achieved (and their resulting astonishment) have been the catalysts for this book.

WHAT THIS BOOK *IS*

This book gives special education teachers (as well as those preparing to be special education teachers) realistic tools to incorporate into day-to-day working relationships with fellow teachers, para-educators, and administrators. Ideas presented in this book can be used to improve successful collaborative teams and work with family members.

This book was written because other books focusing on collaboration often presume that if teachers become better problem solvers and develop their communication skills they can effectively collaborate. This book takes a very different approach. It presumes that it is naive to assume that problem solving or communication skills alone are adequate resources for teachers to overcome collaboration barriers. In this book, better communication skills are a subset of what teachers need to learn, and to use, to collaborate. Other, more substantive strategies are provided. After completing the main project and try-outs, special education teachers and preservice teachers will have a sophisticated set of collaboration insights and capabilities.

This book has a clear point of view. It is structured around a presumption that a collaboration project will take place.

- Special education teachers who pick this book up on their own can use it for self-study.
- Special education teachers who decide to use this book for professional development can use it as the basis for a year-long program.
- Instructors teaching special education teachers in training can use it to structure a course on collaboration.

WHAT THIS BOOK *IS NOT*

This is not a "typical" collaboration book. It has three presumptions:

1. The collaboration project will be the focus of the professional development activity.

2. In most cases, when a professional relationship is unsuccessful, one person in the relationship is more motivated to make changes than the other. It offers the option of shared work on a relationship but focuses on the circumstances in which many teachers find themselves: another person is driving them crazy (or underperforming, or distant), and something has to change. Odd is the notion that "collaboration" can be the primary responsibility of one person in a relationship, but that is the underlying assumption of this book.

3. The book assumes that people reading it are ready to change their attitudes and their behaviors. The relationship upon which they are focusing does not have to be terrible—it could be just getting bad, or it could be new. But if you picked up this book looking for a "quick fix" for a collaboration challenge, you had best put it down and find another one.

SPECIAL FEATURES

This book contains the following special features:

- Text and data-based selections from among the more than 1,000 collaboration projects completed by students in college classes

- Text box "voices" of teachers expressing a wide range of thoughts and feelings, frustrations and successes experienced when collaborating
- Up-to-date references throughout the book, including an overview of literature on collaboration (Chapter 1) and the legislative context for collaboration (Chapter 2)
- Idea Try-Outs: Step-by-step reflection activities designed to promote independent, innovative thinking about collaboration
- Project Try-Outs: Step-by-step research and interview activities designed to give teachers structured, focused ways to test their collaboration skills
- Collaboration notebooks are referred to, so that teachers can systematically record their progress
- Preparation, implementation, and analysis of a collaboration project (Chapters 3 to 10). Teachers at any stage of their career can benefit from this book's focused method of improving a collaborative effort
- Generalization beyond the collaboration project to work with members of families (Chapter 11) and interdisciplinary teams (Chapter 12)

AUDIENCE

This book has been designed for three primary audiences and a fourth secondary audience:

- *Audience 1:* A multi-session professional development series sponsored by a school or district for special education teachers who are interested in improving their collaboration relationships.

- *Audience 2:* Traditional undergraduate and graduate special education teacher preparation programs. Students can best benefit from this book if they are familiar with assessment techniques. Special education teachers-in-training who are close to graduation and special education teachers who are returning to school for advanced coursework can use this book.

- *Audience 3:* Self-study by special education teachers. A collaboration resource network (see Chapter 6) would provide peer counsel. This book could give an independent teacher the structure to use to turn around working relationships at school.

Individuals who are "on their own" have written to me about their success in using this book for self-study. Sufficient materials are provided in the book to enable this approach to work for the motivated reader.

- *Audience 4:* General educators can use this book to examine how their collaboration with others (special educators, general educators, administrators) could be improved.

FOR THE SECOND EDITION

For the second edition, a complete revision of the entire book took place, including the addition of over 400 new articles, books, and Web sites pertaining to the topic. Every line of text of the first edition was reviewed and updated. Chapter 2, focusing on the legislative context for collaboration, was completely revised in collaboration with Dr. Maureen Griffin, University of Wisconsin, Whitewater.

PREMISE AND APPROACH

This book emphasizes *empowerment of special education teachers and teachers-in-training, giving them the motivation, understanding, and skills needed to analyze and improve collaboration relationships.* Full-time teaching requires educators to collaborate every hour of every day with others in their schools (i.e., paraprofessionals, co-teachers, and administrators). The book integrates practical exercises with discussion of relevant research, maximizing the probability of successful collaboration.

After completing self-assessment and assessment of their environments, teachers develop an individualized collaboration project. They can carry out their project in any of a variety of settings—in practica, work, or volunteer settings. The collaboration project helps teachers to generate options that they can use to think and act differently in the collaborative relationship. The collaboration project can take place even if those who are the focus of the project are not similarly motivated toward collaboration. Outcomes of the collaboration project include (a) an improved collaborative relationship, (b) familiarity with literature related to collaboration, and (c) familiarity with a skill set. All three of these outcomes will lead to heightened professionalism and efficacy.

SUMMARY

This book can help teachers who are learning how to collaborate to become curious, self-motivated learners. The long-term benefits of effective collaboration are worthwhile, as shown in the following excerpts from two points in a collaboration project journal:

At the Start

This project is not going very well. I don't seem to be very enthusiastic about it and I'm not sure how to do it. Sally is confused about everything, and I don't know how to explain things differently. I would rather keep things as they are and not do this project.

Later On

I am so glad I chose Sally as the focus of my project. I appreciate what she does for me and the wonderful attitude she has about life in general. I realize that I never noticed this before because I was annoyed at her for little things she did or didn't do. I see that Sally is very good at following a set of instructions that have been thoroughly explained to her. I realize now what I have to do differently. What a change this project has made in my life! (Weisberg, 1995)

This book helps people approach collaboration with optimism, skill, and direction.

Acknowledgments

This book was inspired by the experiences of students who invested themselves in collaboration projects in classes I've taught since 1985. Students' willingness to change their interactions and their resulting astonishment at the satisfying outcomes have been the major impetus for my interest in developing this book. Thanks to Douglas Rife, President and Publisher, Corwin Press, this book is being published. The current edition of the book has been carefully, and helpfully, handled by Kylee Liegl, Acquisitions Editor. During the production of the book, Melanie Birdsall and Diana Breti provided invaluable assistance. Help at Corwin was also provided by Jaime Cuvier, Robert D. Clouse, and Nadia Kashper.

The first edition of this book was promoted by Ray Short, Senior Editor, Education, Allyn & Bacon; he and his editorial assistant, Christine K. Svitila, made every phase of the first edition of the book's production go smoothly.

All the student projects I've supervised have led to my own learning about the complex topic of collaboration. I've appreciated the candor and insights that students in my classes have shared with me. Specifically, I would like to acknowledge the following Buffalo State College graduate students who allowed me to include their work in some form in this book: Cynthia Angelo; Kim M. Arent; John A. Barberio; Barbara J. Barnes; Kim Cudney; Elaine Czenskzak; Kelly Ejnik; Joseph H. Falkowski, Jr.; Ronald Hernandez; Katie Huntley; Kathryn Lovejoy; Jon MacSwan; Marilyn Marfurt; Gail Marzullo; Andrea M. Mrugala; Elizabeth O'Sullivan; Brenda Ott; Susan Paul-Saladino; Channon Piwowarczyk; Michele Plarr; Heather L. Putnam; Marguerite Pyszczynski; Patricia A. Riggi; Shauna Rollinson; Dereth A. Smith; Raquel Smith; Katy Steinwachs; Christopher Tendorf; and Amy Tierney. Their work has improved this book; I am grateful for their willingness to share their experiences.

Dr. Maureen Griffin contacted me regarding use of the book in her classes and assisted greatly in the rewriting of Chapter 2 of the second edition of this book, as well as an exercise in Chapter 8. Her contributions enriched the book. I take full responsibility for any errors or misstatements that may inadvertently be included anywhere in this book.

Writing a book is not easily done during the academic year. The sabbatical I received in 2005 from Buffalo State College enabled me to complete the second edition of this book in tranquility, broken only by the sounds of birds outside my window. In addition, colleagues and friends were encouraging throughout the book's development, and their heartening support made work on this book a learning experience. I am grateful for the distinctive assistance each of them provided: Claire Jones (BSC); Dr. Stan Kardonsky (BSC); Dr. Susan Leist (BSC); Marjorie Lord, Interlibrary Loan Librarian (BSC); Marie Mance (BSC); Dr. Horace Mann (BSC); Dr. Mary Murdock (BSC); Gloria Paul; Dr. Darlene Perner (Bloomsburg University); Mary Jo

Pfeiffer; Elizabeth A. Plewniak, Interlibrary Loan Librarian (BSC); Dr. Dennis Ponton (BSC); Dr. Janet Ramsey (BSC); Val Sharpe; and Dr. Jan Stivers (Marist College).

For the first edition of the book, a group of former students participated in focus group discussions. Their thoughtful reactions and suggestions led to significant improvements. My special thanks to: Joanne Augugliaro, Anna Caci, Barbara Drmacich, Andrea Higgins, Cheri Lesinski, Cindy Masseo, Mary McLean, Kim Mirando, Pat Postula, Mary Ellen Royce, Paula Senio, and Carol Wild. Four former students participated in the focus groups and gave me additional opportunities to test out ideas with them. Their interest and constructive criticism enhanced the book. My everlasting thanks to Karen F. Harter, Belinda Kimmick, Barbara Ann Walsh, and Daryl Weisberg.

Finally, my family members helped to bolster me along the way, using humor, anecdotes, and love to encourage me: many thanks to Eleanor Briggs, Bob Sears, and Joan and Mike Weinstein. My father, Adolph Cramer, is steady in his belief in my capabilities and supportive of every new step I have ever wanted to take. My sister, Barbara Cramer Sears, is always optimistic about my talents and never doubts my ability to succeed. My husband, Leslie R. Morris, married me and the first edition of this book project in 1995. He continues to be a trusted, honest, and loving advisor. I am grateful for his patience, tolerance, friendship, and support.

Corwin Press gratefully acknowledges the contributions of the following reviewers:

Kathy Isaacs
New Teacher Coordinator
Edmund Burke School
Washington, DC

Sancta Sorensen
Special Education Teacher
Monroe Middle School
Omaha, NE

Jacqueline S. Thousand
Author, Professor
Cal State University, San Marcos
San Marcos, CA

Cathy Riggs
Department Supervisor
Pupil Services
West Hartford Public Schools
West Hartford, CT

Alice Parker
California State Director
Special Education
California Department of Education
Sacramento, CA

Heather Walsh
Special Education Teacher
Jackson Elementary School
Lawrenceville, GA

Ruth Ann Gharst
2003 Kansas Teacher of the Year
Cedar Creek Elementary School
Olathe, KS

About the Author

Sharon F. Cramer, PhD, is a Distinguished Service Professor at Buffalo State College, where she has been a member of the Exceptional Education faculty since 1985. Her professional experience includes chairing the Exceptional Education Department and leadership roles in state and national professional organizations, including serving as president of the New York State Federation of the Council for Exceptional Children, and publications chair of the Division of Developmental Disabilities 1997–2001. In 2003, she received the Burton Blatt Humanitarian Award from the Division of Developmental Disabilities of the Council for Exceptional Children. In 2003–2004, she was president of the Northeastern Educational Research Association (NERA), a regional unit of the American Educational Research Association (AERA).

Her publications include this title, *The Special Educator's Guide to Collaboration: Improving Relationships With Co-Teachers, Teams, and Families,* which is a second edition of *Collaboration: A Success Strategy for Special Educators* (1998) and "Keys to Successful Collaboration" in *Special Women, Special Leaders: Special Educators and the Challenge of Leadership Roles* (2005). Further information about her can be found at her Web site, www.sharoncramer.com.

A sought-after presenter, Dr. Cramer has given over 100 presentations and keynotes in 20 states and Canada. She completed her PhD studies at New York University, earned an MAT degree from Harvard University and a BA from Tufts University. She is listed in *Who's Who in America* (60th edition, 2006) and *Who's Who in American Education* (60th edition, 2006).

Why Can't We Just Be Friends?

*S*pecial educators thrive on anticipation. At the beginning of our careers, at the start of the school year, when we move to a different building, or work with a new age group, we spend time and energy wondering what awaits us. We imagine students who will learn from us and be influenced by us. We get ideas for the inspiring lessons we will teach. We foresee professional friendships that will last for decades. As busy as we are, we hardly feel the burden of responsibility as it settles on our shoulders.

As special educators, we want our work to go beyond the classroom—whether our own classroom in which we teach, or those of general education teachers in which our students are included. For that to happen, we must be able to successfully work with the many adults in the lives of our students. Our professional working lives must include an ongoing commitment to develop and sustain effective professional relationships. If our students are to succeed, we must be able to effectively collaborate in our work setting.

How can this be done? This book will provide practical ways to develop and maintain the professional relationships you need for successful collaboration. These relationships make day-to-day work more effective. Ultimately, these relationships benefit our students, their parents, all our school colleagues, and ourselves.

BECOMING PROACTIVE: IMPROVING THE SCHOOL CLIMATE THROUGH COLLABORATION

Beginning teachers must be able to work not only with their students but with many different teachers.

When I got my first teaching position, I was very nervous. I didn't know how to get from one end of the school to the other without getting lost. But as the year went on, things changed. It all became different when I started to work with other teachers. Instead of feeling like I was working in a building, I felt like I was working for my students with other adults. By the end of the year, I could help my students so much better than I could at the beginning because of the other teachers I got to know.

Collaboration is no longer just an ingredient in school life but an essential feature (Burnett & Peters-Johnson, 2004; Villa & Thousand, 2005). Caron and McLaughlin (2002) identified the presence of a "collaborative culture" as an indicator of an excellent school, even though the strategies used in schools might differ from classroom to classroom. Research projects examining collaboration in the context of early childhood education (e.g., Pianta, Kraft-Sayre, Rimm-Kaufman, Gercke, & Higgins, 2001), secondary settings (e.g., Bouck, 2005), as well as those in preservice preparation programs (e.g., Knapczyk, Frey, & Wall-Marencik, 2005) describe the extended interactions between general and special educators. Collaboration has the potential to make these interactions productive and satisfying for all involved, to the benefit of the students.

When interviewing for new positions, special and general education teachers are often asked about their ability to collaborate. Clearly, collaboration skills alone are not enough to enable an individual to be a successful teacher. To get hired and remain employed, all teachers must be effective in the classroom. Before getting their first job, most special educators have completed extensive professional training, mastering all of the following: assessment of students with disabilities, design and delivery of effective learning opportunities for their students, and evaluation of the services provided. Teachers use the instructional strategies they were taught in rigorous teacher preparation programs. Many books are available to help teachers learn to assess student progress (King-Sears, Cummings, & Hullihen, 1994; Mayberry & Lazarus, 2002; Spinelli, 2006). Teachers also learn methods for instruction (Bos & Vaughn, 2006; Eanes, 1997; Reif & Heimburge, 2002; Sailor, 2002; Salend, 2005; Welch & Sheridan, 1995). Teacher preparation course activities and books or guides prepare beginning teachers to be competent in their direct instruction of students.

This same disciplined approach is also needed to prepare special education teachers to establish and maintain effective working relationships with their colleagues. Many factors contribute to making good teachers (e.g., National Council on Teacher Quality [NCTQ], 2004). For both general and special educators, a link between policy and practice is needed, and the NCTQ observes that "many of the policies in place at the state and district levels do not reflect the best research" (p. 2). Their booklet, available for free at www.nctq.org, highlights issues that should be considered when preparing general and special education teachers.

One reality that both general and special educators face is that an increasing number of special needs students are receiving their education in inclusive settings. Collaboration is an essential part of the program planning needed to make such placements effective (Vaughn, Bos, & Schumm, 2005; Walther-Thomas, Bryant, & Land, 1996). When successful, positive collaborative relationships in schools have many rewards. Teachers who experience the long-term benefits of a collaborative school environment are more committed to their profession and more productive (Gerber, 1991). Malone, Gallagher, and Long (2001), reporting on the outlook of 148 general educators who were members of teams supporting children with disabilities, reported that the general educators valued opportunities for discipline collaboration, as well as the personal benefits (e.g., collegiality, improved knowledge, personal support) and positive communication that emerged from the team process (p. 586).

Collaboration skills are increasingly incorporated into teacher education programs for special educators (e.g., Conderman, 2001; Crutchfield, 2003) as well as general educators (e.g., Coombs-Richardson & Mead, 2001). Kluth and Straut (2003) have used a collaborative approach in the university classroom for four years, illustrating different types of collaborative partnerships that general educators and special educators might use in inclusive classrooms.

> How better to prepare students for inclusive classrooms than to demonstrate and model inclusive practice? The university or college classroom can become a laboratory for developing co-teaching and coplanning skills that will undoubtedly be needed in the diverse, inclusive classrooms students are entering. (Kluth & Straut, 2003, p. 239)

As Fisher, Frey, and Thousand (2003) describe,

> Inclusive educators do not maintain separate classroom responsibilities. Instead, they assimilate into the varied settings in which their students participate. The ability to collaborate with general educators, coaches, related service professionals and vocational personnel is fundamental because they are the instructional providers . . . Successful special educators are masters of collaboration. (p. 46)

In the Hamill, Jantzen, & Bargerhuff (1999) survey of 111 educators in 10 schools, and in focus groups conducted with some of these educators, collaboration was identified most frequently as of highest importance (significant at .01) for competencies of teachers and administrators in inclusive schools.

> As this investigation highlights, educators place high value on the need to develop skills in collaboration. If collaboration that supports inclusion is to prevail among both teachers and administrators, their professional development should provide opportunities for interaction and shared experiences across the disciplines of general and special education. (p. 33)

This point is further made by Edmiaston & Fitzgerald (2000), who describe a model program built upon collaboration as the basis for successful inclusion. The designers of the POND program make use of the Reggio Emilia approach, incorporating collaboration directly into their work with young children:

> Collaboration helps achieve the common goal of inclusion. Loris Malaguzzi (1993), the late founder and director of early education in Reggio Emilia, described *relationships to be the fundamental, organizing strategy of our educational system. We view relationships not simply as a warm, protective backdrop or blanket but as a coming together of elements interacting dynamically toward a*

common purpose (p. 10). At the early childhood center, important collaborative relationships develop between teachers and children, children and their peers, general and special educators, and teachers and parents. (p. 66)

Programs like the service-learning experiences that four high schools in Kentucky organized for students with moderate and severe disabilities (Kleinert et al., 2004) could not exist without widespread collaboration.

Cross-agency collaboration is powerful, as described by Little and Houston (2003) as a result of a multischool team-based approached aimed at improving student performance: "The knowledge, skills, and perspectives from each of these partners enhance the common vision, necessary support, and unique roles contributed by each collaborator. However, this critical component is also the greatest challenge, as multiple systems often struggle to collaborate within a single system" (p. 85). How can collaboration more routinely be incorporated into these settings?

Collaboration skills can be learned. Collaboration techniques are presented in this book along with the research that supports their use. Using this book, you can develop and use a detailed set of goals to proactively define your ideals for new working relationships. The following definition of collaboration is used to underscore the goal-oriented nature of a collaborative effort:

> Effective collaboration consists of designing and using a sequence of goal-oriented activities that result in improved working relationships between professional colleagues. The responsibility for collaborating can either be the sole responsibility of one individual who seeks to improve a professional relationship, or a joint commitment of two or more people who wish to improve their working relationship.

Collaboration rests on the ability to accurately assess the demands of a situation, develop appropriate expectations, and initiate actions that will enable collaboration to occur. When this takes place, both students and their teachers benefit. Scribner and Scribner (2001) describe high-performing schools serving Mexican American students in which collaboration is identified as a key component of success.

> Collaborative governance and leadership serving Mexican American students did not seem to be driven by state-mandated accountability measures. Educators held themselves accountable, however, believing that all children can learn and that it was their responsibility to make it happen (Scribner & Reyes, 1999). (pp. 3–4)

Collaboration can enable educators to work together to effectively assist students. The impact of collaboration on students is further supported by Christiansen, Goulet, Krentz, and Maeers (1997): "Collaborative learning communities that build knowledge from within and through interactions with others [lead to] . . . relationships which, in turn, affect teaching practice and educational change" (pp. xvi–xviii). When synergy takes place in the school, students are the beneficiaries.

The assumption that teachers and administrators automatically know how to collaborate may be unrealistic. As Glenn (1989) explains, "the missing ingredient in too many schools is the energy for learning that arises from commitment— commitment of teachers and principal to a *joint* [italics added] enterprise and commitment of teachers and students to a school they have chosen" (p. 779). Programs such as the one described by Sharpe and Hawes (2003) provide a five-step process—based on the work of the Minnesota Department of Children, Families and Learning (2002)—that enables general and special educators to begin the process of working together. The authors characterize the steps as "a simple but effective strategy for bringing general and special education teachers together to address the academic and social needs of students with disabilities in the general education settings" (p. 6). Other, more in-depth resources (e.g., Bauwens & Hourcade, 2003; Friend & Cook, 2002) and this book provide opportunities to consider the challenges teachers face when collaborating and how to overcome them. Special educators need explicit training to enable them to foster and maintain collaborative relationships and to fully participate in joint enterprises.

Davis and Thomas (1989) describe a school climate of trust and good communication between staff and administrators as preconditions for effective collaboration. Kilgore, Griffin, Sindelar, and Webb (2002) made a similar observation when looking at schools that made progress incorporating inclusive practices into their school settings:

> Lasting changes occur when stakeholders build collaborative cultures, rally behind a vision, and build reforms into the organization of the school. When teachers work in relative isolation—without the guidance of a school vision, the assistance of "critical friends," the support of professional development, or the discipline of accountability—they typically resist school reforms, especially those that threaten classroom autonomy. . . . Over time, . . . within [the school's] open and collaborative climate, teachers redefined their roles, accepted greater responsibility for all student learning, shared teaching ideas, allowed others to suggest curricular and instructional modifications, and developed a greater sense of personal and collective teaching efficacy (Webb & Barnash, 1997). (p. 11)

An example of this collaboration model in use is provided by Haskell (2000), who describes the benefits for all students when collaboration between general science teachers and special educators occurs: "A proactive collaborative relationship with the special education teacher can result in a teaching situation which is not only more agreeable to the science teacher, but also more beneficial to all of the students in the classroom." Beginning special educators are generally optimistic. They presume that these preconditions—trust and good communication—exist everywhere. They embark on their new jobs, assuming that "everyone will get along." Many are unprepared when they encounter the unexpected.

On my first day in the building, I went up to people in the teachers' lounge and introduced myself. They smiled at me but went right on talking. After that, I ate lunch in my room. I don't think I said ten words to another teacher that whole first year.

When special educators receive neutral or negative reactions, they often dismiss the opportunity to analyze what has taken place. They may (1) be too busy to examine the encounter in depth, or (2) conclude that difficulties are the exception rather than the rule, or (3) assume that problematic encounters are going to happen all the time and that little can be done. They may use a variety of explanations to justify the encounters—including blame or guilt. Instead of changing their behavior, they may avoid the particular teacher or teachers. If these difficult encounters persist, their optimism can sour and be replaced by pessimism. This negative spiral is defeating.

When confronted with interpersonal problems, teachers do not always employ the systematic approach used in typical teaching situations. For example, when an instructional practice is ineffective, a teacher will assess what happened and make the necessary changes. In a failed collaborative effort, teachers often passively accept the consequences. They may inaccurately presume that (1) they *should* know what to do, or (2) their colleagues are probably people with whom no one could collaborate. The resulting feelings are very similar to those that innovative teachers sometimes experience. Renegar (1993) describes the response of innovative teachers to their colleagues in this way:

> Teachers who have experienced their colleagues' negativity about creative teaching efforts frequently characterize this response as jealousy. Others classify it as negativism motivated by insecurity or laziness. Whatever the cause, the negative peer pressure frequently has the chilling effect of intimidating the innovator and extinguishing the flame of experimentation. (p. 70)

You do not have to be defeated by negativity—there is another alternative. This book provides you with a constructive, proactive approach to collaboration based on four assumptions illustrated by the following example:

My reason for going into teaching was my interest in people. I was always good at figuring out what made people act the way they did. That's why I was so upset when my paraprofessional and I couldn't get along. Things went from bad to worse in a few short weeks. If I hadn't had to do this project, I don't know what would have happened. We got things turned around, and I feel so relieved! I never ran into a problem I couldn't solve before. Now, I know when it happens again, I'll be ready.

The four assumptions are

1. Most special educators have instinctively learned to work effectively with other adults. These instinctive skills will be sufficient for the majority of working relationships to be successful.

2. Problematic professional encounters are *inevitable* barriers that will appear occasionally in the life of every special educator.

3. Developing a positive, proactive approach to overcome or transform these barriers is the responsibility of the special educator.

4. All the necessary components of this type of approach can be learned.

This book provides a step-by-step approach for developing and carrying out a collaboration project. Your collaboration project, described more fully in Chapter 6, will enable you to improve a relationship in which you are currently involved. You can do this improvement on your own, following the steps outlined in the book, or as part of an organized group activity (e.g., a professional development program in your school, with other teachers who get together informally to address collaboration issues, or as part of coursework in your special education program).

Before you begin the design and implementation of your project, you will explore the basic ingredients of collaboration. Throughout this book you will find idea try-outs and project try-outs. Idea try-outs give you ways to reflect on experiences you have already had and review them in light of the ideas presented in this book. Project try-outs are activities that enable you to apply ideas presented in the book to your current situation. Both types of try-outs are designed to help you improve your collaboration skills.

Record your responses to the try-outs in a collaboration notebook (a loose-leaf notebook or an electronic version of a notebook, with a new file for each chapter). It will help if you date and label each entry in your notebook using the try-out number that appears in the book. You can be your own best critic.

The best part of the project was reviewing what I wrote in my daily notes. I was amazed at what I learned by rereading my thoughts just a few weeks later.

OVERVIEW OF THE COLLABORATION PROJECT

Using guidelines provided throughout this book, you will design and carry out a collaboration project that meets your needs. This project gives you the opportunity to change a specific professional relationship by changing your way of interacting with another person. The collaboration project, fully described in Chapter 6, can be completed whether or not you are currently in a school setting. The project focuses on *you*. It helps you to find ways to think and behave differently, even if the person with whom you want to better collaborate remains the same. No one needs to know about the collaboration project other than you and people you choose to inform.

Terminology

To clarify communication about the projects, the following terms are used in this book:

- The "person with whom you want to better collaborate" is called the *target person.*
- You are called the *project planner.*

Typical Questions

Does This Really Work?

The collaboration project has been used by over 1,000 special educators in training to improve their school or work situations. Some of these special educators were at the very start of their careers, and they completed their collaboration projects while they were full-time students. Others were employed as paraprofessionals or worked as volunteers in schools. Still others were established teachers interested in improving their collaboration with others. Approximately 90% of the special educators who completed collaboration projects experienced dramatic changes in either behavior or attitude.

Behavioral Changes. When behavioral changes took place, project planners found new ways to interact with their target persons. Each target person demonstrated a new behavioral response. When the project is underway, patterns of interaction between the planner and the target person begin. Occasionally, unexpected changes take place.

When I started this project, no one could have ever convinced me that it would work. I thought he was a stuck-up snob and wanted to have as little to do with him as possible. But now, I see him in a whole different light. I learned that he is easily intimidated by new situations and is on his guard more than I ever guessed. Other people are amazed that the two of us get along so well now.

Both people begin to behave differently. Sometimes, the target person turns out to be more reserved than anyone had suspected. Other times, the target person responds to new opportunities for planning or co-teaching. Behavioral changes in the relationship are often evident to everyone, even though the collaboration project is not public. Examples of behavioral changes are provided throughout this book.

Attitude Changes. In other collaboration projects, there are no evident changes. To others watching the people who are the focus of the collaboration project, everything may look the same. However, the project planner has a new attitude about the target person. Instead of feeling frustrated, angry, or disappointed by the target person, the planner has some new insights about the target person's motivation. At other times, there is greater acceptance of the limitations of the working relationship.

When I started this project, I decided to pick a problem which I faced with my co-teacher all the time. She loves to share gossip, even though it makes me very uncomfortable. As a result of my project, I learned that in spite of her need to gossip, we could work together. Even though outwardly nothing changed, I didn't get so upset anymore. Instead of trying to fix her, I focused on me. I learned how to avoid those conversations and accept a part of her that used to drive me crazy. When the project was over, I felt a real sense of relief. The gossip still goes on, but it just doesn't bother me anymore.

Usually, the attitude change comes as a direct result of the project. Because of the effort expended in this project, new attitudes emerge. Throughout this book, you will read about attitude changes that improved collaborative efforts.

How Can the Relationship Change
If the Only One Working on It Is Me?

The collaboration project is based on two assumptions.

- *Assumption 1.* Each relationship develops its own kind of balance. Visualize it as a teeter-totter. When both people stay in the same positions in relation to each other, there is little likelihood of change. When one moves, both are influenced. Therefore, the project activities require re-examination of old habits. New activities potentially result in behavioral or attitude change.
- *Assumption 2.* In all relationships, when one person makes a commitment—and takes subsequent action—to improve the working relationship, change results. The improvement is either a behavior or attitude change.

These two assumptions lead to the project. Teachers who have completed the project are amazed that in a relatively short time they are able to see dramatic shifts in their relationships—either in their behavior or in their attitude.

In some projects, the planner talks with the target person about the need for improvement in their working relationship. Together, they agree that they want to make some changes. All of the ideas in this book can work equally well if you conduct your project privately or in conjunction with your target person. However, most of the examples given in the book presume that you and your target person do not discuss the project together.

How Is Working by Myself Collaboration?

In most school situations requiring collaboration, people are not equally motivated. Even though their relationship is asymmetrical, they must find ways to work together. Generally, one person has to put more energy into initiating the working relationship or fixing problems that have occurred. This project gives you the momentum needed for collaborating with anyone in your work situation. You should be able to work with people who see situations the same way you do, as well as with people who don't. The skills you'll develop—to take ownership of your thoughts and actions—will prepare you to be an effective collaborator in all circumstances.

Compare being a collaborator to being a member of a winning sports team. Each member of the team must find ways to be able to perform consistently at the peak of his or her capabilities. Individual excellence is presumed. Only when individual team members are fully in control of their individual performances can the team win. Team confidence must be based on a history of competence. A team can only win when team members can assess themselves accurately and take full responsibility for meeting team goals. The project gives you a means of preparing for your collaboration with others. Part of this process will include helping you to become familiar with both your strengths and your weaknesses. In Blanchard's (2001) highly engaging story about developing skills essential for teamwork, members of a hockey team learn how to analyze what they need to do differently—as individuals and as a team. This project will enable you to examine what you bring to your school setting as well as what you need to learn to contribute more effectively.

Isn't It Unethical to be Doing Something Like This When It Is Kept Secret?

In all working relationships, there are public agendas that are separate from private ones. It is extremely rare for people in a workplace to share every thought or idea that they have about each other. The intent of this project is to help you become an effective collaborator. By investing time and energy in the improvement of a working relationship, which is aimed at yourself, you are contributing to the overall improvement of the relationship. In this way, the project serves a valuable function. Most teachers who have developed and implemented projects feel awkward spending so much time and energy privately focusing on another person. As you will read in this book, nearly all of them conclude that the project's benefits are significant enough to outweigh their initial apprehension.

Some project planners choose to inform their target person that they would like to improve their working relationship and share some aspects of the collaboration plan. That option is open to you.

Idea Try-Out 1.1 is designed to help you consider what you have already experienced. Your review of what you've observed can help you to organize your ideas about collaborative relationships.

Idea Try-Out 1.1

At Work: Yes and No

This idea try-out allows you to identify characteristics of working relationships that you would like to include in your professional future. Think about paid or volunteer jobs you have held over the last few years and people with whom you have worked. If you wish, you may also think about contacts with family members or friends. Remember to date and label this try-out in your collaboration notebook for future reference. Your notebook should be in a format that is easy for you to use—it can either be a paper notebook or an electronic one. Pick one approach and stick with it for all of the activities that reference the notebook in this book.

1. In your collaboration notebook, on the left side of the page, list four or five pairs of people who got along well with each other. Double-space your list of names.

2. On the right side, next to each pair of names, record two or three phrases describing their working relationship. You may want to put down a word or phrase that reminds you of a time you saw them working together well.

3. On a new page, on the left side of the page, make a new list of four or five pairs of people who had trouble getting along with each other. Double-space your list of names.

4. On the right side, next to each pair of names, record two or three phrases describing their working relationship. You may want to put down a word or phrase that reminds you of a time you saw them having problems getting along.

5. After looking over these two lists, turn to a new page and make a chart for yourself, using a line down the middle of the page. Label the left-hand side "YES" and the right-hand side "NO."
   a. On the left, jot down two or three features you would like to have in future working relationships with colleagues.
   b. On the right, put down two or three features you would like to avoid in future working relationships.

As you complete the try-out, you may find that you have trouble putting your thoughts into words. Throughout this book, you will find ideas and suggestions that should increase both your vocabulary and understanding of working relationships. You can add to the lists you created for Idea Try-Out 1.1 throughout your use of this book. You may think of new things you want to include, and those you want to avoid, in future collaborative relationships, as well as your vocabulary for describing collaborative strategies, based on your new ability to attend to working relationships all around you.

The literature pertaining to the field of collaboration is extensive; it is incorporated throughout this book. Embedded in the literature are four major principles of collaboration, which are central to this book. The collaboration project you will carry out incorporates the following principles.

PRINCIPLES OF COLLABORATION

1. The goal of collaboration is to create a climate of heightened professionalism between professionals, with an "indirect impact on student outcomes" (Idol & West, 1991, p. 72) such that the students who are served by the professionals can achieve their highest potential.

The focus of this book will be on maximizing the effectiveness of collaboration between special education and other professionals who work together. The long-term, indirect goal of collaboration is to help students to achieve their fullest potential. This focus is based on the notion of "shared responsibility" that Will (1986) describes as the effective working relationship of general educators and special educators. The benefits to students include use of research-based practices in content areas such as reading (e.g., Schmidt, Rozendal, & Greenman, 2002), improved student achievement (Givens-Ogle, Christ, Colman, King-Streit, & Wilson, 1989; Stewart & Brendefur, 2005), and the successful accommodation of an increasingly diverse student population (Johnson, Pugach, & Devlin, 1990). The results lead to seeing students in new ways. Instead of thinking of them as "yours" and "mine" they become "ours" (Keller & Cravedi-Cheng, 1995, pp. 84–85). More experienced special educators, when interviewed, referred to collaboration and consultation as a strategy used to enhance student outcomes, significantly more often than did novice teachers (Stough & Palmer, 2001; Stough, Palmer, & Sharp, 2001).

2. Collaboration "should provide a vehicle to facilitate independent problem solving on the part of participants" (Johnson et al., 1990, p. 11).

The goal of collaboration is *not* to create an intertwined group of professionals who will work together on joint projects indefinitely. In the following description, a teacher figured out how to improve her collaboration with a hard-to-like counselor.

Whenever teachers talked about our high school guidance counselor, they would get angry. "She never listens!" "She always thinks she knows what's best for students." I knew she had strong opinions that I was never going to change. Still, I was determined to broaden the range of post-high school options for my special needs students. After lots of trial and error, she and I applied for a grant from our local Rotary to identify resource people in our community who could mentor my students during their junior and senior years. It has made a world of difference in the lives of my kids! She's still just as hard to take as she always was, but I didn't let it stop me.

Ideally, collaboration promotes the efficient and effective resolution of problems. Occasionally, work will be done individually—in other cases by collaborative teams.

This collaboration principle underscores one way this book differs from much that has been written about collaboration. Here, there is no prerequisite that collaborators must have identical intentions. It is unrealistic to always find shared collaboration goals in schools. Many teachers must work with colleagues who don't intend to change objectionable interpersonal habits. Yet, "difficult people" must still be involved in the planning of students' programs.

Following this principle is the caveat of Cook and Friend (1991a). They warn that "collaboration is not a panacea." In other words, collaboration cannot be expected to solve every problem educators experience. The following example Cook and Friend describe is a familiar one:

> Collaboration is seldom a means of correcting fundamental problems in an already existing program. The most direct example of this occurs when a special education teacher is asked, under the guise of collaboration, to work with a general education teacher experiencing difficulty with classroom discipline. The risk is great that the general education teacher will resent the special education teacher. (p. 8)

The special educator must be careful to avoid such traps. Therefore, the target of the collaboration effort has to be one that is either a joint concern to both individuals or one that is indispensable for the person doing the collaboration work. Cross-disciplinary models can facilitate new approaches to solving problems (such as the collaboration between special educators, administrators, and school counselors in training, described by Shoffner & Briggs, 2001, involving an interactive CD-ROM). "As the three groups of professionals-in-training shared their ideas, they learned to draw on each others' perspectives and strengths [to solve the case problems]" (Shoffner & Briggs, 2001, p. 199). The collaboration project can be used to improve working relationships with other special educators or others in your school environment.

3. Collaboration is "an interactive process that enables teams of people with diverse expertise to generate creative solutions to . . . problems. The outcome . . . produces solutions that are different from those that any individual team member would produce independently" (Idol, West, & Lloyd, 1988, p. 55).

When attempting to solve problems, some teachers get stuck and fail to improve the situation. Then, individuals often become entrenched in their own belief systems, usually convincing themselves that they are justified—in their frustration, hopelessness, despair, or anger.

As part of the collaboration process proposed in this book, individuals are encouraged to develop effective collaboration resource networks, which can serve many purposes. (In Chapters 6 and 7, various ways to set up and work with these networks are described.) Collaboration resource networks help project planners to feel less isolated. But they can also provide the action orientation toward problem solving, which can lead to improved working relationships. "The facilitating and enabling functions of collaboration provide the foundation from which teacher empowerment can be built" (Johnson et al., 1990, p. 11). An outcome for network members is that they are better able to achieve the goals they set for themselves. These goals can be achieved whether they are working on the collaboration problem indirectly or directly.

4. In the collaboration effort, "vested interests are sublimated to the broader purposes of the . . . strategic agenda" (Lasley, Matczynski, & Williams, 1992, p. 257).

Teachers who make a commitment to a collaborative effort must subsume their personal preferences to the total requirements of the task. Ripley (1998) makes this point very clearly:

> The biggest change for educators is in deciding to share the role that has traditionally been individual: to share the goals, decisions, classroom instruction, responsibility for students, assessment of student learning, problem solving, and classroom management. The teachers must begin to think of it as our class. (p. 16)

The strategic agenda for the classroom is focused on meeting the needs of all students. This can mean that the type or timing of effort that is comfortable for one person may have to be modified when others have conflicting needs. For example, Elliott and Sheridan (1992) reviewed literature on effective teams, and they identified seven characteristics that maximize teams' effectiveness. One of them involved planning before meetings, including distribution of material to team members before the meeting (p. 329). For some teachers, planning in advance may be onerous. However, to benefit others, these burdens may have to be accepted. As Friend (2000) recommends, collaboration "must arise out of an understanding of its potential and pitfalls, and as a system-level standard it can be sustained only through professionals' deliberate use of appropriate knowledge and skills" (p. 131). Collaboration rises beyond the personal to a systemwide commitment to work. Friend goes on to caution that "calling nearly every shared effort in schools collaborative, whether it is or not, diminishes the value of the concept, dilutes professionals' understanding of what it requires, and fosters a false belief that there's not much to collaborating" (p. 131). Collaboration is more than a word.

Incorporating a collaborative approach to education of culturally and linguistically diverse exceptional (CLDE) students was the focus of the study by Roache, Shore, Gouleta, and de Obaldia Butkevich (2003). At the end of their study of 125 education professionals, they concluded that

> The challenge to collaboration in CLDE students' education is to develop democratic, ethical processes with multicultural understanding and respect. . . . However, collaboration efforts may result in conflict between educators, if not done carefully. To avoid these potential areas of conflict, it is important for the collaborative team to establish democratic processes of collaboration and have a clear understanding of the roles, expertise, and responsibilities of each team member. (p. 130)

Roache et al. (2003) recommend that individuals put aside their own issues and look at the broader concerns of the education of students in order to collaborate effectively.

Sometimes, special education teachers may have to consider a broader strategic agenda when it pertains to students with special needs. For example, with reduced federal contributions, communities are evaluating the services that school districts can provide to all students. Special educators will be in the middle of the debate over essential services. The principle derived from the work of Lasley et al. (1992) can be central to many discussions.

The ability to follow this principle may be a challenge that requires extensive self-assessment. Chapter 3 provides a starting point for this process. Project Try-Out 1.2 gives you an opportunity to explore your use of the Collaboration Principles.

Project Try-Out 1.2

Collaboration Principles

This project will give you an opportunity to make use of the four Collaboration Principles. Use one to reflect on a decision you've already made, and then apply it to a decision you will be making in the near future.

   I. Think back to a recent decision of yours that had an impact on other people. This could be a minor or major decision affecting people in any setting—school, work, or home.

2. Select one of the Collaboration Principles that appeals to you.

3. In your collaboration notebook, rewrite the Collaboration Principle in your own words.

4. List two or three ways in which you followed this Principle to reach the decision you selected for Step 1.

5. List two or three things you could have done, or ideas you could have considered, that would have extended the impact of the Collaboration Principle.

6. Identify a time in the next two weeks when you will make a decision with others. Write a note to yourself about it in your collaboration notebook. List two or three ways you would like to handle that decision.

7. In two weeks, respond to these two prompts before and after the decision is made:
   a. While making your decision, review the note you wrote to yourself.
   b. After the event has taken place, write a new, brief note. Include both a self-critique and two or three things you want to remember about the whole experience in the future.

Project Try-Out 1.2 lets you try a new approach for decision making. It gives you a structured way to change your usual process of making decisions. The chance to think about a collaboration principle, and thereby to see things from a different vantage point, may enable you to think about what you would like to do differently in the collaborative process.

Professional Working Relationships: An Analogy

Relationships that special educators form with other adults in their schools and within their school districts can be central to their professional lives.

We've been working together as a team for so long that we depend on each other constantly. When we need to talk, we know what the other person is thinking right away—it's almost as if we have our own code. Secret Santa gave us a big poster of peas in a pod one year—that's us! We hung it right up in our classroom, and it still makes us smile.

I don't know how we could get through some of our tougher days without each other.

This is an example of a teaching team that works together seamlessly. Special educators must work closely with other adults to help students achieve academic goals.

The uniquely intimate professional relationships that special educators have with their paraprofessionals, colleagues, and administrators parallel arranged marriages. People who are expected to be compatible are brought together, with optimism, by their advocates. In the best circumstances, the relationships formed are deep and honest, emerging from shared values. Both parties actively work toward strengthening their commitments, overcoming their differences, and jointly developing a useful frame of reference. In the worst circumstances, shallow or hostile relationships result, leaving both parties feeling cheated and pessimistic.

Special education teachers must learn all they can about collaboration with their general education colleagues—teachers, administrators, and support personnel—so they can succeed in the "arranged marriages" that will be a part of their professional careers. The collaboration project described next shows how one teacher turned a frustrating situation into one that was gratifying.

I didn't realize before I implemented this project how hard it was for me to tell people unpleasant things. I would clench my teeth to avoid reacting negatively. I wanted to have a sense of harmony at work but had no idea how to go about developing it.

I've learned how to let go of many of the negative things that used to get to me. I was surprised that quite a few were not so important and could be ignored. I've learned how to deal with people at school, in spite of ambivalent feelings about some of them. I eat with others in the faculty lounge a few times a week now—I never would have thought I'd feel comfortable doing that at the start of the project!

Special educators must work with others for whom special education is their secondary, rather than primary, focus. These other individuals are like the "extended family"—the school personnel and general education teachers. Often, special educators must advocate for parents as well as for their students. They are likely to work directly with families and also communicate family needs and concerns to other educators. (Chapter 11 provides ideas for improved collaboration with members of your students' families.) By learning to apply the creativity used in their classrooms to contacts with other adults, special educators can develop working relationships that will enable them to eventually serve their students best.

Sometimes, as in an arranged marriage, building a collaborative relationship takes a while. Initial skepticism toward collaboration can be overcome. A school building, or district, must undergo change in order to be fully receptive to the supports administrators must provide in a collaborative environment. Senge's (1990) classic, *The Fifth Discipline: The Art and Practice of the Learning Organization*, illustrates the kinds of transformations that must take place for a building to be able to truly be a learning organization. Mohr & Dichter's (2001) article, "Building a Learning Organization," describes the kinds of changes that take place when a school moves from a hierarchical to a collaborative model. The differences between collaboration, consultation, and teaming are subtle but unmistakable. The following section of this chapter clarifies these distinctions.

DISTINGUISHING BETWEEN COLLABORATION, CONSULTATION, AND TEAMING

The development of collaboration in special education has its roots in the consultation model. Ripley (1998) provides a useful historical overview. Consultation generally designates one person—the consultant—as the "expert." In some interdisciplinary teams, such as those providing physical education services to students with disabilities, the consulting model continues to be used. Shapiro & Sayers (2003) explain that "school-based roles and responsibilities of physical therapists, occupational therapists, therapeutic recreation specialists, and adapted physical education teachers are defined by regulations, guidelines, and philosophies gathered from Federal and state laws, state guidelines, professional standards, and school district policies" (p. 32). Each professional contributes a unique perspective, and together they each "provide additional data and important intervention strategies for the development and implementation of the student's IEP goals" (p. 37). Originally, consultation had a different structure for special educators.

Consultation became part of the service delivery model in the 1960s and 1970s when services to special needs students often had to take place prior to formal referral. Consultation usually occurred in a triad consisting of consultant, teacher, and student (Fuchs, Fuchs, Dulan, Roberts, & Fernstrom, 1992). Pugach and Allen-Meares (1985) explain that "consultation typically denotes an inequality of status between professionals, usually with the implication that the regular classroom teacher is less qualified than a support services specialist to provide input and resolve problems" (p. 4). In many schools, school psychologists were the experts to whom school personnel turned for advice (Reeve & Hallahan, 1994). Although the idea of an expert had appeal, the consultation model was shown to have limitations. These limitations were, in part, due to questions raised about measurable benefits.

Empirical literature on consultation was reviewed by Fuchs et al. (1992). They reviewed articles, book chapters, dissertations, and monographs written between 1961 and 1989 and found that few data-based studies evaluated the effectiveness of consultation. They considered the reasons for the limitations and proposed two explanations. First, there were significant challenges to conducting well-controlled research in the field that were rarely overcome. Second, many studies focused exclusively on teacher or consultant attitudes or satisfaction, rather than on student progress (Fuchs et al., 1992, pp. 162–163). The following situation is based more on attitudes than on student behavior.

Every day at lunch, I heard the same things. Teachers would tell me all the things my kids did wrong on the playground, in the bathrooms. They never had a suggestion or offered any sympathy. After a while, it became so bad that any response I made would just make them start laughing. By October, my students got much better and learned to control their behavior everywhere in the school. Even so, the teachers never bothered to say anything positive. Somehow, "my" kids never became "our" kids.

For effective consultation to take place, both persons (consultee and consultant) need to have some things in common. The lack of joint ownership for student problems or student growth is evident in the example above. Johnston (1990) would classify this situation as "troubled." When evaluating the participation of school psychologists in the consultation process, he recommends several factors as important: "enthusiasm, communication skills, mutual respect for professional abilities, and mutually desired expectations" (Johnston, 1990, p. 53). However, everyone involved in the consultation process did not always view it in the same way. Thus, the effectiveness of the consultation process is severely limited.

In the late 1980s, practitioners began to change the roles taken in their work together. Ponti, Zins, and Graden (1988) described a consultation-based approach to decrease referrals to special education that employed a collaborative process involving psychologists, teachers, and parents. This process "became part of the [school] system's routine functioning, . . . and positive expectations regarding the program were created among those who were involved in it" (p. 99). Teachers and other service providers began to work together more effectively, and these unique configurations became more standard.

The switch from *consultation* to *collaboration* came when the role of the special educator evolved from that of expert to one of a collaborator or joint problem solver. In part, this was a realistic response to situations faced by many beginning special educators. After the passage of P.L. 94–142 in 1975 (see Chapter 2 for a historical perspective on service delivery to students with special needs), the need for special education teachers increased dramatically. Often, special educators were hired immediately after they graduated from college. These beginning teachers were not considered experts when they joined school faculties. Most of their fellow teachers had been teaching for some time, and many were parents of children the same age as the new special educators. This made the establishment of the special educator as the expert frustrating and unrealistic.

I'll never forget the first time I tried to make a suggestion at a faculty meeting about getting parents more involved in our afterschool program. One of the teachers said, "Where do you get those ideas? Are you a parent?" and I looked around the room and realized that almost everyone there was a parent, except me. Four of the teachers had grandchildren! I got really quiet after that.

Twenty-five years after the passage of P.L. 94–142, legislation has supported collaboration in the general education classroom. Austin (2001) investigated the views of 46 pairs of general and special educators who co-taught. Asymmetrical relationships were seen to exist: both general and special educators believed that the general educator

> did the most in the inclusive classroom ($p = .001$) . . . This may be due to the fact that the special education co-teacher is typically the visitor in the classroom and is often viewed as the expert on curriculum adaptation and remediation, whereas the general education co-teacher is often regarded as being more expert in the content area. (p. 252)

The roles the co-teachers took in Austin's view include behaviors both identified as important:

> offering feedback to one's partner, sharing classroom management, providing daily mutual planning time, and using cooperative learning techniques . . . This reality should compel school districts and teacher education

programs to provide training, practices and supports to serve in inclusive classrooms. (p. 254)

Collaboration has become integrated into the work in the inclusive classroom.

With the implementation of P.L. 94–142, schools faced practical realities of changing their faculties, bringing young, beginning special educators together with highly experienced general educators. The timing for a change from consultation to collaboration was right for another reason: collaboration had a philosophical appeal for many teachers. Babcock and Pryzwansky (1983) contrasted the perceived value that principals, teachers, and special education teachers attributed to four different models—Collaboration, Mental Health, Medical, and Expert. The reliance on the expert to provide the answers was presumed in both the Medical and the Expert models. The Collaboration approach was most highly rated, illustrating that education professionals found the opportunity to participate in a problem-solving endeavor preferable to getting answers from experts. As Reisberg and Wolf (1986) stated emphatically at the time, the process of collaboration required shared thinking, often leading to schoolwide change: "The value of cooperative planning and decision making in the development of a school change process cannot be underestimated" (p. 12).

Increasingly, diverse use of the collaborative process was described in special education literature. For example, Donaldson and Christiansen (1990) outlined a cycle in which collaboration could be incorporated at several different decision points, depending on the needs of the student and the team. Idol (1988) modified her definition of consultation to be "collaborative in that all individuals involved in the process are assumed to have expertise to contribute and responsibility to share for instructional outcomes" (p. 48), illustrating the broadening of the original meaning of the term consultation to include a sharing of expertise. The term *interactive teaming* described how coordinated groups of individuals with different perspectives could successfully meet the needs of culturally diverse students (Correa & Tulbert, 1991).

However, the use of the same terms to connote various approaches was confusing. In 1991, Cook and Friend described this period in the field as follows:

> The present status of consultation and collaboration might well be likened to a period of adolescence: Just as teenagers are often a mixture of smooth growth and awkwardness, so, too, is the field as it appears to be striving for conceptual clarity amid its own contradictions. Some services are emphasizing collaboration while successfully meeting student needs. Others are struggling to find an identity. When we look to anticipated adulthood for collaboration and consultation, we hope for a time when all educators understand both concepts and are able to use both effectively to serve our society's children. (1991b, p. 27)

This book illustrates a process by which the "adulthood" of collaboration can be encouraged. It supplies a strategy that fits the request of Bay, Bryan, and O'Connor (1994) to "create a structure that foster[s] reflectivity and analysis among teachers" (p. 18). Through the use of a collaborative approach building on self-reflective activities, you will learn how to successfully collaborate with others. Fennick and Liddy (2001) warn, however, that the need for training in collaboration has expanded beyond the original group of special educators to include general educators. IDEA and IDEA 2004 both support the use of the Least Restrictive Environment for students with disabilities, and increased time for special education students in general education classrooms means increased collaborative teaching.

Teacher preservice and inservice preparation for collaborative teaching must be reexamined if teachers are expected to share responsibilities that affect teaching formats and the curriculum. Although special educators are more likely than general education teachers to have experienced training for collaborative teaching, opportunities for training must increase for all co-teachers. Without extended opportunities to learn collaborative teaching skills, the number of general education teachers who are willing and prepared to teach collaboratively will not increase. (Fennick & Liddy, 2001, p. 238)

In some circumstances, cooperative teaching or teaming is the means by which teachers work together in schools. The focus is on direct instruction to students, often involving both the special educator and the general educator. Reeve and Hallahan (1994) recommend that "the teaching arrangement best suited to the participating teachers, students, and classroom evolves out of close planning and evaluating by the general and special educators" (p. 6). They make the following distinctions:

In cooperative teaching both general and special education teachers are present simultaneously in the general classroom with joint responsibility for instruction. . . . In a team teaching approach, the special educator and the general educator jointly plan and teach academic subject content to all students. (p. 6)

Thus, the location of instruction, and the extent to which both teachers are involved in planning instruction, can vary depending upon the approach that best meets the needs of the students and the adults involved. In evaluating the benefits of cooperative teaching, Bauwens, Hourcade, and Friend (1989) asked 46 general and special educators to evaluate the potential benefits of a cooperative teaching model. Using a 5-point scale, with 5 representing "very likely," the highest benefit (4.37 for general educators and 4.22 for special educators) was "Increase teaching/learning potential" (p. 19). They conclude that "through cooperative teaching, more individualized teaching becomes possible, as each teacher is more able to take full advantage of his or her particular skills" (p. 21).

As Gulledge and Slobe (1990) describe the successful interdisciplinary team, the knowledge base of special educators can provide the general educators with new information to reach students more effectively:

Adding a special educator to an interdisciplinary team does not add to the burdens of the team, but lightens the load. These teachers possess an expertise in the special needs of exceptional children that is often missing in the regular educators' background. (p. 35)

Instead, the development of a successful team is ideally "forged in an intense team-building process. A team is much more than a bunch of people appointed to do a job together" (Maeroff, 1993, p. 514). The commitment of special educators to a collaborative process can be the resource base used to improve the quality of their lives in schools.

Deep commitment and effective strategies for collaboration are essential, as many logistical and ideological challenges may stand in the way of collaborative work. Able-Boone, Crais, and Downing (2003) describe how the collaboration among the preparation programs for early childhood, speech-language, and occupational therapy led to preparation of graduates who were able to benefit from interdisciplinary instruction. Commitment to offering such a preparation program requires a willingness to overcome obstacles, such as "crowded curricula, differing schedules, and different priorities within the individual disciplines" (p. 82). These authors found that collaboration was a solution that bolstered their commitment to interdisciplinary work: "networking among interdisciplinary faculty who have parallel interests and expertise . . . [and] creative solution[s] to ensure that the collaborative efforts achieved will continue to thrive with or without funding" (p. 82). This type of collaboration serves as a strong foundation for other collaborative models teachers are likely to find in their work.

Barnes, Bullock, and Currin (1997) describe the many types of collaboration that are part of the model for assisting students with special needs to make a smooth transition from school to work:

> While the concept of cooperative planning and service delivery appears to be straightforward, community transition teams can be difficult to maintain when there are conflicting priorities and time constraints. The skills that facilitate collaboration need to be intentionally developed. The territorial attitudes that are a barrier to collaboration may originate in the separation of programs at the preservice level.
>
> Special educators and VR [Vocational Rehabilitation] counselors share a common goal, that being the maximum self-sufficiency for young adults with disabilities. . . . Collaborative skills should be introduced and practiced as a part of the preparation of the special educator. (p. 256)

Collaboration moved from the outer circle of options for special educators into the hub of work in schools, with families, and became part of the expectations of community members. Programs like the one described by Simpson and Yocom (2005) include collaboration as one of the strategies that makes the Every Child program successful within the school: a rethinking of the school day to allow for team meetings led to a block scheduling approach, which facilitated better services to students as well as opportunities for faculty meetings during "collaboration times." "Gilbert described the block schedule as key to the program's success: 'Before, scheduling was a nightmare, general education teachers would send kids down at their whim. We had no ability to group students either by skill deficit or subject'" (p. 39). Instead of viewing the special education resource setting as a black hole, teachers in the building began to work together more effectively to keep each other informed about needs and options. The collaborative process became one that was infused into the routines of all educators, and expanded: "With the emerging success of the Every Child project at Mills Elementary School, 10 more elementary schools in Casper have adopted the program" (p. 40). Collaboration offered new resource opportunities to students and teachers.

There is need for further examination of collaboration practices. Duke (2004) reviewed 26 empirical studies of collaboration, which focused on general and special educators, and drew the following conclusion:

> The descriptive key words *special education* and *collaboration* yielded some 934 entries in the ERIC database. Only 41 (4%) of these 934 entries, however,

represented empirical studies published in refereed journals, and only 23 (2%) of these examined collaboration among general and special educators. (p. 315)

More empirical research is needed to evaluate the effectiveness of collaboration. As an example, Duke recommends the following: "This research should explicitly examine systems of privilege/oppression based on skin color, gender, sexual orientation, and disability status. This research would transform the empirical discourse surrounding collaboration" (p. 315). Further research would enable a better understanding of the effects of collaboration on both students and teachers. Simpson (2004), in her discussion of how to reduce barriers to inclusion, identifies collaboration "as an essential element in the development of an inclusive culture (Kuglemass, 2001; Carrington and Elkins, 2002). Building relationships and shared approaches are therefore crucial" (p. 66). Collaboration is identified as valuable, but more is needed to infuse collaboration into practice.

CONCLUSION

Developing a positive outlook on collaboration, or even learning to use collaboration strategies effectively, will not necessarily lead to successful collaboration. Kugelmass (2004) provides a number of examples of the challenges that individuals face when working on establishing a collaborative model within a school: "To develop the kind of collegiality needed for the long-term sustainability of collaborative leadership . . . they needed to understand that it would take time to develop trust for one another" (p. 108). Collaboration is the result of effort and attention; as Gulledge and Slobe (1990) explained, seeing results after several years of effort, "the walls between special and regular educators will not fall simply because they are teammates. The relationships they develop will take time. . . . Teachers new to the building are amazed at the understanding and acceptance that exists between regular and special education" (pp. 35–36). Lenz and Deshler (1990) corroborate the need to have a realistic, patient view when they describe the establishment of new instructional procedures. Their cautions apply to the establishment of an effective approach to collaboration:

Successful use of complex . . . procedures . . . requires a significant investment of time and practice. Frequently, teachers will discard a new instructional procedure before allowing sufficient time for its effects to be realized. In the never-ending search for the "magic widget," teachers often flit from one instructional procedure or material to another. (p. 94)

Collaboration guarantees no "quick fix." Instead, it requires a serious scrutiny of a person's intrapersonal and interpersonal practices (as outlined in Chapter 3). Schmoker and Wilson (1993) report that the incorporation of teaming, based on the Deming model for Total Quality Management, had observable, dramatic results at the end of one year, but the most substantial result—gains in student achievement—took several years (p. 394).

As special educators, our motivation is similar to that of general educators. We all want to see long-term improvement of the educational climate in the schools, leading to effective education of all students. We must learn to be effective collaborators and problem solvers. Golightly (1987) described the need for teaching collaboration skills within special education preparation programs because, at the time, few teacher preparation programs included team-building. Hopefully, with the incorporation of more opportunities for collaboration training into college courses, this situation will change. This book is one approach, making each special educator responsible for taking a proactive role in collaborating with others.

Collaboration is becoming a more routine strategy across the educational spectrum. Bassett (2004) commented on the benefits independent schools experience in such programs as the Breakthrough Collaborative (www.breakthroughcollabora tive.org), involving middle school, high school, and university participants.

It is hoped that as educators, we have come a long way since Dudley-Marling (1985) warned that the Individualized Education Program (IEP) could, if viewed "only as the fulfillment of a legal requirement, become an essentially meaningless exercise" (p. 67). Simpson, Whelan, and Zabel (1993) recommended that special educators in the 21st century must be prepared differently. They predicted that collaboration would comprise much of their work:

> Future collaborative approaches will likely discard the consultant–consultee model, whereby consultation flows from expert to novice, in favor of more transdisciplinary approaches. . . . That is, special educators will be trained not only to provide expertise but also to seek expertise from a variety of sources and coordinate the application of such expertise. . . . In addition, collaborative approaches will not be limited to traditional "educator" roles. Because of the multiple ecological factors that affect children's lives and learning, educators must collaborate with non-school systems. (p. 10)

The concerns raised by Simpson et al. (1993) are addressed in the preparation of special educators. Today's journals are filled with examples of the new roles that special educators take (e.g., Ford, 2004, in relation to interactions of educators with community agencies) as well as the integration of training on collaboration into the preparation of special educators (e.g., Hourcade & Bauwens, 2003). While there is still more to be done for teacher preparation (e.g., Bouck, 2005, in her discussion of the preparation of secondary special educators), progress has been made over the last few decades.

Dallmer's (2004) thoughtful reflections on her experiences collaborating in schools, in higher education settings, and with professional development schools led her to this conclusion:

> What my experiences have taught me is that undergirding collaborative relationships is a value system that honors "human caring, commitment, and justice" (Dickens, 2000). This sort of relationship building is based on trust and respect and every interaction is a part of an ongoing process to reaffirm those beliefs (Miller et al., 2000). It is a process that requires conversation and compromise. It is time consuming, difficult, and requires patience. (Dallmer, 2004, p. 43)

Development of collaboration skills can benefit general educators, special educators, and teacher educators. There will be an ever-expanding need for collaboration and the benefits that it can produce. Collaboration is expected to be an increasing part of the role of the special educator.

My high school juniors had their minds everywhere but my classroom. I tried everything I could think of, but I still couldn't get their attention. When I started talking to a few other teachers, I realized I wasn't the only one who was talking to myself. We've started some new initiatives, using all our contacts in the community. What a difference it made in my outlook! I had actually been thinking about leaving teaching, but now I'm full of ideas again.

Smith's (1992) caution is one we can all benefit from addressing:

> As educators try to meet the continuing goal of changing our practice, the enemies of change and renewal await: inertia, impatience, fear of faddism, misinformation, lack of information, and mistrust. Patience and persistence will be required to overcome the habits of isolation and privacy . . . and to gain the greater good of combined efforts. (p. 254)

We need to heed Smith's advice in order to make use of collaboration. Darling-Hammond (1999) describes the potential benefits of collaboration when she includes it in her list of what teachers need to know, as a tool for their students as well as for themselves:

> They need to know about *collaboration*. They need to understand how interactions among students can be structured to allow more powerful shared learning to occur. They need to be able to shape classrooms that sponsor productive discourse that presses for disciplined reasoning on the part of students. They need to understand how to collaborate with other teachers to plan, assess, and improve learning within and across the school, as well as how to work with parents to learn more about their students and to shape supportive experiences at school and home. (p. 226)

Collaboration can assist you in many aspects of your work as a special educator. Instead of making you the slave of practices you resist and resent, this book will provide you with the tools you need to make collaboration work for you and your students.

2

Background

Making the Case for Collaboration

*I*t has been said that time travel would be no problem for teachers. Unlike heart surgeons, computer programmers, or mechanics, teachers could walk into any room, in any century, and educate. Some might crave chalk, if entering into an open-air dialogue with Socrates, but they would otherwise feel at home.

However, special educators might look at this opportunity for time travel differently than general educators. If we attempted to find our students under the trees where Socrates held some of his most lively seminars, we would be disappointed. Until 1975, when P.L. 94–142 was implemented, few people with disabilities took part in everyday life. It is hard to appreciate how total the shift has been—little over a quarter century ago, people with disabilities were educated in a setting separate from their peers. In many cases, people with disabilities received no education at all. Today, people with disabilities are involved with school, recreation, social experiences, and work with their peers. Inclusion is no longer limited to progressive schools—it is seen in rural, urban, and suburban settings. Parents, siblings, and extended family members take part in activities that special and general education teachers sponsor to maximize participation in life events for family members with special needs.

In this chapter, you will see how collaboration emerged as a cornerstone for special education services. You will read about other events that influenced special education services. By the end of the chapter, you will be more aware of the regulatory and legislative supports provided for students with disabilities and their teachers.

AUTHOR'S NOTE: The author gratefully acknowledges the assistance provided by Dr. Maureen Griffin, University of Wisconsin, Whitewater, in revising this chapter.

LEGISLATIVE MILEPOSTS

Services for children and adults with disabilities began centuries ago. The original medical service delivery model has evolved into a continuum of services, leading toward today's maximized independence for individuals with disabilities. This change in philosophy and service delivery is described in several excellent introductory special education books as well as specialized books on the law (e.g., H. R. Turnbull & A. P. Turnbull, 2000) and collaboration (e.g., Tiegerman-Farber & Radziewicz, 1998; Walther-Thomas, Korinek, McLaughlin, & Williams, 2000). This chapter focuses on the origins of collaboration in special education and illustrates how the goals and standards have dramatically changed.

Day-to-Day in a Psychiatric Institution, 1945

While I was in college, I worked summers in the kitchen in a psychiatric institution. I still dream about it. All day long, the patients waited for meals. Some waited calmly, some screamed, some became physically rigid, and others regressed. We never talked to them, just fed them. We picked food which could be digested easily, but it smelled and tasted awful.

I think back to that time and shudder. I'm grateful we have fewer and fewer institutions now. When I read Burton Blatt's "Christmas in Purgatory," I knew he'd seen what I saw.

Day-to-Day in a Group Home, 2005

I'm in my sophomore year in college, and I'm a nutrition major. I found a great job as an aide in a group home. My shift covers the dinner hour. The house coordinator and I spend a lot of time planning ways to involve the residents in meal preparation. Our goal is to help them become as self-sufficient as possible, as well as become part of the neighborhood. It has been a real learning experience for me in so many ways. I've had to think differently about how to involve people who need tasks broken down into small parts. We all laugh a lot, and we turn out meals we all like to eat. We have become part of the block association and had day-to-day practice in being friendly, but not pushy, with people we see walking by. Neighbors were wary of us at first, but now we just fit in.

The contrasting examples above illustrate the major shift in services for people with disabilities. As a society, we moved from focusing on caretaking in residential settings to a model that helps people with disabilities to do as much for themselves as they can.

Today's legislatively driven service delivery system facilitates education of individuals in the least restrictive environment (LRE). The change in the location of services reflects a rejection of institutional and special class formats. Formerly, the social systems and procedures were often regulated for the benefit of service providers (e.g., the location, the type of food, and the time it was served). Now, regulations are geared to make the social situation as natural as possible, one in which expectations more closely parallel natural settings in schools, at home, and at work.

The improved service model has directly affected every aspect of the lives of people with disabilities. A few decades ago, options available to family members were severely limited.

1982: Looking Back

I am a nurse and my husband is a physician. When our third child was born with Down Syndrome in 1972, everyone urged us to put him in an institution. Both of us had interned in state hospitals. All the people we saw there with Down Syndrome seemed to be incapable of leading full lives. It was a very difficult decision, but everyone told us that it would be best for him, and for our other children, too, if we placed him. Reluctantly, we placed him in a nearby state hospital.

But I worked in schools and saw children with Down Syndrome taking part in things I never thought were possible for my son. In 1982, we brought him home. We have a lot to learn about each other, but it was the right decision for us. He's been with us for a year now, and we are getting to know each other more and more. Thank goodness his lifetime is now, not twenty years ago.

Parents may have felt compelled to place sons and daughters in state institutions. Now, school, vocational, and residential options are very different. Rudd and Ann Turnbull describe their son's experiences:

> As parents of J.T., our 28-year-old son who has mental retardation and autism, we have benefited from his own empowerment. . . . There was a time, not many years ago, when J.T. had "failed" special education, the sheltered workshop, and group home living. The direction of his life was straight down—into an increasingly deep, dark hole of disappointment, segregation, and disability.
>
> Today, some seven years later, J.T. works in competitive employment, with support, at the University of Kansas. He earns enough at his job to pay the principal, interest, taxes, and insurance on the house he lives in. He lives there with two roommates, neither of whom has a disability. He participates in recreation throughout our community and has become a well-known and welcome customer at bakeries and restaurants, music hangouts, and fitness centers.
>
> How did all this come about? . . . There has developed in our lives, and in J.T.'s, a synergy—a combination of action and actors—that has a ripple effect. As J.T. and we are motivated to act, develop necessary knowledge and skills, and then take action—that is, as we act empowerfully—we do so with others as collaborators. (Turnbull & Turnbull, 1997, ix)

The Turnbulls' experience testifies to the power of collaboration as a resource for parents, teachers, and individuals with disabilities. In their 2000 presentation to the Division on Developmental Disabilities conference members in Baltimore, the Turnbulls described J.T.'s new apartment, his work at their center, and their realization that his interests were not always what they expected them to be. They contrasted the old paradigm ("fixing" the individual) with the new paradigm ("fixing" the system) and helped audience members see the ways that family life had changed for people whose members included individuals with disabilities. New outcomes not imagined a few decades ago are now becoming commonplace. The direct effects of the new continuum of services has transformed the lives of people with disabilities and their families.

This change in service focus and delivery has had indirect effects as well. The practice of collaboration has become essential for a new group of people—those with whom people with disabilities live and work. Until the latter part of the 20th century, people with disabilities were, for the most part, served by people who chose to work with them. Professionals and paraprofessionals who worked in residential settings, sheltered workshops, day treatment programs, special schools, or special classes generally made a reasoned decision about working with people with disabilities. These were all settings in which people with disabilities were separated from people without disabilities.

Professionals and paraprofessionals chose their work for many different reasons—commitment to the less fortunate, being of service, or more practical reasons (hours, benefits, finances). They rarely found themselves in work situations that they had not anticipated. People working with individuals with disabilities before 1973 generally found that their job choices brought them into contact with coworkers who had made similar employment decisions. In this period, collaboration focused on the same issues as in other fields, such as cooperation, personal responsibility, and problem solving. Changes in the location of service delivery meant that collaboration with a whole new group of diverse service providers had to take place. The time frame and reasons for these changes are described in the next section.

Civil Rights for Individuals With Disabilities

Collaboration among those working in the field of disabilities changed dramatically in 1973. During that year, Congress passed P.L. 93–112, the Rehabilitation Act of 1973. Professionals and paraprofessionals working in the field of disabilities suddenly had more contact with individuals who had not been trained to work with the disabled. Thus, collaboration went from being an "optional extra" to being a mandate. Why?

Section 504 of the Rehabilitation Act (P.L. 93–112) was the first federal law to protect the civil rights of people with disabilities. It provided in part that

> No otherwise qualified handicapped individual in the United States shall, solely by reason of his/her handicap, be excluded from participation in, be denied the benefits of, or be subjected to discrimination under any program or activity receiving federal financial assistance.

Although limited in its impact to federally funded projects, Section 504 meant that all education institutions that had not previously accepted people with disabilities were now required to do so. School programs were impacted (preschools through colleges and universities) as well as all federally funded programs not previously serving the disabled. If program directors wanted to continue to receive federal funds, their programs had to change. They would have to make programmatic changes to include "otherwise qualified" individuals. Section 504 was the beginning of the shift from separate settings to naturalized settings for people with disabilities. There was an increase in the number of options available to people with disabilities, bringing them into society as a whole.

Section 504 is referred to as a statute that protects the civil rights of individuals with disabilities. It was significantly expanded by the Americans with Disabilities Act (ADA) of 1990 (P.L. 101–336), which extended the scope of the civil rights of people with disabilities even further. ADA entitled people with disabilities to an enforcement mechanism for their civil rights in private sector employment, public accommodations, transportation, state and local government services, and telecommunications. These changes opened up new opportunities for people with disabilities.

What the ADA Meant to Me

The Americans with Disabilities Act (ADA) changed my life. I was fifteen when it was passed, and I've been in a wheelchair since I was six. When I thought ahead to my future as a computer programmer, it always included my mom. I knew I could never get a job in Silicon Valley because I would have to stay near home and work for a federally funded project where they would "have to take me in." All of a sudden, things changed. You have no idea how small the world looks to you when it has your mother in it all the time. The ADA meant that I could get any job for which I was qualified!

When ADA was implemented, employers and employees in the newly identified career areas were unprepared for the changes they would have to make. Implementation of ADA meant that workers with little or no prior training (and in some cases no interest) in accommodating people with disabilities were suddenly faced with new responsibilities.

Since both Section 504 and ADA meant that people with disabilities had options in typical settings, people in all professions were encountering people with disabilities—in some cases, for the first time. Lou Brown often tells the story of his early effort to give students with disabilities options in a natural work environment—a Howard Johnson's in Madison, Wisconsin. Brown explains that he convinced a manager to allow his group of students with moderate and severe disabilities to clean a motel room. He promised that his students would clean the room as well as other room cleaners in the motel. He describes taking pictures of the way the finished room would look and helping his students develop the capabilities to clean the room. They progressed from taking seven hours to do the job to completing it in three hours, and finally, to one hour. And then, Brown explained, they were ready to begin to interact with the other room cleaners. Brown knew that the integration of people with disabilities into a normalized setting had to involve collaboration between the service providers (himself and the motel manager) as well as socialization between his students and their peers at the motel. The workplace was changing. However, for workers in settings like this Howard Johnson's, the impetus for collaboration was obligation, rather than self-initiation.

The workplace was not the only place in which changes were taking place: the educational options offered to students were transformed, as described in the next section.

Education for Individuals With Disabilities

Another series of laws exponentially increased the need for collaboration. These laws focused on the education of students with special needs. In 1975, the Education for All Handicapped Children Act (EHA) of 1975 (P.L. 94–142) was passed. This is generally agreed to be the legislative act "that would significantly expand the educational rights of children and youth with disabilities" (National Information Center for Children and Youth with Disabilities [NICHCY], 1991, p. 3). It was an amendment to P.L. 89–10, the Elementary and Secondary Education Act (ESEA), which was passed in 1965. All subsequent legislation amended P.L. 89–10 and included name changes as well. Generally, P.L. 94–142 is referred to by numbers rather than the initials, since it is an amendment, not the original legislation.

P.L. 94–142 was the result of collaboration between parents, teachers, administrators, and legislators. Professional organizations, like the Council for Exceptional Children (CEC), persistently worked with members of Congress, resulting in passage of this amendment. The focus of this amendment was on services to individuals with disabilities in school settings. Each of the four major features of P.L. 94–142 required collaboration in new ways.

Feature 1 of P.L. 94–142

Free and appropriate public education (FAPE) for all children with disabilities, ages 5–21, in educational settings that reflect a continuum of service delivery options.

Collaboration Issues. Because the options included resource rooms (where students would spend at least a portion of their school day) and general education classrooms, teachers were going to have to work together in new ways. General and special education teachers were encouraged to work together to serve all students. Solutions that were previously satisfactory (e.g., separate settings for students with disabilities) were no longer sufficient. General educators also had to learn to work with others in the lives of students with disabilities (e.g., therapists, aides, family members).

Feature 2 of P.L. 94–142

An *Individualized Education Program (IEP)* must be developed by a multidisciplinary team that includes parents, therapists, general education teachers, and special education teachers.

Collaboration Issues. Professionals with various backgrounds and professional expertise had to learn to work with parents to develop mutually acceptable educational programs. This meant that everyone had to learn to share their perspectives and to listen to each others' ideas. "Turf issues" had to be addressed, and mutually acceptable solutions had to be developed.

When Vaughn, Bos, Harrell, and Lasky (1988) contrasted initial placement conferences "ten years after mandate involvement" (before and after the implementation of P.L. 94–142), they found that the number of people at the conference had increased (from 3.7 to 6.4), and that the percentage of verbal interaction with the parents had gone down (from 16.8% of the meeting to 14.8% of the meeting), and parents only spent 0.9% of the meeting asking questions. Clearly, more collaboration solutions would be needed.

Feature 3 of P.L. 94–142

To the maximum extent possible, students with disabilities are to be educated in the *least restrictive environment (LRE) that is appropriate*. This feature corresponds to similar language in Section 504 regarding "neighborhood schools." Whenever possible, the students are to attend the school they would normally attend if they were not disabled. Students educated in their own neighborhoods are more likely to be able to make friends who will be conveniently available for afterschool activities. These relationships are harder to achieve if students with disabilities are educated far from home.

Collaboration Issues. General and special educators had to find new ways to meet the needs of students. Service delivery meant redefining appropriate education for each student individually. The least restrictive environment in each school setting had to be identified, and the supports needed to educate the student had to be provided. This often meant collaborating with administrators, parents, and other service providers.

Feature 4 of P.L. 94–142

Parents have the right to participate in all aspects of the identification, evaluation, and placement of their child. Due process procedures assure parents' rights.

Collaboration Issues. General and special educators had to find ways to make parents partners in the placement process. Many different efforts were undertaken to make this partnership a substantive one. Parent Network Centers were established in each state. The mandate of the centers included improving parent-professional partnerships and helping parents to become better consumers of services offered by professionals in schools and agencies.

Summary

In each of these four features of P.L. 94–142, the need for collaboration is embedded. New groups of individuals had to learn to communicate, to share ideas, to exchange viewpoints without anger. These challenges were formidable and were evident in the actions of the courts as well as in schools (Huefner, 1991; Yell, 1992).

The ongoing responsibilities and privileges of P.L. 94–142 are more easily met with recent technological advances. Special education law CD-ROMs enable educators and family members to stay current (Maloney, 1996).

Mandate Extended to Younger Children: P.L. 99–457

In 1986, the mandate contained in P.L. 94–142 was extended to younger children. P.L. 99–457 was another amendment to P.L. 89–10 of 1965. Under this amendment, children ages 3–5 are guaranteed a free and appropriate public education, to the maximum extent appropriate. In addition, Part H of P.L. 99–457 established Early Intervention Programs for children with disabilities aged 0–2.

The Individualized Family Service Plan (IFSP) was a new approach included as a requirement of P.L. 99–457. This requirement is intended to ensure that professionals collaborate with families when planning services for young children with disabilities. The IFSP is parallel to the IEP for school-aged students with disabilities. To the maximum extent appropriate, all children with disabilities are to receive services in the least restrictive setting.

P.L. 101–476, Individuals With Disabilities Education Act (IDEA), and IDEA 2004 (P.L. 108–446)

In 1990, P.L. 101–476 was passed. This amendment is referred to by the acronym IDEA, which stands for Individuals With Disabilities Education Act. Two new classifications of children with disabilities were identified—those with autism and those with traumatic brain injury. Many of these students require services that have not been needed by previous special education students (e.g., assistive technology). If assistive technology devices and services were needed, they were included in the student's IEP. Transition services were also a part of IDEA. Schools were required to give students with disabilities opportunities (before they reached the age of 16) to develop plans for their lives after their public schooling ends on their 22nd birthday. Students were to be taught to be informed consumers of public and private services. In addition, P.L. 101–476 emphasized the importance of educating students with their nondisabled peers to the maximum extent appropriate. Of particular importance to collaborative efforts was the promotion by IDEA of the involvement of students with disabilities in the general education curriculum.

Early intervention and early childhood special education were strengthened in the IDEA Amendments of 1997.

> To meet the mandate of the reauthorized IDEA, states and localities must provide early intervention services for children with disabilities within natural and inclusive settings. Child care now provides an increasingly prominent role in both the Individualized Family Service Plan (IFSP) and Individualized Education Program (IEP) as the natural or least restrictive environment in which early intervention or early childhood special education (EI/ECSE) services are provided. (Osborne, Garland, & Fisher, 2002, pp. 43–44)

Caregiver training, such as the SpecialCare program designed by Osborne, Kneist, and Garland (2000), is an example of the redefining of services that took place across the educational spectrum. "Model efficacy data offer strong evidence that this training results in increased knowledge about and comfort with caring for children with disabilities and expanded placement options for these children" (p. 44).

An increasing awareness of the need for collaboration between general and special educators emerged with the passage of IDEA. For example, the 1999 National Association of State Directors of Special Education's 62nd annual meeting "brought together a selection of speakers from a range of education fields to discuss how to collaborate better on the education of children with disabilities" (Sack, 1999, p. 6). New thinking on the role of special education was taking place.

The reauthorized IDEA (IDEA 2004) was signed into law on December 3, 2004 by President George W. Bush, with provisions of the act taking effect July 1, 2005. In order to increase the probability that children with disabilities will have the same opportunities for education as their nondisabled peers, IDEA 2004 includes more than 60 references to the Elementary and Secondary Education Act (ESEA) of 1965 as amended by the No Child Left Behind Act of 2001 (NCLB). Both amendments have the goal of improving education—IDEA 2004 for children with disabilities and NCLB for all children—and share emphasis on early intervention, informed parents, highly qualified teachers, and accountability systems. IDEA looks at the individual child with a disability with an emphasis on developing an IEP and specific services, while NCLB takes a more global view with an emphasis on closing gaps in achievement test scores.

As IDEA 2004 strives to improve educational success for children with disabilities, it asserts that success can only be achieved in an environment that supports high expectations for success, increased parent participation, support of the regular curriculum with special education and related services when required, and increased efforts to reduce mislabeling and high dropout rates of minority students with disabilities. Additionally, IDEA 2004 expanded the methods used to identify students with learning disabilities, streamlined IEPs and other paperwork requirements, and provided funding for professional development for special educators to deliver research-based academic and behavioral interventions. The gap between research and practice was highlighted, and numerous efforts are underway to bridge the gap with practices that have been proven to be effective.

Collaboration Issues. Many new collaborative relationships have been formed among educators, families, students, and the employment community as a result of IDEA and IDEA 2004. These collaborative relationships have expanded the opportunities for students as well as the circles of concern for special educators, students, and their families. Collaboration will continue to be a cornerstone of services to individuals with disabilities as we seek to equalize educational opportunities. Collaborative structures, such as student assistant teams and cooperative teaching, are key elements in the delivery of comprehensive services. These structures require general and special educators, school psychologists, speech and language clinicians, principals, families, community agencies, related services, and others to work collaboratively to provide a free and appropriate education. Each structure serves a distinct purpose, requiring distinct collaboration skills, with the goal of adapting curriculum and instruction to accommodate students' special needs in the least restrictive environment through a coordinated delivery of service. Comprehensive collaborative efforts require discussion of personnel and material resources, maintenance of a continuum of services, and ongoing evaluation. All of these elements are needed in the many IDEA requirements that require collaboration (e.g., developing IEPs, classroom accommodations/adaptations, transition plans, and behavior intervention plans) as well as when selecting related services and using a response-to-intervention model for determination of specific learning disabilities. The goals and vision of IDEA and IDEA 2004 are clear, and the means to achieve those goals depend on the ability of educators and families to work together in a collaborative and cooperative fashion.

Dieker (2001a) identified a challenge that many districts faced in implementing IDEA–disjointed service delivery. In many ways, disjointed service delivery is an example of a failure of individuals to effectively collaborate. She recommended five steps for addressing this problem, which can be generalized to address broader collaboration issues:

1. Start small but ensure that key players within and across grade levels are involved.

2. Involve children and their families in the development process.

3. Develop a comprehensive plan for change across the school and the district.

4. Focus on preparing students and their families as well as staff.

5. Continuously evaluate the plan. (pp. 266–268)

These five steps engage stakeholders within the school and district with family members to work toward coordinated service. "New tools may need to be developed to ensure that students are not victims of disjointed service delivery" (Dieker, 2001a, p. 268). The opportunity to evaluate services, and improve them, emerged from legislation over the past quarter century.

Summary of Legislative Mileposts

Legislative mileposts from 1973–2005 transformed the lives of people with disabilities and others in their lives. Service providers, educators, and community members had new roles requiring involvement with individuals with disabilities and their families. Reflecting on the 20th anniversary of P.L. 94–142, Braaten, Gable, and Stewart (1995) commented that

> what constitutes an "appropriate education" and "the least restrictive environment" for students with disabilities has been the subject of widespread debate and frequent reinterpretation. . . . [Nonetheless], schools across the country are at work dismantling barriers that have long separated students with disabilities from their classmates without disabilities. (p. 4)

Collaboration remains at the core of IDEA 2004, and, in fact, the ability of adults to work effectively together may become the determining factor in what constitutes effective schools (Barth, 1990).

COLLABORATION: RELEVANT TRENDS AND EVENTS

Educators and politicians who were attempting to improve services to people with disabilities also used means other than legislation. Four influential trends and events are discussed in this section: *A Nation at Risk* report, the Regular Education Initiative, Goals 2000, and CEC/INTASC standards for the preparation and certification of special education teachers.

A Nation at Risk

The 1983 National Commission on Excellence in Education (NCEE) published a report titled *A Nation at Risk: The Imperative for Educational Reform*. This report raised questions regarding services to typical students, recommending such benchmarks as higher academic standards and more time in school. The report suggested specific measures that would result in typical students who were better prepared to achieve in school and also succeed in life after school. In his 2004 book, *Are We Still a Nation at Risk Two Decades Later?* Hayes observes that "there is widespread agreement among those who have studied the history of education in the United States that the publication of *A Nation at Risk* . . . was instrumental in creating a significant school reform movement during the last two decades" (p. vii). Hayes details the stimulus that the 1983 report provided for a number of initiatives that are now part of the educational climate, including standards, choices of charter schools, as well as other initiatives.

In 1984, President Reagan translated *A Nation at Risk* into five recommendations. Three of the recommendations focused on student outcomes, including higher standards for high school graduates with improved graduation requirements and rates. None of the recommendations mentioned students receiving special education services. The fourth recommendation focused on teacher preparation with the intention of "improving the preparation of teachers . . . to make teaching a more rewarding and respected profession" (NCEE, 1983, p. 30). Collaboration issues were not mentioned. These national recommendations were to be accomplished by 1990.

While policy makers were examining education, a self-study was being conducted among teacher educators. The Holmes Group published *Tomorrow's Teachers* in 1986 and challenged educators to reconsider teacher preparation programs. The authors of the report highlighted the need for more integration of research into teaching practices; encouraged partnerships between classroom teachers, administrators, and teacher educators; and recommended that several principles be followed. Among the principles were "reciprocity, or mutual exchange and benefit between research and practice," and "experimentation, or willingness to try new forms of practice and structure" (p. 67). Implicit in the notion of abiding by these principles was the commitment to collaboration among professionals.

In 1986, the National Governors' Association reviewed the progress to date on achievement of the recommendations in *A Nation at Risk*. They also identified populations that had been omitted—students at risk, special education students, and young children in need of early intervention. The report, titled *A Time for Results,* was the blueprint for the Regular Education Initiative (REI).

Regular Education Initiative

The Regular Education Initiative was a movement that focused on ways special educators and general educators could jointly provide services to students with disabilities and promoted the placement of students in the general education classroom. The initiative created a great deal of controversy and turned national attention to collaboration.

Maynard Reynolds, one of the originators of the "continuum of service options" that was a cornerstone of P.L. 94–142, rejected his own notion of the continuum in favor of general education placement with supports. In a 1986 article, former Assistant Secretary of the Office of Special Education and Rehabilitative Services, U.S. Department of Education Madeline Will moved from a firm support of the continuum toward individually determined general education placement. And inclusion proponents such as Lou Brown and Alan Gartner (Gartner & Lipsky, 1987) stressed the value of full, unqualified inclusion of all students, all the time, in general education classes.

When special education teachers and parents of students with disabilities heard more about the REI, debates began. Some special educators viewed the REI positively, while others became concerned that the REI was a cover-up for diluting services to students with disabilities.

What the Regular Education Initiative Meant to Me

When I began teaching in 1980, I was the only special education teacher in my junior high building. By 1984 there were five of us. The other teachers called us "you" and never let us in on what they were doing in their classes. When the Regular Education Initiative started to be discussed in the late 1980s, I was thrilled. I thought it was finally time for us to be included. I was wrong! Instead, the five of us began to fight among ourselves. At the end of the year, I asked for a transfer. I still can't believe how mean we became. And all our hostility was because we disagreed about the REI.

The REI was prominently featured in special education journals, and many concerns were voiced about its benefits and its drawbacks. Two articles published in 1988 (Hallahan, Keller, McKinney, Lloyd, & Bryan, 1988; Kauffman, Gerber, & Semmel, 1988) illustrate educators' rigorous examination of the REI.

In retrospect, REI had and continues to have an impact on special education. Kubicek (1994) analyzed 24 federal and state court decisions involving the REI that have established legal precedent in special education law or have raised relevant issues that educators must consider. From the time the REI was first introduced, many educators used it as a convincing rationale for program changes.

The REI forced to the surface a related concern for special educators. The idea that general educators and special educators might jointly educate students led some to be concerned that special educators would lose their unique identities associated with service to students with disabilities. In 1989, Jeptha Greer, during his term as Executive Director of the Council for Exceptional Children, wrote a commentary titled "Partnerships: What Is Our Contribution?" This commentary explored the roles special educators were developing in partnership with others—members of the business community and also general educators. Greer urged special educators to build on, not abandon, their areas of expertise:

> It is wise to remember our contributions in all these partnerships. Certainly, arrogance is not called for, but neither is the hat-in-hand approach. Partners must realize what each side has to contribute to, and what each side must be able to take out of, a partnership. Only then does a partnership become a team. (p. 393)

Concerns about the preparedness of general educators were also being expressed. Teachers were aware that a shift was taking place in the roles of special and general educators. General educators were moving from their role of identifying students in need of special education services to teaching all children. Simpson and Myles (1990) expressed the concern shared by many general educators at the time: "Many general educators feel imposed on by mainstreaming, considering themselves unprepared to teach students with disabilities, and are put upon by mainstreaming practices" (p. 4). They went on to describe the need for support and discussion, because "a supportive general educational environment for students with disabilities is best developed by combining information with discussion opportunities" (p. 5). The authors concluded by recommending "a multifaceted system that takes into consideration shared input, responsibility, and decision making between general and special educators" (p. 8). Recently, this movement has expanded to include students receiving other support services, such as Chapter 1 reading and migrant education.

Idea Try-Out 2.1

Ripple Effect: REI in 1991

This idea try-out will give you an opportunity to experience the impact that the REI had on people in 1991, when it was being introduced.

1. At the top of a page in your collaboration notebook, list the connections between a teacher and other activities in school and the community that might be influenced by the REI. List as many different types of connections as you can. You can identify relationships between teachers and students, content specialists, discipline specialists, homework, parent/school communications, leisure recreation, sports, arts, and basic daily living tasks. Number the items in your list. You'll use this list in three different ways.

2. At the bottom of the same page of your collaboration notebook, draw three pairs of circles next to each other. Each pair will consist of an inner circle surrounded by an outer circle.
   a. Draw an "inner" circle (about the size of a quarter). The inner circle will represent you in several different roles.
   b. Draw an "outer" circle (about the size of a large doughnut). The outer circle will represent the outer limits of the school in which you teach (e.g., all academic and recreational programs, staff relations, home/school partnerships).

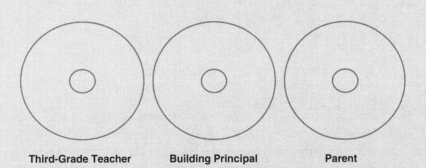

| Third-Grade Teacher | Building Principal | Parent |

3. Now, imagine that you are a veteran third-grade teacher. Until now, the extent of your relationship with the three special education teachers in your building has been to say hello and to see them at building meetings. Over the years, one or two students have been mainstreamed smoothly into reading groups in your class. You aren't sure exactly what the REI will mean for you and your students.
   a. Look over all the items on the list you created that would be part of the relationship between you, as the third-grade teacher, and the school at large.
   b. Label the first pair of circles *Third-Grade Teacher*. Draw spokes between the inner circle and the outer circle to represent the many relationships between

you and your school. Label each spoke, using the number you assigned to each item in Step 1 above.

  c. Use a highlighter (or a series of *x* marks) to draw attention to those items that might change as a result of implementing the REI.

4. Next, imagine that you are the building principal of a smoothly running elementary school. There are three special education classes in your building, and implementation of the REI means that the general educators will be working more closely with these classes than they ever have before.

  a. Look over all the items on the list that you created that would be part of the relationship between you, as the building principal, and the school at large.

  b. Label the second pair of circles *Building Principal.* Draw spokes between the inner circle and the outer circle to represent the many relationships between you and your school. Label each spoke, using the number you assigned to each item in Step 1.

  c. Use a highlighter (or a series of *x* marks) to draw attention to those items that might change as a result of implementing the REI.

5. Finally, imagine that you are the parent of a girl in third grade who has been diagnosed as moderately mentally retarded. Your daughter has been receiving services from special education professionals since she was born. She has been happy in her special class, even though she has to take a 45-minute bus ride to and from her school each day. You are concerned that she might not receive the same services from a general education teacher, and you don't know what the REI would mean for your daughter.

  a. Look over all the items on the list you created that would be part of the relationship between you, as a parent, and the school at large.

  b. Label the third pair of circles *Parent.* Draw spokes between the inner circle and the outer circle, to represent the many relationships between you and your school. Label each spoke, using the number you assigned to each item in Step 1.

  c. Use a highlighter (or a series of *x* marks) to draw attention to those items that might change as a result of implementing the REI.

6. Look back over the circles and spokes that connected you, in your three different roles, to your school.

  a. What differences did you see between the number of items you identified for each role?

  b. How many items showed up on all three lists?

  c. How many appeared on only one list?

  d. What role do you think would have been the most difficult during 1991, and why?

Connection to Collaboration

The REI was the first national push in the direction of collaboration between general educators, special educators, and all the members of other professions who were beginning to work with students in schools. The expanding school community included many more individuals and new sources of information about services for students. Fears surfaced regarding the implementation of the REI and implied consultation skills that general and special educators were expected to have. Little was spelled out in the Initiative to describe the development of these skills.

Exploring the impact of the REI on different groups in Idea Try-Out 2.1 may have helped you to see that it did not have the same impact on everyone. For example, did the REI make as big an impact on the building principal as it did on the parent? How about on the classroom teacher? The way in which you imagined people reacting may have shown you how it is possible to use the REI as a benchmark when you look for the start of collaboration as a feature in schools. As you probably observed when completing Idea Try-Out 2.1, it was difficult for you to determine what *definitely* would be changed by the implementation of the REI. You aren't alone. Most teachers, administrators, and parents were struggling. Some assistance was provided through a training component for teachers, as discussed in the next section.

Goals 2000

Goals 2000 is a national plan to improve student capabilities. It was approved by the U.S. Congress and includes both regulations and funding. Goal 4, a part of Goals 2000, focuses on Teacher Education and Professional Development. It was the first national goal that specifically addressed teacher preparation as it relates to collaboration. Goal 4 was tied to budget bills (e.g., the 1996 budget bill signed into law on April 26, 1996) that enabled the plan to move from theory to action.

Background

In 1989, President George H. Bush brought the 50 state governors to Charlottesville, Virginia to discuss educational concerns. This meeting has been referred to as an "historic education summit." An outcome of the meeting was a list of six national education goals. Bill Clinton, then the governor of Arkansas, attended the summit and participated in translating the goals into a proposal to Congress called America 2000. After his election, President Clinton worked with Congress to turn America 2000 into Goals 2000: The Educate America Act. The legislation was passed by Congress and signed into law in March 1994. During debate, Congress added Goal 4, which is related to teacher education and collaboration:

> By the year 2000, the Nation's teaching force will have access to programs for the continued improvement of their professional skills and the opportunity to acquire the knowledge and skills needed to instruct and prepare all American students for the next century. (Goals 2000: The Educate America Act, 1994)

Three selected objectives relevant to collaboration follow:

- All teachers will have access to preservice teacher education and continuing professional development activities that will provide such teachers with the knowledge and skills needed to teach to an increasingly diverse student population with a variety of educational, social, and health needs (Objective 1).
- All teachers will have continuing opportunities to acquire additional knowledge and skills needed to teach challenging subject matter and to use emerging new methods, forms of assessment, and technologies (Objective 2).

- Partnerships will be established, whenever possible, among local educational agencies, institutions of higher education, parents, and local labor, business, and professional associations to provide and support programs for the professional development of educators (Objective 4).

These objectives illustrate how Goals 2000 was being translated from general areas of concern to more specific targets of professional activity.

What Goals 2000 Means to Me

When I look at Goals 2000, and think of me in the classroom, it is hard to see the fit. I guess I'm saying that I feel small next to these statements. But when I translate Goal 4 into my life, it sounds like someone is saying that I don't have to do everything on my own. That's good! I don't know exactly who is going to help me, or how, or when, but whenever they are ready, so am I!

Connection to Collaboration

The implementation of Goal 4, and its related objectives, forms the foundation for effective collaboration between regular educators and special educators for three reasons. First, unlike America 2000, it identifies a diverse student body that is in need of services. Second, it presumes that teachers will need additional training to meet Goals 2000. Through the coordination of teachers, professional organizations, teacher educators, and labor unions, it is expected that teachers will be able to acquire the skills and knowledge that will be part of their new responsibilities. Third, with associated funding, it enabled activities to take place across the country.

Project Try-Out 2.2

Goals 2000 and You

1. Select one of the objectives for Goal 4 that interests you.

2. Arrange to interview three or four teachers. Plan to spend 10–15 minutes with each one to find out what kind of help they are currently receiving (or have received in the past year) to implement the objective you have selected. Give each teacher a copy of the overall goal and the specific objective on which you want to focus when you set up the interview. Ask each teacher to look it over prior to your interview. If the teacher has never received any assistance, switch the focus of the interview to the type of help the teacher *would have liked* to receive.

3. When you meet with each teacher, restate the purpose of your interview. Record your interview notes in your collaboration notebook. Discuss each of the following types of assistance, either as a format that was actually available

to the teacher within the last year to help in achieving the objective, or as something the teacher would have liked to have used:

   a. coursework at a college or university that included topics related to the objective
   b. national, state, or local conferences for which a fee had to be paid to participate
   c. teleconferences or inservice presentations for which *no* fee had to be paid
   d. training provided through the school or district
   e. electronic bulletin boards or telecommunication through electronic networks
   f. journal or newsletter articles
   g. curriculum materials that can be used to help teachers to meet their students' needs more effectively and also address the objective in question
   h. mentoring or networking among professionals, either through professional organizations or through the district
   i. other assistance

4. At the conclusion of each interview, thank the teacher for sharing ideas with you.

5. Summarize your interview results by tallying the types of formats that teachers used or would have liked to use. Make some notes for yourself regarding formats you think you might like to seek out later.

As a special educator, you will find that your education does not end when your professional training is completed. You will be responsible for keeping current with many topics that directly influence your delivery of instruction. When you interview teachers as part of Project Try-Out 2.2, you may be surprised at their varying levels of enthusiasm for their work. Some may be very positive and upbeat, while others may sound more discouraged. You will find a wide range of attitudes and feelings among educators—special and general. Your responsibility to remain up-to-date will be the same, no matter how you feel about your job.

International Standards for the Preparation and Certification of Special Education Teachers

The CEC first published *What Every Special Educator Must Know* in 1995. The current edition, the fifth, was published in 2003. Each edition was the result of a massive collaboration project among special educators across the country. The original set of standards were designed to provide "content" standards for teacher preparation programs and "knowledge and skills" for teachers who work directly with students. These competencies were originally designed to dovetail with Goals 2000. The current standards "are the result of a 3-year process to refine the 1996 standards and to build on them to create standards that address changes in the field" (CEC, 2003, p. ix). "The Interstate New Teacher Assessment and Support Consortium (INTASC) standards are compatible with the [fifth edition] CEC content standards" (Crutchfield, 2003, p. 41). Collaboration has appeared as a content area in all five editions of the CEC standards, and is the tenth set of standards included in the "knowledge and skills" domain areas. This document has continued to have an important influence on special educators (Crutchfield, 2003).

Background

The challenge posed by Goals 2000 for special educators and related teacher preparation programs was to determine what teachers needed to know, and to be able to do, in providing education to individuals with disabilities: the 1995 CEC publication was a response to the challenge. The 2003 edition reflects a shift to coordination with the INTASC standards, performance-based accreditation standards, and a new approach to the evaluation of teacher preparation programs. With this set of standards, CEC was providing explicit guidance for all teacher preparation programs in terms of expectations for educators across special education disciplines.

The original method used by CEC to generate the competencies reflected a model of collaboration. The method used to develop the competencies is described in the preface of *What Every Special Educator Must Know:*

> This collaborative effort of members of CEC, its Divisions, and others reflects our belief that standards for the profession should emanate from the field and represent the wide diversity of the field. The thousands of special educators and others who served on committees, subcommittees, and working groups and responded to exhaustive surveys gave freely of their knowledge and time to develop and validate these standards and guidelines. (1995, p. v)

For the first time, input was sought from professors in teacher preparation programs as well as classroom educators. The results of their work helped to provide standardization. The fifth edition also was based on a collaborative approach: "Over 100 CEC members helped directly to develop and evaluate the standards and thousands of CEC members and many other individuals affiliated with other organizations helped validate the standards" (2003, p. ix).

Connection to Collaboration

The centrality of collaboration is shown in the document. Standard 10 of the CEC's 2004 definition of a well-prepared special education teacher is titled "Collaboration." The following overview statement is provided:

> Special educators routinely and effectively collaborate with families and other educators, related service providers, and personnel from community agencies in culturally responsive ways. This collaboration assures that the needs of individuals with exceptional learning needs are addressed throughout schooling. (p. 10)

These broad requirements are described in much more detail throughout the book, with specific knowledge and skill standards for teachers working with students with special needs as well as a "self-evaluation tool" for students preparing to become special education teachers of students in general education settings.

Project Try-Out 2.3

Planning Ahead for Collaboration

1. Access the Special Education Standards developed by the Council for Exceptional Children, either on the Web (www.cec.sped.org/ps/) in the Professional Standards section of the site, or in the hard copy guide.

2. Review Standard 10, which focuses on collaboration.

3. Summarize the resources and information you have obtained for each item included in Standard 10 from (a) your special education courses, (b) your experience in schools, (c) your personal reflections. Stretch beyond the facts to examine the meaning of these standards and how you have deepened your understanding of collaboration.

4. Select 2–3 items that you know are gaps in either your knowledge or understanding. Make a commitment to yourself that one year from today, you will have deepened your knowledge or understanding of these items.

CONCLUSION

Legal and historical events in the twentieth century have transformed the lives of people with disabilities, their teachers, and their families. In part, this has been a function of changing the vision of what life could be like for people with disabilities. Collaboration alone is insufficient for substantial paradigm shifts to take place. Major changes emerge from the availability and use of new resources (e.g., Web-based portfolios; Cramer, Krasinski, Crutchfield, Sackmary, & Scalia, 2000) and a commitment to institutional change (e.g., Cramer, 2003). The changes in the lives of people with disabilities have moved the issue of collaboration from an optional extra to a crucial part of the delivery of services to people with disabilities and their families. Throughout the rest of this book, you will see many examples of how collaboration makes a difference. Teachers who collaborate effectively are better able to

- advocate for their students
- work with other professionals and paraprofessionals in their school district and community
- communicate with parents and family member of their students
- seek out resources in the community

Collaboration is a key that will help you unlock many doors. The remainder of this book will show you how to develop your own collaboration skills and to apply them to your collaboration project.

3

Ingredients for Successful Collaboration

Intrapersonal and Interpersonal Characteristics

There are surprising similarities between collaboration and cooking. Consider this: there is no one "right" way to collaborate or cook. Instead, we evolve our collaboration and cooking styles based on our interests, capabilities, and experiences.

Think about making a favorite recipe. If you view collaboration in schools comfortably, like a "natural" cook concocting at the stove, you are likely to be a relaxed and confident collaborator. On the other hand, if you dread collaboration, you may avoid it, just as some people avoid cooking. Many people imagine that any collaborative (or cooking) contact is a disaster waiting to happen.

Whether you are a confident or abstaining collaborator, Chapter 3 will highlight features of collaboration that pertain to your work with others. This chapter will examine successful ingredients for collaboration, ideally leading to an expanded definition of "professional world" to include collaborative encounters. Ultimately, the results of collaboration have the same potential to make people smile as do the aromas emanating from a kitchen—familiarity, comfort, and anticipation!

Lopez, Torres, and Norwood (1998) mention both intrapersonal and interpersonal competence as contributors to successful collaboration. Rubin (1993) describes both intrapersonal and interpersonal motivations for communication patterns. When you collaborate, communication must be a key ingredient. These two motivations are quite different.

First Day of School: Professional Goal Setting

Responses to the question, "How will you make this year better than last year?"

I realize that I have lots of great ideas, but they stay in my head. I'm going to do a much better job this year of putting those thoughts into action.

I am going to do a better job of communicating with other teachers this year. Instead of saying over and over that we never have enough time, I'm going to make time each week for conferencing. I ended last year on a frustrating note—I don't want that to happen again.

The first response reflects *intra*personal motivation, which is based on the internal issues each person brings to a situation. The second response emphasizes contacts with others. More *inter*personal, the motivation is external, based on the person's desire to communicate with others.

Neither approach is "right." However, one may appeal to you more than the other. We will explore these two very different motivation sources to distinguish what impels people to collaborate. Collaboration does not occur in a vacuum. Herrity and Morales (2004) describe a collaborative endeavor at Learning Together Charter School, which existed within "a trusting and nurturing environment . . . where school members are considered as professionals and given meaningful opportunities . . . to participate in shared decision making with colleagues and parents" (pp. 76–77). Little and Crawford (2002) describe modeling a collaborative approach in teacher education involving an interdisciplinary planning team as well as a collaborative course delivery approach: "From the successful implementation feedback of this pilot course, [it can be concluded that] the collaboration across disciplines and educational institutions can serve as a source of continuous renewal within the university and public school" (p. 324). In this chapter, we'll look at both intrapersonal and interpersonal foundations for collaborative work.

INTRAPERSONAL FOUNDATION FOR COLLABORATION

Getting up each morning, many special educators are awakened by their internal vision of the school day. When the alarm clock goes off, many immediately begin reviewing their visible and invisible job responsibilities. While some eagerly anticipate the day ahead, others find themselves anxiously anticipating collaboration challenges that await them at work. They picture themselves running into a principal who has a habit of being argumentative, conferring with a paraprofessional who lacks initiative, or coordinating schedules with a co-teacher who hasn't set up a time to discuss a difficult student. "If only it were Saturday," many special educators sigh, as they work their way out of bed and into the shower.

In this section, the effects of intrapersonal characteristics will be discussed. Internal motivators can help teachers change their personal outlooks about collaboration from "half empty" to "half full."

Attitudes Make a Difference

Like the little engine who could, the teachers who "think they can" have an advantage over those who just "wish they could." Teachers looking at collaboration with optimism are focusing on what they *can* do rather than what is beyond their control. In research terms, this perspective parallels teacher efficacy, or teachers' belief in their ability to affect student learning. Efficacy is an internal belief system that has intrigued researchers for some time. Most researchers attribute the origins of teacher efficacy to the work of Bandura. In 1977 he introduced the concept of efficacy to the field of cognitive social learning theory. Bandura differentiated between expectations of *outcomes* (the probable consequences of behavior) and expectations of *efficacy* (the belief that one could accomplish certain things). Subsequent research has often made use of the instrument developed by Gibson (1983), which specifically tests teacher efficacy. Woolfolk and Hoy (1990) provide a thorough history of the development of the concept of teacher efficacy. Bangert (2004) discusses the concept in relation to constructivism and effective teaching. While research has not explicitly matched collaboration beliefs with beliefs about efficacy (and resulting actions), the following discussion highlights relevant parallels.

Most research in the field examines efficacy as a measure of an individual's conviction that it's possible to produce a specific outcome by successfully performing necessary behaviors. The following is an example of a method of tracking individual success.

When I started teaching, I set up a file box. In it, I used blue cards for things I did that worked. I used white cards for things I tried that had to be improved. When I made a refinement, I stapled a pink card to a white card. Every Friday, I reviewed all my cards, adding and changing based on what I'd tried during the week. When I finally got it right, I stapled a blue card on top.

At the start of the year, almost everything was white or pink. But I remembered something I'd read, that a goal was to double your mistakes, to keep trying new things, and extending yourself. And, as the year went on, I had more blue cards. By the end of the year, I had a lot of ideas which I could reuse. And I felt more confident about my trial-and-error approach.

Efficacy, which begins as an internal belief system, influences external behavior. The example with the white, pink, and blue cards shows a highly self-disciplined teacher who systematically analyzes his effectiveness. This teacher reviews what he does and makes necessary adjustments. A methodical review process—comparing what you think you can do with what you actually do—is an informal way to examine your own efficacy. Idea Try-Out 3.1 is an opportunity to look back on what you did, focusing on communication with others.

Idea Try-Out 3.1

This Week in Review

This activity allows you to reflect on the effort you put into several different projects/ activities you accomplished in the past week. Divide this page in your collaboration notebook into four vertical columns. Use the following guidelines:

- If you are currently working or volunteering in a school as a student teacher, paraprofessional, or a classroom teacher, use the school as your frame of reference.
- If you are not currently involved with a school, think of a setting in which you have recently spent a lot of time or invested a lot of energy. This could be a sports team, your living arrangement, or a part-time job you have that is not in a school. Use this setting as your frame of reference.
  1. Think back over the past week, and pick out *four* projects/activities you completed. Two should be projects/activities you looked forward to doing, and two should be projects/activities that were difficult or new. In the column on the far left side of the page, label them, adding a few brief descriptive words. Space them out down the entire page.
  2. Think back to the start of each task or project. Evaluate how well you thought you'd do. Give yourself a grade of A, B, C, D, or F. Put these grades in the middle column, along with one or two words summing up your outlook at the start.
  3. Evaluate the ways in which you sought assistance or used your inner resources to accomplish your goal. Record the answers to the following questions in the third column:
     a. How many people did you ask for information? _____
     b. How many people did you ask for advice? _____
     c. How often did you mentally explore options before taking action? _____
     d. How many other types of resources did you use (e.g., books, articles, the Internet)? _____
     e. How many times did you revise your approach based on your success, or lack of it? _____
  4. In retrospect, how would you describe the impact of your initial outlook on the results you achieved? Put a brief description in the fourth column.

As you reflected on these four activities, you may have observed that your outlook at the start was more predictive than you would have guessed. You may need to find ways to increase your own efficacy in difficult situations. The collaboration project that is the focus of this book will enable you to develop a new, confident approach toward a person with whom you interact regularly. Your inner belief system should become a support for you—your attitude can become a help rather than a hindrance.

Strategies for changing attitudes can include pairing individuals whose outlook on a specific challenge differ. In the study conducted by Sprague, Cooper, and Pixley (2004), university faculty were paired with K–12 teachers for a "high tech mentoring" experience. The K–12 teachers, whose experience with technology was extensive, helped change the outlook of faculty members, as individualized support experiences and practice helped them to become more adept at using technology.

> This project resulted in several collaborative relationships. Many of the faculty continued to meet with their teacher partners even after the year of participation had ended. . . The mutual respect that developed allowed them to see themselves as partners with the ultimate goal to improve preservice education. (p. 19)

Although concerns existed at the outset of the project ("At the start of this project there was concern expressed about whether or not faculty would be willing to learn from a teacher and whether or not teachers would be intimidated by the idea of mentoring a faculty member," p. 18), the carefully structured program and opportunities for learning led to attitude change.

Teachers who can connect their inner belief systems to their external behavior can be successful in several different ways. Agne, Greenwood, and Miller (1994) conducted research examining the correlations between teacher belief systems and teacher effectiveness. When they compared outstanding teachers (88 teachers rated as Teacher of the Year) with excellent teachers (92 teachers who had been selected to provide inservice training to others), the outstanding teachers had significantly higher evidence of teacher efficacy than the excellent teachers (p. 148). This comparison is based on completion of several scales measuring teacher efficacy, including the scale developed by Gibson (1983). Outstanding teachers believed in their capabilities, and their capabilities were significantly more widely recognized by others than those of excellent teachers. The following is a description by a coworker of a teacher who views herself as capable and competent.

> *I have always liked to work with Karen. She can always put a positive spin on things. Whenever we get stuck trying to help out a student, she always says, "We'll find a way!" And, the amazing part is, when she's around, we do.*
>
> *I've told Karen that sometimes I find her optimism to be kind of sickening, and we laugh. But really, I envy her ability to keep on keeping on.*

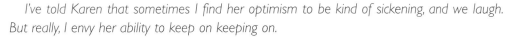

Others rely on her perseverance.

Teachers with a high sense of efficacy exude confidence. In her study of 200 special education teachers from four Midwest states, Allinder (1994) found significant correlations between the teachers' efficacy and their classroom behavior. Teachers who had greater belief in their abilities to teach were more likely to be confident and enthusiastic about teaching. As collaborators, these teachers' confidence and enthusiasm would be an inner resource for them. When working with others, they might sound like Karen.

Allinder's findings about the relationship between teacher efficacy and confidence/enthusiasm confirm those of previous studies (Anderson, Greene, & Loewen, 1988; Gibson & Dembo, 1984; Guskey, 1988; Woolfolk & Hoy, 1990). Allinder (1994) recommended that teachers in training should work toward developing self-reflective skills; "preservice teacher education programs should emphasize a framework for analyzing one's beliefs and actions" (p. 94). In other words, teachers in training should take time to look at their attitudes, because a belief in their own abilities is likely to correlate with "maximizing academic and social gains for students" (p. 94). The try-outs in this book offer you opportunities to examine your attitudes and beliefs.

Allinder's work is also in keeping with an earlier study by Ashton and Webb (1986). Ashton and Webb reported that "teachers with a high sense of efficacy were more likely than their low-efficacy counterparts to define low-achieving students as reachable, teachable, and worthy of teacher attention and effort" (p. 72). The attitudes that empower teachers help them in many different aspects of their professional lives. This constructive outlook can be an asset when collaborating.

Teachers with a strong sense of efficacy express their confidence to others. Hoover-Dempsey, Bassler, and Brissie (1992) reported that teachers who demonstrate efficacy are able to interact with parents more confidently and less defensively. This relationship is improved if the parents also have a sense of their own efficacy. In their review of literature discussing collaboration between teachers and parents, Robinson and Fine (1994) commented on how the collaboration between home and school can be strengthened through the presence of efficacy.

Practices observed by Dieker (2001b) for effective teaming in middle and high schools to include students with disabilities include preparing a positive climate, clarifying the roles of all team members, securing common planning time, and developing an effective evaluation plan. Details about the specifics of strategies used are provided in Dieker and Berg (2002). All of these would be most effective if the teachers involved had a high sense of efficacy.

Being a confident teacher is not only an inherent trait; it can be developed. Fritz, Miller-Heyl, Kreutzer, and MacPhee (1995) involved 241 teachers in a training program called DARE To Be You to enhance feelings of personal and teaching efficacy. Their results show that teachers can learn how to approach teaching more constructively. They concluded that teachers need to explore "issues of confidence and involvement in their professional roles. Programs such as DARE, which foster teaching efficacy, have a continuing positive impact on participants' interest and commitment to their professional growth" (p. 207). Participating in a structured program is one way to increase your sense of efficacy. This book will provide you with many ways to increase your confidence and ability to collaborate, through the collaboration project. You can use this book as the start for an ongoing commitment to your own professional development.

Consider investigating your outlook on the collaboration process using the scale developed by Bauwens and Hourcade (2003). They include several items that are needed when developing a predisposition toward collaboration:

- tolerance of failure and mistakes while seeking results
- high level of confidence in own abilities
- respect and trust for others
- inner pressure to achieve results

Teachers who become increasingly aware of their own attitudes can use their ideas and inner-directed motivation to become more purposeful, effective teachers and collaborators.

Self-concept is another feature of the intrapersonal foundation of collaboration. The self-concepts of many teachers can be fragile.

> *When I think back to my first years of teaching, I remember how hard it was to "be myself." I spent most of my time trying to figure out what other people expected of me. It was very hard for me to ask others for help. I think the first time I really felt like I fit in was when a newer teacher came to me for advice. That's when I could really share my ideas!*

Although we may think that self-concept exists on the inside only, Sparks and Rye (1990) reported that students could differentiate between teachers whose self-esteem scores were higher and those whose scores were lower. The teachers who were "enthusiastic, bold, group-oriented, relaxed and extroverted" (p. 32) received the highest satisfaction ratings from 163 eighth-grade students, and these were the same teachers who received the highest total self-esteem scores on two separate indicators. Teachers with the lowest total self-esteem scores were rated lowest by the students and described as "submissive, shy, tense, and introverted" (p. 33). The authors concluded:

> Modeling is one of the most effective ways students learn, so it could be assumed that the teacher who feels good about himself or herself and who expresses warmth, genuineness, and congruency in communicating with students will be the most influential in helping students become fully functioning in school. (p. 33)

Our students and fellow teachers watch us. As Sparks and Rye found, our self-concepts are more public than we would guess. Do you wonder what others see when they look at you? See what you learn from Project Try-Out 3.2.

Project Try-Out 3.2

Test Your Attitude

This activity gives you several ways to look at attitudes you have that are related to your outlook on collaboration.

1. Use one or both of the following published research instruments:
   a. The Teacher Efficacy Scale (TES) was developed by Gibson (1983). It is included in the article by Gibson and Dembo (1984) describing the validity of the scale. Get a copy of the article. Make two copies of the TES. Complete one copy and evaluate your current efficacy. Keep the other copy and complete it at the end of the semester.

> b. You can also rate your collaboration readiness using the scale developed by Bauwens and Hourcade (2003). It is included in Chapter 5 of their book *Cooperative Teaching: Rebuilding and Sharing the Schoolhouse.* Make two copies of their scale. Complete one copy and evaluate your collaboration readiness. Keep the other copy and complete it at the end of the semester.
>
> 2. Put both the completed and blank copies of the instruments in your collaboration notebook. Review the ratings you gave yourself. Identify *one* way that you would like to see yourself change in the coming year. Include your comment in your collaboration notebook.

Were the outcomes of Project Try-Out 3.2 as you expected? Were there some things that you predicted and some that surprised you? As you design and carry out your collaboration project, you will have many opportunities to look at yourself critically. This type of self-reflective activity is an ongoing requirement for successful collaboration. Ideally, when you complete the rating of yourself at the end of the semester, you will have fewer surprises because you'll know yourself better. Some people incorporate in-depth reflection into many aspects of their lives, as Bateson (the daughter of anthropologists Gregory Bateson and Margaret Mead) shares in the fascinating set of biographies she presents in *Composing a Life* (1989). Reflection is part of the lives of all of the individuals in her book, and it serves as a precursor to major transitions and life changes. Reflection can be a tool for you as you develop your teaching practices.

Activities of a Reflective Practitioner

The process of reflecting on teaching appears frequently in the literature and is quite similar to the development of intrapersonal skills described so far in this chapter. Stefani, Clarke, and Littlejohn (2000) observed that there are numerous descriptions of reflective practice, and use this definition: "To reflect on their learning, students need to evaluate their performance against clear criteria such that they are then measuring their progress against targets which are self-identified or negotiated in collaboration with tutors or peers (Stefani, 1998)" (p. 165). Their research project with a group of postgraduate students led them to the following conclusion:

> This case study has re-enforced the importance of formative feedback to student learning. It is often the case that students feel aggrieved at the level of emphasis on summative feedback in higher education at the cost of formative feedback . . . This project has provided . . . considerable insight into the importance of sharing an understanding of the purpose of formative feedback . . . Students could recognize the value and importance of reflection, when contextualized to a specific learning task for which the students had been involved in setting out their own learning goals. (p. 169)

The ways in which the reflective practitioner is directly engaged in the reflective process influences its likelihood of being successful.

Ross, Bondy, and Kyle (1993) present seven basic assumptions for the reflective practitioner that are consistent with the development of intrapersonal skills, building on Ross (1989). Abernathy and Cheney (2005) provide a tool for reflection that enables teachers to analyze their work. They recommend that this analysis be the start of further training. Reflection is an important starting point but requires follow-up: "Teachers noted surprise at their personal results but were unsure how to make changes" (p. 56). Reflection alone is not enough.

The idea of reflecting on teaching is not new. In 1933, John Dewey encouraged teachers to incorporate reflection into their work to promote professional growth. However, reflection is not intended as simply a rehashing of the past. Garman (1986) described it this way: "[Reflection is not] a mental reexamination of past events aimed at justifying or defending the consequences. Neither is reflection a way of determining what should have been done—a way of replaying scenarios with a slightly different script" (p. 15). Gabel's 2001 extraordinary article, based on a year's work with three novice teachers who were themselves disabled, illustrates the power of reflective practice. "They have begun to realize the potential for engaging themselves and their students in explorations of personal identity and lived experience" (p. 45). Reflection served as a tool for personal and well as professional growth.

Consider reflection to be an organized process for evaluating information. Rather than reflecting while on your drive home from work, record your analysis in a journal. Participants in Dieker and Monda-Amaya's 1995 research project maintained journals and used a content analysis approach to review their reflections. (See Chapter 8 for a description of how to use content analysis in your collaboration project.) The project staff trained six full time master's-level students in the Collaborative Resource Teacher (CRT) Training Program at the University of Illinois to become more reflective in their practices. Teachers learned to analyze their journal entries systematically and also participated in interviews. At the end of the study, "all CRT students indicated that they would continue to use a structured reflective process in their own teaching. . . . One CRT student noted that she reflected on her teaching continuously throughout the teaching day, a practice that exemplifies reflection-in-action as proposed by Schon (1983)" (p. 251).

Ongoing reflection can be incorporated into daily teaching activities. Carter and Doyle (1995) encourage preservice teachers to reflect on their intrapersonal motivation and to clarify their expectations about their future classrooms. The ideas they generate can be used as future resources: "[Novice teachers'] preconceptions clearly cannot be ignored or pushed aside in favor of more academic understandings of the issues surrounding teaching. . . . Preconceptions should not be seen as obstacles . . . but rather as the basic resources novices have in learning to teach" (p. 194).

Teachers' hopes and positive preconceptions about collaboration can be harnessed and contribute to making the collaborative effort successful. Teachers' expectations, based on prior experiences, can influence their views of what they can accomplish with their colleagues and their students. Idea Try-Out 3.3 provides an opportunity for you to reflect and make use of your positive attitudes and experiences.

Idea Try-Out 3.3

Idea Transplant

This exercise invites you to reflect on two different situations. Record your reactions to the items below in your collaboration notebook.

1. Think back over the last few months. Recall a situation in which you were successful in your school or work setting.
   a. List two or three adjectives that you or others might have used to describe your outlook *before* you entered the situation.
   b. List two or three adjectives that you or others might have used to describe your outlook *during* the situation.
   c. List two or three adjectives that you or others might have used to describe your outlook *after the situation was resolved.*

2. Repeat the three steps, but this time consider a situation that did not turn out as you wished.
   a. List two or three adjectives that you or others might have used to describe your outlook *before* you entered the situation.
   b. List two or three adjectives that you or others might have used to describe your outlook *during* the situation.
   c. List two or three adjectives that you or others might have used to describe your outlook *after the situation was resolved.*

3. Imagine that you could have received an idea transplant from the first situation to use in the second. Write down one thought or idea you found to be helpful in the first situation that could have improved your outlook in the second situation.

4. Compare your attitudes in the two situations using the following questions:
   a. If you could have received the idea transplant, *when* would it have helped you most in the second situation—at the outset, in the middle, or at the end?
   b. What difference do you think the idea transplant might have made in the outcome of the situation?
   c. Given what you have considered so far, what might you try to do differently in the future?

Your review of these two situations may give you ways to examine your typical approach to situations. Ideally, this will enable you to become more familiar with your predisposition toward success and failure. This kind of analysis can enable you to adjust your outlook during the collaboration process and more routinely become a reflective practitioner.

Although the collaborators' attitudes can highly influence the outcome of the collaboration effort, they are only one part of the picture. The interactions in which you engage are important to you as a teacher. As Howey (1985) explains, "teaching is largely an interpersonal activity. The degrees of understanding teachers have of their own behavior and how they have changed over time is directly related to the nature and quality of interactions in schools" (p. 59). When teachers give themselves time and permission to improve their interpersonal relationships with others, they incorporate key ingredients needed for collaboration. Their self-awareness is an important foundation for collaboration, fitting in with the work they do with others, as discussed in the next section of this chapter.

INTERPERSONAL FOUNDATION FOR COLLABORATION

Do administrators and general educators expect effective, ongoing communication with special educators? The answer is a resounding "Yes." Angle (1996) describes an effective approach to collaborative teaching and enrichment remediation: "Steps evolved systematically when teachers collaborated with each other on a continual basis. *Communication is the key to enrichment remediation*" (p. 8). This is true even if communication is not explicitly included in the job description. Friend and McNutt (1987) compared the actual job descriptions in 776 school districts to administrators' identification of job activities on a questionnaire. "Consulting with school staff" was identified significantly more often by administrators as an expectation than it appeared as a part of the job description. All the administrators viewed the consultation process as an expected part of the job description, yet it was only included in 76% of the written job descriptions, a difference significant at the .01 level (p. 226). The unwritten expectation for dialogue places the burden on the special educator. Hourcade and Bauwens (2003) recognize the challenges that most special educators will face in creating an effective interpersonal foundation:

> For most educators, the single most significant change . . . is the new professional relationships they must develop with their teaching partners. This may well represent the single greatest challenge . . . It takes work and skill to develop and maintain a harmonious and productive working relationship with another professional. (p. 166)

In the following example, the teacher realizes that conflicting priorities interfere with communication at school.

"When can we get together?" It seems like that is the question I am always asking teachers at school. Some days I really feel like a broken record. But I have to remind myself that what is a high priority for me—discussing a student's progress—may not be at the top of their lists. How can I bring my expectations for me and their expectations for me together?

The problem facing teachers can be a function of the gap between expectations. This is true regardless of the kind of relationship you are trying to establish with your fellow teachers. As described in Chapter 1, there *is* a difference between consultation and collaboration. That difference may be decisive in characterizing the nature of communication (e.g., is one teacher expected to be an expert in the interaction?).

Instead of focusing on whose expectations are right, or blaming someone else for having the wrong expectations, shift to a different approach. Develop routines to make expectations explicit—your own and those of your teaching partner(s). Thompson (2004) describes such a process for developing a collaborative relationship with a research partner. Her collaboration surprised her in that "laughter became a significant factor in shaping research relationships and a necessary factor which cemented the possibilities for research action" (p. 18). Laughter helped her to avoid becoming discouraged and to avoid the "individual blaming focus" (p. 29) that her study might have prompted. Thomson et al. (2003) provides a very different collaborative model in a graduate program of 500 special education teachers (the Resource Teachers Learning and Behavior, or RTLB) in the New Zealand schools. New legislation (Special Education 2000) required a shift in the services teachers were to provide, and explicit discussion of the new roles, in a teacher training program and with general educators, led to very positive outcomes.

> Despite the difficulties, there are many situations throughout the country in which the implementation of this new role has been sound and robust. This is occurring where RTLB have enthusiastically embraced the inclusive paradigm and have worked with high levels of skill and with receptive class teachers who also are committed to inclusive education. (p. 109)

You can work successfully with others only if all involved know about (and agree on) what is expected. In the 1995 case study of a Kentucky elementary school using teaching partnerships to create an inclusive school, this kind of communication was essential. Phillips, Sapona, and Lubic (1995) reviewed transcripts of collaborating teams that worked together to develop inclusive practices within their school. They drew the following conclusions:

> Collaborative efforts between special and general educators tended to progress through identifiable phases or stages . . . (a) experiencing anxiety, (b) working out the logistics, (c) determining classroom roles, (d) sharing planning and curriculum development, (e) recognizing and articulating the benefits of collaboration, (f) learning to recognize when a more restrictive setting may be appropriate, and (g) evaluating the overall effort. (p. 265)

In other words, the collaborative process does not take place immediately once the commitment to collaborate has been made. Instead, ongoing dialogue is needed.

Friend (1984) studied 126 three-person teams, asking resource room teachers, general education teachers, and principals about their expectations for resource room teachers' consultation practices. All three groups had high expectations for the resource teachers' consultation skills. The most highly rated item (rated as number one by 98% of the group) did not vary by group. All agreed the top item should be "systematically evaluating interventions to determine effectiveness." This item is clearly related to student needs. The second item, rated as important by 96% of the group, focused on the resource room teachers, charging them with the task of "establish[ing] a climate of mutual trust" (p. 248). Friend concluded,

> Resource teachers appear to be expected to be "super teachers," that is, in addition to the primary responsibility of providing direct instruction to handicapped students, they are expected to confer with regular education teachers,

observe students in mainstream settings, conduct inservice training, and so on, through a seemingly endless list of job duties. (p. 249)

Her conclusion still rings true for many teachers today. The obstacles special educators must overcome to collaborate are part of an already crowded job description. However, overcoming those obstacles leads to observable outcomes, which benefit teachers as well as students. Lopez et al. (1998) recommend the development of "interprofessional competencies," which include "shared vision, . . . awareness of professional differences, . . . knowledge of and skills at collaboration, . . . and collective power" (p. 170). They recommend that

> there must be ongoing monitoring of each partner's commitment to the collaborative process and the successful functioning of the team. This can only be accomplished by scheduling a time for the discussion of arising issues or concerns. The management of conflict as it emerges would also be helpful in maintaining the goals of the collaboration. Unresolved conflict continues to serve as an obstacle to the collaborative process. (p. 173)

The development of a professional, collaborative work style depends on effective communication.

Friend and Cook (2002) recommend that teachers involved in co-teaching "talk about classroom matters that you might take for granted, . . . make time to discuss how co-teaching is going, . . . [and] don't set unrealistic expectations" (p. 13). Co-teaching may take place in relation to specific content (e.g., secondary mathematics co-teaching is described by Magiera, Smith, Zigmond, & Gebauer, 2005) when the collaboration on content and strategies would be needed. Magiera et al. have recommendations for discussions that include explaining the nature of the disabilities to the general educator and discussion of teaching issues:

> Discuss every aspect of teaching with your co-teaching partner, including management of the classroom, critical elements of the mathematics curriculum, pet peeves, and how to provide feedback to each other. The special education teacher should be truly invested in how the class is conducted. (p. 23)

The use of this, or any other strategy, must be analyzed carefully to make sure that you are effectively intervening with your students. In Murawski and Swanson's 2001 meta-analysis of the co-teaching research, they found that only 6 of the 89 articles reviewed allowed for in-depth analysis, using effect sizes related to students with disabilities. The authors concluded,

> The fact that the research on co-teaching is lacking does not mean that co-teaching in schools should be eliminated altogether. . . . It is imperative that data be gathered in classes where the merger between general and special education faculty members has been successful, as well as in those where it has not worked well. (p. 266)

A key factor in success in the classroom is communication between teachers. How can this communication take place effectively? Chapter 7 provides explicit suggestions for communicating well. In the next section of this chapter, some of the fundamentals of communication are discussed.

Communication and Its Relationship to Effective Classroom Performance

An effective communication style coincides with effective teaching. Sallinen-Kuparinen (1992) reviewed the empirical studies of teacher effectiveness that appeared in the speech communication literature. Two major trends could be observed: (1) effective teaching and communicator style are positively correlated, and (2) there is no single communication style that is effective. The following illustrates how two different listening styles can be almost contradictory, and yet each can be successful.

> *I remember being confused during student teaching. My cooperating teacher and I were so different from each other. He was outgoing, joked with the students, and made them feel like he was really listening. I am much quieter, and wondered how I would ever become a good teacher. My supervisor told me that I had what it takes, that I would grow into my style.*
>
> *Looking back, ten years later, I'm glad I didn't just try to imitate someone else. I'm very different from him, but I've found my way to pay attention to my students. Each time my students tell me that I'm a good listener, I think of him. I've learned that you can be a good listener in lots of different ways.*

What does this mean for you, as a teacher and as a collaborator? It means that there *is* a need for you to evaluate your effectiveness as a communicator, rather than imitate the communication style of others.

Chrystal (1988) corroborates the idea that there is no single acceptable approach for teachers to use. He describes four different helping styles that teachers use:

- *Moral Style*: Students are considered primarily responsible for both creating and solving their learning problems.
- *Compensatory Style:* Students are considered the source of their problems, but teachers are involved in developing the solution.
- *Medical Style*: Students are responsible neither for the creation nor the solution of their problems.
- *Enlightenment Style*: Teachers have responsibility for solving the problems created by students. (pp. 9–11)

These different approaches illustrate the range of interpersonal communication and helping styles available to you when you teach. They show that there is no single answer for interpersonal communication by teachers in their classroom work.

In a study that examined these same four communication styles, an additional feature was brought into consideration. In literature on gerontology, there were several studies that supported the help and communication styles of "natural helpers . . . relatives friends and neighbors who have earned reputations within their social networks as caring competent problem solvers. . . . They typically help others free of charge and are not affiliated with an organization" (Memmott, 1993, p. 11). Memmott investigated the preferred communication style of trained and untrained helpers. His study consisted of interviewing 48 rural natural helpers and

48 trained social workers. In addition, each participating subject completed the Coping Orientation Questionnaire and the Helping Orientation Questionnaire. Both questionnaires examined preferred interpersonal communication styles. Memmott's findings suggested that all helpers endorsed the moral and compensatory models significantly more than the enlightenment and medical models. Natural and professional helpers differed in terms of the type of problems on which they focused.

In an earlier study, Patterson and Brennan (1983) contrasted natural and professional helpers, comparing 42 paid helpers with 108 natural helpers in rural Kansas. They supported the value of the natural helpers' work, commenting on their "interesting data on the range and richness of techniques used by natural helpers" (p. 60). They concluded that the match between the person giving the help and the one receiving it is very important: "Attention must be paid to the match between helper and recipient needs and satisfactions to promote mutually beneficial helping relationships" (p. 64). These studies suggest that there are many different interpersonal communication styles that teachers can use when providing assistance to students. One approach cannot serve all students.

As we will see, this need for variety is also true of communication styles in the collaborative relationship. Morford and Willing (1993), in suggesting communication strategies for administrators, had the following recommendation:

> Communicate in various styles. Send memos. Hold meetings. Use the telephone. Drop in. Manage by walking around. With each of these strategies, pay close attention to reactions. Be sensitive to the other's style, then communicate appropriately. Be always aware that effective administrators use a variety of communication styles. (p. 10)

Training in communication skills takes place in many contexts in higher education. Dinnebeil & McInerney (2001) incorporated instruction in interpersonal communication skills into the consultation and collaboration training provided to early childhood educators in their project. Mallette, Maheady, and Harper (1999), in their analysis of peer coaching by preservice general educators of students with special needs, included tracking improvements in the correct responses of the students as well as the behavior of the preservice peer coaches. They observed that

> almost every coaching-related interaction was positive in nature. It was extremely rare to hear any critical comments regarding a partner's performance. Instead, coaches focused specific praise statements on particular things their partners did well during the session. This suggests that given an opportunity to collaborate around educationally related topics, most preservice general educators will do so in a positive and, generally, constructive manner. (p. 214)

With communication training incorporated into higher education classes and practicum work, preservice teachers learn communication best practices and are able to practice these skills in a safe setting. Webb (2004), Salend and Sylvestre (2005), and others incorporate teaching communication skills (including both vocal and nonverbal strategies) to students with disabilities as part of social skills instruction. Thus, attention to communication skills can take place prior to, and during, full-time employment as a special education teacher.

Varying your communication approach can enable you to broaden your reach—you can more effectively connect with people who count on you for information or feedback. The ability to communicate effectively is a component of most recommended collaborative training programs (Hudson, Correa, Morsink, & Dykes, 1987; Price, 1991). Chapter 7 will provide a thorough analysis of the specific communication skills required to be successful in a collaborative venture. Below is an overview of two major types of communication—verbal and nonverbal.

Verbal Communication Strategies

Effective communication strategies bring better collaboration results. Gresham and Kendall (1987) reported increased likelihood of success if several things happened during the collaboration process. First, the collaborator should *ask* rather than *tell* how to identify and use resources. Second, effective collaborators were skilled in active listening and paraphrasing. Third, they were more likely to use colloquial language than technical jargon. Tannen (2001) recommends consideration of linguistic style, related to gender and other individual characteristics, to enhance communication.

The collaboration process requires special educators to be effective communicators, especially in team meetings. Bailey, Heisel-DeWert, Thiele, and Ware (1983) observed 160 participants in meetings with interdisciplinary teams. The researchers concluded that members were relatively well-prepared before the meetings and provided information effectively during meetings. However, they demonstrated group process behaviors (e.g., suggesting goals, objectives, or strategies for implementing goals and providing feedback on suggestions made by others) much less frequently. Preparation for these meetings can be incorporated into coursework and professional development activities in school. The graduates of an interdisciplinary program at University of North Carolina at Chapel Hill (described by Able-Boone et al., 2003) valued the "opportunities to work with 'real families' embedded in the seminars and coursework" (p. 81).

Sunderman (2000) studied four schools in the Chicago area to examine how standards and school reform were incorporated into their "already complex policy environment" and found that each school used collaboration as part of the process. "While teacher collaboration was an important strategy for aligning the curriculum with standards, standards were not the major impetus for reorganizing schoolwide programs" (p. 371). Two of the schools already had collaboration in place, and in the other two, "collaboration was introduced as part of the . . . plan but remained weakly developed in both schools" (p. 371). She drew the following conclusion:

> Teacher collaboration may be a useful strategy for aligning the curriculum with the standards. Through collaboration, teachers were more likely to teach the same things in the same grade and be more aware of what was required in the next grade. However, standards do not ensure that schools put in place the necessary structures to support teacher collaboration. (p. 372)

Administrative support is essential for collaboration to be successfully used, to align curriculum with standards, or to facilitate cross-level collaboration among teachers.

The following team initially faced difficulties but was able to overcome them. The team-based skills needed for effective collaboration with members of multidisciplinary teams are described in detail in Chapter 12.

When Maria chaired our team meetings, we found that we all moved along together. She was very good at summarizing and checking to see if everyone was in agreement.

She got transferred to another school, and we had a terrible time at first. We argued and got nowhere. Finally, we realized that we could teach ourselves to use the techniques she'd used. We make sure at the start of every meeting to appoint a chairperson. And we keep a list of group process techniques posted in our meeting room. We still miss Maria, but we're doing pretty well on our own.

The intent of the communicator may not be accurately perceived. Babad (1991) examined the ratings of 520 students regarding presumed teacher intent toward hypothetical students. The same behavior ("calling on the student") had different meanings, depending upon the capabilities of the student. If the student was seen as high-achieving, the teacher behavior was viewed as "emotionally supportive." However, if the student was identified as low-achieving, the same teacher behavior was viewed as "pressure."

Tschantz and Vail (2000) looked at the success that peer coaching had on the rate of responsive teacher statements in an inclusive setting. "Teachers embed individual objectives into the child's chosen activities with use of specific questions, reflective statements, open-ended questions, specific praise statements, modeling with the same materials, and other responsive teaching techniques" (p. 191). They were concerned that there was limited collaboration between early childhood specialists and early childhood special educators: "With the increase in inclusive environments there is also a need to improve communication and collaboration between general and special education teachers" (p. 191). Following the use of a peer coaching approach, and a multiple probe design to evaluate the effectiveness of peer coaching, over a two month period they saw increase in responsive statements and a positive response to peer coaching. In addition, "teachers found peer coaching helpful in increasing communication and wanted to continue sessions. . . . Peer coaching has the potential to become a powerful tool in improving teaching behaviors and communication between regular and special education teachers" (pp. 198–199). Their study illustrated how a coordinated approach could increase communication between teachers and also improve teaching practices.

Byers (1985) describes various communication analogies, illustrating the variety of expectations for effective communication. In some cases, the focus is on individual skill (e.g., in a game of tennis), while in others, the focus shifts to team coordination of individual skill (e.g., in a game of baseball). He concludes,

The individual and the cooperating group are not two extremes of some continuum in which we are trying to find a working middle. . . . It is not a matter of finding a middle ground. Both forms of human relations are facts of life and require recognition in our education enterprise. (p. 75)

The communication skills needed by an effective collaborator working in a group include both verbal and nonverbal capabilities.

Nonverbal Communication Strategies

Special educators must be able to express their ideas accurately and effectively, and this requires more than a good vocabulary. As Hudson and Glomb (1997) advise, "It is essential that teachers be aware of how their facial expressions, eye contact, gestures and body posture communicate their feelings and attitudes to their colleagues (Cook & Friend, 1996; Miller, 1986)" (p. 443). Banbury and Hebert (1992) comment on the need for special educators to make their nonverbal messages consistent with what they are saying. Body language and facial gestures must be congruent with comments—the "words" and the "music" must go together. Accurately understanding nonverbal communication has been the focus of study in many fields—linguistics, anthropology, psychology, and business. In the classic book *Kinesics and Context: Essays on Body Motion Communication* (1970), Ray Birdwhistell coined the term "body language" and examined the need for culture-specific examination of body and facial gestures:

> Insofar as I have been able to determine, just as there are no universal words, no sound complexes, which carry the same meaning the world over, there are no body motions, facial expressions, or gestures which provoke *identical* responses the world over. A body can be bowed in grief, in humility, in laughter, or in readiness for aggression. A "smile" in one society portrays friendliness, in another embarrassment, and in still another may contain a warning that, unless tension is reduced, hostility and attack will follow. (p. 42)

Birdwhistell's work inspired more research in the field. In *Bodytalk: The Meaning of Human Gestures* (1995), Desmond Morris provides a series of drawings of specific gestures worldwide. Scheflen (1972) used pictures to illustrate meaning, and Axtell (1991) combined text and drawings. All authors agree that the context of nonverbal communication, combined with the cultural characteristics of the people communicating, must be taken into account to interpret what is being said. As collaborators, we can train ourselves to develop sensitivity to the alternative meanings of nonverbal gestures.

Bernieri and Rosenthal (1991) examined research studies focusing on the coordinated responses between people, which they label "interpersonal coordination." They report that "evidence is slowly accumulating to suggest that . . . synchronization of one's behaviors with those of another may be one of the earliest forms of human communication and may even be present at birth" (p. 404). In other words, our instinct to communicate precedes our development of language. Examples they give for adult interpersonal coordination include "synchronization of head nods to the vocalization of the speaker, . . . behavioral or postural similarity, . . . mimic[ing] of another's behavior" (pp. 406–407). There are many different kinds of nonverbal coordination. Bernieri and Rosenthal conclude,

> Interpersonal coordination . . . is associated with many important social, cognitive, and developmental phenomena . . . The most empirically demonstrated result involving interpersonal coordination has been its relationship with social rapport. People seem to get along better when their behavior is well coordinated. . . . For schoolteachers, an understanding of interpersonal coordination could help identify teaching styles or rhythms to which children may be differentially receptive. Teachers then could be assigned

students who are more likely to coordinate with their particular teaching behavior. (pp. 428–429)

While assignment of students to classes is one possible solution, another is an increased sensitivity to students' nonverbal responses. Banbury and Hebert (1992) describe body language that teachers in classrooms can use to their advantage to better understand what their students are communicating. They provide recommendations for teachers—to pair nonverbal behavior with particular verbal messages. They differentiate approving/accepting from disapproving/critical and assertive/confident from passive/indifferent (p. 36).

Physical distance between speakers is another aspect of nonverbal communication. Banbury and Hebert (1992) define ways that students may use physical distance and personal space to communicate different messages. Beale (1990) also examines the physical space between individuals as a nonverbal message related to listening.

Clifton (2004), in discussing the challenges of involving students of diverse backgrounds in the inclusive classroom, discussed how observation enabled her to better understand students "who are not able to express themselves easily through the usual channels" (p. 81). She encouraged teachers to try to take the perspective of students in their classes, as prerequisite to working with them: "Pupils' voices talking about experiences when starting school are seldom heard, especially when communication is difficult. The methodology I decided to use involved observation and informal interviews followed by reflective conversations with critical friends" (p. 81). Incorporating observation into the communication process can assist you in broadening your options for understanding your students.

Learning to read body language can also help you assess your effectiveness as a speaker. Body language of your listener can be a signal that the person to whom you are speaking is attending to the conversation (or not attending) fully. Reading body language can be helpful when you are working with other adults as a collaborator or with your students. Both verbal and nonverbal communication are needed in the collaborative strategy of problem solving.

PROBLEM SOLVING: INTRAPERSONAL AND INTERPERSONAL SKILLS

Problem solving involves both intrapersonal and interpersonal capabilities. The interpersonal characteristics that coincide with effective problem solving overlap with the establishment of effective collaborative relationships (Elliott & Sheridan, 1992; Idol et al., 1988; Patriarca & Lamb, 1990; Polsgrove & McNeil, 1989) and putting problem solving in broader contexts of such concepts as common sense and intuition (Cacioppo, 2004). In their analysis of responses from 1,000 secondary special educators, Foley and Mundschenk (1997) reported that

in practice, educators appear not to be using or reporting problem solving as a major activity during collegial interactions . . . The lack of highly skilled collaborators may thwart attempts at meaningful collaboration activities, which may ultimately degenerate to mere exchanges of information among colleagues. (p. 58)

Problem solving is a skill that must be taught. Problem-based learning is described by Levin, Hibbard, and Rock (2002) as follows:

> Problem-based learning (PBL) is one instructional approach that encourages teachers to apply their developing knowledge base to real-world issues as they try to solve complex problems and dilemmas related to teaching and learning (Dean, 1999; Gerber, English & Singer, 1999; Levin, 2001; Pierce, 1999; Sage, 1999; Shumow, 1999). It is also a method that allows participants to practice needed skills, such as working in groups, collaborating, sharing information, and problem solving, as they apply information they gather to real-world, practical problems (Levin, 2001). (p. 278)

In their study of problem-based learning, the researchers involved 44 preservice teachers in problem-based learning activities in cohort groups. They found that as a result of their experience with this approach,

> many preservice teachers participating in the PBL unit began to perceive the role of an inclusion teacher as a member of a team, rather than as an isolated teacher trying to make the class work on her own, and many participants expressed that cooperation and collaboration is the only way they could see themselves being successful in an inclusive setting. (p. 287)

Problem solving and problem-based learning both support a methodical approach to real-life problems.

While there are some differences about the sequence to be followed in effective problem solving, there is agreement that generally problem solving follows a predictable pattern, including these four stages:

- Problem Identification (including gathering of information)
- Project Development
- Implementation
- Feedback/Evaluation

In each of these stages, persons doing the problem solving must focus on a specific part of the problem—either defining the problem or working on the solution. The ability to learn what the problem really is, through listening, is essential, as shown in the following example.

> *When I switched from working with elementary students in a resource room to being a consulting teacher, I was terrified. I was sure that everyone would think my ideas were terrible. I was amazed that I could give up the "expert" expectations I had for myself. That was the turning point for me. From that point on, I listened to the teachers more than I talked. I found that the pressure I felt was lessened. And listening made me much more effective.*

(Listening skills are described in more detail in Chapter 7.)

Interestingly, the skills that collaborators bring to the problem-solving process are not always connected to formal training, according to Memmott (1993) and Patterson and Brennan (1983). Memmott (1993) analyzed the difference between "naturals" (people who have a reputation within their friendship and work groups as "caring competent problem solvers"; p. 11) and those who received professional training. The natural helpers reported feeling closer to those they were helping, both before and after solving problems, than did the professionals. You and other beginning collaborators may feel linked to others in your school setting, even if you are not proficient at carrying out all the responsibilities involved with problem solving.

In Lazenby and Morton's (2003) description of "facilitating transformation through collaboration," two educators describe how collaboration between special education majors and nursing majors took place, with techniques that included problem solving and reflective learning. "Through problem-based learning, students were given case studies and questions that required collaboration to develop an effective educational plan" (p. 92). Students from both academic majors brought insights to the problems, which led to novel solutions neither could have developed alone.

As you will find in Idea Try-out 3.4, assistance can come from many sources.

Idea Try-Out 3.4

Helping Naturally

This activity will give you an opportunity to reflect on a time in your life when you received help from others.

1. Think back over your life, and identify three or four times in your life when you needed help. "Help" may have consisted of giving you information, listening to your concerns, or directing you toward other resources.

2. Identify one or two people who helped you in each situation. In your collaboration notebook, jot down their names on the far left side of the page. Next to each name, record several adjectives that describe the ways in which they helped. Record only how they helped.

3. Review in your mind the training these people received.
   a. How many of them were "natural" helpers or trained problem solvers?
   b. How did the natural helpers differ from people who had received some training in helping others?

4. Look over your work on this idea try-out and record one or two suggestions for yourself—ways you would like to behave when you are giving help to others in the future.

As you completed this exercise, you may have found that you learned something about how you solve problems. As part of your coursework in higher education, you may have studied "problem-based learning." In their meta-analysis of problem-based learning studies, Gijbels, Dochy, Van den Bossche, and Segers (2005) trace the origins of problem-based learning, or PBL, back to ancient Greece (p. 28), but state that

> PBL, as it is known today, originated in the 1950s and 1960s in response to dissatisfaction with common practices in medical education (Barrows, 1996). Although originally developed for medical training at McMaster, the McMaster version of PBL has been applied globally in many disciplines not necessarily related to the study of medicine. (p. 28)

Gijbels et al. identified "three levels of knowledge structure that can be targeted by assessment of problem solving . . . (a) understanding of concepts, (b) understanding of the principles that link concepts, and (c) linking of concepts and principles to conditions and procedures for application" (p. 27).

Ochoa and Robinson (2005) describe it as a simulation or case-based analysis. PBL is based on three assumptions:

1. Students learn more in groups than in lecture.

2. Ideas will be vetted by the group and will prevail on their merits.

3. Students' learning is maximized when they learn from tutors, not instructors. (p. 12)

Gijbels et al. (2005) concur with these as the first three principles and add three more:

4. Authentic problems are present at the beginning of the learning sequence, before any preparation or study has occurred.

5. The problems encountered are used as tools to achieve the required knowledge and the problem-solving skills necessary to eventually solve the problems.

6. New information is acquired through self-directed learning. (p. 30)

In other words, the process of solving problems involves a sharing of ideas, in a structured format, with a goal of authentic learning.

In teacher preparation programs, in controlled environments, PBL can be highly effective. Steinkuehler, Derry, Hmelo-Silver, and Delmarcelle (2002) incorporated a PBL Web-based approach into an undergraduate course, making use of a resource designed for PBL tutors (STEP Project Group, 2000). Their model—individual pre-analysis, group investigation, and individual final analysis and reflection—included reflection on both the process for problem solving as well as the specific problem itself. "Our site development strategy is very simple: *Accumulate wisdom and practical skill through repeated trials and then distribute it across resources, tools, and artifacts*" (p. 35). Their approach incorporated such items as

> worked example of each "product" for the students, a register of frequent misconceptions students bring to each problem and the common difficulties

students have had while working with various cases in the past, and a collection of problem-specific research suggestions that tutors can share with students who get stuck. (p. 35)

Sharing resources enables iterative reviews of the same problems, with instructional improvements taking place as resources are incorporated into the PBL activities.

In their analysis of studies that reported on the effects of PBL in medical education, Gijbels et al. (2005) carefully analyzed the methodology, outcomes, and statistical values of 40 published studies. They were interested in finding out how effective PBL actually was. After outlining the limitations of their work, they concluded that "the effect of PBL differs according to the levels of the knowledge structure being measured" (p. 45). They make the following recommendation: "If PBL aims to educate better problem solvers, more attention should be paid to the third level, during both the learning activities that take place and during students' assessment in PBL" (p. 46). The way in which students apply what they have learned to situations requiring problem-solving, they suggest, "must be considered in examining the effects of problem-based learning and probably in all comparative education research" (p. 27).

Think about how you handle problems in your current setting. You may work through problems primarily on your own. You may have a few people to whom you consistently turn, no matter what problem you are trying to solve. Or, you may have a wide range of people you use as a resource group. The design of a collaboration resource network is part of your work on your collaboration project, described in more detail in Chapters 6 and 7. Your team is likely to be part of your work at all stages of your collaboration project, but they may be especially helpful during the initial part of problem solving, problem identification.

Problem Identification

Problem identification is the first stage of the problem-solving process. Snell and Janney (2000), in their report of teachers' problem solving with students with moderate and severe disabilities in elementary classrooms, began with problem identification (p. 480). Problem identification involves the clarification of the issues to be addressed. Success in this stage requires a combination of intrapersonal and interpersonal skills. Snell and Janney reported that "Like subsequent steps, problem identification was not always done collaboratively by team members; however, the special education teacher expressed the need for consensus with the classroom teacher" (pp. 480–481). Snell and Janney observed that teachers used an iterative process, whereby they often refined the problem they had originally identified.

Tindal and Taylor-Pendergast (1989) also studied the problem-solving process. They analyzed the amount of time and the types of activities that collaborating teachers spent in each of the four stages of the problem-solving process. Half the total time was spent on problem identification, the most time spent in any single stage. Of the total time spent interacting with others, the vast majority (86%) was spent in this stage of the problem-solving process. The authors concluded "the need for a well-focused identification of problems that others are responsible for remediating . . . is critical" (p. 15).

Problem Identification

We begin every one of our team meetings with a five minute free-form discussion of what is going well on our teams. That helps us realize that there are positives.

From there, we move to problem identification. We've found that it helps if each of us comes to the meeting with three or four things that are of concern to us. These are sometimes our students, curriculum problems, behavior management issues—we've covered lots of ground over the years. We select the problems we can address best as a full team, or as subgroups. It takes us a while to figure out what to do, because our time to work together is so limited. But, by the time we are done, we feel like we are all going to be going in the same direction.

Tindal and Taylor-Pendergast (1989) were looking for ways to determine exactly what teachers did when problem solving. It is not clear whether the teachers in their study were able to be more successful because of the time spent in problem identification or if they subsequently ran out of time to accomplish the tasks that occur in the other stages. Further examination of how you divide your time between each stage of problem solving might reveal trends that will surprise you, either reinforcing your approach or pointing to a need for change.

Tindal and Taylor-Pendergast's study was designed, in part, to analyze the competencies developed by West and Cannon (1988). West and Cannon had a panel of 100 experts rank the top competencies for consulting special educators. The top five categories included a combination of intrapersonal and interpersonal capabilities: "interpersonal skills, personal and professional attitudes and beliefs, and personal attributes necessary for collaborative communication" (p. 61). All of these skills and characteristics are needed during the problem identification stage. Use Project Try-Out 3.5 to look at some of your habits during the problem identification stage.

Project Try-Out 3.5

Problem Solving for Friday Night

This activity will give you an opportunity to reflect on some of your recent problem-solving experiences. Think back over the past few months to a situation in which you had to solve a problem with a friend. The questions below focus on a relatively simple decision such as deciding what to do together on a Friday night.

I. What were some of the ideas you tossed around alone, to figure out what might be best? Check off all the ones below that apply.
    a. Looking in the newspaper for ideas
    b. Looking at the amount of time you were going to spend together
    c. Prioritizing the kind of activity you wanted to share
    d. Deciding on the amount of money to spend
    e. Throwing out different ideas and seeing what appealed to you
    f. Other possibilities

2. How did you and your friend consider these options—on the phone, talking while looking through newspapers or magazines, leaving each other messages, or other?

3. In what ways did your participation in this activity differ from similar types of discussions you have with others at school or in your work setting?

4. Identify two or three intrapersonal characteristics of your own that you would like to use the next time you have a problem to identify with other teachers. Record the results of this exercise in your collaboration notebook.

5. Identify two or three interpersonal strategies you would like to incorporate the next time you have a problem to identify with other teachers. Record the result in your collaboration notebook.

6. Summarize one or two suggestions for yourself, describing what you would do differently next time.

The results of this exercise could have reflected at least two options. You may have found that you are more likely to do your problem identification alone, using your intrapersonal skills. Alternatively, you may have found more success defining the problem when working with another person, using your interpersonal skills. Ideally, you want to develop your skills so that you can use the most appropriate one when it is needed rather than just because it is easier for you to do. By the end of this book, you should be more "ambidextrous" than you are now. You should be able to use your dominant skill set less automatically and your less-dominant set more often.

As part of problem identification, you will need to learn more about the situation. In the information gathering phase, Snell and Janney (2000) observed teachers "watch, think and talk" (p. 481). This phase afforded all a chance to consider what they were seeing and analyze the behaviors together. "Since teachers had to move quickly from thinking to doing, taking this step seemed somewhat automatic to these experienced teachers, despite the absence of formal collection of student performance data" (p. 481). This phase could, for some individuals, precede the "problem identification" stage if the problem to be solved is very unfamiliar.

Project Development

In the project development stage, ideas generated in the first stage are translated into action steps. The following outcomes are generally the goals of the project development stage: "description of target behaviors that have been operationally defined, specification of a time frame, provision or description of materials and management strategies, consideration of data collection techniques, and incorporation of data analysis/interpretation" (Tindal & Taylor-Pendergast, 1989, p. 10). These outcomes serve to guide the project. After these have been agreed upon, baseline data are collected.

Designing a project is a combination of "action and reflection" (Patriarca & Lamb, 1990, p. 229). In Snell and Janney's study, this phase included "generate potential solutions" and "evaluate potential solutions" (p. 482).

Teachers reported the step of "thinking and throwing out ideas" either alone or with team members during the school day . . . Once teachers developed an idea or one was suggested to them, teachers and staff called upon their recent experiences and, often during the same interaction, made quick predictions about the likely success or failure of the idea in order to determine if it was "worth a try." (p. 482)

The example below is an appropriate combination that can serve as the foundation for the project development stage.

Project Development

Our new team motto is "naturally." That means something special to us. It combines the first let-ter of each of our names, and adds in "look" and "talk." We make sure that whenever one member of our team tries out something new, we have someone there to watch. Before we decide whether or not the strategy is right for the whole team, we get together and talk about it.

As a result, we've been able to develop quite a few new approaches through a very positive trial-and-error method. We always laugh when we use the word "naturally" in notes or in com-ments to each other, but it brings our intention to communicate back into focus.

Patriarca and Lamb (1990) describe the collaborative planning phase as one in which the collaborators are "focusing and clarifying the nature of the task and . . . develop-ing a shared language. . . . Group norms and working relationships became estab-lished" (p. 231). One team's use of the word *naturally* is an example of shared language. The way in which the collaborators work together in the project develop-ment stage is highly dependent on the intrapersonal and interpersonal capabilities of the members.

Polsgrove and McNeil (1989) bring the need for interpersonal skills sharply into focus for this stage of the process, which they refer to as the problem analysis phase. "A critical aspect in the problem analysis phase . . . involves establishing effective working relationships" (p. 8). The ability to establish these relationships is not nec-essarily tied to demographic characteristics of the collaborating teacher. West and Idol (1987) concluded that

investigations of the influence of various consultation input variables such as consultant and consultee characteristics (e.g., age, teaching experience, knowledge, training and competence in consultation skills, readiness for con-sultation and preference for consultation style) and nature of the problem pre-sented have yielded mixed, somewhat contradictory results in terms of their impact on the use and effectiveness of consultation in school settings. (p. 399)

West and Idol's conclusion was corroborated by Polsgrove and McNeil (1989).

Elliott and Sheridan (1992) recommend the use of interviewing during the project development stage.

Relevant questions posed during this stage are concerned with who, what, where, when, and under what conditions the problem occurs. In many cases, consultants and consultees will need to collect additional information. . . . Problem analysis often enhances, refines, and consequently, redefines the target behavior and the variables that influence it. (p. 318)

The give-and-take of questions and ideas that inevitably occurs during the project development phase requires patience and open-mindedness. To reflect on your own habits, review a recently completed project by completing Idea Try-Out 3.6.

Idea Try-Out 3.6

Together and Apart

In this activity you will have a chance to review a project that you developed with another person. Record your answers to the following questions in your collaboration notebook:

1. Think back to a lesson plan, other teaching activity, or study activity that you developed with another person—a co-teacher, a paraprofessional, a friend. Select a project in which the final product was quite different from the initial ideas that either of you had.

2. What aspect(s) of the joint development did you find frustrating?

3. What aspect(s) of the joint development did you find stimulating?

4. What grade (A–F) would you give yourself on each of the following items:
   a. open-mindedness during the planning process
   b. flexibility
   c. building on the ideas and suggestions of the other person
   d. willingness to modify or give up own ideas
   e. patience with the process
   f. acceptance of the final product

5. After reviewing what you have written, record one or two suggestions you would like to remember to follow in the future.

Completing this exercise may have evoked a vivid memory of what the planning process is like when working with one or more other people. However, designing a solution is different from implementing a solution.

Implementation

During the implementation stage, new program plans are actually used. Implementation depends on careful completion of the previous steps in the process. Snell and Janney (2000) refer to the "implementation" stage as "give it a shot."

This step involved one or several team members agreeing to stop discussion, go ahead with a plan, and then put the plan into place. Plans specified one or several actions and who would be responsible for taking action. . . . The length of the implementation was related to the plan's success, and thus was connected to the next step of evaluation. (p. 483)

To teachers who are new to the problem-solving process, it seems as if a great deal of time is spent before the actual problem is solved, but for those experienced in the process, this investment of "up front" time makes good sense.

Project Implementation

For a solid week, I tried to convince the other sixth-grade teachers that Donella could join the other sixth-grade students for the end-of-the-year field trip, but I got nowhere. I could tell from the looks on their faces that they thought I was expecting too much.

Then, I shifted gears. We took time to outline the potential problems and explore some options for solutions which put Donella in a role of increased responsibilities. When I told them about the time she spent, all on her own, helping Kyle with his spelling words, I knew I'd helped them to understand her much better. That was a private part of her I realized that they had never seen but I saw all the time.

We finally were ready to put our contingencies into place. We tried them out first in an in-school career fair, and they worked well. Everyone was nervous about the field trip, but we had our back-up plans in place. And everything worked! The smile on her face when she got on the bus that day was something to see. We knew the time we'd taken to make everything go well had paid off. I realized, too, that all that time we had invested in the planning process was important, because we had strategies in place I never would have developed. We all learned a lot from each other.

In this example, with the focus on increased student responsibilities, the teaching team instructed the student in all the methods to be used to practice the target behavior, gave the student the necessary feedback, and provided support along the way. Working together required a clear, coordinated plan, developed during the first two stages of the problem-solving model.

As Elliott and Sheridan (1992) describe the implementation stage activities, there are a variety of ways to provide training and support: "With teachers, these efforts range from providing verbal or written instructions to actually modeling for and coaching teachers in the delivery of the treatment" (p. 324). Idol, West, and Lloyd (1988) describe this stage as one of "Teaching/Learning" in order to highlight the corrective cycle, which is an inevitable part of the implementation stage.

There is some difference of opinion as to whether data collection procedures designed during the project development stage should be carried out during the implementation stage or should wait until the feedback/evaluation stage. Tindal and Taylor-Pendergast (1989) recommend waiting, while Idol et al. (1988) recommend an ongoing data collection procedure "which is continuous, beginning at the time of assessment and continuing throughout all phases of intervention" (p. 59). Polsgrove and McNeil (1989) merge the implementation and feedback/evaluation stages into one. This book recommends that baseline data be collected in the project development stage, after target objectives and evaluation procedures have been established. Data documenting the effectiveness of the procedures carried out are collected in the implementation stage. While ongoing review of the formative data collected takes place during the implementation stage, a summative review does not take place until the final feedback/evaluation stage.

Project Try-Out 3.7 allows you to reconsider a recently implemented task, the one you considered for Idea Try-Out 3.6.

Project Try-Out 3.7

Doing and Debriefing

This activity gives you an opportunity to make some changes in a project you recently designed.

1. Review the lesson plan, teaching or study activity that you previously designed and analyzed in Idea Try-Out 3.6.

2. Agree to try it out again with your colleague, or with a different person if your original colleague is unavailable, following all the guidelines in this try-out.
   a. Agree to repeat the activity, or series of activities, within a week.
   b. Agree to spend 10 minutes debriefing the format at the end of the day each time you repeat the activity.
   c. Plan necessary modifications, based on your debriefing.
   d. At each debriefing meeting, complete the written activities described in steps 5 and 6 below, and share the results with your partner.
   e. Carry out the planned changes the next day.

3. At the end of each day, record the number of changes *you consider making* in your collaboration notebook.

4. Keep track (a brief description) of the *actual changes* you incorporate into the activity the following day.

5. Separately jot down two or three adjectives that summarize your feelings about
   a. the activity each day, before debriefing
   b. changing the activity, at the start of your debriefing meeting
   c. the modified format for the following day, determined at the end of your debriefing meeting

6. Share your adjective lists with your partner and circle those you both think accurately describe your feelings.

7. At the end of the week, review the implementation stage you have just completed.

8. Summarize two or three ideas you would like to remember in the future.

This activity can show you benefits of continuously monitoring a change effort with another person. You may see how collaboration led to change, as well as how you worked together. By necessity, the implementation stage is full of trial and error. In the final stage, feedback/evaluation, collaborators make decisions about what should be incorporated into the final product and what should be omitted.

Feedback/Evaluation

By the time you reach the feedback/evaluation stage, the project has been more fully defined and refined. This is the period when formal review of collected data takes place. New decisions follow information analysis during feedback/evaluation. Snell and Janney (2000) refer to this as the "more watch, think, talk" evaluation stage.

> Evaluation involved team observation of the outcomes and whether a plan was continued unchanged or tinkered with. When teachers reflected on their criteria for determining whether something was successful, all of them talked both about the child's reaction and their knowledge of the child. . . . Described as "checking back," "comparing notes," and "touching base," the ongoing communication about children's progress was a primary responsibility of the special education teacher. (p. 483)

Although the centrality of the special educator in this process emerges at this crucial stage, the team must work together to make a decision about what happens next.

Feedback/Evaluation

My paraprofessional and I worked hard to find ways to be more considerate of each other. At the start of year, we both agreed that we didn't want another year like the past one, where we put all our positive energy into the students in class and had none left for our conversations with each other.

Since I was working on this project, I decided to propose that we collect baseline data on our interactions. We each kept track separately and then shared our results. Amazingly, almost all our interactions focused on exchange of information. We never stopped to give each other compliments or even ask for assistance.

During our implementation stage, we made an effort to end each day with a review of what had gone well and write down one question about the students that we would try to answer at the end of the week.

When we got to our feedback/evaluation stage, we knew we had been successful. The project changed our moods. Even the students mentioned that we seem happier, more relaxed. Collecting data helped to point us in a new direction.

In the project development stage, specific target behaviors and ways to measure progress were defined. Modification of the measurements, based on changes made while the project is being conducted, takes place in the implementation stage.

During the feedback/evaluation stage, formal and informal methods are used to determine whether the project has worked. As Elliott and Sheridan (1992) suggest, a combination of methods can be used. A comparison of results to a "quantifiable standard" can be used, if appropriate. Comparison, via observation, is "a pragmatic and socially valid method of measuring outcome effectiveness. Feedback from . . . others . . . although generally less quantitative, provides another socially valid method of determining the outcome(s) of treatment" (p. 324). Major plan modifications are based on an analysis of the results. Minor adjustments required to continue the plan also take place. Generally, the feedback/evaluation stage marks the end of the intensive collaboration period and a transition to a modified, less demanding working relationship. The Creative Problem Solving Model, described in detail by Isaksen and Treffinger (1985), illustrates how groups can meet the responsibilities of all of these stages.

BRINGING IT ALL TOGETHER

Chapter 3 provided an overview of ingredients for successful collaboration. Self-analysis, the focus of the first part of the chapter, enabled you to look at what you do that is independent of the other people in the collaboration—a view of your personal ingredients. Gilbert (2004) incorporates your knowledge of yourself into a personality analysis, which is incorporated into your problem-solving approach.

If you use the approaches outlined in this chapter, you can become a better self-observer. Gilbert (2004) provides a strategy to enable you to become effective at solving problems, especially those requiring conflict resolution. Use "three competencies of leadership:

- *Diagnosing,* the cognitive competency—understanding the situation.
- *Adapting,* the behavioral competency that helps close the gap between where things are and where you want them to be.
- *Communicating,* the process competency that allows others to understand and accept the situation and its need for resolution (Hersey, Blanchard, & Johnson, 1996)." (p. 113)

The ability to bring cognition, behavior, and communication together fits with the ideas expressed in this chapter. As Gensante and Matgouranis (1988) suggest, "We believe that to *reflect* on their practice, teachers must first be able to describe what they are doing. . . . We expect authentic, sustained improvements from our efforts" (p. 28). We need to reflect on what we can do differently as well as what is holding us back. This insight about limits that restrict us—"Creativity is the ability to modify self-imposed constraints" (Ackoff & Vergara, 1988)—became the basis for a keynote address I developed for women leaders in collaboration with Gerard Puccio (Cramer & Puccio, 2004).

The remainder of this book will outline how you can use your "ingredients" to your advantage to modify a collaboration partnership. You can begin to design your personal self-assessment. This will enable you to practice using a technique to identify the positive features of your intrapersonal and interpersonal resource base and those you would like to adjust. Each month, you can develop your own self-awareness habits by analyzing your behavior in three ways: looking at a *unique moment,* a *productive pattern,* and a *counterproductive pattern.*

The unique moment refers to a novel way you react to a situation. You may react in a way that meets the demands of the situation very well or poorly. Either way, you are surprised at what you did. These surprises can give you opportunities for insight that happen at no other time.

A productive pattern is a familiar behavior that meets the demands of the situation successfully. You may find yourself doing something you have done many times before. Reviewing a productive pattern can give you a chance to reflect on some of your positive capabilities.

The counterproductive pattern is also familiar, but it is ineffective. When it takes place, you know you are doing something that you've done before but you would rather not do again.

Taking a look at all three of these ways in which you behave—by yourself, or with others—on a regular basis can give you a quick, realistic analysis of your collaborative skills.

Analysis of a Unique Moment

Take a minute to think back over the last few months to see if you can remember a time when you did something that was very unusual for you—a time when you got angry, were deeply compassionate, or were able to approach a problem in a way that felt unfamiliar. The following is an example of a unique moment that transformed a working relationship.

Unique Moment

She and I never seemed to see eye-to-eye. It seemed as if we were always quarreling. I got to the point that whenever she opened her mouth, I disagreed with her. I never listened to her anymore.

Then, my brother was in a terrible car accident. I was out of school for a week, and when I came back, she came over to me and told me that she had been praying for me and my family. She looked at me, and we both started to cry. I knew I would never see her in the same way again. I found a picture of a huge pair of glasses, and I put it in my notebook, to remind me to never look at people superficially again.

She and I aren't really friends, now, but I listen when she talks. The way she treated me after that accident taught me that she was much more empathetic than I'd ever suspected.

The collaborative process requires you to capitalize on self-knowledge, using times like these unique moments as indicators of how you might be able to behave intentionally in the future. Although an identical circumstance might not recur, you might, based on a previous experience, try to change your future mode of action or belief. Kouzes and Posner (2002) refer to a similar concept for leaders who reflect on a positive unique moment, a "personal-best" leadership experience.

The exercise of analyzing their personal-best leadership experiences was enlightening for them: by highlighting key lessons from the past, they were able to generate insightful road maps for leadership highways still to be explored. . . . It's the knowledge gained from direct experience and active searching that, once stored in the subconscious, becomes the basis for leaders' intuition, insight, and vision. (pp. 122–123)

See whether something has provoked an unusual reaction in you recently. In your collaboration notebook, analyze the situation using the following steps:

1. Briefly describe what happened in the unique moment.

2. Explain what you did in the situation and what other alternatives you considered.

3. List the ways in which the unique moment was new for you.

4. Sum up what you want to remember about this moment and how you can help yourself to remember it.

The unique moment can illustrate some unexpected options that you have for thinking, feeling, or behaving. The results may be surprising.

In spite of good intentions, it is often hard to recall what we remind ourselves to do. By selecting a way of visualizing what you learned from your unique moment, you can help yourself remember it. Cut out a picture or buy a card or postcard that has special meaning for you. This could help you, as the picture of the glasses helped the teacher in the example. This simple action can help you to remember something that you don't want to forget. You may find that a song, word, or phrase that has special meaning to you can work as well as a picture. Include this "memory jog" in your collaboration notebook to enable you build up your knowledge base about yourself.

Analysis of a Productive Pattern

A productive pattern is a recognized part of your intrapersonal or interpersonal resource base. It may be the way in which you ask questions for information, your ability to pay attention, or your use of humor to lighten a difficult moment. A need for deliberation can be a productive pattern.

Productive Pattern

One thing I've come to respect in myself is that I don't make hasty decisions. When I started to work as a consulting teacher, people would come up to me all the time with a problem to be solved right then. I always gave them the same answer—let me think about it, and I'll get back to you tomorrow.

At first, everyone was put off. But when they saw that I stuck by my word, and always made sure to give them my response the next day, they became more trusting.

Now, it's a common thing for someone to come up to me and say, "I know you can't decide right now, but. . . ." They trust me, and I trust myself.

Your productive pattern is an aspect of your personal style that you use confidently. It is helpful to use this analysis of a productive pattern for two reasons: (1) it highlights a resource you want to remember to employ, and (2) it helps you to evaluate whether the productive pattern is as effective as you believe it to be.

To complete the following steps, identify one productive pattern that you have displayed within the last few weeks. Think back to one specific situation, and answer the following questions in your collaboration notebook.

1. Briefly describe the productive pattern and the circumstance in which you used it.

2. How well did the productive pattern meet the requirements of the situation?

3. Briefly analyze how the productive pattern was received by others, both verbally and nonverbally.

4. Explain how automatic the productive pattern is for you and whether you have other easily used options in your resource bank.

5. List two or three features of the productive pattern that you might change in the future.

6. Describe what you can do to help yourself remember what you want to change.

As you did with the unique moment, select appropriate words or pictures to help yourself remember. In this way, you can develop a habit of focused self-observation and self-reflection that is not too time consuming. This can lead to a very directed procedure for identifying what you want to include in your collaboration plans in the future.

Analysis of a Counterproductive Pattern

As shown in the following example, a counterproductive pattern is one that is familiar to you.

Counterproductive Pattern

I know that I shouldn't interrupt people, or finish their sentences, but I do it all the time. I wish I could stop.

A counterproductive pattern does not meet the demands of the situation appropriately. For example, you may be able to relate to the habit of interrupting people. Or, you might realize that when others around you are being critical of a student or a fellow teacher, you have a habit of being quiet or joining in the conversation with examples of your own—even if you would like to prevent this negative talk from continuing. You may find that you have a habit of being impatient around certain people who take a long time to say anything. We all have habits like these.

Counterproductive patterns can be modified or discarded. Use the following steps to review a recent time when you used one of your counterproductive patterns:

1. Briefly describe the counterproductive pattern.

2. List the physical and social features in the environment that contributed to the display of the counterproductive pattern.

3. List alternative reasons or motivations for the display of the counterproductive pattern.

4. Explain how automatic the counterproductive pattern is for you and whether you could replace it with other options in your resource bank.

5. Are you open to changing the counterproductive pattern?

6. List two or three features of the counterproductive pattern that you want to change in the future.

7. Describe what you can do to help yourself remember what you want to change.

By narrowing your scope for the changes you want to make in your counterproductive pattern, you may find that you become more motivated to make the necessary changes than you would be if you tried to do too much all at once. Above all, when changing a counterproductive pattern, you want to avoid feeling guilty and getting immobilized.

Use of the unique moment, productive pattern, and counterproductive pattern self-assessment processes has two major benefits.

1. You can stay alert to what you do well and to what you wish to change without being overwhelmed. Teachers who have used this system for self-assessment report an increased tolerance for their own behavior. They also find that they are motivated to target specific behaviors that they want to change.

2. By increasing self-awareness through self-assessment, you are more empathetic and patient when considering your collaboration partners. Instead of presuming that *they* should change their ways, you grasp the complexity of making changes in professional habits.

Eventually, this self-assessment process can lead you to "inquiry knowledge," as described by Krutilla and Safford (1990). You are able to know and connect your technical knowledge of the "craft" of teaching with your "personal reality, . . . uncovering . . . taken-for-granted thoughts posited in light of new experiences and insights" (p. 217). This new thinking can enable you, as a collaborator, to maximize your teacher efficacy and to enjoy collaboration more fully, resulting in use of collaboration throughout your career (see Cramer, 2005 for a discussion of collaboration and mentoring for special education leaders). As described in the next chapter, you can use your knowledge of yourself in conjunction with your knowledge of the situation to improve your chances for successful collaboration.

4

Evaluating Your Situation Honestly

Appraising Your School as a Context for Collaboration

We all imagine working in the perfect school—one that welcomes students, families, teachers, and members of the community. When problems occur, we want to know that we are not alone when trying to solve them. When successes happen, we want to be able to share them with people who can appreciate what they mean. How often do we teachers find ourselves in such a place? And, even if we are lucky enough to find the perfect school, it can suddenly change when an administrator leaves or a new paraprofessional begins. The wish for a perfect, ever stable school is real for all teachers. However, when we don't get our wish, we still have the opportunity to make collaboration happen. This chapter describes what to look for in all schools—even the less-than-perfect ones—to improve your chances for successfully collaborating with others.

ASSESSING RESOURCES AVAILABLE TO COLLABORATORS

Change—this word is often heard in school corridors and offices. When administrators pair it with "collaboration," interest is sparked in a few teachers; in fact, many instantly stop listening. You are more likely to hear bitter, sarcastic jokes in response to an administrator's comments than inquisitive questions. Why? Teachers often assume that both change and collaborative efforts will inevitably fail.

Honig and Hatch (2004) thoughtfully describe the overwhelming demands that schools face before they can create an environment capable of "crafting coherence" to address policy initiatives. Sarason (1990) connects attitudes of personal failure and failures of educational reform to power relationships. Without new kinds of relationships among teachers and with principals (Leithwood, 1992), teachers can become discouraged. They anticipate the limited result of their efforts. Pessimistic teachers expect that little meaningful collaboration will happen, no matter how hard they try.

All teachers in the same situation do not draw identical conclusions. Teachers interpret their experiences to develop either optimistic or pessimistic views of what can happen in their school. In the example below, the teacher, experiencing difficulties, decided not to remain powerless. Instead, she imported something that she'd seen succeed in another setting.

> *When I began teaching, all the teachers in my building warned me that we would never be able to get together to conference our difficult students. They said, "We tried it before, and it never worked."*
>
> *But at the end of one terrible week in October, I was desperate! I thought back to my student teaching days. I remembered how my cooperating teacher used to meet early in the morning with other teachers. They got together in our room because they could never find any other time to talk about students.*
>
> *So, I volunteered to pick up fruit and doughnuts for anyone who would meet with me before school on Monday. Several people showed up to give me ideas and encouragement. We were all surprised that we felt better after starting the week together. We agreed that our "doughnut whole" would get together again. We've met a few times since.*

You, too, may find that sometimes your prior experiences are motivators. Other times, these experiences provide little or no help. However, available resources may go unrecognized. By the time you reach the end of this chapter, you will be better able to identify existing resources. As McBreen and Polis (1996) describe, collaboration can take place on a wide range of topics—sharing data, bringing different perspectives to the planning process, establishing networks, creating professional development activities (p. 12). Law et al. (2001) found that collaboration across and within agencies was extremely beneficial for individuals offering speech and language services to children. Their findings, based on 189 surveys and follow-up focus groups, included an overarching conclusion: "[there is a] need for enhanced collaboration at a range of levels" (p. 133). What separates a setting in which collaboration is effective from one where it is not? After you finish reading this chapter, you should have your eyes opened to many opportunities for collaboration in your current situation. Factors that suppress resources, as well as what can be done to identify them, are discussed below.

Factors Impeding Collaboration: Pragmatic and Conceptual

Johnson, Pugach, and Hammittee (1988) distinguish between *pragmatic* barriers and *conceptual* barriers to effective consultation in schools. This same distinction was referenced by Doelling, Bryde, Brunner, and Martin (1998). Their approach is a useful structure for examining collaboration barriers.

Pragmatic Barrier 1: Inadequate Time

Most special educators can corroborate the first pragmatic barrier—inadequate time to spend on the collaborative process. "From a purely practical standpoint, lack of time may be one of the biggest barriers" (Johnson et al., 1988, p. 42). Bulgren et al. (2002) report that 70 high school teachers, employed in nine inclusive high school districts, reported that general and special educators collaborated on average only 12 to 24 minutes *per week*! Without sufficient time to share informal and formal information about students, collaboration can become a burden rather than a benefit. The following example sums up the feelings teachers share in schools all across the country.

> *I can't count the number of times I've heard teachers in my school say, "If only I had an extra day, all to myself, I could get everything done." When I look around at a faculty meeting, when the principal asks for volunteers, I am amazed at how everybody avoids eye contact. If I could find a way to add an hour to everybody's day, I'd be a millionaire.*

Cambone's (1995) discussion of time as a key resource in schools highlights problems collaborators face. There are many practical problems that teachers must overcome if they are going to find ways to meet in schools. He cites Hargreaves's (1990) definition of time: "a finite *resource* or *means* that can be increased, decreased, managed, manipulated, organized, or reorganized in order to accommodate selected educational purposes" (Cambone, 1995, p. 514). He goes on to use Hargreaves's work to consider time conflicts in new ways:

> While administrators often conceive of time as a commodity that can be managed to render tasks complete, teachers' work is highly context-dependent and individualized. . . . [Hargreaves] offers examples from his study of preparation time for teachers to demonstrate how these two time frames can conflict. He explains instances where administrators scheduled time for teachers to "collaborate" without reference to the compatibility of the people that have been co-scheduled, or to the utility of that particular collaboration. Similarly, teachers may be scheduled to collaborate at times of day that they would prefer to use for doing other tasks—to phone parents or copy materials, and the like. (p. 516)

The problem of limited time is faced by others in schools (e.g., school library, media specialists), as described by Buzzeo (2003). They also seek ways, and time, to develop collaborative working relationships.

Absence of meeting time—the explanation that many teachers give for the lack of collaboration in their buildings—may, however, be only part of the difficulty. Buzzeo (2003) encourages an examination of the school culture to make sure that "a collaborative work culture, teaching partnership, and team planning" (p. 29) are all included in school norms. An effective solution would involve many people looking at the problem from all angles. Administrators and teachers would need to jointly consider their needs (using issues such as those presented by Cambone, 1995) and generate mutually acceptable solutions.

Pragmatic Barrier 2: Language Barriers

The second pragmatic barrier is verbal. Because of their specialized orientation, special educators and general educators often don't "speak the same language." This is not a clash of cultures, but instead is a problem of jargon. It can lead to a more serious problem of not understanding each others' perspectives.

Problems can develop when professionals use terms that are familiar to them but unfamiliar to others.

> I never thought anyone would notice! The speech pathologist in my school always confused me when she gave an update on my students' progress. From the very first day, she acted so confident and assumed I knew what she meant. I kept hoping that someone on my team would ask for an explanation, but no one ever did.
>
> When I got a student teacher, I realized I was going to have to learn more. So, I started asking questions—supposedly for the student teacher's sake, but really for mine. Getting answers really helped me out.
>
> I found out that I shouldn't have waited so long. After one of our team meetings, the speech pathologist came up to me and said, "Thanks so much for asking questions. I always noticed this blank look on your face after I said something, but I couldn't think of how to explain things to you without being insulting." We both started laughing.
>
> The student teacher's assignment ended two months ago, but I kept asking questions. I never imagined it would be so easy, or I would have done it long ago.

"There is generally poor communication among professionals of different backgrounds; as professionals achieve higher educational levels, they are less willing to collaborate or recognize each others' expertise" (Allen-Meares & Pugach, 1982, p. 32). This may be a problem based primarily in their educational training, as Allen-Meares and Pugach suggest. Or, it may be a problem that has to do with lack of familiarity with others' frames of reference. In either case, the practical outcome is that in many school situations teachers don't understand each other.

How many times have you been in a situation at school in which people were using words or acronyms that you didn't understand? How often have you asked for an explanation? Many people keep listening, hoping to be able to figure things out through context, but this can create problems. Collaboration activities can force unclarities out in the open, but until they do, people may be guessing rather than knowing what is really being said.

Pragmatic Barrier 3: Lack of Administrative Support

The third pragmatic problem is the absence of support from the school's administrators and administrative structure. Although many principals and building administrators welcome the opportunities to meet challenges (e.g., Bolman & Deal, 2002; Crow, Hausman, & Scribner, 2002; Jentz & Murphy, 2005), some do not. Allen-Meares and Pugach (1982) describe the goal for leadership as follows:

> The [collaboration] process must be viewed as significant by those within the school who determine policy, develop role definitions, assign tasks and make schedules. The building principal can be the key person to provide support and leadership in shaping the collaborative process. . . . As the educational leader of the building, the principal can set the overall tone for staff interaction and in this capacity can model respect for diverse expertise. (p. 33)

Like a train conductor, the building principal makes sure all aspects of the program run smoothly and effectively. This responsibility requires the principal to be attentive to detail, to anticipate upcoming deadlines, and to demonstrate other "calendar" skills.

However, for a schoolwide collaboration agenda to move steadily forward, more is required. Gerber and Popp (2000), based on their interviews with over 250 individuals in 10 schools in 7 districts, wanted to learn how to make collaborative teaching more effective. The role of the principal was central:

> The principal can set the tone for acceptance of collaborative teaching as one component of collaborative school improvement. Allocations of resources including appropriate staff, scheduling considerations, and guarded planning time send the message that the collaborative teaching program is supported by the administration. Support is emphasized further through communicating the successes of the program to internal and external audiences and evaluating the program to promote ongoing improvement. (p. 234)

Leadership means engaging others in a new direction (Barr & Barr, 1989; Gardner, 1990). Charismatic qualities of the leader alone are insufficient for developing commitment to a new direction. An effective administrator must be able to address all pragmatic problems—logistics, scheduling, assigning tasks. The issues that are central to leadership cross over into a different category: conceptual barriers.

Conceptual Barrier 1: Administrative Tone

Conceptual barriers may seem less formidable than pragmatic problems. It is frustrating when administrators communicate in formats we have trouble using. For example, if meeting notices arrive late and contain grammatical errors, inaccuracies, or incomplete information, you can become irritated. But, in many ways, these annoyances are just pebbles on the road. Conceptual barriers can block the highway altogether. The first barrier discussed is the tone set in the school. This tone, established by the principal and the teachers, becomes a problem if it does not support collaborative, innovative efforts but instead undermines them. Consider this example:

> When Ann, a fourth-grade teacher, mentioned a cooking idea she planned to use with a particularly difficult class, other teachers in her building laughed at her and told her she was crazy. The project worked beautifully, but even then the other teachers thought maybe Ann was not telling the whole truth. They greeted her reports of the project's success with skeptical comments

and facial expressions communicating disbelief. The cynical negativism of her teaching peers eroded her self-satisfaction. (Renegar, 1993, p. 68)

This situation illustrates two problems—absence of colleague support and competition as a norm in the school. Both undermine innovative efforts. Ann and her fellow teachers clearly have different conceptual views about trying new things in the classroom.

Support needs to be present to encourage innovation. It is impossible to expect that every strategy tried by teachers will succeed. Being open-minded about experimentation is a conceptual cornerstone for collaboration. Without it, teachers and administrators may give lip-service to working together, but few substantial collaborative efforts may take place.

In their study of a mentoring model at the University of Missouri Teaching Fellowship Program involving mentors for beginning teachers, Gilles and Wilson (2004) found that mentors learned how to work with their mentees gradually. Like administrators, mentors had to explore ways to set the right tone with their mentees:

They learned to listen . . . and hear the implications. . . . They learned how to judge when to offer mentees unconditional support and when to probe to challenge their thinking. It takes time, instruction and support for mentors to do these things well. All groups spoke of "learning on the job," and implied that even with a university liaison and monthly mentor meetings, much of the job must simply be learned by engaging in it. (p. 103)

Even with the extensive supports that the University of Missouri program provided, mentors had to take time to learn how to listen, how to support. For administrators, such support is often unavailable. Daresh (2004) discusses at length the need for an administrative atmosphere in schools that facilitates self-reflection and support for administrators. He analyzes how mentoring for (and by) administrators can only take place in a supportive circumstance.

Conceptual Barrier 2: Power Struggles

Establishing a building tone that is supportive of experimentation is related to a second barrier, described by Dietz (1990) as power struggles instead of power sharing. The issue of shared power in the collaborative effort means moving away from the notion of being an expert (Dunlap & Goldman, 1991) and toward facilitative power between principals, staff, and nonprofessionals in schools. Within this context, teachers who collaborate feel free to experiment, knowing that 100% success is not expected. The reciprocal peer coaching approach used by Mallette et al. (1999) could go a long way toward enabling a sharing of power that would reduce conflicts.

Conley and Bacharach (1990), in discussing school-site management, explained that "the issue is not simply how to achieve school-site management, but how to achieve *collegial* and *collective* management at the school level" (p. 540). For collaboration to become part of the fabric of the school, teachers and administrators must find ways to communicate differently.

Conceptual Barrier 3: Credibility of Special Educators

A third conceptual barrier is the credibility of special educators in the eyes of the general educators. Although more frequently special and general educators are participating on teams together (e.g., Malone et al., 2001), the separate training programs in which most general and special educators are prepared lead to different skills and priorities. As Johnson et al. (1988) describe it, special education teachers may have to prove their abilities in thinking about, or working in, the general education classroom:

> Classroom teachers often perceive that . . . [special educators] have difficulty *really* being able to understand the demands of the general education classroom; in its most blunt form, this criticism is exemplified in the comment, "She doesn't know what it means to have 25 kids all day long!" While this retort may be used as an excuse by poor classroom teachers who have failed to make a concerted effort to provide for the needs of individual students, it also reflects a realistic concern on the part of highly skilled classroom teachers. (p. 43)

Through discussion and demonstration, teachers can begin to better understand their different philosophies and backgrounds. Rather than increasing the distance between them, differences can be used as a basis for strengthening the services provided to students in the school. As discussed in the following section, changing the model for thinking about the collaborative team can be a starting point for more effective work together.

FACTORS PROMOTING COLLABORATION

Factor 1: Collaboration Topics

Teachers who want to assess, and eventually improve, the climate for collaboration in a school can start by considering and introducing *collaboration topics*. In the following example, a teacher who focused his collaboration project on increased communication with another teacher found that students in his classroom benefited.

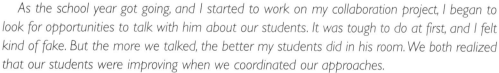

If we saw each other in the hall or the lunch room once a week, that's a lot. And at the start of the school year, that was more than enough for me. I had nothing good to say to or about him.

As the school year got going, and I started to work on my collaboration project, I began to look for opportunities to talk with him about our students. It was tough to do at first, and I felt kind of fake. But the more we talked, the better my students did in his room. We both realized that our students were improving when we coordinated our approaches.

We have continued to meet weekly, even though my project is done.

Collaboration topics are found in everyday, informal conversation as well as during formal meetings. Think about situations in which you find yourself in a school. How often do you find yourself talking with others about what is going well? How often do you discuss what is going poorly? Which conversation is more animated and interesting? If you are like most groups of educators, your complaints outnumber all other topics, often by as many as three to one.

As McLaughlin (2002) points out, the topics on which you need to collaborate are part of planning for all students in the class.

> In recent years, the push for collaboration has intensified as part of new special education requirements in the Individuals with Disabilities Education Act (P.L. 105–17). . . . Under these new policies collaboration means more than just helping an individual student be present in the classroom. Collaboration must now involve teachers planning and problem solving around specific curricular goals to ensure that every student is given an opportunity to learn challenging content in the schools. (p. 280)

Consider how changing topics might change the collaboration climate in your building. McLeskey and Waldron (2002) used a qualitative research approach in six schools that were incorporating curricular and instructional changes for elementary students. Discussions of curriculum changes, student expectations, grading, and grouping patterns took place as the teachers involved in these efforts participated in teaming, collaboration, and co-teaching.

> Teachers reported that they collaborated and teamed with other teachers much more frequently as a result of the ISP [Inclusive Schools Program]. The teaming process was described by many respondents as an opportunity to share ideas, brainstorm about problems, and plan how instruction would occur. It was acknowledged by many that this approach to teaching was quite contrary to their previous experiences, because prior to the program their collaboration with others was very limited. (pp. 48–49)

The teachers involved in this initiative needed to talk to each other to make the program function.

> Interviews with teachers involved in the development and implementation of the ISP revealed that, in contrast to add-on programs that were used in the past in an attempt to implement "mainstreaming" programs, teachers perceived that fundamental changes in the school setting occurred as inclusive school programs were implemented. These changes affected the day-to-day, hour-to-hour professional activities of teachers of students with disabilities as well as general education classroom teachers. (p. 50)

The topics that these teachers incorporated into their work emerged naturally from their observations of their classroom functioning.

The finding of McLeskey and Waldron (2002) is consistent with an earlier study by Meyers, Gelzheiser, and Yelich (1991), in which 12 special education teachers involved in "pull-in" programs (in which special education teachers provided instruction in the regular education classroom) were compared with 11 special education teachers who used "pull-out" programs. They found differences in what teachers discussed. Teachers involved in pull-in programs discussed *specific strategies* and *instructional concerns* in their collaboration meetings. The teachers involved in the pull-out programs had more general discussions, and they had fewer collaborative meetings. Meyers et al. described the implication of their results:

> Pull-in programs seemed to be successful in modifying norms where teachers are not likely to collaborate about instruction, and where general and

supplemental education teachers are assigned different roles. Pull-in programs required teachers to work collaboratively to plan instruction and solve instructional problems; as a result, they were forced to adopt new roles. . . . Therefore, both teachers contributed to plans for introducing new skills and content, as well as activities designed to reinforce or reteach, for less successful students. Another consequence of this combined program was that both teachers contributed to whole class and individualized instruction. (p. 14)

The opportunity to work on specific problems gave collaborators in this study ways to invest in joint outcomes when both persons provided instruction in the same classroom. The study by Mason, Thormann, O'Connell, and Behrmann (2004), in which topics in 29 general and special education association journals were analyzed, led the authors to this conclusion:

Our results indicated that topics such as (a) inclusive classrooms, (b) IDEA, (c) differentiated instruction and (d) transition were not top priority items for general education staff. . . . We found that (a) technology, (b) curriculum alignment, (c) shortage of personnel, (d) improving teaching, (e) teacher quality, and (f) staff development were either topics of great interest to general education association staff or are topics frequently mentioned in their literature. (p. 227)

The differences in topics does not have to mean that general educators and special educators are unable to communicate:

Meaningful collaboration among general and special education associations may be furthered if special educators not only discuss the specific issues with key general educators, but also scan their Web sites, read some of their association reports, and keep track of articles that are published in at least some of their journals. (Mason et al., 2004, p. 227)

This is a practical suggestion leading to creating joint ownership of specific topics that can become part of *your* collaboration agenda. You can use Project Try-Out 4.1 to get started.

Project Try-Out 4.1

Your Way, My Way, or Our Way?

In this exercise, you will have a chance to see what effect the *topics* of conversations have on your general satisfaction with the conversation.

Background

- Think about recent satisfying professional conversations you have had with fellow teachers, fellow students, or friends. Review in your mind a few of the topics that have an impact on both of you and topics that need further exploration.
- Jot some notes down in your collaboration notebook.
- Select the topic of most interest to you.

- Do a short online search of topics you have identified. Review articles in both general and special education journals.
- Set up a time in the coming week to follow up on the topic with the coworker, friend, or fellow student with whom you had the original conversation. Explain your interest in pursuing the unresolved topic and agree to brainstorm some alternate ways to approach the topic.

Try-Out

1. As you go through your discussion, remember that your joint commitment is to do things differently to specifically address your topic.

2. Take notes and see how many of the solutions you generated are general approaches and how many are specific approaches you can use in the next week or two.

3. At the end of the conversation, review the following with your coworker, friend, or fellow student:
   a. How satisfied was he or she with the solutions generated?
   b. How does his or her satisfaction compare with yours? If you disagree, why do you think you saw things differently?
   c. Look over the notes you used to keep track of your discussion, and evaluate the areas of commonality as well as those of disagreement.
   d. Identify how you can build on some of the areas of difference to come up with some areas of agreement, or mutual respect.

What you may have found in this exercise is that your attention to the specifics of your solution required more effort than you were accustomed to exerting. The research of both studies cited above showed that the ability to become more specific became more automatic over time. As a teacher in the McLeskey and Waldron (2002) study said, "This has been my toughest year, but also my most rewarding" (p. 41).

Factor 2: Expectations for Team Building

A second factor that can promote change is your expectation for teambuilding. Consider how teams in a school are put together. Some are based on *what* teachers do (e.g., all fifth-grade teachers, or all social studies teachers). Some are based on the *way* teachers do their jobs (e.g., a creative person is balanced by a practical person). Sometimes, teams may consist of people randomly selected because they missed a meeting and have been "volunteered" by others. Discussions of the frustrations of life on a team can be counterbalanced by an understanding of how powerfully teams enable progress to occur (e.g., Wheelan, 2005).

Reflect on your experiences with successful school-based teams. Your review can help you assess your school's collaboration environment. You may find that some teams function under the forceful direction of one leader. Others may spend a lot of time and energy on consensus building. Still others may be chaotic at times but pull together at critical times. Consider not only how they function now, but strategies that have helped them to bring out the best in their members. Horton, Wilson, and

Gagnon (2003) recommend four collaboration "best practices" for physical education teachers—collaboration with special educators, therapists, families, and the community—leading to a broad-based commitment to the collaborative model. "Partnerships such as [these] function with a collaborative effort recognizing that one person cannot do everything" (p. 16). These kinds of team structures and collaborative efforts provide the basis for shared work in the service of students.

In the end, you may find, as Drucker (1994) suggests for business and government agencies, that it is possible to transform the design of collaboration teams, with positive results:

> There is a great deal of talk these days about "teams" and teamwork. Most of it starts out with the wrong assumption—namely, that we have never before worked in teams. Actually, people have always worked in teams; very few people ever could work effectively by themselves. . . . Much discussion today assumes that there is only one kind of team. Actually, there are quite a few. But until now, the emphasis has been on the individual worker and not on the team. With knowledge work growing increasingly effective as it is increasingly specialized, teams become the work unit rather than the individual himself. The team that is being touted now—I call it the "jazz combo" team—is only one kind of team. It is actually the most difficult kind of team both to assemble and to make work effectively, and the kind that requires the longest time to gain performance capacity. We will have to learn to use different kinds of teams for different purposes. (p. 68)

Drucker's recommendations can apply to education. If we change what we expect of individual team members and instead look to the team as a *whole*, we can upend what schools expect of every teacher. If, like the "jazz combo" described by Drucker, each team member is expected to have a unique area of expertise that must spontaneously harmonize with all others, beginning collaborators are at an immediate disadvantage. Instead, the team could be more like a volleyball team—all members have an equal opportunity to contribute to the score. The goal of the teaching team would be to give beginning and experienced collaborators the chance to work together effectively.

I wanted so much to be a part of the team that was working with area businesses, to do transition planning for students in our district. As the only special education teacher in the building, I felt that I had a lot to offer. But, it was only my second year, and no one invited me to come to the meetings. A few weeks went by, and the principal asked me to join the group because he realized that I was the only teacher who had been actually looking for a job within the past few years. No one expected me to be an expert, but they were willing to listen to what I had to say.

A team works best when members have varied skills and interests; when putting the team together, ensure the heterogeneity of the talents and experiences of team members. McLaughlin (2002) examines the many different types of teaming and collaborative approaches general and special education educators have developed.

> Collaborative practices were among a handful of . . . features that emerged . . . in exemplary schools, including both specific teaching practices as well as a climate and culture that supported a community of professionals working together to improve teaching and achievement for all students. (pp. 279–280)

Villa and Thousand (1988) make the following point regarding the value of training team members:

> Members of collaborative teams frequently are at different levels in terms of their competence and confidence in performing collaborative skills. However, all of these skills can be taught or learned. In some school districts, direct instruction in collaborative teaming skills has been arranged for staff. Teachers also have chosen as annual professional growth goals the development of specific collaborative teaming skills. (p. 151)

When teachers take collaborative training one step further and incorporate their interest into annual goals, they show ownership of the teaming process. This will lead to teams that function successfully.

Both the "formally" defined teams and the informal networks that develop can provide special education teachers with opportunities to display their capabilities. Adamson, Cox, and Schuller (1989) described the changes in perceptions of two resource room teachers who made an effort to become more involved with other teachers in their school:

> They ate with the teachers, attended faculty social events, dropped into their classrooms before and after school, took duty and committee responsibilities, and made themselves available in the faculty work areas. It was in these informal relationships that ideas and suggestions were shared and nonjudgmental offers to assist were made. The informal network among the faculty actually seemed to help in the development of new relationships and requests for assistance. It appeared that as the word got around the faculty that these two teachers had ideas that worked, others would risk asking for help. The result was a much more responsive and consistent program for resource children. (p. 54)

Rather than waiting for formal requests for assistance from their fellow teachers, the resource room teachers in this study went out of their way to be available. This action, combined with the successful help they offered, changed the roles they took in relation to the other teachers in their building.

If you find, however, that the collaborative initiatives are absent in your school, you need to be proactive. Beck and Kosnik (2001) discuss the benefits of collegiality and collaboration as embedded in Goodlad's cohort work (e.g., Goodlad, 1990a, 1990c) and Darling-Hammond's (1999) PDS models, but observe that team building is still outside the norm in many educational settings:

> More recent commentators do not see the situation as having changed significantly since . . . Goodlad's studies were conducted. If anything, the increased pressure on teacher educators today to conform to general university norms

of research and publishing leaves even less time for "soft" activities such as community building (Whitford & Metcalf-Turner, 1999). . . . The communication and collaboration that occur are often just among the participants in each PDS rather than among everyone in the teacher education. To a significant degree the scenario of limited community experience in teacher education . . . still holds true. (pp. 927–928)

If you are going to try to create a circumstance in which you can capitalize on working with others in your school setting, you will have to be prepared. Use Idea Try-Out 4.2 to consider potential concerns you may face.

Idea Try-Out 4.2

Experiences, Questions, Hopes

This activity is designed to help you consider what you have to offer a team at the start of your teaching career. Imagine that you wanted to join a team in your school that was planning transition services for students with and without disabilities. In your collaboration notebook, list the following:

1. Three experiences you've had (e.g., as a student, a teacher, or a family member) that could be the basis of suggestions to the team.

2. Three questions you could ask team members to help them address the needs of students with disabilities.

3. Three hopes you have for meeting the transition needs of students with disabilities you could share with the team.

As you completed this exercise, you may have been surprised. Although your experience may be limited, you can still significantly contribute to a team that focuses on transition. As you review your contributions, consider expanding the number of opportunities already available to you on the job, while volunteering, or in other settings. This can be a natural byproduct of changing your expectations for team functioning.

Factor 3: Specific Classroom Environment Instruments

A third factor in assessing the school's context for collaboration is to use specific classroom environment instruments to evaluate what is taking place in classrooms. Data gathered as a result of using formal instruments can help you and others in your school look at the various collaborative working environments teachers have developed in their classrooms.

Formal instruments can give you information that can be used in different ways. McCormick, Noonan, Ogata, and Heck (2001) made use of the Early Childhood Environment Rating Scale (ECERS; Harms & Clifford, 1980), which they cite as "the global measure most often used . . . in both small- and large-scale studies in the U.S. and other countries" (p. 121). This instrument enabled the researchers to look at the quality of socialization and communication, with a focus on the students in the classroom. They also used the Co-Teacher Relationship Scale (CRS) they developed for their pilot study, which "explored the association between program quality and the co-teacher relationship in inclusive preschool programs" (p. 128). Their findings encouraged them to continue their research.

> The present research suggests that the extent to which co-teachers perceive themselves to be similar to one another in personal characteristics and traits, professional style, and philosophical beliefs and biases may affect their ability to provide a quality environment. This, in turn, points to the importance of giving prospective teachers more specific preparation for the role of co-teacher. (pp. 129–130)

Fraser (1991) evaluated six different instruments that help teachers to learn more about the types of relationships they create in their classrooms. The "My Class Inventory" (Anderson & Walberg, 1974) was reviewed in Fraser's article. The same inventory was used in a study conducted by Prawat and Nickerson (1985) that looked at the relationship between teachers' intent and action and students' affective development. The inventory was completed by students in 40 classes. The results showed teachers how effectively they were expressing their priorities regarding the students' affective growth. DeLuke and Knoblock (1987) included environmental assessment in their study of ways that teacher behavior can be used to improve classroom discipline.

In each of these research studies, the activities that teachers used in their own classrooms were indicators of the priorities teachers had developed for their students. As you look around at schools with which you are currently involved, watch what teachers do with their students. Teachers who value group or team projects often bring those same priorities to their work with adults.

Factor 4: Time

A fourth factor in promoting collaboration is time. Caron and McLaughlin (2002) are clear about the need for time:

> Among the most important elements for successful collaboration is time. . . . Effective collaborative planning, consultation and classroom co-teaching require considerable time commitments on the part of staff members. . . . Quality collaboration should include opportunities for teachers to spend time in other teachers' classrooms, to teach jointly, and to attend outside professional development opportunities together. Time is also needed for schoolwide exploration of the norms of collegiality and instruction that guide the staff. (p. 300)

Although time was identified earlier as an impediment to the collaborative process, Cambone (1995) classifies it as both a problem and a resource. He explains that when allocating time for learning new approaches, we need to expand our ideas beyond the actual hours spent by teachers on the collaboration process:

Without a doubt, teachers . . . need time to understand new concepts, learn new skills, and develop new attitudes and tolerances. . . . Adult learning time in schools can be sliced two ways. It can be time that is allotted for the purpose of learning, say in the form of a workshop, an inservice session, or even a course; or it can be the time that it takes—weeks, months, years—for a person to experience or digest new ideas or ways of working. (p. 527)

Cambone encourages people in schools to evaluate how time is being viewed and how it is actually being spent in schools that are trying to carry out innovation (or "school restructuring," which is the focus of his article):

Of course, even the teacher who is in full support of a program change will, in the course of the . . . day, have his or her concentration drawn into myriad other problems and interactions. He or she will consider administrative time lines to be too aggressive, and Hargreaves claims that the teacher will work to slow things down in order to sort things through and integrate classroom efforts. This can result in administrators becoming more impatient for implementation, and subsequent calls for acceleration of the change process. In turn, the teacher slows down even more, and the political battle is engaged.

This clash between administrators and teachers over how teacher time will be used, and how quickly it is used, highlights the role of power and politics in understanding time for teachers in school restructuring. Reformer or administrator notions of how teachers ought to be spending their time are often at sharp variance with how teachers prioritize and use their time. When reformers attempt to carve time out of the teaching day for restructuring meetings, they bump up against the curricular time of teachers. (p. 521)

Teachers and administrators face difficulties when trying to collaborate with each other during the school day. These difficulties do not happen in all settings. Doelling et al. (1998) describe how the administrative support for inclusive, collaborative efforts "became a district priority. Some faculty meetings and district inservice days were reserved for team meetings as educators schedules were organized to promote collaborative planning [to reflect] . . . inclusive practices" (p. 38). Differences of opinion can be minimized when the meetings become priorities; if time to be spent on innovation can be verbalized, and consensus reached, a commitment can be made, minimizing difficulties. You can use Project Try-Out 4.3 to begin to describe your use of time.

Project Try-Out 4.3

Tick, Tock

This activity is designed to help you look at your own use of time and the "unwritten" priorities for use of time.

1. Identify an innovative project that is underway or that you want to get started. This could be something you are trying to do in your school, with friends, or with family members.

2. Look at the time resources available to you and others in your situation, and try to answer the following questions. First, look at the questions by yourself, and then discuss them with others involved:
   a. How much total time is needed?
   b. Over what span of time would the project development take place?
   c. What other things might have to be limited or temporarily stopped so this project can move forward?

3. Examine how the other people working on the project decide on the time to be spent on this project and when the project will take place.

4. In your collaboration notebook, summarize the ways in which you and the other people involved in the project looked at time. Jot down two or three reminders for yourself of what you learned about the difficulties of finding time for a favorite project.

Although you and the other people involved in the project may have agreed on some things, this exercise may reveal that the discussion of time allocation offered some surprises. Priorities that appeared one way to you may have looked very different to others. When designing a way to allocate time in a school, use what you learned in this exercise. You may be better prepared for different points of view.

Factor 5: Technology

A fifth resource that may be available in your school to promote collaboration is technology. Hourcade and Bauwens (2003) discuss many uses of the Internet for collaboration, both synchronous (at the same time; strategies such as conferencing via chats, audio, and video conferencing) and asynchronous sharing of materials (at times convenient for the participants, uncoordinated with others, such as electronic bulletin boards and electronic mailing lists). Technology can reduce time problems if teachers and administrators use electronic networks to communicate and plan rather than trying to discuss ideas face-to-face. Through e-mail and electronic bulletin boards, they can share ideas or raise questions without having to coordinate schedules. Technology can make the collaborative process more interactive, for example, in the use of cases to explore issues.

> Collaboration between the university and a local school makes it possible to use a real-life case and case teacher on the Web. This collaboration bridges the communication and application gap and may begin to reduce the steepness of the learning curve from novice to expert. (Andrews, 2002, p. 34)

Chapter 11 discusses ways to involve family members of students using technology. Andrews (2002) describes the use of online assistance with lesson planning that moved beyond the "surface" adaptations to "intense" adaptations. With the opportunities for multiple interventions, the preservice teachers participating in the project "especially liked the asynchronous nature of the collaboration because it added a highly valued factor, contact time" (p. 38).

However, simply having access to computers and electronic networks is not enough. Instead, as Boe (1989) correctly predicted, schools must put their money where their collective mouth is and agree to help staff members to learn about and use technology. "Technology Staff Development" must be part of the total inservicing plan for the school:

> The [technology] staff development plan . . . must be a long-term commitment; personal and organizational change does not occur overnight. Second, the progression of activities and involvement by teachers in this program starts with experiences designed to meet personal needs, then concentrates on instructional strategies, and finally develops into a collaborative effort of innovation. (p. 42)

Evidence of partnerships between industry and education, such as Hewlett Packard's program to support K–12 schools through a combination of donated hardware and professional development, is the kind of support Boe had in mind.

Technology can serve as a vehicle for bringing teachers together, if it has its base in meaningful instructional interests of the teachers. Seabrooks, Kenney, and LaMontagne (2000) used collaboration (via video conferencing and virtual mentoring) as strategies to enable graduate students to mentor undergraduates (from two separate universities). Pre- and post-surveys indicated that "building consensus on my team" and "listening skills" were evaluated as having improved by both mentors and mentees. The authors concluded that "Regardless of age, culture and background experiences, virtual mentoring appeared to be a viable format for exploring classroom challenges, possible solutions, and the effectiveness of applied strategies" (p. 232). This model offers possibilities that expand the potential resource base in any single building and can facilitate inter-university collaboration.

> In an age in which there is a need to prepare future teachers to become resourceful consumers of information and ideas, virtual mentoring offers the opportunity for novice professionals to access mentors beyond their own immediate environment, thus broadening their community of support. . . . An increased community of support builds confidence in teaching, enabling preservice and beginning teachers to feel positive about their career choice and their ability to teach their students. (p. 234)

Participation in an innovative effort like this one can engage teachers in their work. Shea and Babione (2002) incorporated Webcams as well as e-mail into student teaching supervision and found that the opportunity to involve exemplary teachers who were a distance from special education student teachers changed the dynamic of field supervision: "The wisdom, as well as the process of electronically collecting it, benefited the university faculty as well as the exemplary special educators themselves" (p. 3). The collaborative activity engaged individuals in multiple settings in supervision in new ways, through the use of technology.

The "collaborative effort of innovation" enables teachers to pool their resources, to problem solve, and to streamline their efforts. Using technology, collaboration can avoid the problems faced by teachers who are looking for timely suggestions for solving a problem or looking for support after a hard day. Models like the virtual mentoring described by Seabrooks et al. (2000) and Shea and Babione (2002) have been in use for some time. Merseth (1991) described the use of computer networks to support 39 beginning teachers. Her findings showed that the network was most helpful in providing moral support, reducing the sense of isolation often experienced by beginning teachers. This study, limited to first-year teachers, provided limited curricular or technical help, unlike the study by Odell (1988), in which experienced mentors staffed the electronic network. In the Odell study, technical support was more highly valued by participants than emotional support among network users. All of these studies illustrate how networks can foster different kinds of communication.

Technology can, however, have the opposite effect, as Friedman (1994) cautions: "Too frequently, technology is allocated to 'fiefdoms,' thereby leading to inefficient utilization. It is often the most useful tact to share new technology, and to reassign old technology, but that cannot be accomplished without a coordinated strategy for utilization" (p. 89). Technology, instead of opening up new forms of communication between teachers, can be divisive. Best (2002) describes challenges that the information technology (IT) specialists can face while trying to assist teachers:

> The IT professionals were hired to install, support, and manage the technology resources of the school district as a system. They believed that more efficient and compatible technology would facilitate teachers in improving student learning. This assumption often collided with each teacher's need to customize learning to meet individual needs of students. (p. 20)

In the long run, a new paradigm must be developed in which teachers, rather than being the repository of knowledge and experience, communicate with each other, sharing knowledge that can be a basis of new discovery (Branson, 1990, p. 9). Best (2002) recommends "new cultural norms" to assist IT professionals and teachers to collaborate effectively, with "the new infusion of technology and technologists into the school system provid[ing] the educational culture the opportunity to reflect on its protocols and practices" (p. 20). Collaboration via the Internet has become a means by which physically isolated people can communicate in a timely manner, using collaborative tools and video conferencing (Ozer, 1996a, 1996b). Although challenging (as Bonk, 2004, describes), such collaboration is part of the lives of individuals in schools today. Teachers finding themselves in charge of, rather than the prisoners of, technology can exponentially increase their opportunities for collaboration.

APPLICATIONS TO USE IN YOUR SCHOOL SETTING

How well teachers overcome barriers described at the start of this chapter predicts some of their collaboration success. Success is also a result of how thoroughly teachers look for hidden resources. Cheng (1996) analyzed the results of a survey sent to teachers, principals, and students in 62 schools in Hong Kong. The most significant factor associated with professionalism was the human leadership observed in the building principal. Professionalism influenced student educational outcome, classroom management, teachers' job attitudes and feelings, and school organizational factors. "In addition to supporting the significance of teachers' professionalism to the professionalization of teaching and education quality, the profiles may provide a useful pattern for undertaking staff development and school development" (p. 170). You may learn a lot about your school by looking at it from a new point of view. Professionalism, for example, may be one of the invisible resources upon which you can build in your school. You can look for the other factors as well.

Consider some of the following approaches, which others have used to assess the school environment for collaboration.

Use the Lunchroom

While you are in the faculty lunchroom, do some informal data gathering. This way, you can assess the climate for collaboration in your setting. Review the items in this chapter. Focus on one barrier to collaboration or one collaboration promoter. See how often a particular topic (positive or negative) comes up. You can do your data collection right in the lunchroom after you've finished eating your lunch. Collect data for about 10 minutes while you and other teachers are sitting around. You can use either of the following methods:

1. When preparing your lunch, count out a certain number (20 or 30) of food items. These could be sunflower seeds, bite-sized pieces of celery, sugar-free candy, or other small items. Each time the topic you are listening for is mentioned, eat one of your food items. Count how many you have left at the end of your meal and subtract them from your original number to create your baseline. Go back to your classroom and record your baseline data.

2. Take out a pad of paper and do some doodling. Make a decision about the doodle symbol (a filled-in triangle, a dot with a circle around it) that represents the topic for which you are listening. At the end of the meal, take your doodle back to your classroom and put the date on it. Calculate the frequency of the topic and record your baseline data.

Ideally, you would collect baseline data for three days before you start your collaboration project.

Review Written Samples

Review a sample of three or four memos or reports from school personnel regarding collaboration-related topics. Take some time to develop a few questions to assess the environment for collaboration in your building. Questions such as the following, applied to a sample of memos, letters, and reports in your building, can give you a sense of the communication patterns:

1. How are receivers of memos grouped? Are they members of the same content area, grade level, rank? Or are other collaboration-related characteristics considered?

2. In what ways does the content of the memo include or exclude people in the building? In the broader school community (e.g., parents, PTAs, other interest groups)?

3. To what extent does the written material's topic or timeframe reflect joint decision making?

4. How would you describe the tone of the written message—supportive of a collaborative endeavor, dismissing collaboration as a possibility, or somewhere in between?

These reviews can give you a sense of the explicit and implicit messages related to collaboration that are present in your school environment. You may find that there are some team-builders in action whom you never noticed. Peters and Austin (1997) describe autonomous groups ("Skunkworks") that work within many large organizations. Quietly, they work purposefully to accomplish change. You may be able to discover some of these in your school.

Compare Work Among Colleagues

Compare work on two similar projects involving more than one teacher in your building, and note differences. Contrast how two projects (e.g., Open House for students or family members and another schoolwide activity later in the year that recognizes excellence among students at different points in the year, or gathers teachers and staff together for special events) or two different extracurricular activities reflect the collaboration orientation of their designers. You can identify how the events involve people differently. Use the following questions to compare the two events:

1. How do the materials communicating information about each event, from initial notice up through and including the event itself, differ? Which one reflects a greater effort to involve and welcome others who might be new to the initiative or event?

2. How were the planning groups for each event formed? In what ways were the issues related to "team building" that were discussed earlier in the chapter put into action?

3. How much flexibility was there for people to participate in each event? Did the flexibility seem to have any relationship to maximizing ways to enjoy the event (e.g., preset start/stop times, options for types of participation, mandatory vs. optional participation)?

4. Based on what you observed, would you make any recommendations to the planners of the next event?

The events taking place all around you in your school may contain indicators of collaboration. By scrutinizing situations, you may be able to make use of the subtle, almost invisible evidence of collaboration that fellow teachers and administrators are offering. Although you may not find yourself in the perfect school, you should find ways to use what is available to you right where you are.

Farmakopoulou (2002) analyzed inter-agency collaboration to address the special education needs in Scotland. She examined how power over information and resources, as well as interdependence, limited the extent and quality of the collaboration that took place across agencies. The complex relationships could be improved, but "only if changes in the internal and external conditions take place simultaneously is there a chance of improving the existing collaborative relationships" (p. 57). In other words, change has to take place at several levels in order for collaboration to take place. In the description below, just such initiatives are undertaken in a rural community in Michigan and in Gosport, Indiana.

COMMUNITYWIDE COLLABORATION EXPERIMENTS

Mariage and Garmon (2003a) describe Project PREPARE, a five-year project in which eight collaborative structures were incorporated into a rural primary school, creating a method for general and special education teachers to work with two area universities. The use of a collaborative structure was designed to improve the way teachers worked together, improve student progress, and create a culture that welcomed parents and local community members. By incorporating teacher study groups, a model summer school program, home-school partnerships, mentor-intern and mentor-mentee programs, as well as a professional development center (with new computers), it was hoped that changes would occur.

They found the following changes: improvements in reading and math achievement in relation to 10 comparison schools, in relation to end-of-year data from computer-assisted programs. The interconnected nature of the collaborations were cited as the key:

> The work that was accomplished in curricular alignment, adoption, and targeting professional development was essential to the improvement of student achievement . . . Project PREPARE has drawn upon special education and other literature to play an important role in developing a collaborative site of practice and inquiry that has demonstrated the ability to affect student achievement in powerful ways. Developing systems of individuation, the ability of a school to adequately address the academic and sociobehavioral needs of each student and faculty member may be a critical framing concept for helping universities work with schools . . . through the implementation of curricula that provides calibrated support, a collaborative infrastructure that has multiple entry points for teacher learning and autonomy, and support structures for extending opportunities to learn. (p. 232)

The changes observed in this school were incorporated into all aspects of the school's daily activities, and "stakeholders were affected in a number of ways" (p. 232).

Mariage and Garmon elaborate on their work further in 2003b:

> We have seen that the systemic change process has benefited from having both mandatory and voluntary collaborative structures. Specifically, the mandatory structure of the North Central Outcomes Accreditation/School Improvement target area teams created a collaborative problem-solving space where faculty had to examine core standards at the state level. . . . Voluntary structures created energy points that were believed to be critical for sustaining the change process, creating momentum, and providing sites for individual teachers to take instructional risks and/or create a professional identity. (p. 67)

The schoolwide nature of this change initiative was a critical aspect of its success.

Wiggam (1992) describes the work done in a small rural school in Gosport, Indiana; the school made a commitment to a collaborative process for change. In explaining the three-year process, Wiggam underscores the importance of raising critical questions at the beginning of the process:

> As the staff at Gosport began preparing to bring about change, we reviewed many of the previous attempts throughout the country to establish meaningful improvement in education. . . . We were concerned and perplexed by the short life spans of those earlier attempts to change the system. We began taking a closer look to find the causes of their eventual abandonment. One thing that we noticed was that there was not community understanding or support. We could not find any evidence that the community had been involved in the planning. . . . Therefore, the decision was made to initiate and develop new approaches to two-way communications. (pp. 54–55)

In taking this approach, the school personnel in Gosport followed the first two principles that Mauriel and Lindquist (1989) include in their framework for effective leadership in schools. First, they spent time determining priorities influencing school systems, and second they examined social and educational trends. The Gosport group also incorporated the principles Wilson (1993) later outlined in her description of teacher leaders: "In common with other leaders, teacher leaders seek challenge, change, and growth. . . . At the same time, teacher leaders feel like family: informal, reassuringly dependable, and supportive of colleagues" (p. 24). The Gosport group did not approach collaboration as an "add-on." Instead, they viewed gathering information from others as an essential part of consensus building, leading to outcomes in which all had ownership. Their strategies included team building, open meetings, distributing and collecting surveys, use of the community newspaper to report their progress, and initiation of a student newspaper. All these approaches culminated in a successful presentation of their proposal to the school board (Wiggam, 1992, pp. 55–56). The collaborative process expanded beyond its original scope:

> The teachers extended their communications beyond just the parents of their students. They visited other schools in the district to share the school's goals, activities, and purpose. . . . The school helped form a network of schools that were also designing changes of their own. This network allowed the exchange of ideas, concerns, and strategies. (p. 56)

In the approach taken by the participants in this process, visible leadership was key. As the members of the school and the community worked together, they focused on joint outcomes. In Gosport, the definition of leadership that Barr and Barr (1989) provide was demonstrated: "Leadership is the process of influencing people to give their energies, use their potential, release their determination, and go beyond their comfort zones to accomplish goals. . . . Leadership draws trust, acknowledgment, risk, and loyalty from the led" (p. 9).

In the description of the Gosport effort, concurrent outcomes were achieved. Although the stated goal was improved delivery of school services, a commitment to collaboration was developed:

There has been significant improvement in effective communications. The information shared among staff members has grown to include more about what is working for individual students. There is more collaboration in designing strategies and materials . . . There is a new willingness on the part of the local professionals and businesses to become open supporters of the school. (Wiggam, 1992, p. 57)

The collaboration process went far beyond lip service to include the exchange of substantive ideas. Gardner (1990) cites "the release of human possibilities" (p. 73) as a task of leaders:

In all of us there are undiscovered gifts, untested strengths. Sometimes capabilities remain hidden simply because the circumstances of life do not evoke them, the challenge never arises, the call never comes. . . . It is a matter of self-interest in every society to remove obstacles to human growth and performance. (p. 74)

Morocco, Walker, and Lewis (2003) describe the use of a schoolwide thinking curriculum to facilitate changes within one building, which enabled change to occur within the district. These transformations influenced the students, teachers, and community:

The district leaders . . . view the school as a lever for change, a continual reminder that an economically and culturally diverse group of students, including students with disabilities, can engage in rigorous thinking about hard questions. Finding the resources to support districtwide change is extraordinarily difficult for district leaders at this time. Yet having a strong middle school example helps to inspire continuing progress toward schoolwide, inclusive practices. (p. 14)

Gardner (1990) asks us to extend ourselves and to reach our potential. This call was met in the rural district of Gosport. The initiative in Gosport met the "lessons learned" that Fuchs and Fuchs (2001) identified as critical for "adoption and sustainability of research-based practices: the importance of a key individual, control of resources, accountability for student outcomes, participation in development, improving implementation with practice, and recognition of accomplishments" (pp. 309–310). Momentum developed in Gosport helped to bring change about.

The next chapter will help you set the stage for your initiative, which may eventually expand to broad-based collaborative activities in your building or district.

5

Developing an Effective Collaboration Strategy

Half Empty or Half Full?

"**H**ow much of what happens at school is due not to the students, not to the principal, not to the curriculum, but just to me?" This question may pop into your head at odd times. It may even cross your mind as you walk into your classroom. In Chapter 4, we identified the features of the school environment that can both slow down and speed up the collaboration process. In this chapter, we'll identify what you contribute to your personal collaboration agenda. This is your personal collaboration 30,000-mile checkup. Included in Chapter 5 are the items for you to address as you begin to plan your collaboration project—your own professional Indy 500 Race. Just like race car drivers, you may have a sinking feeling in your stomach as you consider what is ahead. But you can also anticipate what they do as they climb into their cars—the flag down at the finish line, being the winner. Your race begins in the driver's seat. You will figure out what you need to do to be a winner.

COLLABORATION COMPONENT CHECKLISTS

Self-examination is a difficult but rewarding process. Learning about yourself through a systematic exploration of what you do when working with others can give you new ways to approach familiar situations. This kind of self-study will ultimately make you a better collaborator and a more effective teacher.

Consider the following collaboration project that was completed by Kathryn Lovejoy, a graduate student who had been working as a teacher for some time. When she received the collaboration project assignment, she immediately knew who her target person would be. She selected a fellow teacher with whom she had not developed a successful working relationship. For several years, she'd been concerned that her feelings were poisoning her teaching, leading her to feel unsatisfied on the job and making her unhappy about going to work. As a result of carrying out her collaboration project, she found ways to change the situation. Her attitude toward her situation evolved, even though her coworker made no behavioral changes. She used self-inquiry as the focus of her collaboration project. Learning more about herself enabled her to reconceptualize her situation.

> When I began this project, I thought I knew a lot about myself. Only as I got into it did I realize how much some of my biases influenced my relationship with Priscilla. For example, it is very important to me that I have visible relationships with my co-workers. I enjoy working with people who show their feelings in complex ways. Priscilla is a blank screen—I never know what she is thinking! I was also surprised to discover how much I dislike disharmony. I get upset when conflict occurs. However, it is easier for me to live with conflict than with the unknown. What upsets me most is when I can't tell what someone else is thinking or feeling.
>
> After I realized all this about myself, I was better at evaluating my working relationship with Priscilla. She is the only person with whom I work who doesn't respond positively toward me, because she doesn't react at all! I have had a hard time relating to her because she always appears so apathetic.
>
> Once I realized that much of the problem came from my expectations, I stopped hoping for the impossible. I came to accept her for what she is. She is hardworking and responsible. I never really noticed that before because I was so preoccupied with her distance. I realized that although we will never really like each other, we can still work well together.
>
> Now, I can accept what is good about her. I've trained myself to ignore the rest. As a result, our working relationship has really improved. (Lovejoy, 1994)

Lovejoy's insight about her contribution to the problem led to the development of an improved working relationship. The following is another example of self-exploration and the resulting changes that are independent of others.

> *When I think back on that year, I feel grateful. I thought I was being normal—but I was bad-mouthing my principal every chance I got. It was only when someone asked me if I was planning to transfer that I realized how negative I sounded to others. In fact, everywhere I'd ever worked, we'd made mincemeat of the person in charge. I never thought it could be any other way. Once I decided to think and sound more positive, even though nothing had changed, I was surprised that then I felt better about everything.*

In both situations described above, attitude changes led to successful outcomes without any changes on the part of the other person in the situation.

Your attitude might be influencing *your* effectiveness. In this chapter, you will explore your own predispositions toward collaboration in many different ways. You will find out whether your biases are undermining you (making your glass half empty) or getting you ahead (making your glass half full). By the time you finish Chapter 5, you should have new ways to assess yourself. Whether you decide on a formal approach (e.g., moving from paper to a portfolio, or eventually to a Webfolio, as described in detail by Love, McKean, & Gathercoal, 2004) or stay within the boundaries of the simple data collection approach suggested in this chapter, you will discover ways to document your changed attitude and behavior.

The ability to change your outlook about a person, or the people, with whom you are working in schools can have an enormous benefit. Unlike many professions, teaching requires us to interact with others. Goldring and Greenfield (2004) make these observations about life in schools:

> Schools are highly normative organizations . . . [involving] people-intensive activities. The goals of schools are cultural and developmental, and getting things done in a school requires heavy reliance on face-to-face interactions with teachers and others; people themselves are the medium and the focus of a school's efforts. More than most other institutions, virtually all of the daily work that occurs in schools involves people working with and through people to influence people—students, parents, teachers, school principals, and superintendents, working with and through others, ultimately and more importantly to enhance the cognitive, social, emotional, and physical development of children. (p. 6)

Becoming adept at working with others can assist you in meeting the needs of your students and in making your work environment more personally and professionally satisfying. You may also be able to incorporate ideas from your collaboration project into classroom content. Imada, Doyle, Brock, and Goddard (2002) describe the positive outcomes that emerged from infusing leadership skills into their secondary classrooms in rural Nebraska. Their bimonthly leadership conference was co-led by a special educator and general educator. Data they maintained over a two-year period showed student improvement in many areas (including adult/peer relationships and leadership skills). Teaching on such topics as communication, goal setting, plan of action, and risk taking (p. 51) could enable you to use what you are learning in this book with your students.

Assessment of your collaboration skills is important in terms of your satisfaction on the job. It also has direct and indirect impact on the success of students in your classroom. In their analysis of a decision-making approach that depended on partnerships between professionals and students, Thomson, Bachor, and Thomson (2002) described the positive outcomes that occurred for students when a collaborative approach was used during IEP meetings.

> While it is recognized that there are limitations and barriers to collaborative consultation, primarily over territory and the use of "jargon" by special educators, the potential benefits make such an approach appealing. Benefits include the use of the least restrictive environment, a student-centered

approach to service delivery, staff development opportunities, and a shared responsibility for design and implementation of programs. Staff were able to reflect on all of these points and felt that the decision-making model had indeed encouraged such benefits. (p. 42)

Benefits to students were also the focus of an analysis by Villa and Thousand (1988) of the practices associated with success for students with disabilities in typical classrooms. They concluded that

one content area in which all school staff need instruction is collaborative teaming . . . . School personnel need to become skillful in implementing a collaborative teaming model and using interpersonal and small group skills to function optimally as collaborative team members. (p. 152)

In Chapter 1, the first principle of collaboration was *to create a climate of heightened professionalism between professionals, with the "indirect impact on student outcomes" (Idol & West, 1991, p. 72) such that the students who are served by the professionals can achieve their highest potential.* Villa and Thousand (1988) and the following example emphasize the value of collaboration among professionals in serving special needs students.

One of the reasons I went into teaching was because I liked watching my teachers, Mr. Martin and Mrs. Farrell, work together when I was in sixth grade. I probably learned more from them than I did from my books. Carol was a student in our class who had many problems learning. I watched how my teachers talked to each other and helped Carol. They were patient and creative. They inspired me. I don't think either of them ever knew what an effect they had on me, but their behavior led me toward teaching.

This kind of collaboration is also a crucial component when working toward the seamless transition for students as they move into society. Repetto and Correa (1996) make the following point: "The success of transition service provision rests on the building of strong interagency and intra-agency partnerships. Collaboration among all the service providers seems to be one of the most important components in the development and implementation of transition programs" (p. 558). Turnbull, Turnbull, Erwin, and Soodak (2006) state that the "collaborative team climate, in which everyone works cooperatively with mutual respect and equity, is essential for reaching successful outcomes for students, families, and professionals" (p. 186). This is the case with the school-based teams as well as those that serve students in their transitions to post-school life and work. Thus, the impact of effective collaboration reaches beyond the school years into the adult lives of our students.

For teachers to become better collaborators, they need to identify exactly what is inhibiting effective collaboration. You can begin by finding out whether the way in which *you* like to collaborate fits with the collaboration needs of those around you.

COMPATIBILITY CHECKLIST

In the following example, the teacher is surprised that collaboration habits are different at different schools.

The difference between my old school and my new one is incredible. My old school was where I had my first job. I thought every place was like that. We never got anything done without at least one teacher bursting into tears. Everything was a fight. In this new school, we take turns chairing the Student Welfare Committee. Not every idea is accepted, but people listen. I haven't had to take one aspirin after work so far this year—what a difference.

Think about your own recent efforts to work with family, friends, and coworkers over the past few months and consider these questions.

- Have you experienced collaboration styles that are compatible with yours?
- When did you last feel as if everything "clicked" when you were trying to collaborate with someone else?
- How long ago did you feel that you were at cross-purposes and the only result of your efforts was frustration?

If, as you answered these questions, you found yourself thinking about situations that were problematic more often than those that were successful, you may need to consider ways to improve your compatibility rating. Your approach to collaboration may be different from that of your colleagues. In the following section, you can consider a range of possible problems and solutions for improving your collaboration compatibility rating.

Compatibility Item 1: Using Clarifying Questions

Collaboration Stumbling Block

For many teams, habits used for giving and getting information create problems and are potential stumbling blocks.

Collaboration Ramp

The use of clarifying questions can help you give and get information effectively.

Imagine the following situation: A building team is meeting to decide how to increase parent involvement in the graduation ceremony. Many ideas have been suggested, but there is little consensus among the teachers at the meeting. Ten minutes before the end of the meeting, a teacher comments to the meeting coordinator, "Well, we can just forget the parents of the kids in the special education classes."

As a special education teacher at that meeting, which of the following do you think you would do?

1. Pretend you didn't hear the comment.

2. Accuse the teacher of stereotyping special education students and their parents, either during the meeting or to your friends on the faculty immediately after the meeting.

3. Ask the teacher to describe the problem further.

In this difficult situation, you may feel as if your options are limited to 1 or 2. Option 3 may not even occur to you, given the tenor of the meeting. Yet a question such as "What do you think makes the parents of students receiving special education services different from our other parents?" or "What have you noticed over the past few years?" could be used to get more information about the teacher's perception of the problem. Option 3 involves the use of *clarifying questions.*

Kennedy, Higgins, and Pierce (2002) provided teachers with a set of questions either to be used during a preliminary meeting or to be completed and shared in written form. These questions were designed to assist teachers at the start of their collaborative planning process. They observe that

> good communication is the key to a well-functioning collaborative relationship. . . . Because many [teachers] are itinerant within school districts, it may be difficult to contact them. Often, communication forms are necessary. Communication forms provide tangible evidence of the request for assistance and the response provided. (p. 45)

Tschantz and Vail (2000) used peer coaching to increase the use of responsive communication strategies in early childhood settings (see Chapter 3 for a further discussion of their work). Pugach and Johnson (1988b) included clarifying questions in the early stages of the peer collaboration process (p. 75). In 1991, Johnson and Pugach became even more explicit, identifying clarifying questions as the first of a four-step process for peer collaboration: "The first step in the process is the longest and provides the foundation for subsequent steps" (p. 456). They recommend the use of questions "to clarify all aspects of the problem" (p. 456). These questions can be used to help collaborators accurately assess how well they are understanding other people with whom they interact. Teachers can prevent confusion or misunderstanding through the use of clarifying questions. These can be followed up by such strategies as "self-questioning, summarizing, and predicting" (Pugach & Johnson, 1988b, p. 75); all these can help teachers to give and get information more effectively.

Pugach and Johnson (1995) continued their research, training 95 experienced teachers in the use of peer collaboration (which included clarifying questions) in pre-referral conferencing. When the 95 teachers trained in peer collaboration compared their referral rate to the rate the previous year, they had 50% fewer referrals than they had the year before. In the same two-year period, a comparison group of 96 teachers (who had received no training) had a slight increase in overall referrals.

The teachers trained in peer collaboration also were more confidently able to handle problems. The authors conclude that "this group of teachers was able to use a structured problem-solving process to engage in a dialogue about classroom concerns and in most cases develop solutions to those concerns" (p. 109). Clarifying questions were effectively used in this research study.

Clarifying questions were also very valuable in a collaboration project. Lovejoy, the teacher you read about at the start of this chapter, used clarifying questions with her classroom paraprofessional. She wanted to better understand her part in frequent power struggles with a particular student:

> A final aim of my project was self-discovery. I wanted to answer the question, "Why do I get so angry when this student is noncompliant?" In order to learn more about how I responded to this student, I set up a series of opportunities to use clarifying questions with my paraprofessional.
>
> I wanted to get her insights about what she thought was happening between me and my student. I asked her questions about what she saw, and thought a lot about her answers. Because of the questioning process, I was able to get out of the guilt-blame cycle I'd been in over this student all year long.
>
> I've been a teacher for five years. I've prided myself on my sense that students generally wanted to do a good job because I had developed rapport with them. In most cases, rapport had been a successful tool, to encourage good behavior and to motivate my students. I had to admit this student was not motivated by any of my tried and true strategies.
>
> Through the back-and-forth of questions and answers with my parapro-fessional, I discovered I had a need to control. I also came to see that encour-aging motivation and controlling are different. I think I am more relaxed and effective now, since I am allowing students to make clear choices. I'm becom-ing more comfortable letting them make those choices. As a result, the power struggles have almost disappeared. I don't think this would have happened without the conversations with my paraprofessional. (Lovejoy, 1994)

Using clarifying questioning enabled Lovejoy to honestly assess the difference between her idealized version of what was happening in her classroom and what was really taking place. Her paraprofessional's questions raised new areas to con-sider. Lovejoy recognized that she was not reaching her student. However, when she tried to think her way out of her old habit, she found that she was stuck. She got her-self unstuck by reflecting on what could be different in her classroom, via the answers her paraprofessional provided. This led to more management options and better rapport with her problem student.

Compatibility Item 2: Using a Structured Self-Assessment Process

Collaboration Stumbling Block

Teachers often have difficulty translating the clarifying questioning process into an ongoing self-study approach, one which can be used flexibly at any point in the collaboration process.

Collaboration Ramp

You can use a standard indicator, like the Tuckman Teacher Feedback Form (Tuckman, 1995, p. 179), to compare your perception of yourself with the perceptions others have of you. While this 30-item form was designed to be completed by students, you can complete it yourself. Your self-rating can serve as a basis of discus-sion with colleagues about how you are viewed by them. Tuckman's results, includ-ing descriptions such as "organized," "dynamic," "flexible," "warm/accepting," and "creative," can provide you and your colleagues with an opportunity to evaluate the accuracy of your self-perception.

You might also find it useful to discuss with other teachers how you would like to be seen. Tuckman explains that "the criterion for excellence has been individualized by allowing each teacher to rate his or her ideal" (p. 182) and then compare the ideal rating to the self-rating or the rating given by others. As the basis for ongoing professional development, it can be helpful to consider how you would like to be seen and to work toward achieving your goal with like-minded others. Project Try-Out 5.1 will give you a chance to do just that.

Project Try-Out 5.1

Mirror, Mirror

This exercise will give you an opportunity to compare your inner picture of yourself and how you teach with some more objective information.

1. Get a copy of the Tuckman Teacher Feedback Form (Tuckman, 1995, p. 179).
   a. Complete the form based on your recent teaching or volunteer experiences.
   b. Complete the form as you would *like* to behave as a teacher.
   c. Score each version of the form using the key provided.

2. Discuss the differences between the two ratings with a friend who knows you well and jot down your observations in your collaboration notebook, or privately review the differences and jot down your observations in your collaboration notebook.

3. At the end of your review, identify two or three specific things you can do to move closer to your ideal. Record these ideas in your collaboration notebook.

4. Optional—On the Job: If you are currently working in a school, include this step; if you are not working in a school now, come back to this step when you begin teaching:
   a. Ask a person in your school who is familiar with your teaching style to think about the strengths seen in your teaching. Ask the person to complete the Tuckman Teacher Feedback Form.
   b. Take time to meet with the person and discuss the differences between the person's ratings and your ratings of how you would like to behave as a teacher.
   c. At the end of the discussion, agree upon two or three action steps you could take to become the teacher you want to be.
   d. Record the suggestions in your collaboration notebook.

If you can't find an indicator that suits your needs, you might use a mapping process to analyze your thoughts about your collaboration situation in advance of, and following the implementation of, your collaboration project. Trent and Dixon (2004) describe the use of concrete mapping and comparative essays to look at whether or not there had been changes in the attitudes of preservice teachers enrolled in a special education course that emphasized multidisciplinary concepts. Their article shows the process they used to assess change.

Either of these self-assessments can help you compare your current collaboration style with your idea of the collaborative teacher you would like to be. In addition, you can do any of the following:

1. Use the unique moment, productive pattern, and counterproductive pattern questions at the end of Chapter 3 to examine your behavior.

2. Modify Try-Out 5.1 without a standard form; instead, use ideas you've generated in other try-outs in this book.

3. Talk with someone who has known you for a long time and discuss the questions in Try-Out 5.1.

As you become more familiar with self-assessment, you will find that it becomes automatic. You will be able to identify what you are doing effectively and also what you're doing that you'd like to change. One potential area of change is the way you interact with others in meetings.

Compatibility Item 3: Clarifying Expectations for Meeting Styles

Collaboration Stumbling Block

When people in schools meet, they do not always explicitly share their expectations. They may not explain what is to be accomplished or even clarify their timelines. This can lead to frustration before, during, and after meetings.

Collaboration Ramp

Making meeting expectations explicit and establishing consensus for meeting formats can improve meetings significantly. The following example illustrates both the collaboration stumbling block and the collaboration ramp.

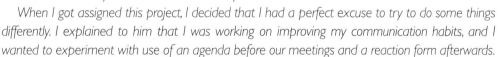

At the start of the year, each meeting with my principal felt like time wasted. He never knew what he wanted to discuss, and there were always a million interruptions. Since I already have tenure, I didn't really care too much one way or the other.

When I got assigned this project, I decided that I had a perfect excuse to try to do some things differently. I explained to him that I was working on improving my communication habits, and I wanted to experiment with use of an agenda before our meetings and a reaction form afterwards.

The difference it made has amazed both of us. We're more efficient, and I'm much more satisfied. I'm planning to use it with other teachers, too.

Thousand and Villa (2000) developed a tool ("Are we really a team?" worksheet) for team members to use to analyze their meetings. A total of 100 points can be "earned," but items (e.g., "Have we publicly discussed the group's overall purpose?" "Do we distribute leadership responsibility by rotating roles [e.g., recorder, timekeeper, encourager, facilitator]?") can only be earned if all group members agree on the answer. An adapted version of their form is provided in Turnbull et al. (2006, p. 188). Elliott and Sheridan (1992) looked at meetings in schools and suggested a way to help the collaboration team function effectively:

> At the outset, . . . it is important for the group to establish an appropriate agenda. Among the relevant issues, the leader should help the group decide which topics they will address, the order of priority, and how much time will be devoted to each topic. (p. 329)

Resources like the one produced by Cleese and Jay (1993), a humorous video depiction of effective and ineffective meetings, can help turn a familiar, often boring topic (meeting agendas) into one that clearly links expectations and meeting organization.

For many teachers, the idea of making meeting expectations explicit is appealing because things to be done are clearly laid out. If the agenda serves the group well, teachers share their ideas before the agenda is set. The translation of their ideas into items on the agenda leads to ownership that is demonstrated during the meeting. By the end of the meeting, they can look back and agree that the meeting time was well spent.

Is this compatibility approach right for you? You may want to experiment at a formal or informal meeting. Think about your usual approach. Establish a set of expectations to share with your colleagues that is different (either more or less structured) from the approach you usually use. Share it with others at the start of the meeting to see what effect it has on your compatibility with your colleagues. You may be surprised. Van Meter and Stevens (2000) examined the role of different theories in relation to peer collaboration, considering such factors as cognitive conflict, gender, and the conditions that promote collaboration. Their article may give you some insights about the kinds of issues that are getting in the way of working well with some of your fellow teachers in meetings.

Developing a meeting style that is comfortable for you, and for others with whom you are working, is challenging. For example, your expectations for an agenda and the expectations of others may be quite different. Susan Paul-Saladino's collaboration project focused on a coworker. She realized that she had to make her agendas (and her general decision-making approach) more compatible with that of her target person:

> I strive for consensus, and see very little as being written in stone. I think I may spend too much time agonizing over decisions, and often postpone having to make a decision. My target person likes to stick to her agenda and gives set amounts of time for each item on the agenda. When time is up, time is up. There is no more discussion and a decision is made, good or bad. I found her approach to be very troubling.
>
> Through my project, I got a heightened sense of how she operates. This has made a world of difference for me. Things aren't perfect—I still have a hard time with some of what she does. But now I have a much greater understanding of why she might conduct herself a certain way. (Paul-Saladino, 1994)

Paul-Saladino learned that she and her target person had contradictory expectations for meetings, which led to a very low level of compatibility between them. Through her collaboration project, she came to realize that there is not necessarily a right or wrong way to set up a meeting. Her comfort level is higher with a looser format, while her target person is more comfortable with a highly structured agenda. When they work together, Paul-Saladino realizes that she will need to develop a greater acceptance of her coworker's style:

> At the very beginning of my collaboration project, I took responsibility for part of the problem, but felt that there was no possibility that things could ever get any better. I was forced, through the project, to take a closer look at what was actually going on between us. I had to make some changes in the way I asked for her ideas. In doing so, it became obvious to me that one person cannot take full responsibility when a relationship is strained. Still, focused effort to improve the relationship did make a difference. (Paul-Saladino, 1994)

Paul-Saladino's experiences fit together with the recommendations that West and Cannon (1988) identified. They encouraged teachers to "match consultation approach(es) to specific consultation situation(s) and need(s)" (p. 59). These essential competencies would be needed while collaborating as well as while consulting. Tindal, Shinn, and Rodden-Nord (1990) provided an overview of influential variables in three categories: people variables, process variables, and procedural implementation variables. While these were developed to focus on a consultation model, they are relevant to collaboration.

Trent (1998) provides a multiyear follow-along study of a secondary teacher who has co-teaching experiences with several different learning disabilities specialists. Two created challenges for the teacher; while she overcame "startup problems that could be 'worked out'" (p. 507) with one teacher, the problems were more substantial in the second case. "The two had different ideas about the need to plan together . . . lack of openness and incompatible beliefs prevented the development of a more mutually satisfying relationship between the two teachers" (pp. 509–510). Trent concludes as follows:

> Analysis of the data collected in this study suggests that, in implementing the collaborative teaching model at McGinnis High School, too much was left to chance. . . . These two teachers were unable to move beyond a superficial dialogue to change their pedagogy and facilitate improved learning outcomes for their students. (p. 511)

Trent's description of the "lost opportunity" is one that this book hopes to help you avoid, as you investigate how to make the most of co-teaching or other opportunities to work with fellow educators in your school setting.

Congruence of expectations of people in meetings would be one way to ensure that meetings are successful. In her collaboration project, Paul-Saladino (1994) modified her habits and expectations. Eventually, the meetings met her needs as well as those of her target person. Her experience is consistent with the leadership program in which Castro (2004) found this challenge for rural school leaders: "School leaders want an environment that fosters professional growth in teaching strategies, honest two-way communication between administration and faculty, and shared team leadership development" (p. 338). The development of trust, and use of two-way communication, can lead to the type of congruence of expectations that can foster productivity and satisfaction. Collaboration can be easier when such an atmosphere exists.

In a year-long study, Phillips et al. (1995) trained and interviewed six general education and four special education teachers. In describing collaboration, teachers used the analogy of "cooking in someone else's kitchen" (p. 268), a vivid image that can connote chaos or teamwork. The authors commented that "negotiating roles and figuring out their partner's style of instruction was challenging for all the teachers" (p. 268). Suggestions from the participating teachers included the following: "Maintain flexibility" and "be prepared to 'put in time' getting to know your teaching partner; this phase cannot be rushed. It takes time to learn about each other's styles and preferences" (p. 269).

Almost 10 years later, Trent, Driver, Wood, Parrott, Martin, and Smith (2003) studied the efforts of a pair of general and special education teachers to co-teach; the researchers studied them and the supervising principal via interviews, observations, and a review of archival data. The in-depth analysis of the experiences in the schools illustrates the complexity of collaborative relationships, planning, and teaching, observing (in substance, very similar to the recommendations of Phillips et al., 1995, provided in the above paragraph) that "implementing and sustaining a cooperative teaching relationship is complex and requires dynamic and sustained communication on the part of teachers and administrators" (p. 217). Both teachers involved in the study were experienced (the special educator had 6 years of experience, 5 years in the building where the study took place, and the general educator had 13 years of experience, 5 years in the building where the study took place).

At the end of the year, Trent et al. (2003) drew the following conclusions:

> Despite problems, constraints, and uncertainties, both teachers agreed that the changes they experienced due to cooperative teaching resulted in many benefits for them, their students with disabilities, and their students who were not labeled. . . . These educators believed that, as a result of on-going communication, sharing, and planning, they became better teachers. In addition, they believed their changed teaching methods resulted in benefits for the students in their classroom. (p. 211)

These experienced teachers had to take time to make sure that they were coordinating their approach in working with students in their class.

You can come out ahead if you review the differences between team members' ways of doing things. It also helps if you familiarize yourself with your own habits in decision making. An opportunity to do just that is provided in Idea Try-Out 5.2.

Idea Try-Out 5.2

New Year's Resolutions

This activity will give you an opportunity to look at your habits in decision making and a chance to identify some things you would like to do differently.

1. Think back to a time when you were stubborn about getting something done your own way. In your collaboration notebook, jot down a brief description of

the event and as many adjectives as you can think of that describe how you behaved.

2. Think back to a time when you capitulated too quickly on a decision. In your collaboration notebook, jot down a brief description of the event and as many adjectives as you can think of that describe how you behaved.

3. Think back to a time when you felt good about a decision you made. You collected necessary information in advance, considered options in a way that felt right to you, and the decision was one that worked out well. In your collaboration notebook, jot down a brief description of the event and as many adjectives as you can think of that describe how you behaved.

4. Review these lists. Put together a short list of "New Year's" resolutions describing how you would like to behave in the future.

By completing this exercise, you have identified a few things to do differently. Unlike the usual New Year's resolutions—the list you make and feel guilty about for the rest of the year—try to find ways to include one resolution in a meeting soon.

As you improve the clarity of your expectations for meeting styles, you may discover additional personal and professional characteristics that you would like to eliminate or improve. It is not possible to change everything all at once. Instead, continue to keep track of ideas you have. Generate a sequence of goals for yourself. In developing your goals, you can consider not only how your meetings take place but topics you discuss. You may be able to improve how you get along with others by discussing role prescriptions.

Compatibility Item 4: Developing Workable Role Prescriptions

Collaboration Stumbling Block

Like the teachers in the following example, many teachers experience frustration on the job.

"It's more work for me to give something to my aide than for me to do it myself. Whenever I ask for something, I get back less than I expected."

"Me, too. I've almost given up altogether. My aide and I almost seem to speak different languages at times, in spite of everything I've done."

"I really like my aide as a person, but to tell the truth, I'd rather have the classroom to myself."

When these teachers sat down to analyze their situations, they were surprised to find that no one ever sat down with their paraprofessionals and decided point by point who would do what in the classroom. Many teachers make the same discovery—what was obvious to them about the partnership between teacher and paraprofessional was never clarified. No wonder so many teacher-paraprofessional partnerships are like marriages headed for divorce courts!

Collaboration Ramp

Upon reflection, many people discover that they expect those with whom they work and live to be mind readers. The process of consciously sharing work expectations is one that can become a routine part of a classroom or school-based team. Making the implicit explicit can be the start of a new working relationship. Vaughn and Coleman (2004) found that the use of a mentor partner was much more effective than the typical professional development model in a rural school. Four themes emerged:

> The themes are that most of these teachers (a) valued working with a partner, (b) preferred partnering to traditional inservice, (c) perceived themselves as successful in their roles, either as mentors or mentees, and (d) had definite opinions about the ideal professional development experience. (p. 33)

Teachers in this study had an opportunity to clearly explain their ideas and concerns to each other and to benefit from a model that "was more efficient and less time-consuming . . . more individualized, directed, and applied with ongoing support" (p. 34). Vaughn and Coleman provide five steps to use when setting up the mentoring program (p. 35), which can be incorporated into your work with colleagues in your school. They might enable you to set up some shared expectations for how you will work together.

In Friend's 1984 study of principals, resource teachers, and regular education teachers, the groups differed dramatically in their identification of consultation skills needed by resource teachers. This lack of consensus is likely to occur in collaborative relationships as well. It can translate into dissatisfaction with what others in the school setting are doing, similar to the conversation between the two teachers presented in the previous example.

In addition to the frustration that coworkers experience, teachers who are missing clear role prescriptions may find that they don't get much done. Maeroff (1993) describes how disagreement can impede progress toward a common goal:

> Lack of a clearly defined mission can defeat a team as readily as having unsuitable members. No matter how thorough the training in the academy, it may not be clear how the team is to go about putting into practice what it has learned. Some teams are not provided with a sufficiently detailed process for pursuing change. They are equipped with new ideas, but not enough is said about how these ideas are going to reach others. (p. 519)

Existing materials can be used to get beyond general ideas to identify specific ways to divide job responsibilities.

A paraprofessional can be given very explicit orientation. McKenzie and Houk (1986) described a four-step process for placing a paraprofessional in a classroom. The first two steps involve self-inventories for both the teacher and the paraprofessional. Examples of each inventory are provided in their article. After a third step, in which a third person helps the team to review their inventories, an individualized job description is developed. (See Welch, Brownell, & Sheridan, 1999 for research on teacher teaming [gaining an overview of research methodologies and results, as well as looking at suggestions for future research].) This type of approach can help you and others in your school setting to list the "what, where, and how" of joint responsibilities. Idea Try-Out 5.3 gives you an opportunity to do just that.

Idea Try-Out 5.3

Mind Reader

This exercise helps you look at the extent to which expectations in work situations are clear. Think back over jobs you have held in the past or projects that you have worked on with others. Record your answers to the following questions in your collaboration notebook:

1. How often did you find yourself wishing that someone else would just figure out what should have been done?

2. How easy was it for you to meet with the other person(s) and discuss what parts of the job still needed to be done?

3. How often did you find yourself resenting the amount of work another person was contributing?

4. How often did you find yourself doing extra work rather than discuss alternatives with other people on the project?

Did you find that the set of questions in this try-out reminded you of a situation in which collaboration was difficult for you? That is certainly true of the description in the following example. Is this true for you, also?

I was so used to doing things my own way in my classroom. It never even occurred to me that there were other ways to organize my desk, do my bulletin boards, contact the families of my students, or teach.

When I got my very first student teacher, I was excited! I was finally going to be able to share the things I had learned with someone. The more time we spent together, though, the more I realized that I was losing the feeling of "my" classroom. I found myself making decisions without explaining them to her, just to reassert myself as the classroom teacher.

When she left, I was really confused by how little I'd shared with her while she was here. Looking back on it now, I realize I expected her to read my mind. Next time I have a student teacher, I'm going to speak up.

Look for specific job descriptions that you and your fellow collaborators can review before beginning a task. This can take the pressure off you and put it on the written job description. Others with whom you work may have materials that you can use as a springboard for discussion.

When clarification of roles is done at the start of the year, it helps everyone to agree to the same ground rules. For example, if beginning teachers who have been assigned experienced paraprofessionals have job descriptions to use to establish clear roles and responsibilities, they are more likely to develop common expectations than if they have no such materials. These clear expectations can make an enormous difference in the quality of their interactions. It can also be part of the initial discussions that teachers who are teaming, or assigned to a Consulting Teacher role, have early in the year.

Broer, Doyle, and Giangreco (2005) describe the important recollections former special education students have of special education paraprofessionals, and recommend involving students in the decision-making process:

> Models need to be explored and studied that actively involve students in contributing to decisions about their own supports, specifically paraprofessional supports and related services . . . virtually no data exists in the paraprofessional literature in which students with disabilities have a substantial voice in making decisions about their paraprofessional supports. (p. 427)

Involving students in discussions of decisions and role descriptions can engage them in thinking about what they want and need in the classroom. The push toward developing a workable role prescription is, to some extent, restricted by the constraints of teachers' daily activities. Little (1990) differentiates independent activities from interdependence. "Under conditions of nearly complete independence, teachers satisfy the demands of daily classroom life by occasional forays in search of specific ideas, solutions, or reassurances" (p. 513). She distinguishes this from "joint work," in which "professional autonomy resides collectively with the faculty; put more forcefully, each one's teaching is everyone's business, and each one's success is everyone's responsibility" (p. 523). The preceding example shows a teacher who was used to more solitary (independent) planning. He did not comfortably develop the routines necessary to collaborate with his student teacher.

Firestone and Pennell (1993) synthesized Little's view, explaining that collaboration opportunities are limited by two things: (1) "the 'egg-crate' organization of classrooms" that gives teachers separate, clearly compartmentalized responsibilities, and (2) "strong norms of privacy that allow for social interaction but inhibit discussion about the teaching craft" (p. 505). Graseck (2005) makes a similar observation:

> Teaching is humbling, hard work, often performed in isolation. It requires the wearing of many hats: manager, thinker, counselor, innovator, planner, critic, learner, diplomat, inspirer. It is a job that calls for the dexterity of a top-level executive yet is performed without the help of a secretary. (p. 375)

Firestone and Pennell (1993) conclude that pragmatic policies are needed to increase the possibilities for collaboration among teachers. These policies should be used in concert with changes in working conditions that will attract more collaborative teachers to the profession. Miller, Ray, Dove, and Keinrich (2000), reflecting on work in a professional development school, describes the professional benefits of collaboration:

To be able to share insights and work with other colleagues helps to break the isolation and keep us alive as educators. In a global system that changes so quickly, the only hope for education is to be able to serve the needs of our students by creating teacher networks to question and develop the practices in our field. (p. 146)

Collaboration is not an exercise but a vital part of work.

Although teachers touch base with each other throughout the week, the time needed to thoroughly discuss a mutual concern is scarce, as shown in the following example.

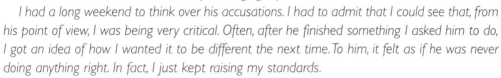

When I think back on trying to get along with my paraprofessional all last year, I am mystified. I thought I was being clear and realistic with him whenever I gave him instructions. But I was wrong.

On the Wednesday before Thanksgiving, he blew up at me. He said that he never understood what I wanted, that I was always changing my mind.

I had a long weekend to think over his accusations. I had to admit that I could see that, from his point of view, I was being very critical. Often, after he finished something I asked him to do, I got an idea of how I wanted it to be different the next time. To him, it felt as if he was never doing anything right. In fact, I just kept raising my standards.

After Thanksgiving, we had a long talk. We decided that we would keep any new procedure in place for at least a month before changing it. His outburst gave us both a chance to reconsider our classroom routines.

Scarcity of resources with details about activities makes crafting descriptions of work very difficult. Articles like the one by Causton-Theoharis and Malmgren (2005) provide the basis for conversation between teachers and paraprofessionals that could enable them to consider a wide range of options for promoting peer interaction and select the behaviors appropriate for students in the class. Such a resource would have been very helpful to the teacher and paraeducator described above.

Lack of available time to collaborate and confused role prescriptions can severely cramp the collaboration habits you develop. When Karge, McClure, and Patton (1995) surveyed 124 California resource room teachers, teachers were asked to state the percentage of time spent collaborating. Eighty-six percent reported spending less than 40% of the week collaborating with general education teachers. The researchers went on to summarize the comments teachers added to the questionnaires:

It seems that the teachers believe they have adequate time to conference about an individual child or technique; however, they do not have the amount of time needed to effectively implement a collaboration program. The middle school/junior high school teachers in this study reported that although collaboration is expected by school administrators, official preparation time is not provided. The time spent collaborating is often on a catch-as-you-can basis and is usually initiated by the special education teacher. (p. 83)

These teachers were not able to develop either the mental habits nor the routines needed to collaborate.

In the mentoring program for school leaders that Williams, Mathews, and Baugh (2004) describe, time was taken so that

> interns verbalize their own knowledge, reasoning and thinking processes while solving problems; in so doing they access deeply rooted unconscious implicit knowledge and transform it into explicit knowledge. Articulation leads to reflective thinking, which helps interns adapt what they know and do to the shifting conditions of school leadership. (p. 62)

The mental clarification precedes actions that meet the demands of the school situations.

Teachers face difficulties when trying to agree on role expectations. This process is made even worse by the limited time they have to devote to collaboration (Raywid, 1993; Stump & Wilson, 1996). Teachers must cope with problems of time and other constraints that limit their ability to develop explicit descriptions of "who does what." Absence of effective descriptions can lead to confusion or resentment. In analyzing your own collaboration predispositions, consider whether the development of clearer role prescriptions would help you to be more comfortable and effective in your school setting. Clear role prescriptions have been found to lead to more equity in interactions between coworkers (Cohen, 1994) and more satisfaction overall.

Satisfaction may also be increased if you find new ways to define success for yourself in your work with others, as described in the section below.

SUCCESS CHECKLIST

As you develop and carry out your collaboration project, one crucial area to self-monitor continuously is your ability to be realistic. How realistically are you defining success? An overly ambitious plan has as many chances for failure as a poorly developed plan. Consider the process you will use to develop your collaboration project as follows:

- Your actions are the bricks
- Your attitudes the mortar
- The combination of the two is the foundation for success in your plan

We'll look at each of these items separately. Taken together, they are a comprehensive basis for designing your collaboration project.

Success Item 1: Changing Your Actions

Archer and Isaacson (1990) looked at how teacher trainers provide instruction. They found that "good [college] instructors teach in the same manner that they would like teachers to teach" (p. 64). In other words, there's no gap between what effective educators expect from others and how they routinely behave. Welch and

Brownell (2002) incorporated technology into a course designed to provide students with information and strategies for collaboration: "The technology-enhanced course consists of 10 video presentations interspersed with breakout activities, 10 CD modules, and support materials. . . . A comprehensive description of the beta-test and field test evaluation is provided elsewhere (Welch & Brownell, 2000)" (p. 135). They found that use of these strategies was helpful: "This evaluation study indicates that technology-enhanced course work can increase teacher candidates' knowledge and attitudes toward collaboration" (p. 143). This finding was similar to the results reported in an earlier study (Welch & Sheridan, 2000), in which it was concluded that "teleconferences are cost effective and promote professional dialogue" (p. 238). These studies by Welch suggest that watching successful collaboration can assist you in developing your own collaboration habits. Does your behavior mirror the way you would like others to behave when they are collaborating with you? Use Idea Try-Out 5.4 to examine your actions:

Idea Try-Out 5.4

Two Sides to Every Coin

This activity will give you ways to reconsider both effective and ineffective working relationships.

1. Think back to a time when you successfully worked cooperatively with another person with whom you have a good professional relationship. In your collaboration notebook, record a brief description that you think the other person might have used to describe how you behaved in the interaction. Write it as if the other person was writing a short note to you reflecting on this memory.

2. Think back to a time when you were unsuccessful when trying to work with another person. In your collaboration notebook, record a brief description that you think the other person might have used to describe how you behaved in the interaction. Write it as if the other person was writing a short note to a friend about you.

3. Compare the two descriptions. Circle the words that appear in each. Consider the differences between your behavior in the two situations. Identify a goal that you think is realistic for you to include in your collaboration project based on this exercise.

Identifying and working toward realistic goals, as you did in this activity, can help you to develop your collaboration skills more automatically. Archer and Isaacson (1990) provide several different methods that teachers can use for self-analysis of their behavior using a combination of goals, procedures, and weekly monitoring. Their approach might work well for you.

Another approach is to follow the model of Westling, Cooper-Duffy, Prohn, Ray, and Herzog (2005) based on collaboration between teachers and faculty members at an area college. Their project focused on "helping teachers use better, research-based practices and delivering reality-based, effective procedures to preservice teachers" (p. 12). They describe a teacher support program (TSP) that connected university faculty at Western Carolina University (WCU) with teachers. A coordinator is needed for this model to work effectively. The authors report that "data collected over the past 3 years have shown that teachers report benefiting from the WCU TSP and have been satisfied with its structure and supports" (p. 13) and provide suggestions for seeking funding to set up such a program.

Alternatively, consider using a self-management approach. Carter (1993) describes such a model for special education students. This approach can be used to self-assess your expected actions. Her nine-step planning approach, when modified slightly, can be used to both define target behaviors and assess change. Carter's steps are presented below, matched to the student collaboration project developed by Joseph Falkowski, which focused on his work with a co-teacher, Mr. R.:

Falkowski: I work as a Crisis Counselor with Mr. R. My role is to help students in de-escalating their behavior before possible disciplinary actions. Mr. R. is a sensitive, caring educator. However, upon witnessing an inappropriate student behavior, Mr. R. immediately redirects and/or disciplines the student instead of ignoring the behavior in the hope of extinction. Most times his actions escalate the student behavior to the point where the student must be sent to my office. I have tried to politely make subtle hints to Mr. R. about ignoring student misbehaviors, and having him understand that my availability is to many classrooms and not only his. However, nothing has worked. We both know that we need to find a new way to communicate.

Step 1: Select a target behavior; (a) identify the target behavior, (b) identify the replacement behavior.

Falkowski: I will convey my feelings to Mr. R. regarding our problems in communicating. Instead of avoiding Mr. R. (as I have been doing lately), we will develop a format in which he and I can give immediate feedback to each other regarding what needs to be done in a crisis situation.

Step 2: Define the target behavior; write a clear description of the behavior (including the conditions under which it is acceptable and unacceptable).

Falkowski: I must find a new way to communicate with Mr. R. We need to discuss ideas for how to handle crisis situations. I want to be able to convey my feelings about how to handle the students' inappropriate behaviors. I want to receive feedback from him about weekly problem situations. I will try to focus on as many positive situations as possible so that we may work side-by-side in a confident manner.

Figure 5.1 Recording Form

RECORDING FORM   **Student Name:** _____   **Date:** _____   **Time:** _____

Inappropriate behavior exhibited by student: _____

What happened right before the student's inappropriate behavior?

_____

_____

_____

Student report:

Mr. R.'s report:

How Mr. R. reacted in the situation:

How Mr. R. evaluated his reaction:

How I reacted to the student:

How I communicated with Mr. R.:

How I rate the situation overall (A for best rating, F for worst):

How would I behave differently next time?

SOURCE: Falkowski, 1992

Step 3: Design the data recording procedures; (a) identify the type of data to be recorded, (b) identify when the data will be recorded, (c) describe the data Recording Form.

Step 4: Teach the student to use the Recording Form; briefly describe the instruction and practice.

This step was modified. The teachers developing the Recording Form (Falkowski and Mr. R.) would take time to make sure they were both accurate and comfortable using it.

Step 5: Choose a strategy for ensuring accuracy.

Falkowski: Another teacher in the school will be involved in collecting baseline data and in periodic checks throughout the plan.

Step 6: Establish goal and contingencies; (a) determine how the student will be involved in setting the goal, (b) determine whether or not the goal will be made public, (c) determine the reinforcement for meeting the goal.

Falkowski: (a) Set up weekly meetings with Mr. R., using need to improve our interactions as reason. During Week One, discuss our reactive behaviors toward students and staff, including lists of how each of us reacts to student behaviors. During Week Two, discuss progress to date, and brainstorm other solutions. Start program to express ourselves using a gesture or signal, to give immediate feedback on how each other handled the crisis situation. Continue this in subsequent weeks of the project. Incorporate feedback from Mr. R. (b) Mr. R. will be informed about the overall purpose of this effort, but not about the collaboration project, per se. (c) Self-satisfaction is the only reinforcement needed.

Step 7: Review goal and student performance; (a) determine how often the student and teacher review performance, (b) identify when and how the plan will be modified if the goal is met or is not met.

Falkowski: (a) Weekly meetings will take place in which the tallies of implementation of the feedback system and evaluation of the new approach will be shared. A log will be maintained in which I will record inappropriate reactive behaviors I demonstrated, or Mr. R. demonstrated. Also, I will include any modifications I will make to help me be a better model for Mr. R. I will note any modifications that Mr. R. and I have agreed upon in the implementation of our program; (b) to be determined during implementation.

The last two steps of Carter's (1993) planning form would be developed after the collaboration project was put into effect: "Step 8: Plan for reducing self-recording procedure" and "Step 9: Plan for generalization and maintenance."

Carter's approach spells out steps that you might take to modify your actions in the work setting. You can quickly learn whether or not you are developing a realistic plan for success in your collaboration project. Use Project Try-Out 5.5 as a starting point.

Project Try-Out 5.5

Self-Management Strategy

This Project Try-Out will give you an opportunity to examine the self-management approach from a more personal perspective.

1. Select the step from Carter's self-management approach that would be the *easiest* one for you to complete successfully. In your collaboration notebook, record the step in your own words. List the strengths you have to implement this step.

2. Select the step from Carter's self-management approach that would be the *hardest* one for you to complete successfully. In your collaboration notebook, record the step in your own words. List the personal obstacles that you have to overcome to accomplish this step.

3. List three people who would easily accomplish the step you selected for Question 2, the step that would be hard for you. In your collaboration notebook, jot down four questions to ask each person to find out how they do what would be difficult for you.

4. In the next two weeks, schedule and complete your interviews. Record the results of your interviews in your collaboration notebook.

5. Summarize your findings by listing three generalizations that can be drawn from what these individuals told you. Record your responses in your collaboration notebook.

6. Finish this Project Try-Out by reviewing the strengths you identified in answer to the first question in the try-out. Match each of your strengths to one or more of the generalizations you've recorded.

This try-out was designed to give you an overview of what you do well, as well as potential areas for improvement. When you develop your collaboration project, you should focus on a behavior that limits your ability to work effectively with a specific person. You will be responsible for accurately selecting a behavior (or behavior pattern) on which to focus that will help you and another professional in your school setting to work together in the best way possible. This does not mean that you have to change entirely. As in the following example, your approach should include a new behavior that will facilitate improved collaboration in the work setting.

When I started my project, I thought that I was going to have to learn how to be more accepting. I tend to be disappointed with the people around me, and keep feeling let down by them. As I got further along, I found out that I didn't have to get rid of my high standards—I just had to have better timing when communicating them to others. I used to wait until I was disappointed to say anything. Now, I work hard to set up ground rules ahead of time.

If you have developed your ability to self-monitor, you are working toward the goal of independent problem solving, which Pugach and Johnson (1988a) advocate:

> The suggestions and prescriptions teachers and consultants offer to their colleagues during . . . interactions are well-meaning, made in a spirit of helpfulness and sharing. In the short term, they may be a source of useful ideas. But the long-term outcome of this kind of prescriptive, external advice-giving as the major mode of assistance is likely to work against teachers' gaining independence in solving classroom problems. . . . To reach this goal of long-term independence, the concept of consultation can be redefined to include not only prescriptive, advice-giving interaction, but interaction that facilitates independent problem solving as well. (pp. 4–5).

Pugach and Johnson's (1988a) advice for consultation pertains to collaboration as well. They describe the difference between an information giver/receiver and an independent problem solver. While the "prescriptive, advice-giving" approach can be reassuring, eventually you want to be able to work with teachers who are thinking for themselves. Gable and Manning (1999) incorporate evaluation of the effect of the plan on student performance, as well as evaluation of the meeting, into their problem-solving process. The following situation illustrates the benefits of improving problem solving.

> *When our Grade Level Team started to meet to work on pre-referrals, it took us two months until we could finish a single case in one meeting. I was terrified that this committee work was going to take over my life. But the more we did, the better we got. Now, we are able to do a lot of our thinking before we even get together. We've all become better at thinking things through ahead of time.*

Self-monitoring can help you develop goals for yourself. The approach that you take in establishing an effective working relationship with another teacher needs to build long-term plans that take short-term concerns into account.

Teachers see different benefits in collaboration. As Laycock, Gable, and Korinek (1991) suggested,

> For school professionals, collaborative approaches sometimes have the goal of helping them to expand their repertoires of assessment and intervention strategies so that they can address a broader range of student needs. Participants may also learn more explicit and effective problem-solving skills. Finally, collaboration offers educators personal and professional support to persist in their work with difficult-to-teach students. (p. 15)

Thus, teachers can expand their attitudes in a number of different directions.

In some cases, as implied in the above paragraph, behavior is combined with attitude. As illustrated in the following example, a particular attitude can be schoolwide or present within a single classroom.

One of the only good things I can say about that year I spent substituting was that I got to see many different schools. What amazed me was how unique each one was. Until then, I'd figured all schools were more or less the same. But looking at the messages which visitors to the building saw ("Visitors: Report to the Office Immediately" or "Welcome to Our School"), as well as the kinds of things which hung in the hall, let me know that you can tell a lot from the outside. I learned from what teachers left behind for me to do, too. Some rooms were friendly places, while others were heartless.

Cabello and Terrell (1994) spent time in schools observing 10 exemplary elementary school teachers. They specifically looked for coincidence of behavior and attitude that reflected "warm and caring classroom climates." Their summary of behavior observed in the classroom illustrates that exemplary teachers integrated their philosophies of "justice and respect for self and others" (p. 19) into their daily activities as well as into the content of their lessons. To be realistic in setting goals for your collaboration project, you may find that you need to combine change in action with a clearer statement of the attitude you are trying to modify. This success can have a dramatic effect on you and those around you.

Success Item 2: Changing Your Attitude

If the situation in which you find yourself is not to your liking, reconsider it. You might have inherited difficulties that you didn't create—these are not quickly modified. A humorous example of this type of situation is presented by Forbes (2004), whose status in the eyes of her doctoral advisor was problematic. She had to explore how to change her own attitude because her advisor was not going to change. Her new insights led to a change in her circumstances, and a successful outcome.

Everyone has experienced difficult situations at one time or other and found a way to adapt to or change the situation. Think back. You will likely find that you have been able to overcome problem situations in the past. Change is possible. Often, a shift in your actions is accompanied by a change in attitude, as shown in the following example.

I used to feel that I was a victim of my teaching partner's moods. Some days, she would come into the classroom and it would be as if the sun had just come out from behind the clouds. She was so positive! Other days, we knew we had to watch every word we said or she would snap our heads off. She was as unpredictable as the weather in the Midwest.

As the year went by, I kept getting more and more frustrated. Finally, in April, I realized I was tired of being a prisoner of something that I couldn't control. I decided I wouldn't let her get to me any more, and I didn't. On the good days, I enjoyed her positive energy. On the bad days, I made myself scarce and used gentle humor to minimize her caustic remarks. She hasn't changed a single bit, but I just don't let myself get upset like I used to. It has made me feel like a free man again.

The modification of a "can't" to a "can do" approach is visible both to you and to others.

Attitudes are contagious. Fleming and Love (2003) describe the SLIM model (Systemic Change Model for Leadership, Inclusion, and Mentoring) in which insights about an early childhood program led to changes, including improved collaboration to serve children with special needs. Change in the outlook of the director (as a result of goal setting with a mentor) led to these changes.

A different effect related to attitude was reported by Sparks and Rye (1990). They reported the results of a study in which 163 eighth-grade students rated their comfort levels in the classes of 33 teachers. The student ratings were compared to the teachers' ratings on the Tennessee Self-Concept Scale.

> Students assigned the highest satisfaction ratings to teachers with the highest total self-esteem scores and who were enthusiastic, bold, group-oriented, relaxed, and extroverted. Students assigned the lowest ratings to teachers who had the lowest total self- esteem scores who were submissive, shy, tense, and introverted. (pp. 32–33)

Although the students did not know how the teachers viewed themselves, there was a pattern of "higher comfort level in classes" that corresponded to "higher teacher self-concept." The authors conclude as follows: "This study illustrated that eighth-grade students can differentiate between teachers who displayed a higher level of self-esteem and those teachers who scored considerably lower in their feelings about themselves" (p. 33). Attitudes of the teachers were visible to the students. As the previous example illustrates, a change in mood shouldn't hold everyone hostage.

In the section of their overview of collaboration, Walther-Thomas, Korinek, and McLaughlin (1999) identify "considerations for effective collaboration," and they include

> coherent vision . . . a clear, well-defined, and shared view among administrators, teachers, specialists, students, and families of what the school's future should be like—a collective sense of why the school is moving toward more collaborative and inclusive services and what team members are trying to accomplish. Such a vision enables teams to make more informed decisions and facilitates collaboration toward common goals. (p. 9)

A building that has this kind of common vision could promote "comprehensive planning" and "sustained implementation"—two of the other considerations identified by the authors. They state that "time and commitment are necessary to become an effective collaborator. This enables teams to develop positive working relationships" (Walther-Thomas et al., 1999, p. 13). The positive working relationship would be evident not only to the team members but to the students, staff, administrators, and family members involved with the school.

Positive moods, and also negative ones, are visible to others. Bettencourt, Gillett, Gall, and Hull (1983) conducted several studies in which teachers were trained to be more enthusiastic when instructing. While there was no achievement difference between the two groups of students, the students in the classes of the more enthusiastic teachers were on-task more of the time than students taught by less enthusiastic teachers. The authors concluded that the more purposeful behavior of the students was a reflection of the ways in which their teachers were interacting with them. The teachers' attitudes influenced their students' behaviors.

And the influence of attitudes isn't limited to students. Teachers in the study by Karge et al. (1995) ranked good teacher attitude the factor most likely to make collaboration succeed and bad teacher attitude the factor most likely to hinder collaboration. However, teacher attitude can be influenced, but it cannot always be easily controlled. In some cases, you must look to another way to make gains—you must find new ways to define success.

Success Item 3: Re-Evaluating Success

The way in which teachers define whether they are effectively collaborating with others is, in part, a function of how they evaluate their success. Some teachers may look at any effort they make and see it fall short. Others refuse to see any room for improvement.

The self-fulfilling prophecy, for satisfaction or dissatisfaction with the outcome of an effort, can be modified by focusing on how success is defined. One of the assumptions of this book is that the responsibility for successfully collaborating with others in your school setting is within your control. By changing either the nature of the interaction (behavior change) or your response to it (attitude change), you can become more effective at work. This can take place whether or not the other people in your work setting want (or are able) to collaborate. Kegan and Lahey, in their 2001 book *How the Way We Talk Can Change the Way We Work: Seven Languages for Transformation*, contend that

> the forms of speaking we have available to us regulate the forms of thinking, feeling, and meaning making to which we have access, which in turn constrain how we see the world and act in it . . . We have a choice whether or not to be thoughtful and intentional . . . to make much of the opportunity or little. (pp. 7–8)

They encourage us to consciously work—through language and action—toward commitment, personal responsibility, and ongoing regard (pp. 8–9).

As special educators, we have the obligation to make ourselves available to work with many people whose level of investment in the educational outcomes of our students differs from ours. The burden of responsibility falls on us. One way to make sure that we shoulder the burden willingly, not begrudgingly, is to redefine what we mean by success at the end of our efforts. Here are several alternatives to consider.

The first way to define success is to *understand the collaborative effort better at the end than we did at the beginning.* Krutilla and Safford (1990) identified how the use of student journals enabled student teachers to develop *"inquiry knowledge* [italics added] [which] is a direct connection to a personal reality, the *uncovering of taken-for-granted thoughts posited in light of new experiences and insights* [italics added]" (p. 217). As special educators, we need to develop inquiry knowledge. Sometimes, the resulting inquiry knowledge is the source of a sense of accomplishment. Instead of looking at a situation with no visible results after we have invested considerable effort, we can feel encouraged by what we have discovered. Turnbull et al. (2006)

illustrate a number of partnership principles and practices that can enable teachers to build trust with parents. Their suggestions include outlook (e.g., respect and commitment) as well as behaviors (e.g., professional competence that includes setting high expectations for students and advocacy to prevent problems) (p. 273).

The second way to define a successful project is to *build on our strengths and overcome our weaknesses better at the end than we did at the beginning.* This can translate into being better able to individualize our efforts. Kegan and Lahey (2001) encourage us to take stock of what we do and believe, and challenge our underlying assumptions about what we are doing in relation to colleagues, family, and friends. Much like the collaboration project you will complete, we need to find ways to look at what we are doing and can do differently.

Adamson, Matthews, and Schuller (1990) summarized approaches used at Hillside Elementary School in Salt Lake City, in which collaboration among faculty members has worked extremely well. Two strategies that have been very successful are "working with individual students using alternative techniques and methods" and "demonstrating to the regular teacher alternative techniques in teaching academics and monitoring behavior" (p. 75). These strategies involve redefining success in collaboration by expanding the definitions of student participation and by *showing* rather than *telling* other teachers what to do.

Dickinson and Adcox (1984) also identified individualization of approach as an outcome of a highly effective process. When reviewing a successful school consultation program, they noted the variety of approaches for individualizing—during both planning and interventions:

> [They] used a number of different activities with the same group of referral problems. In some cases, programs were developed with teachers alone, and in others, programs were planned with the students. . . . The consultation program was designed according to the uniqueness of the child and the resources in his/her environment, with no one activity working best for every youngster. (p. 341)

The success of individualization in this school highlights the need for a variety of approaches needed for the collaboration process.

A third alternative for redefining success is to *work better within the confines of the collaborative environment at the end than at the beginning.* This means making full use of available resources. Look more carefully at the context in which you are attempting to collaborate. Sometimes, you may have to redefine the resources to which you have access. Packard, Walsh, and Seidenberg (2004) and Baugh and Scandura (2000) examined the benefits of multiple mentoring relationships rather than a relationship with a single mentor (146 first-year students and 115 seniors in higher education in the Packard study and 275 executives in the Baugh and Scandura study). Baugh and Scandura state that

> The results of this study add to the mounting evidence that it is important to encourage mentoring relationships within organizations. . . . Organizations can facilitate the development of informal mentoring relationships by promoting interactions between newer and more experienced employees, thereby increasing the probability that mentoring relationship will result. In

addition, the focus should not be exclusively on new organizational entrants, but also on more experienced managers, who could benefit from mentoring relationships with well-established [individuals]. (p. 515)

They encourage the consideration of a developmental model: "Mentoring relationships should unfold differently, then, depending on the needs of the protégé. The mentor's ability to assess the protégé's current level of development is essential in order to provide appropriate developmental experiences and support" (p. 516). This developmental model is similar to the conclusion drawn by Packard et al. (2004): "Developers of mentoring initiatives can take a developmental perspective in their creation of programs so that the developmental needs and experiences of students are taken into account. A one-size-fits-all approach to mentoring may not be appropriate" (p. 82). The value of mentoring in settings outside schools raises the possibility for a mentoring and supportive relationship within schools.

The goal of redefining success and accessing resources (such as multiple mentors) is to help teachers to feel more confident and take full advantage of their situations. This idea is the cornerstone of Bonstingl's (1992) application of Deming's concepts of Total Quality Management (TQM) to education. He redefines success for educators by applying TQM principles to schools instead of to business settings. For example, he uses one of the tenets of TQM—Think of the consumer as the customer—to reconsider success for a teacher:

In education we are particularly prone to personal and departmental isolation. "When I close the classroom door, those kids are *mine*!" is a notion too narrow to survive in a world in which teamwork and collaboration result in high-quality benefits for the greatest number of people. (p. 6)

In other words, he encourages teachers to reconsider success more broadly. Defining success only in terms of the events in individual classrooms is no longer viable. Having a better understanding, by the end of the collaborative endeavor, of the educational environment in which you are working can enable you to define "success" thoroughly. Cheney and Demchak (2001) describe how the use of both formal and informal communication tools, easy to find and use on a daily basis, enable general and special educators to collaborate effectively.

The benefits of collaboration can be significant. In the Winooski School District in Winooski, Vermont, collaboration was the foundation of systemwide change in service delivery. All students (including those with moderate and severe disabilities) receive their educations in regular education settings (Villa & Thousand, 1992). The district operationalized Villa and Thousand's recommendation that "educators who expect children to support and respect one another in heterogeneous educational groupings must model similar collaboration" (1990). As a result of these changes, services to all students have been enhanced: "Winooski educators consistently identify collaboration and teaming practices as the cornerstones of their success. This new arrangement of instructional resources has benefited students and teachers through improved instructor/learner ratios and an ongoing exchange of knowledge, skills, and materials" (p. 40). Winooski is an example of collaboration at its best.

Agness, Sharpe, Sebald, Turner, Simon, and Vaughan (2004) reported on the values of co-planning for achieving quality inclusive education. By facilitating a more thorough collaborative process in the Howard County Public School system, general and special educators incorporated each others' knowledge of learners, pedagogy, and curriculum into an effective academic environment for all students. Agness et al. found that the planning and problem-solving process became the center of their collaborative work:

> We have characterized teacher collaboration as a problem-solving process. In fact, the collaboration process is moving away from being simply a problem-solving tool toward becoming the basis for restructuring schools so that all students have an equal, though not the same, opportunity to succeed (e.g., Pugach & Johnson, 1995). The generative efforts of collaboration can benefit all students, as educators work together to eliminate ineffective classroom practices and to address the differentiated instructional needs of a heterogeneous population of students. (p. 186)

Collaboration has been integrated into the vision that teachers can have for their work with all students.

CONCLUSION

By expanding the ways you look at yourself—separate from any specific collaboration effort—you had the opportunity to examine your options. Your ability to be both accurate and realistic when assessing the viability of work with another person in your school setting is a crucial part of the success of your effort. Your confidence in your own accuracy can be increased with practice. You can begin this practice when you get underway with your own collaboration project in Chapter 6.

Don't neglect your own willingness to be honest with yourself about your areas of strength and weakness. As you have done in this chapter, you will have opportunities to consider what is hard for you to do and also what you do well. Your insights about yourself are fundamental prerequisites to the success of your effort.

Finally, your definition of success is within your control. Examples throughout the chapter have shown alternative outcomes for effective collaboration. None require that the two educators become friends for life. Instead, increased insight or greater tolerance for the abilities and needs of others may be an acceptable improvement over what previously existed. As you begin your collaboration project, draw on both your enthusiasm and your curiosity. You never know what you will learn in a project like this one!

6

Designing a Plan for Change Starting With You

*I*t happens all the time. People talk about their difficult jobs and loudly complain, comparing themselves to others who have it easier or contrasting the present with "the way it used to be." This may be a situation in which they feel they are doing all the work—everyone else is lazy. Or, perhaps they describe an awful person with whom they have to work. You listen and commiserate, saying, "Too bad—it sounds terrible." Privately, you think to yourself, "Thank goodness it isn't me. In that situation, what could I do except quit?" In this chapter, you will be identifying a specific professional relationship that you want to improve. You will develop and carry out your plan so that you can do the best job possible collaborating with the other person in your professional setting. Even if the other person's behavior does not change, the possibilities for improvement are within your grasp. Reach out and take hold of a new set of opportunities as you begin your collaboration project.

GUIDELINES FOR THE COLLABORATION PROJECT

While reading the first five chapters of this book, you analyzed your options for collaboration in the abstract. However, you need to know how to improve specific situations. Imagine the following scenario.

You've been teaching for 10 years. It is 7:15 A.M. on a sunny Monday morning in October. You have come in early to work on your pile of paperwork. This week, you will be meeting with parents, teachers, and students for your annual Committee on Special Education (CSE) meetings. Your classroom door swings open, and George pokes his head into your room. You have gotten to know George over the past year. George is a second-year special education teacher in your building. He is an excellent teacher, and his students learn a lot from him.

"Do you have a minute?" George asks tentatively, and you realize that his voice is shaking.

"Sure," you say, reluctantly putting down your work. "You look upset. What's the matter?"

"I have no idea how I'm going to do my job!" George explodes. "I have three CSE meetings this week, all of them with teachers who won't give me the time of day. What can I do?"

You think back to last year and remember a friendly, happy George. He got along well with most of the other teachers. He used his sense of humor to make others smile and he was always able to explain his students' needs clearly. He had come to your classroom in June and talked excitedly about coming back in the fall. He shared his enthusiasm about being in the building as a special education teacher.

You can hardly believe that you are listening to the same person. He moans, "The teachers have been telling me that I know what I'm doing, and so we don't have to meet beforehand. We haven't even discussed the students' IEPs. I hardly believe that I'm in the same building."

"Well, George," you say aloud, desperately trying to buy yourself some time, "maybe they have a point. Perhaps you don't need to go over everything in quite so much detail. After all, the teachers are the same ones with whom you worked last year."

"Yes, but everything feels different. I feel so much more pressure because now I'm supposed to know everything. I don't know what to do."

George's situation is familiar to many special educators. The problems we have to face, and overcome, feel urgent. We know that our collaboration activities are essential for the progress of our students, and yet we know that true collaboration takes more than good intentions. This chapter will give you the approach you need—and which George could have used—to be able to work more effectively with fellow teachers. You may not have a situation that is problematic right now. No problem—you can focus on getting to know a fellow professional better, to develop a more substantial working relationship.

You will learn to improve a specific professional relationship by designing and carrying out your own collaboration project. Use three basic guidelines.

1. The project focuses on *you.* You will develop ways to examine and change *your* thoughts, feelings, and behaviors in relation to another person. Your goal is to improve your ability to collaborate. You can reach your goal by changing the only person in your collaboration relationship over whom you have total control: you!

Although you want your relationship to be different, permission has not been given to change the other person's behavior. However, you don't have to give up. Instead, you shift your focus in this project to yourself. You will learn to modify the ways you organize and initiate your collaborative efforts. In the end, you want to have confidence that you made the best effort you could to be an effective collaborator. By the end of the project, you may have changed your behaviors, your attitudes, or both. This will prepare you to be an excellent collaborator.

In George's case, he would probably have the same agenda for his CSE meetings with or without his collaboration project. He, his fellow teachers, the parents, and the special education student would most likely focus their meeting on jointly developing an IEP. However, what would be different is that George would take ownership of his behavior. He would have found a way to address his resentment and anger before the meeting, using a collaboration project, so that he could participate in the meeting as effectively as possible.

2. The target of the project should be a person with whom you must collaborate. Select a person with whom you regularly interact. Most likely, you do not have an option—you and the other person must work together. During the period when you will be carrying out your project (see Time Frame for Collaboration Project, below), you should meet or work with your target person at least once a week. To select your target person, look over the following possibilities and pick one that fits your current situation:

    a. If you are currently employed or volunteer regularly in a school setting, select a person who supervises you, a peer, or an adult you supervise.

    b. If you are currently employed or volunteer regularly in a nonschool setting, select a person who supervises you, a peer, or an adult you supervise.

    c. If you are not currently employed or volunteering regularly but are taking at least one college course, select a target person who is (1) an instructor in one of your courses, (2) a fellow student with whom you must collaborate involuntarily (e.g., you have been assigned to work on a group project together) or voluntarily (e.g., you work together in study groups or volunteer projects related to college), or (3) a professional or staff member at your college with whom you have an ongoing school-related relationship (e.g., your advisor or a person who works with you to provide academic assistance).

    d. If you do not fit into any of the above categories, you will have to consider your family or friends to find a target person for this project. It is difficult, but not impossible, to carry out your collaboration project with someone with whom you have a personal relationship. However, project planners are most successful if they select a friend or member of their extended family with whom they are not currently living. If you are selecting a personal friend or relative, make sure you will be able to see the person weekly while implementing your project.

3. The relationship you select should be one which, if improved, will be beneficial for you in the setting you have chosen. Right now, the collaboration relationship should be one that you find less than fully satisfying. You could describe what you'd like to see improve in any of the following ways:

a. If your collaboration relationship is *overtly negative,* you and your target person have areas of disagreement (either recent or longstanding) that are apparent to people who know you both. These disagreements could take the form of angry words, hostile looks, or general inability to work together well. You may find that you interact with this person in a way that is upsetting—to you, to your target person, and even to other people who (directly or indirectly) become involved. In some cases, you may be able to identify reasons for the problems you have with your target person. These reasons may justify the negative relationship in your mind or in the mind of your target person. In other cases, you may not really understand why the two of you don't get along. Although the origins of the difficulties remain outside the scope of the collaboration project, the relationship can still be improved.

The collaboration project that George would design would not fall into this category. So far, he and his fellow teachers are not behaving rudely toward each other. However, if left unattended, his working relationship with them could deteriorate into this kind of hostility.

b. If your collaboration relationship is *covertly negative,* you may be doing a good job of hiding your true feelings from your target person. It may not be evident to the other person, or to others around you, that things are not to your liking. However, you know that your collaborative efforts with the other person are not as sincere as they might be. This may be due to the personality characteristics of your target person or differences in your work habits.

This is the correct category for George's collaboration project. So far, the situation is not out of hand, but he is feeling resentful toward his colleagues. Therefore, his working relationship is covertly negative.

c. If your collaboration relationship has *potential that has not yet been fully realized*, you and your target person may have a noncontroversial working relationship. While considering this person for your collaboration project, you may have realized that you don't know your target person very well. You may know little about the person's priorities regarding your work setting, what the person likes or dislikes, or how the individual's background relates to the work setting. If you knew more, you could probably become better collaborators.

During his first year, George might have been able to use a collaboration project like this one. He might have discovered more about his fellow teachers, and these discoveries might have helped him to develop more realistic expectations for his second year.

After reviewing these options, select the target person for your collaboration project.

DESIGNING A SELF-REFERENTIAL PLAN FOR COLLABORATION

In the design of your collaboration project, consider how to plan for the relevant changes in your interactions with, and your attitudes about, your target person. The time frame you will follow is described below.

Time Frame for Collaboration Project

Planning Phase: 2–3 Weeks (see Chapters 7 and 8)

During the planning phase, you will design your project. You will review your objectives, activities, and evaluation methods. Only you will know whether you have selected the key issues for improving your interpersonal dynamic. You are in charge of selecting the goals and objectives and identifying resources that can help make your collaboration project a success. You will ensure that you set reasonable expectations for your project. You will also learn how to document both your efforts and the outcomes of your efforts, considering both objective and subjective criteria.

Project Implementation: 4–5 Weeks (see Chapter 9)

During project implementation, you will carry out your project. After collecting your baseline data, you will carry out the plan that you designed for your project. Throughout this period, you will make use of the evaluation methods you selected.

Project Review: 1–2 Weeks (see Chapter 10)

During project review, you will analyze what you accomplished and decide how to continue a modified relationship with your target person.

Throughout the weeks planning and carrying out the project, you will work to improve a specific relationship. There are many safeguards to make sure that you don't design and carry out activities that will result in a *worsened* relationship. Throughout the project, *you* are the reference point on which the plan must depend.

Identification of Pragmatic Goals

By the time you complete this chapter, you should have selected your target person. Next, identify the goals to use as the focus of your project from among those presented in the next section of the chapter. Goals should, if achieved, make a difference in the way you feel about your target person and also how you interact together. Six different types of goals are described below. Before you review them and select your collaboration project goals, use Idea Try-Out 6.1 to imagine how things might be.

Idea Try-Out 6.1

Importing the Best

This activity will give you a way to visualize a new kind of working relationship. It should result in an image that will enable you and your target person to work more effectively together.

1. Reflect on your experiences with your target person in the past few weeks. In your collaboration notebook, list all the positive interactions that took place.

2. Reflect on your experiences with another person with whom you interact easily and well. (This relationship of choice could be a person in your work setting, in your recreation setting, or in your family.) In your collaboration notebook, list as many positive interactions as you can that took place between the two of you in the past few weeks.

3. Compare the two lists:
   a. Which is longer?
   b. If you were to compare your behavior in situations with the two individuals, in what ways did it differ (e.g., your enthusiasm, assertiveness, comfort level)?
   c. How do the situations on the two lists differ in terms of their relative importance to you? To the other person involved? To people other than the two of you?

4. Imagine that you could import your positive traits in your relationship of choice into the relationship you have with your target person. List the traits and characteristics you would select. Briefly describe the difference each new trait or characteristic would make.

As you worked your way through this exercise, you may have found it to be like standing in front of a three-way mirror. You may have seen parts of yourself that you don't ordinarily see. Like looking in the mirror, you may have been surprised (either pleasantly or unpleasantly) by what you discovered. The purpose of this Idea Try-Out was to give you an opportunity to identify what already is going well in your relationship. These are the things upon which you can build. The exercise was also designed to help you to consider what might be missing in your relationship, or certain behavior with others that you can add to your relationship with the target person. Now, let's look at the other side.

Idea Try-Out 6.2

Exporting the Worst

This activity is designed to enable you to begin the actual work on your collaboration project by getting some of the ideas about what you'd like to change down on paper. Use your collaboration notebook to record your ideas.

1. Jot down, in a few words, what you think is *wrong* with your relationship with your target person. It could be what your target person does that you don't like or what you think you could do differently. If you and your target person have an unexplored relationship, list questions you have about your target person.

2. Select three or four episodes in your relationship that show it at its worst. List these episodes on the side of a page in your collaboration notebook. If you and your target person have an unexplored relationship, list situations in which you and your target person failed to take advantage of opportunities.

3. Imagine a few traits you would like to eliminate from the relationship. Would you like to be less angry? Less assertive? Less shy? List three or four things you would like to be able to do differently to make your relationship work more successfully.

4. Describe a surprise that symbolizes how you hope your relationship with your target person could work out. Take a few minutes to finish this sentence: "Even though things had not changed between us, I had the strangest dream last night. We were leaving school together when I had the most amazing insight. I turned toward _____, shook my head, and I said, 'You know, if only . . .'"

Exploring what is wrong with your relationship, as well as your hopes for how things might be different, was intended as a warm-up for your collaboration project. Now, you can translate what you've learned through both Idea Try-Outs into action:

- Review the Overview of Pragmatic Goals below.
- Pick the pragmatic goal that best suits your situation. If you think that more than one may be right for you, read through each pragmatic goal. Your goals and objectives can come from more than one section.
- Review and follow the recommended steps for Development of Pragmatic Goals and Objectives in the following part of this chapter.

OVERVIEW OF PRAGMATIC GOALS

Communication-Related Projects

Are there important things missing from your communication with your target person? As you look over the results from both Idea Try-Outs 6.1 and 6.2, perhaps you could improve the ways you share information, ask questions, or communicate in general. If this sounds right to you, review the sample goals and objectives below under Development of Pragmatic Goals and Objectives: Communication-Related Goals and Objectives, and pick the ones that are right for you.

Assertiveness-Related Projects

You may have realized that part of the problem in the relationship corresponds to your inability to clearly ask for what you want or need with your target person.

You privately expect your target person to be a mind reader or a person who seeks you out. In fact, you can change the nature of the relationship by taking more responsibility for (and ownership of) the relationship. If this sounds right to you, review the sample goals and objectives below under Development of Pragmatic Goals and Objectives: Assertiveness-Related Goals and Objectives.

Clashing Values Projects

If you are considering a Clashing Values project, you may have realized that all of the worst moments between you (when you explored them in Idea Try-Out 6.2) involved different core values. You and your target person may have times when you can get along without any problems. However, you may find that when certain topics come up, your relationship is in trouble. The difference in values may have to do with your professional work (regarding inclusion, or expectations regarding test modification) or other, more personal values (issues related to race, ethnicity, gender, religion, or politics). If this sounds right to you, review the sample goals and objectives below under Development of Pragmatic Goals and Objectives: Goals and Objectives Related to Clashing Values.

Different Work Styles Projects

If you are considering a Different Work Styles project, you may have realized that you and your target person have very different work habits and expectations. You may prefer to work at the last minute, and your target person may find that troublesome (or the opposite may be true). You may like to write out what to do and include many details, while your target person may prefer broad outlines. If this sounds right to you, review the sample goals and objectives below under Development of Pragmatic Goals and Objectives: Different Work Styles Goals and Objectives.

"Clean Slate" Projects

This type of project may interest you if you and your target person have a long-standing relationship. You may have had your ups and downs, but you aren't really sure what you can do to start all over. If this sounds right to you, look over the sample goals and objectives below under Development of Pragmatic Goals and Objectives: "Clean Slate" Goals and Objectives.

"Getting to Know You" Projects

If you are thinking about this type of project, you may be realizing that you know very little about the person you have selected as your target person. The relationship you've selected may have been going on for a long time, or it may have just begun. In either case, you can improve your collaboration if you know more about the person's likes, interests, and professional concerns. This type of project is not designed to turn you and your target person into friends. Instead, it should give you a more effective base from which to work together. If this seems right to you, review the sample goals and objectives below under Development of Pragmatic Goals and Objectives: "Getting to Know You" Goals and Objectives.

DEVELOPMENT OF PRAGMATIC GOALS AND OBJECTIVES

This section of the chapter provides goals and objectives that can be used for projects in a variety of settings. Some of the project goals and objectives meet all the criteria for specifically stated behavioral objectives. Others are more generally stated. You can adapt the project goals and objectives to meet your particular needs and interests. You might also like to review other resources. For example, Goor and Santos (2002) developed a series of short cases to enable intern and beginning special educators to think about different challenges they face in their work. Chapter 2 of their book is devoted to short cases that focus on communication and collaboration, and some of the follow-up questions might assist you in focusing your project.

Remember, the goal of this project is not to brainwash your colleague (even if you'd *like* to). Instead, you want to learn to better appreciate your differences and find ways to consider your situation from a new perspective. Keep the focus of the project on yourself. Evaluating success is crucial. Chapter 8 contains many examples of evaluation of all types of objectives.

Communication-Related Goals and Objectives

In many collaboration projects, the success or failure of the project rests on the ability of the two people involved to exchange ideas or information in a timely, complete, and respectful manner. Contrast the following two descriptions.

I hate my student teaching placement! No one listens to me. I've attended every single faculty meeting, but no one ever talks to me. I feel like I'm invisible. I'm even wondering if I still want to be a teacher.

I can't believe my luck. My new principal really cares about my ideas. Even though I'm just a student teacher, he asks me questions about what I'm doing and why. He even goes out of his way to get my opinion about staff meetings. It has made me think about what I say because I'm afraid I might sound stupid. I really feel like I'm learning a lot by being here.

Both student teachers have focused on communication as a key feature of their placements. However, they are having very different experiences. What they have in common is that they are assuming that the burden for communication rests on other people. Instead, each of them could take ownership for communication in his or her setting.

If this sounds like an approach that you could use, review the goals (and related objectives) provided below. Each goal corresponds to communication skills that could be part of your collaboration project. You can use the goals and some or all of the objectives exactly as shown below, or modify them to fit your situation.

Goal 1: I will examine and strengthen my communication skills in order to improve my interactions with _____.

   Objective 1.1   I will brainstorm new techniques for developing communication skills that could possibly be used to communicate with _____.

   Objective 1.2   I will assess my communication patterns and decide which of them need improvement and which are currently acceptable.

   Objective 1.3   I will improve my communication with _____, based on the results of Objectives 1.1 and 1.2.

   Objective 1.4   I will get feedback from others regarding my improved communication patterns and determine what I need to do next.

Goal 2: I will become more positive in my communications with _____.

   Objective 2.1   I will assess my communication patterns and calculate ratios of positive:negative and focused on self:focused on _____.

   Objective 2.2   I will generate alternative ways to become more positive in my outlook with _____.

   Objective 2.3   For _____ days, I will practice more positive responses with people I talk to regularly.

   Objective 2.4   After completing Objective 2.3, I will identify what I can incorporate into my communications with _____ that will make them more positive.

   Objective 2.5   I will incorporate strategies identified in Objective 2.4 into my conversations with _____.

Goal 3: I will incorporate new types of communication into my conversations with _____ so that we have more active exchanges of information than we have had to date.

   Objective 3.1   I will keep track of different types of communication patterns (e.g., comments made, suggestions or feedback given, questions asked, compliments exchanged) and examine my own patterns in relation to _____ and in relation to another person with whom I get along well.

   Objective 3.2   I will compare the communication patterns I had with each person and identify two things that I could do differently in my work with _____.

   Objective 3.3   I will incorporate two new communication patterns into my work with _____ at the end of each day and assess how successful each approach has been.

   Objective 3.4   I will decide what I want to continue to do differently at the end of my project to ensure that my work with _____ will be more active and effective.

Assertiveness-Related Goals and Objectives

As you think about your collaboration project, you may identify certain things that are difficult for you to do. For some people, it is difficult to initiate interactions. Asking for or offering assistance is not easy. As a result, it takes a great deal of energy for some people to decide whether to act. Sometimes so much energy is invested in the decision process that nothing actually gets done. Consider the following example.

> I remember when I first started teaching in this building. I went into the teachers' lounge several mornings during the first month, but I didn't know anyone in the room.
>
> I decided that if anyone spoke to me when I went to get a cup of coffee, I would stay, but otherwise I'd go back to my room. No one even looked in my direction, so I left. Hard to believe it now, but I was almost shaking, I was so upset. I thought no one liked me, but the truth is, no one noticed me.
>
> Now, I get my coffee and look around the room before I sit down. If anyone smiles at me, I introduce myself. I've met lots of people that way.

The teacher went from feeling unwelcome to deciding to make herself welcome on her own terms. She found a way to adapt that felt comfortable for her.

For some people, assertiveness is not only a problem in social situations but has to do with other areas of concern. For example, some teachers are reluctant to ask for supplies, materials, copies of memos, or other information that they may not automatically get. It is hard for some people to speak up for themselves. If this is a familiar issue for you, review the goals and parallel objectives from the following list. Use them as they are presented here, or adapt them so that they better fit your situation. Two examples of assertiveness goals and objectives are included from student projects.

Goal 1: Define my role with _____ in my words and actions (Walsh, 1995).

Objective 1.1 List a minimum of five ways to carry out my job that _____ and I agree upon.

Objective 1.2 Identify a minimum of five options for expanding my role, which I could discuss with _____ .

Objective 1.3 Based on the success of the conversation(s) used to achieve Objective 1.2, identify three specific new behaviors to use on a regular basis.

Objective 1.4 Use three new verbal and/or behavioral strategies in the execution of my role.

Objective 1.5 Experience fewer episodes of guilt resulting from inconsistency between my role and my words/actions.

Goal 2: Express myself clearly so that there are no misunderstandings (Walsh, 1995).

Objective 2.1 Outline the major issues I want to include in each conversation with _____ prior to our meetings/conversations.

Objective 2.2 Brainstorm with coworkers new strategies I could use to improve my clarity.

Objective 2.3 Identify alternative ways to explain each major issue, and list pros and cons for each approach.

Objective 2.4 Objectively review my communication skills and pinpoint those that need improvement to increase clarity.

Goal 3: Remain well-focused on the relevant topic.

Objective 3.1 Be able to recognize when I am drifting off a subject and to redirect my attention.

Objective 3.2 List topics I need to discuss with _____.

Objective 3.3 Create (and continue to add to) a vocabulary list that will help me to return to relevant topics.

Goals and Objectives Related to Clashing Values

When you see the phrase "parent involvement," you might think that it connotes a situation with which no one would disagree. However, in school settings, we must often face deeply held beliefs. We must examine our own beliefs, those of our fellow teachers and administrators, and also those of our students and their families. These beliefs come to the surface as *values.*

When others' values coincide with our own, we tend to consider them sympathetically. For example, when we talk with others who see parent involvement as we do, we empathize with their frustrations. We tend to read positive meaning into their silences. Gartin, Murdick, Thompson, and Dyches (2002) conducted focus groups in four states and found that taking advocacy roles on behalf of students was difficult for many special educators. "Teachers perceived that there was considerable risk in advocating for students. . . . One teacher noted 'There was pressure to support the party line'" (p. 11).

When others' values clash with ours, we are often intolerant. We may find ourselves referring to others' values in negative ways, even characterizing their statements as stereotypes or as evidence of prejudice. For example, frustrations expressed about lack of parent involvement may be seen as lack of sympathy for the pressure that parents face.

Consider the following experience. This event could take place in schools all over the country.

> *I was waiting in the principal's office for a meeting with my student teaching supervisor when I overheard a heated conversation in the principal's office. A parent of one of my special education students was yelling at the principal, saying her daughter wasn't being challenged in class. The principal was yelling back! I was torn—I could see both of their points of view.*

What the student teacher in this situation realizes is that at times two strongly held, opposite values can each be "right." It is possible to acknowledge this even while seeing that those values clash with each other. Hopefully, with the help of a third person (e.g., the school guidance counselor, a parent advocate from a local special education organization) these two people can learn to appreciate each other's positions.

It is difficult, but not impossible, to achieve a good working relationship when you work with someone with whom you differ about values. Values clashes can occur in relation to many different topics relevant to or outside your educational setting. For example, passionate views about inclusion often reflect deeply held values. These values are sometimes based on actual experiences and other times are the result of stereotypes. In some schools, there is open hostility toward the participation of students with special needs in general education classrooms because teachers must balance the needs of those students with the pressures they face in meeting state standards or preparing for state examinations. Such hostility has to be addressed.

Conversations that allow all members to hold sharply opposing views can be tense. For example, curriculum modifications are considered tantamount to cheating by some, a necessary fact of life by others. The opportunities in schools to discuss and implement curriculum modifications can be overshadowed by emotional value-based conversations. If this is the case in your setting, you and the relevant teachers would have to come to an understanding, or the experiences of students receiving extended time are likely to be very negative. Your role as a student advocate would have to include addressing this tension-filled topic.

Think about your own situation, and review the following goals and objectives. Adapt them to fit your particular situation.

Goal 1: Create opportunities in which professional sharing is part of my interaction with _____ (Harter, 1994).

Objective 1.1 Meet with others in my professional network, and brainstorm alternative topics for me to explore with _____, in order to better understand _____'s perspective on topics related to special education.

Objective 1.2 Identify three or four alternative settings at school (or another appropriate place) where I could have conversations with _____.

Objective 1.3 Identify two or three people who might be part of my conversations with _____ at school (or another appropriate place).

Goal 2: Expand on and improve the working relationship with _____, based on mutual professional interests that are different from the ones about which we disagree.

> *Objective 2.1* Identify two or three specific ways to build on mutual professional interests that have not thus far been areas of collaboration.
>
> *Objective 2.2* Identify a project on which _____ and I could work that is consistent with our professional interests and job responsibilities.
>
> *Objective 2.3* Initiate the project with _____, and throughout our time working together, attend to the positive ways in which we are collaborating.

Goal 3: Realize that having different opinions can be something positive (King, 1994).

> *Objective 3.1* Brainstorm, or generate in a journal, the pros and cons of having different opinions.
>
> *Objective 3.2* Analyze the next five episodes of values clash with _____ in terms of pros and cons.
>
> *Objective 3.3* During three episodes of "values clash" taking place within a specific timeframe, build on the "pros" of values clash in my mind and incorporate into the end of each conversation something positive and genuine about our differences of opinions.

Different Work Styles Goals and Objectives

Many collaboration projects are developed to help you to learn to work more effectively with a person whose work habits differ from your own. You may have found, as you worked on completion of some of your course requirements in college, that people around you treated assignments differently than you did. They may have started on them earlier or later, used more or less detail in developing drafts of their work, and even reacted differently to feedback from professors than you did. Consider the following situation.

You are a confident special education teacher and have been teaching for three years. Recently, you received word that you have been assigned a student teacher for the fall. You eagerly await your first meeting, scheduled for a week before school is to begin in September. All three of your previous student teachers were outstanding. Their eager, honest, and curious approaches to the classroom benefited you and your students. You enjoyed watching them grow and develop during their placements.

You are taken a bit by surprise when your new student teacher arrives. She is poised, pleasant, and your mother's age. She explains that she has been serving as a full-time teacher in a parochial school for the past five years and is doing her student teaching in special education "just to get certified." "Since I have so much experience," she goes on, "I thought we would be more like peers than anything else." She then proceeds to show you some of her sample lesson plans, and you realize that she is going about the planning process very differently than you do. What do you do?

In this situation, there would probably be many possible considerations. As with any student teacher, you would naturally meet with her college supervisor to find out what competencies she is expected to accomplish in her placement. You would also have to help her to find a way to get invested in the role of student teacher and to feel challenged during student teaching. But in this case, you might also have to decide how to deal with a work style that differs from yours.

As you look over the list of goals and objectives included here, you may find some that match your areas of concern. Adapt them as needed to make sure the ones you select fit your situation.

Goal 1: Feel comfortable [instructing _____/receiving instruction from _____] regarding daily/weekly/monthly duties.

Objective 1.1 Identify obstacles to my [overseeing _____/being overseen by _____].

Objective 1.2 Identify ways in which _____ and I coordinate our work styles successfully.

Objective 1.3 Identify times of the day/week when we are least successful as well as times we are most successful in working together.

Objective 1.4 Target a particular project or time of day on which to focus to become more confident and comfortable in communicating my expectations and concerns to _____.

Goal 2: Evaluate how I am presenting responsibilities to _____/ receiving responsibilities from _____ (Weisberg, 1995).

Objective 2.1 Meet with _____ and explain that I would like to experiment with [giving/getting] instructions differently.

Objective 2.2 Jointly generate an activity checklist, which will include a way for each of us to evaluate both how well the activity was accomplished and how clearly it was presented.

Objective 2.3 Jointly find ways to let each other know about what is going well (through a dialogue journal, humor, little notes, etc.).

Objective 2.4 Jointly assess our outcomes at the end of _____ weeks, and decide which of our strategies we want to continue.

Goal 3: Find ways to be more patient and understanding when working with _____ (Pyszczynski, 1995).

Objective 3.1 Identify and become aware of the strengths that _____ displays in our interactions.

Objective 3.2 Find ways to build on her strengths in our work environment so that we have a more professional, positive working relationship.

Objective 3.3 Use relaxation strategies as well as refocusing techniques to avoid getting upset with _____.

Objective 3.4 Evaluate ways in which I am patient with others in my life and generalize those approaches to work with _____.

"Clean Slate" Goals and Objectives

Some projects focus on "old business" between you and your target person that is getting in the way of your current working relationship. Old agendas may be long forgotten by one of you but hotly remembered by the other. They also might be concerns that were once important but really aren't relevant to your lives today. Although old feelings are not always appropriate, they may still linger. The following situation is similar to O. Henry's short story "Gift of the Magi," in which the two people involved don't really understand each other as well as they think:

It was a long time ago, but whenever I see her, I remember the day she first came into the building. She'd gotten soaked in a rainstorm. She had this horrified look on her face because a bunch of us were there to see it while we waited with the students for the buses. I said something stupid, I don't even remember what it was, and we all laughed. Now, she's one of our very best teachers. Each time I see her, I smile to remember how she started out and how far she's come. It makes me feel old, but it makes me feel happy, too.

I rarely see him in the hall without remembering the first time we met, my first day of student teaching. I was just coming into the school building, and I'd gotten caught in the rain. I was soaking wet! He was standing with about five other teachers, waiting for the buses to arrive. He looked at me and said, "Well, here's one we know is wet behind the ears!" Everyone laughed, except me. If I could have walked right out of that building, I would have. I've been teaching here now for five years, but I still remember that day…I could have killed him then, and I think I feel exactly the same way today.

In these examples, two colleagues reflect on an event that is full of meaning for each of them, but the meaning they ascribe is very different. The former student teacher is still angry. Her hostile feelings are keeping her from moving past an awkward moment. A Clean Slate collaboration project would enable her to let go of some of her anger and to take advantage of the fondness her colleague has for her. Because Clean Slate projects are unique, you will probably have to modify the goals and objectives listed below for your own use.

Goal 1: Limit or eliminate my defensive (or other problem) behaviors around _____ (Steinwachs, 1995).

Objective 1.1 Learn why I respond so defensively (or other problem) around _____.

Objective 1.2 Watch other people and compare their working relationship with _____ to mine.

Objective 1.3 Generalize one or two things I observe others do when interacting with _____ and incorporate them into my relationship.

Goal 2: Find ways to stop focusing on the events of the past (e.g., something unfortunate that was said, an episode of anger or misunderstanding) and move on.

Objective 2.1 Review the events from the past that continue to bother me and list alternative explanations for each event.

Objective 2.2 List ways in which my continued preoccupation with the past is helping me and hurting me.

Objective 2.3 Decide how to proceed in ways that are not too demanding of my time and energy to continue to focus on the "here and now" with _____, rather than on the past.

Objective 2.4 Write an imaginary letter to _____, describing the past event(s) and also my plans to stop perseverating about the past. End the letter with a realistic description of how I hope our new relationship will benefit each of us, now that I have moved on from my preoccupation with the past. Save the letter and reflect upon it at the conclusion of the project (e.g., after Goal 3 has been completed).

Goal 3: Start afresh with _____.

Objective 3.1 List ways in which a fresh start would help me and hurt me.

Objective 3.2 Commit to a fresh start with _____ on a specific date.

Objective 3.3 Evaluate the fresh start period after two weeks by listing what is working for me about this new approach and what is working against me.

Objective 3.4 Make the necessary modifications to maintain this fresh start, based on what was learned in Objective 3.3.

Objective 3.5 Identify an episode that took place between us, one that embodies the new directions I hope I will be able to sustain. Incorporate into the letter I began earlier in the project a description of this episode.

Objective 3.6 End the letter by imagining myself five years from now, thinking about all this. How important will it be? What will I have learned to do differently as a result of putting this episode to rest? Put a date five years from today on the outside of the envelope, put the letter inside, and seal up my feelings and old memories while I seal the envelope.

"Getting to Know You" Goals and Objectives

For many people, the collaboration project stimulates them to ask questions that were never asked before. It is human nature to pay attention to problems as they come up and to take untroubled, calm situations for granted. We often see this in our classrooms—the students who get most of our attention are those who are having trouble. At the end of the first month, we often find that we know a great deal about the noisy, difficult students and much less about those who are well-behaved.

When I first began teaching, I met a first-grade teacher who had a Friday afternoon ritual. At the end of the week, she took out a list of the students in her class. Beside each name she wrote a word or two to note a personal contact that she had with each student during the week. If there were no words written beside the student's name, she made it her business to interact with the student in the coming week. By October, she knew each of her students very well.

Most of us are less disciplined than she was. We hope we will get to know our students, our colleagues, and the support staff in our buildings but do not always do so. A collaboration project that is designed to help you to know more about another person can take the form of a realistic set of interactions using (or modifying) the following goals and objectives.

Goal 1: Establish a working relationship with _____ that will be an improvement over what we have now (Walsh, 1995).

Objective 1.1 Use active listening when working with _____.

Objective 1.2 Interact effectively with _____.

Objective 1.3 Incorporate a positive, optimistic outlook into our working relationship.

Objective 1.4 Build on our successes or mutual interests to establish a better working relationship.

Goal 2: Self-monitor in order to avoid emotions or expectations that I know can get me into trouble (e.g., frustration, discouragement, wanting perfection).

Objective 2.1 Identify problems I have seen in myself when starting a working relationship that I think could get in the way of working with _____.

Objective 2.2 Identify ways I have previously started relationships successfully that I could adapt to this relationship.

Objective 2.3 Develop a way of building on the positives and avoiding my personal pitfalls so I avoid a negative attitude in the relationship.

Goal 3: Identify a project that we could work on together that will enable us to develop shared history.

Objective 3.1 Evaluate upcoming events in our building, or in one of our lives, that are candidates for a joint project.

Objective 3.2 Select two or three projects from the list that have timeframes compatible with the collaboration project.

Objective 3.3 Approach _____ with the suggestion of joint work on these projects.

Objective 3.4 Complete the project together, focusing on getting to know _____ in addition to completing the project.

INCORPORATING EXPERTISE: MARSHALING RESOURCES

As you finish this chapter, you should be well underway in designing your collaboration project:

- You should have selected your target person.
- You should have selected two or three goals and accompanying objectives for your project. Note that these could come from different sections of the chapter, so that you are addressing more than one way to improve your relationship (e.g., one from assertiveness and one from communication).

As you recall, your focus is on changing *your* part of the interaction, demonstrating the following skills identified in the Council for Exceptional Children (CEC) Standard #10, which focuses on collaboration:

Collaborate with families and others in assessment of individuals with exceptional learning needs; Collaborate with school personnel and community members in integrating individuals with exceptional learning needs into various settings; Collaborate with Network members to plan transition to adulthood that encourages full community participation. (CEC, 2003, pp. 66–67)

As mentioned earlier in the chapter, most people conducting collaboration projects do so entirely on their own. As far as your target person is concerned, you two will have the same work agendas, or contacts, and work together to solve problems, meet student needs, and jointly accomplish what you can. If you chose to tell your target person that you'd like to work jointly on a project, or you'd like to see how your working relationship could be improved, that is up to you. In order to achieve some of the objectives, you will need to explicitly ask for your collaboration person's involvement.

Even if you do not discuss your collaboration project at all with your target person, you will be progressing toward the achievement of the objectives. As you learn more about yourself and what inhibits and promotes effective collaboration, you and your target person will be able to accomplish more together. Your project will enable you to transform your working relationship. Part of the transformation will come about through use of new resource people.

Creating a Collaboration Resource Network

Assistance for your collaboration project will come from new sources of feedback and advice. You can identify fellow students, teachers, or other professionals who can help you think about how to adjust your part of the working relationship. As mentioned in Chapter 5, it is helpful to think of the collaboration project as a teeter-totter. You and your target person may have been going up and down at the same rate, maintaining the same relative positions, with little change. In some cases, this may have been going on for a long time. Your collaboration resource network can help you to see that there are other options. For example, you can get on a jungle gym and expand your choices! Idea Try-Out 6.3 is designed to help you select your network members.

Idea Try-Out 6.3

Human Scavenger Hunt

This Idea Try-Out is designed to help you identify new people to whom you can turn while carrying out your collaboration project.

1. Imagine that you are on a human scavenger hunt. Fill in the name of a person who fits each of the following descriptions. You can use the same name more than once. If you wish, you can have more than one name per description.
   a. A person who knows how you *really* feel about your target person: _____.
   b. A person who has known you for a long time and has seen you through some hard times: _____.
   c. A person who has given you good advice with whom you don't have very much contact these days: _____.

> d. A person who is a good problem solver: _____.
> e. A person who has an open mind when it comes to thinking things through: _____.
> f. A person who acts toward others as you would like to act: _____.
> g. A person with a good sense of humor about human limitations: _____.
> h. A person you've had limited contact with, but who you think might have some insights about your collaboration project: _____.
> i. A person who knows your school building (or the setting in which you will carry out your collaboration project) very well: _____
>
> 2. From this group of people, identify three or four who could be members of a collaboration resource network for you as you work on your collaboration project.

As you develop your collaboration project using activities in Chapter 7, you will find different ways to involve the people you identified in Idea Try-Out 6.3. When you are trying to solve a problem in your collaboration project, people may come to mind who you may not have previously felt free to contact for assistance. A person whom you identified as one who "acts toward others as you would like to act" might be someone to call when you are trying to develop new ways to interact. Some teachers who completed the collaboration project found that the use of the collaboration resource network was one of the most surprisingly helpful parts of the whole project. As one teacher said, "Having other people share their ideas with me when I got stuck made all the difference in the world."

Identifying Reference Points for Success

As you design your collaboration project, you may find it hard to change the way you have done things up to now. One way to expand your thinking is to read relevant articles listed in the References section of this book. At this point, research articles and discussion of particular collaboration topics in the literature can give you new perspectives on your situation with your target person. These articles can help you to examine your progress at critical points as you design your project and also while you carry it out.

An excellent example is Gajda's 2004 article about collaboration as a strategy for organizations (including schools) to use to achieve their objectives (e.g., the Safe Schools/Healthy Students initiative). In her article, she identifies five collaboration principles (collaboration is an imperative; collaboration is known by many names; collaboration is a journey not a destination; with collaboration, the personal is as important at the procedural; and collaboration develops in stages; pp. 67–69). She put these principles into action, using a data-driven plan to implement and assess collaboration. This article, and many others, will provide you with insight into your work on your collaboration project.

Jentz and Murphy (2005) look at the experience of being confused and "embracing" (rather than denying) the confusion as a growth experience. As you consider the vulnerability that this project evokes, you may find their article extremely thought-provoking. Here is their description of "Oh, No!" moments: "They are caused not only by emergencies but also by a wide variety of everyday situations that regularly arise out of the blue and call into question our fundamental assumptions. We just can't make sense of what's going on" (p. 361). Their suggestions for how to face, rather than run from, these moments may assist you in thinking about your project options.

Phipps's (2005) article about electronic journaling highlights some of the options, as well as some of the challenges, you may face if you decide to incorporate an electronic journal into your project. Phipps distinguishes between different types of journal work, including *"reflection in/on action"* or *"contemplating better ways of implementing what the writer has already done or observed"*; *"deliberative reflection,"* in which *"the writer's opinions, along with others [are weighed] in order to determine the best solution in a specific situation"*; *"personal reflection* [which] encourages learners to examine motives related to their . . . basic beliefs about who they are and what they want to become"*; and *"critical reflection* [which] is the highest form of reflection because it does not just stimulate personal understanding but also has the potential to instigate social change" (p. 62). Consider using an e-journal to share your ideas with the members of your collaboration resource network, but beware of overburdening your network members with too much information.

You may also find it useful to think about how things might look a month from now when you and your target person are communicating differently. Although it may be tempting to rely on your old way of doing things, look ahead to how you might feel at the end of your project. This is what Angelo, a teacher who implemented a collaboration project, wrote when it was finished:

> As I look back over the last few months, I find myself feeling surprised. I see what was then, and how things are now. It is almost amusing to reflect on what I see. At the beginning, I felt that there was no change needed on my part. The problems we were encountering were all in Michael's hands. If only he would "stop," things would be better between us. When thoughts of change would pop into my head, I would feel defensive, almost angry, because as far as I was concerned, it wasn't my problem.
>
> As things between us became more tense, and my attitude toward Michael became worse, I knew that change would make our lives easier. I had this sense that once I really began the project, things would get better. I had a lot of enthusiasm, which helped me to design my collaboration project.
>
> When I actually began to implement my project, the immensity of it, and my doubts that there would be any improvement, made the project seem impossible. My excitement, energy, and optimism seemed to waiver. The good days were offset by bad, and this up and down roller coaster was very nerve-wracking, to say the least.
>
> By now, after six weeks of implementation, certain behaviors are becoming so familiar! I find that it is improving my relationships with others, in addition to Michael. I am more confident in my ability to deal with others who exhibit the same kinds of irritating behaviors as Michael, because I can control my response to them much better. There are still those days that I go back to pre-plan thoughts, but I try to remind myself of how far I've come. This helps me to keep going forward. (Angelo, 1994)

By the end of this project, you, too, may be able to look back with a wry smile on what you have accomplished! In the next chapter, you will find out how to translate your objectives into activities, which can be used to help you achieve your goals.

7

What Now?

What Works and What Doesn't When Collaborating

I t is so familiar—a project begins with certainty and resolve. "I will exercise five times a week." "I will finish my lesson plans before I leave school on Friday, rather than taking them home over the weekend." "I will remember to keep my paraprofessional informed each day about changes in plans." But our resolve does not come with a starter kit. When you come right down to a task, like the collaboration project for which you have chosen your goals and objectives, you have to define how to do what is needed. Although you may wish for a set of instant solutions, you must develop a sequence of activities.

Chapter 7 will fall somewhere between the "genie in the bottle" solutions that you may hope for and developing the "how to's" entirely on your own. You can review general communication strategies to incorporate into your project, whatever its focus. Then, you can review activities included at the end of the chapter that have been specifically designed for all the pragmatic goals presented in Chapter 6.

Chapter 7 will also help you to design your collaboration resource network. You will learn how to ask for and receive assistance from others who can help you. With all these resources, you can put your project into action.

Now that you have completed Chapter 6 and designed your collaboration project's goals and objectives, you should have a clearer picture of how your working relationship with your target person could improve. Instead of thinking very generally, as you may have done at the outset of the project, that you "want things to be different," you now have some specific ideas like the teacher in the following example.

I knew that I wanted to have a better relationship with my principal. But every time I tried to think of improvements, I came up with a million reasons why nothing would work. I think I spent the first two weeks of my project walking around with a frown on my face.

Then, one day, it came to me. I didn't have to do everything differently. Instead, I had to learn to speak up without second guessing my principal's reactions. That's when I felt better, and the frown disappeared. Instead of needing to change everything about myself in order to make this project work, I just had to stop censoring myself. Suddenly, it became doable.

The teacher is ready to look for the "how to's" now that the "who and what" have been selected. The teacher's confidence increases because the scope of the project has been narrowed. This change can result in an improved working relationship. The goals and objectives you selected are practical and have been used by many other people. Now you will match them up with activities designed to help you achieve your objectives. Stay open to the observations you make throughout your project. An excellent example of the reflective process of analyzing written journals and other assignments is presented by Edwards and Bruce (2004), illustrating observations made while maintaining a reflective journal.

Keep your collaboration project goals and objectives in mind as you read Chapter 7. The ideas presented here are designed to help you adjust your project goals and objectives, if needed. Then, you can select activities for your project from those presented at the end of Chapter 7.

Nearly all projects include some activities leading to improved communication with your target person. Guidelines to consider in developing these activities are provided in the following section.

EFFECTIVE COMMUNICATION STRATEGIES: SOMETHING FOR EVERYONE

In reviewing contacts with your target person, you've had to scrutinize the way you think, speak, and act. It may be the first time in your life that you have investigated yourself so thoroughly. Ideally, you are developing habits that can help you to permanently be a self-reflective, self-correcting teacher. This is a worthy goal long after your collaboration project ends. Pultorak (1993) examines the development of habits for being a reflective teacher, and notes that "It is a difficult task.... The ability to look back and learn from one's experiences within a classroom environment is extremely complex and difficult to acquire" (p. 288). Abernathy and Cheney (2005) support the use of reflection as a "tool [teachers] can use to self-assess their own classroom practices" (p. 56). Chase and Merryfield (2000), reconsidering their collaboration in a professional development school setting, encouraged use of many different tools for reflection, including writing (journaling), reviewing the work of others (reading, discussions), and structuring your own thoughts via constructing cases or developing portfolios (p. 128).

Manouchehri (2001) analyzed the reflections of teachers in their journals and created a model distinguishing five levels of reflection (all of which relate to the type of communication taking place in the situations upon which they were reflecting):

Describing, Explaining, Theorizing, Confronting, and Restructuring. In Manouchehri's 2002 research project, she did extensive analysis of reflective journals of two preservice teachers over a period of 11 weeks. She observed the following regarding their reflections about the 16 meetings that took place over the 11 weeks:

> During these meetings, they discussed various professional matters ranging from school culture to specific classroom events. These interactions directly influenced the initial habits and conceptions they brought to the experience and helped them modify their ways of talking about practice. . . . These discussions facilitated a shift in their level of reflection, moving them from describing-explaining, to a theorizing and restructuring phase. (p. 723)

The attention the two participants were paying to *what* they were saying helped them to improve their attention to each other, as well as to *how* they were working together.

Developing habits of automatic self-assessment can result in more effective, ongoing self-correction. Here are ways to analyze the communication patterns you use on a daily basis. We'll begin with the precursor to effective communication, listening.

Listening to Others: Why

Bush (2003) describes "inquiry groups" as an opportunity for reconsideration of lessons to jointly "unpack, dissect, investigate, digest, contemplate, ponder, reflect, share, elicit, adjust, and grow together. . . . Some form of inquiry groups exists in every school reform movement" (p. 52). Price (1991) makes the case for listening in the opening paragraph of his article:

> Although school reform may be designed with the best interest of students in mind, the path to its achievement is pitted with potential for personal stress. . . . To reduce the . . . stress, educators need to further develop their abilities in the art of communication by acquiring greater knowledge, skills, and experience in the total process, with an emphasis in the area of listening. (p. 25)

Price's choice of listening, rather than speaking, as a cornerstone for communication is illustrated in schools every day. Educators seldom have the luxury of having only one thing to do—they are almost always juggling simultaneous responsibilities. As a result, listening can often get pushed to the bottom of a seemingly endless To Do list. Yet, it is very, very important. Graseck (2005), in his list of the 10 ways effective school administrators "can enhance teacher happiness, which in turn contributes to improving the quality of the learning environment," has as his number one recommendation "They listen to their teachers, and, through such attentiveness, they 'are listening people into existence'" (p. 377).

Covey (1989) describes different ways people can sabotage their listening efforts by just going through the motions. He explains how real listening differs from the less successful efforts. You might be able to think of specific times within the past week that you have seen examples of each.

First, Covey describes the starting point, nonlistening. He describes this as "ignoring another person, not really listening at all" (p. 240). If you have walked into a lunchroom in a school or a cafeteria in a college you have seen this go on. Very often, people are sitting together, and one person is telling a long, involved story. The other people are paying no attention at all, and yet the speaker goes on talking. No listening is taking place, but the speaker needs to talk—even without the attention of others.

This obvious disinterest is different from what Covey describes as "pretending." Instead of ignoring the speaker, the listener responds with occasional appropriate comments. The listener's part of the conversation consists of words such as "Yeah," "Uh-huh," "Right." Have you walked by two people in a hallway who seem to be having a conversation, but when you look more closely, you see that one is delivering a monologue? One person talks, but the other is hardly part of the conversation. Offering a few, insincere, interjectory comments is considered participation, but it is actually pretending.

Covey also describes "selective listening, hearing only certain parts of the conversation" (p. 240). When a person with whom you live or work talks about a topic in which you have marginal interest, pretending may not be appropriate. You may need to engage in selective listening. You may comment about parts of the topic that interest you but ignore others. You may be keeping a part of yourself outside the conversation, thinking about something you will be doing later in the day. By tuning in to the conversation occasionally and making a pertinent comment or two, you can probably get by.

But these listening approaches do not improve the communication between you and the other person. To do that, you need to employ one of the next two types of listening that Covey suggests. "Attentive listening, paying attention and focusing energy on the words that are being said" (p. 240) is a way in which communication begins to cross over from "one way" to "two way." Covey agrees that this is preferable to the other options, but he recommends that we work toward "empathic listening." He describes this form of listening as follows:

> listening with intent to *understand*. . . . Empathic (from empathy) gets inside another person's frame of reference. You look out through it, you see the world the way they see the world, you understand their paradigm, you understand how they feel. . . . The essence of empathic listening is not that you agree with someone—it's that you fully, deeply understand that person, emotionally and also intellectually. . . . Empathic listening is so powerful because it gives you accurate data to work with. Instead of projecting your own autobiography and assuming thoughts, feelings, motives and interpretation, you're dealing with the reality inside another person's head and heart. You're listening to understand. (pp. 240–241)

The experiences that Covey categorizes as "empathic listening" illustrate what most people seek at times of stress. When facing a major illness or serious problem confronting a friend or family member, many would welcome the chance to "be heard" by another who was listening empathically. If you think about the people in your life who are good listeners, you could probably identify times when they pay attention to you fully—whether you are facing a difficult decision or just need to talk. They give you their undivided attention and can serve as a useful sounding board.

Do you use empathic listening with your target person? If you incorporate it into your contacts, it could enable you to develop your project. If you include empathic listening in upcoming conversations, you can collect data needed to better understand things from your target person's point of view.

As you read about these different types of listening, you may connect them with people you know. In the Human Scavenger Hunt (Chapter 6) you identified people you might be able to turn to in new ways. Idea Try-Out 7.1 will give you some ways to consider them as potential members of your collaboration resource network.

Idea Try-Out 7.1

The Listeners

In this Idea Try-Out, you will start to build a collaboration resource network by selecting some people who demonstrate attentive or empathic listening skills. The resource network members may be people with whom you will talk directly, or they may be people you only watch. Watching may help you get ideas about how to listen differently.

1. List the names of three people (whom you see at least weekly) who you think are attentive or empathic listeners.

2. List the names of three people who you think could give you honest opinions about your listening skills.

3. List two situations in which you could observe or interact with the people listed in #1 to observe their listening habits.

4. Briefly describe one time in your life when someone was an attentive or empathic listener. At the end of your description, list five adjectives or adverbs to describe how their listening made you feel.

5. Briefly describe an important time in your life when someone was an ignoring listener. At the end of your description, list five adjectives or adverbs to describe how that person's half-hearted listening made you feel.

6. Summarize in a note to yourself three suggestions for improving your listening that you would like to accomplish in the coming month.

As you worked on this Idea Try-Out, you may have found differences between the reflections on good listeners and those who dismiss the importance of listening. You may decide to choose some of the good listeners to become part of your collaboration resource network. In Project Try-Out 7.2, presented later in this chapter, you will have an opportunity to explore how to change your own listening habits.

In the following example, the advantages of demonstrating empathic listening are supported by the paraprofessional's description of his experiences.

I knew that the teacher with whom I worked found Monday mornings extra hard. He'd always spend time over the weekend thinking about our class and had some new idea to try out. His enthusiasm was amazing to me! We'd always start the week out with new energy.

One Monday morning in April, he started in his usual way to describe what he wanted me to do with the students, but then he stopped in midsentence. I didn't know what to do, so I just waited.

> *Then he started talking, using a much more serious tone of voice. He talked non-stop about the progress he'd seen in some students and his disappointment in what others had been able to accomplish. He must have gone on for ten minutes or more.*
>
> *I didn't say a word, didn't take my eyes off him. I knew that we had to get ready for the students, and for the week, but I decided what he had to say was more important.*
>
> *Finally he said, "I guess I need to figure out where to go from here with the whole class, between now and the end of June. I need to pick something I know we can do." He thanked me for helping him sort things out. All I did was listen, but I knew that was the most important thing right then.*

This is an example of a time when empathic listening was of value and more formal problem solving was unnecessary.

Price (1991) goes on to explain the difference between listening and hearing:

> People tend to think of listening as an inactive process and equate it with hearing, which it is not. Hearing is a natural process in which auditory stimuli are received, whereas listening is a learned skill that involves concentration, analysis, and evaluation through extensive practice. (p. 26)

The act of listening takes more than passing a hearing test. It is one that requires use of specific strategies. Listening guidelines are presented below.

Listening to Others: How

Snell and Janney (2000), in their guide to collaborative teaming, make the following comments about listening:

> The skill of listening to or receiving a message has two fundamental requirements: (1) communicating, primarily through nonverbal behavior, that you want to understand the speaker's message and feelings, and (2) actually understanding the speaker's message and feelings (Johnson & Johnson, 1997). . . . The biggest barricade to effective listening is the evaluation of messages as they are being received. When a receiver makes immediate judgments regarding a speaker's message without first confirming his or her understanding of the message, he or she often stops listening or leaps to conclusions based on a premature or erroneous evaluation of the message. Trust is consequently eroded. Premature evaluations by receivers also cause senders to be defensive and closed and less able to explain or expand on their message. (pp. 111–112)

How can you overcome the temptation to make up your mind about what you are hearing and really focus on what is being said? The following guidelines, based on Price's article (1991, pp. 27–28), can lead to attentive or empathic listening:

1. *Decide your purpose for listening in advance.* Is your role one of providing a shoulder on which to lean, as in the previous example, while the person speaking

"thinks out loud"? Or instead, are you trying to get information? The decision you make will help you determine whether attentive or empathic listening is needed.

2. *Select an appropriate context for listening.* Make sure that you and the person to whom you intend to listen have sufficient time, energy, and privacy to have the necessary conversation. A question that Price raises—"Is it so late in the day that participants may lack the energy and patience needed to be effective?" (p. 27)—is one to which every teacher can relate. However good your intentions to be an excellent listener, listening at the end of a difficult day or week takes more than many people can give. You and the person to whom you are listening should decide if the time is right.

3. *Focus on the speaker.* "Concentrate on *what* the speaker is saying and *how* it is being said. . . . Nonverbal gestures from the speaker including gestures, facial expression, and posture contribute to the meaning of the message, often as much as the speaker's words" (p. 27). Attend to the facial cues, arm position, and position of the hands to better understand the speaker's feelings. Refer back to the discussion of nonverbal cues presented in Chapter 3.

4. *In your own words, repeat important ideas.* Paraphrasing the speaker's main ideas can serve two purposes: (1) it can help you decide whether you are correctly understanding what the speaker means, and (2) it can illustrate that you are listening attentively. Paraphrasing rules are as follows:

   a. To help you to get started, use an "opener." Use a nod, a smile, or simple statement such as, "It sounds like . . ." or "I understand what you are saying to be . . ." or "I see."
   b. Use your own words to highlight what you just heard without exactly repeating (or "parroting") what was said.
   c. Restate the speaker's ideas by organizing the ideas presented or summarizing what you heard.
   d. Avoid inserting your own ideas or opinions.
   e. End with a question or statement that enables the speaker to feel comfortable making any corrections.

It is very difficult to respond to what is being said without including your own ideas, but that is a requirement of effective paraphrasing. Let's look at two examples of the same new teacher's efforts to listen and paraphrase.

In the following example, the principal (the primary speaker) is enthusiastic—verbal and nonverbal participation in the conversation show that the topic is of importance.

Situation: *A school corridor, in August, before the school year begins*

Players: *Principal, New Teacher*

Principal: One of the programs that we began last year was a Homework and Help Web site. Each classroom has a page on the school's Web site, and parents can use it each night to find out what assignments are due.

Teacher: Oh, a homework Web site for each classroom!

Principal: (shaking his head in amazement) We've monitored how often parents use these sites, as well as the links we provide to additional resources (gesture of disbelief). Would you believe that after school hours, more than 50% of our parents click in per night?

Teacher: Fifty percent per night! Parents really use that Web site.

Principal: True. Well, good talking to you. Let me know if you need any help getting materials for your room.

Although the teacher is displaying attentive listening, it is at the "parroting" level rather than "paraphrasing." However, on the positive side, the teacher is following the rules of paraphrasing, especially the rule that cautions about inserting your own ideas into the conversation. On the negative side, the teacher's manner is very forced and stiff.

What this new teacher is doing is typical of how most people sound when they first begin to paraphrase. It is best to practice your paraphrasing skills on family members, friends, or members of your collaboration resource network. You may have to practice for a while until you feel comfortable and flexible. Then, you will be ready to paraphrase when listening to your target person.

The new teacher in the previous example could make improvements in paraphrasing through the use of summarizing and proposing a way to organize the ideas being heard. The following dialogue takes place after the new teacher practiced paraphrasing techniques.

Situation: *School corridor, one morning in September*

Players: *Principal, New Teacher*

Principal: Our procedures for classroom field trips are in your packet of forms. We started including parent volunteers on the trips last year.

Teacher: Parent volunteers?

Principal: (shaking his head in amazement) It was an eye-opener. Parents really never understood the classroom dynamics until they joined us for these trips. (gesturing with open hands) It really helps us out, too.

Teacher: (nodding in agreement) I see. It sounds like there are two different benefits. One is for the parents, helping them to see what the students are like, and the other is for the school. Getting extra hands has to be a big help.

Principal: (nodding) That's exactly right. It is a two-way street. I remember one time, when we had a trip to the zoo . . .

The teacher pulls ideas out of the principal's comments without adding any new interpretation. The teacher inserts emphasis at strategic points in the conversation without overstepping the bounds of paraphrasing. As a result, instead of abruptly ending the conversation, as took place in the first instance, the principal goes on to present another example. This often indicates that good paraphrasing has taken place.

Remember, participation in paraphrasing is part of the listener's role in communication. This is different from the roles that are described in the next section of the chapter in which, as the communicator, you share your own ideas.

Not everyone is convinced that paraphrasing is a good strategy. For example, Covey (1989) has strong warnings about paraphrasing:

> "Active" listening or "reflective" listening . . . basically involve[s] mimicking what another person says. That kind of listening is skill-based, truncated from character and relationships, and often insults those "listened" to in such a way. . . . You listen with reflective skills, but you listen with intent to reply, to control, to manipulate. (p. 240)

To avoid these problems, practice the techniques of active listening. In journal articles specifically mentioning listening skills, as well as in articles cited in this chapter, you can find exercises that can help you avoid some of the pitfalls of this technique.

5. *When reasonable, take notes to improve the quality of listening.* Price (1991) suggests two valuable outcomes of taking notes: "[taking notes] compels the listener to concentrate on and remember what was said for a longer period of time. The retention rate for most listeners after the first 48 hours is only 25% of what they have heard" (p. 28). By increasing concentration and improving retention, taking notes can work out well. However, he cautions that notes should only be taken "if the note-taking process is not disruptive to the speaker" (p. 28).

Listening is an important component of effective communication. Use Project Try-Out 7.2 to test your listening habits. After you've practiced, you can use it to collect baseline data with your target person.

Project Try-Out 7.2

My Favorite Show

This Project Try-Out has been designed to give you a chance to practice your paraphrasing skills in private and then with others you know. You can decide whether you feel more comfortable taking notes or using a tape recorder. Eventually, you will want to get to the point when you can "think on your feet." For now, pick the way to begin that suits you best.

1. Pick a favorite half-hour television program and tape it using video or audio tape, or rent a video and watch it.

2. Select three or four conversations between the characters that are good examples of paraphrasing. In your collaboration notebook, jot down what made the paraphrasing effective. (Remember, script writers spend weeks perfecting dialogue. Don't expect all your efforts to be equally smooth and polished.)

3. Select two different points when speeches made by characters in the program were not paraphrased. Try paraphrasing the comments by writing your ideas down or by using a tape recorder to record your paraphrases. Remember to try to highlight, organize, or summarize what has been said, rather than just "parrot" the statements.

4. Review what you've written, or listen to your paraphrases. Answer the following questions:
   a. Were new ideas or opinions left out?
   b. Did the tone of the paraphrase match the speaker's nonverbal and verbal cues?
   c. Was the vocabulary sufficiently different from that of the original speaker that the paraphrases were not "parroting"?
   d. Were techniques of highlighting, organizing, or summarizing effectively used?

5. Go back over your work and make adjustments. If you have put your work on audio tape, transcribe your efforts and put them in your collaboration notebook.

6. In the next week, practice paraphrasing in two or three real-life situations.
   a. Record a brief summary of what you did in your collaboration notebook.
   b. Evaluate your efforts using the questions listed in Step 4 above.
   c. At the end of the week, record three reminders for yourself of points that you want to remember in future paraphrasing efforts.

This exercise can help you practice an important part of the communication process. You will not always have the luxury of analyzing your responses so carefully. With practice, effective paraphrasing can become a part of your professional skill set, but it is only one part. The next section of this chapter provides effective communication strategies in which you are the initiator.

Tips for Effective Communication: Making Statements

Your plans for improving your relationship with your target person extend beyond listening to include times when you share your own ideas. The way you've been communicating thus far can be improved even if the relationship you have established is a good one. If you and your target person have had problems, then attending to how you convey your ideas is a reasonable starting point.

We've often been told that we need to avoid "jargon" when talking with family members of our students, as well as with fellow educators. Mason et al. (2004) make the following recommendation, based on what they'd observed in reviewing journal articles from general and special education associations:

> Our research confirmed that for the most part special educators are "addressing themselves." If we are interested in furthering collaboration with general educators, then perhaps greater efforts should be made to publish articles on topics of relevance to us in *their* literature. Certainly this is not a new recommendation and a review of the database confirms that particular researchers appear to have made a concerted effort to do this. . . . We may be missing an important vehicle to further communication and collaboration. If special educators used terminology that is "user friendly" for general educators, perhaps collaboration would be easier and more effective. (pp. 226–227)

Successful communication is, in part, a function of what you are discussing, but it is also related to more general skills.

The ability to be an effective communicator is closely related to one of the pragmatic goals presented in Chapter 6, the ability to be assertive. As Canning (1991) describes the use of reflection to student teachers, "students often said, 'Yes, but what do you want us to *do*?' Almost everyone felt a need for structure, since none was specified. . . . In retrospect, however, this latitude helped participants to figure things out for themselves" (p. 19). Determining how to cope with ambiguity and translating your ideas into clear statements may be one of the most challenging tasks of your collaboration project.

Expressing your ideas to your target person can take place in any of the following important contexts: informal/social, informational, and convincing/persuasive.

Informal/Social

Does the example sound familiar?

> When I began my collaboration project, I was skeptical. I was convinced that my working relationship with my co-teacher was no big deal to either of us. But, I had to do something for the project. So, I decided to plan an increase in the number of informal contacts I had with her over the course of the week. On Thursday of the week when I was taking my baseline data, she said to me, "What's going on? You only used to talk to me when you wanted something." I don't know what I said to her—something about being in a better mood these days—but what she said really made me think. I did talk to her only out of necessity—I guess I never noticed before, and it never occurred to me that she was keeping score. After that, I realized that I had to be a lot more aware of what I was doing. Other people noticed things that I ignored. I took my project much more seriously after that.

Your contacts with your target person may be limited. In reflection, you may find that you never talk when you don't have to. Your contacts may be exclusively work-related questions or answers. Think back over the past few weeks. Ask yourself whether you have shared anything about yourself with your target person or learned anything new about your target person's interests or habits. The goal of informal communication is not to become friends with your target person. Instead, take a baseline measure to learn the extent to which you have polite, optional contacts. This can help you evaluate how you balance required and optional contacts. You may be surprised at what you learn.

Idea Try-Out 7.3

Yours, Mine, or Ours?

This Idea Try-Out will give you an opportunity to review your comfort level with casual conversation—with people at work or school, as well as with friends and family members. You will examine your tolerance for casual conversation and also consider its benefits.

1. Think back over the past few weeks. In your collaboration notebook, list the people you've talked with informally or socially. Put this list down the middle of the page.

2. On the right-hand side, put a letter next to each name to show who took the major responsibility for the conversation: mark an "M" for Me, an "O" for Other Person, or a "J" for Joint.

3. Next to each name on the left-hand side, rate your satisfaction with the casual conversation. Think about whether or not you were glad to hear what the other person had to say, whether sharing your own experiences was pleasant, and whether you felt comfortable doing so. Use "VS" for Very Satisfied, "SS" for Somewhat Satisfied, or "U" for Unsatisfied.

4. Look over all the information you have assembled for yourself about the informal conversations you've had. Think ahead to having an informal/social communication with your target person, and consider what you've recalled about informal/social communication with other people in your life. At the bottom of the page, make a chart with "Pros" on the right and "Cons" on the left. List as many items on each side of the chart as you can that relate to incorporating informal/social communication with your target person.

5. Review your list of "Pros" and "Cons" and circle those that you would address in an activity if you included informal/social conversation with your target person.

6. Write a note to yourself about what you need to remember in informal/social conversation that will help you make the most of the experience with your target person.

Expressing yourself in an informal/social context can serve as the basis of one of your activities for your collaboration project. If you work with students or volunteers, you may be able to practice with them. Informal/social contacts can add to your relationship with your target person.

Informational Statements

There are times when you and your target person need to share information. Descriptions of successful information sharing can follow Strunk and White's classic, succinct suggestions in *The Elements of Style* (2005):

- Put statements in positive form (p. 34)
- Use definite, specific, concrete language (p. 37)
- Omit needless words (p. 39)
- Be clear (p. 113)

Strunk and White provide guidance for writers that can be profitably followed by all communicators of information. These four guidelines distinguish effective from ineffective statements. Try monitoring your communication with your target person to assess your success in meeting these guidelines. You may see that you have a harder time with one of the guidelines than another. This insight may help you to design an activity for your collaboration project.

The suggestions for writers pertain to the needs of collaborators who are trying to share information. As the following example indicates, the format chosen for conveying information can also have an impact on the outcome of the conversation.

> *When I tried to talk to my paraprofessional, it rarely worked out. Whenever I'd start to talk to him, his eyes glazed over. I realized, when I started to work on this project, that I had been getting more and more frustrated. Things had deteriorated between us since the start of the year, but I hadn't really paid attention.*
>
> *One day, as I was setting up dialogue journals for the students in my class, I thought I would suggest to him that we could use a "dialogue journal" with each other. I figured nothing could get worse than it already was.*
>
> *Since he likes to use the computer, I set up our journal as a file on our shared drive, which we'd established on the computer in our class to be able to review students' work. What a difference it made! We each have our times of the day to check the file, and it has improved our communication 100%. Until I started this project, I was planning to ask for a new paraprofessional for next year. Now, I don't have to.*

You may find, after completing Project Try-Out 7.4, that your success in communicating information differs depending on the format you use to convey information.

Project Try-Out 7.4

Where and How

This activity will give you an opportunity to examine different formats for conveying information. You can experiment with a family member or friend with whom you feel comfortable. The purpose of the try-out is to give you a basis for comparing different formats for giving information.

1. Over the course of the next week, you will probably need to share information with the person you've selected for this exercise. Experiment with the following formats:
   a. Leave a message on an answering machine or on voice mail.
   b. Leave a written message.
   c. Have a conversation and leave time for questions.
   d. Give a message to the individual through a third person.

2. To evaluate your success with each of these formats, create a chart with a column for each format. Answer all of the following questions for each format:
   a. How effectively did you convey information?
   b. How clear were you? How well were you able to deal with confusion that arose?

c. What evidence do you have that your recipient accurately understood the information you intended to convey?

d. How comfortable were you with the format?

e. What would you do differently next time?

3. Look over your answers and put a star next to the format that was best overall for conveying information. Write yourself a suggestion for how to generalize from this try-out to your contacts with your target person.

Clarity, opportunity to resolve questions, and format: these are the keys to developing your personal guidelines when you need to convey information to your target person. Generate a list of alternatives to use so that you can eventually make effective informational statements. Monitor how you communicate information to ensure a high degree of congruence between how you *want* to sound and how you *do* sound.

A problematic habit that some teachers have is asking a question as a preface to an informational statement. "Can I tell you about something?" may seem like a lead in to a conversation, but if you are going to "tell" the person no matter what answer is given to the question, your question sets up some false expectations. A better preface is, "I have something I need to explain to you/tell you. It shouldn't take more than a few minutes. Is now a good time?" This introduction does several things:

- It alerts your listener to your intention
- It gives the listener a real option—to participate in the conversation now or later

Later in this chapter you will have an opportunity to look at your problematic habits when asking questions and find ways to improve them.

As you reflect on the skills you need to converse with others in your school setting, you will realize that informational statements alone are clearly insufficient. At times, you must convince or persuade the person to whom you are talking.

Convincing/Persuasive

It is rare that any two people agree on everything. During conversations with your relatives, friends, and coworkers there will be times when you see things differently. As you and your target person work together, you may have areas of disagreement. At times, you may have to present your point of view. The following steps can help you prepare for and conduct a discussion that leads to an outcome acceptable to both of you.

1. *Get background information.* Before you can persuade another person about a particular point, you must be prepared. Your preparation can be done in private or with a friend who is part of your collaboration resource network. Use the following steps to analyze the situation, leading to your own version of Figure 7.1:

a. Review the situation; include both what has taken place and what you would like to see happen. Think about the situation. Chart your ideas on paper, or describe the events in conversation with a friend and ask your friend to act as your transcriber. Use the headings of the pie chart in

Figure 7.1   Looking at a Tough Situation I: My Point of View

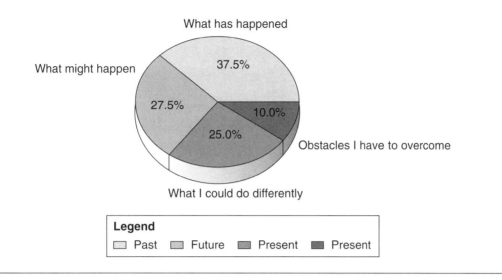

Figure 7.1 as a guide: What has happened? What might happen? What obstacles need to be overcome? What could I do differently? Generate as many items as you can.

After you have finished generating your list, translate your items into percentages and create a chart like Figure 7.1. This visual presentation can help you see where you need to focus more attention. You may have lots of details for the section of the chart titled "What has happened," but very few for "What might happen." You may have many ideas for "What obstacles do I have to overcome," but have a blank page for "What I could do differently." This approach could help you expand your thinking so you can fully understand the problem.

b. Organize your ideas before you start communicating (orally or in writing). After looking at things from your point of view, follow up with a similar activity from the point of view of the other person. With your collaboration project in mind, think about things from your target person's point of view. In Figure 7.2 you can see a representation of the viewpoint of the target person. You may find that this view of the situation enables you to see the problem differently. More obstacles may be present, for example. After reviewing the ideas you have generated, you can get yourself organized before you begin the conversation.

2. *Clearly present your rationale for your point of view, including points you want to be sure to cover.* As you talk with the other person, be prepared to support the ideas you are presenting using specific, recent examples.

3. *Be clear about the points upon which you are willing to compromise, as well as those upon which you need to stand firm.* Have this in mind: After your discussion, your goal is to walk away from the situation with an outcome that both you and the other person understand. Each of you may not exactly agree at the outset about what will take place, but you should both be able to understand the reasoning for it.

Figure 7.2 Looking at a Tough Situation II: Target Person's Point of View

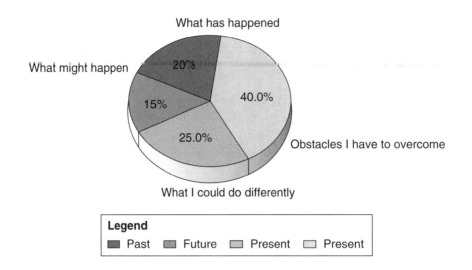

In thinking through the conversation in advance, try to make your thoughts as clear as possible. Roger Fisher's work, particularly *Getting to Yes: Negotiating Agreement Without Giving In* (Fisher, Ury, & Patton, 1991), provides a clear, thorough description of what is required to be an effective negotiator. This bestseller details what you need to do to persuade or convince. For example, Fisher, Ury, and Patton describe the centrality of communication to help people with differences of opinion negotiate a mutually acceptable outcome:

> Without communication there is no negotiation. Negotiation is a process of communicating back and forth, for the purpose of reaching a joint decision. . . . There are three big problems in communication: First, negotiators may not be talking to each other, or at least not in such a way as to be understood. . . . [Second], if you are not hearing what the other side is saying, there is no communication. The third communication problem is misunderstanding. What one says, the other may misinterpret. (pp. 32–33)

These cautions pertain to the collaboration project. If you are attempting to persuade your target person to approach something in a new way, you may find yourself facing one or more of the difficulties described above. As depicted in the following example, the two teachers had trouble finding ways to listen to each other—both were convinced that they were right and the other person was wrong.

When I found out that I had to work with the fifth-grade team to find ways to make test modifications for the science exams next May, I was nervous. I had good experiences with two of the teachers, but nothing I'd ever tried with Mr. X had worked out. In every discussion I'd had with him, he told me that he'd "tried it before, and it had been a dismal failure." Everything I brought up got shot down. He sat through every meeting like he was getting a root canal.

After a while, I made excuses to stop going to the meetings. I knew my principal would get on my case, but frankly, that was better than listening to Mr. X tell me how stupid my ideas were.

Finally, I realized the people who were getting hurt by our problems were our students. I decided to give it another try. I caught up with him in the teachers' lounge one morning and told him I wanted to explain why test modifications were so important to me. I told him what I'd heard about two of our students who'd graduated. He'd worked closely with both of them on a project for the United Way. Both were successful in high school as a result of some of the modifications their high school teachers were using. For the first time, I got his attention. We finally got away from the power struggle between the two of us and got back to the students. We started talking. Everything isn't perfect between us, but we're both trying to help the kids.

Fisher, Ury, and Patton (1991) make the following suggestions for (1) dealing with the communication problems described above and (2) setting your own priorities in the conversation:

- Listen actively and acknowledge what is being said
- Speak to be understood
- Speak about yourself, not about them
- Speak for a purpose (pp. 34–36)

By incorporating these suggestions, the teacher in the example above was able to turn the situation around.

4. *Be prepared to generate alternate outcomes and to use as many listening strategies as possible to reach a mutually acceptable decision.* The development and use of good listening skills can enable you to capitalize on points upon which you agree, eventually leading to a conclusion that is mutually satisfying. The following example illustrates the outcome of a carefully planned conversation.

When I began my collaboration project, I had little confidence in the whole idea of trying to change my behavior without trying to change the other person. How could that really work? But then I watched the Consulting Teacher who worked with my class come close to tears twice in one week in my classroom. I realized that I didn't like the way things were going.

I wasn't trying to be difficult, or even particularly demanding, and yet she kept getting upset. I realized that I would have to find a new way for us to resolve differences in our discipline habits. I thought things through as well as I could and scheduled time for us to meet during a Teacher Conference Day. We sat down and developed some new ground rules. As a result, we've both gotten our senses of humor back. The students in the class are more comfortable, and so are we. The big change was in my head—instead of staying frustrated, I tried something new. And it worked!

The teacher's preparation led to some novel results, which were not altogether pre-planned. Being prepared can open up new options, leading you in the right direction.

The types of statements reviewed thus far—informal/social, informational, and convincing/persuasive—give you a solid base for most of the conversations you will have with your target person. However, there will also be times when another type of communication will be required—asking questions.

Using Questions

When working with your target person, you can extend the range of your contacts with effective questions. Some research studies incorporate interviewing as a primary strategy. Gwynn (2004) provides a detailed account of her preparation for, and completion of, interviews with adolescents with disabilities. She provides transcripts and illustrates how she "made sense of the voices," leading to further investigations: "Raising voices and finding out about student relationships was central to my research, but they also prompted me to scrutinise my own practice" (p. 119).

Think back to when you started to get to know students in your classes at the beginning of the year. Were you able to get a sense of their interests and opinions from their answers to your questions in an interview or on an interest survey? You can incorporate questions using informal/social and informational formats.

Informal/Social

You can expand your knowledge of your target person by increasing the types of questions used and number of circumstances in which questions were asked. Consider the following options.

1. *Direct, closed-ended questions* (asked to an individual): "Did you always know you were going to be a teacher?" "How many children do you have?" "What is your favorite hobby?"
   - Pros: These questions will get you the specific information you seek.
   - Cons: These questions might be perceived as intrusive. They also may serve to limit, rather than open up, conversation.

2. *Indirect, closed-ended questions* (asked to a group, rather than to an individual): "What is the best place for me to go to get my car repaired?" "Who got to the gym last week?" "In what parts of this country—or other countries—were people here born?"
   - Pros: These questions may open up conversation if people go beyond the one-word answer.
   - Cons: People other than your target person may answer the questions and you may not accomplish your goal of getting to know your target person better. Another problem is that the conversation may drift far from where you intended it. As with the direct, closed-ended question, these questions might be perceived as intrusive.

3. *Direct, open-ended questions* (asked to an individual): "What ways do you find to relax after work to take your mind off things?" "What kinds of vacations do you enjoy?" "How do you think our school differs from others its size?"
   - Pros: Since these questions are open-ended, you can expect a more comprehensive answer than you would get to a closed-ended question. You may be able to use paraphrasing or another open-ended question to keep the conversation moving.

- Cons: These questions may lead to more personal disclosure than you intended. Because the questions are somewhat less focused, you may not get the answer for which you were hoping.

4. *Indirect, open-ended questions* (asked to a group, rather than to an individual): "What plans do you have for summer vacation?" "What do you think our Parent-Teacher Association does well?" "When students come back after a long weekend, how do you get them refocused on their schoolwork?"
   - Pros: Same as direct, open-ended.
   - Cons: Same as direct, closed-ended.

As you can see, there is no perfect question format to use in informal or social conversations with your target person. Each of the four types of questions can be used successfully if it is clearly connected to your overall collaboration project objectives. You can decide in advance what you'll do if the conversation stops or what you will do if you find that your target person is telling you more than you want to know. MacSwan summarizes one of his project goals and how it was achieved:

> My third goal for this project was to develop an effective communication channel for us to use to discuss concerns we share for our students. At the onset of this project, I thought that this was going to be the hardest goal to achieve. The minimal communication that Melissa and I shared didn't seem very expandable.
>
> To my surprise, that was not the case at all. My realization that I am often in a rush, and that I can be impersonal at times, seemed to make a great difference. When I forced myself to slow down, and take those few extra moments to talk and communicate with her in a more personal manner, communication channels seemed to be very easy to find. I now find us communicating with ease, not only about common concerns we share for the students, but in many aspects (professional and personal). (MacSwan, 1996)

In reviewing his project, MacSwan identified the following as a turning point, which took place right before the winter break:

> Melissa was in her room setting up a science project, and I was walking past her door. After hesitating for a moment, I decided to walk in. After a few short words, I asked her if she had any special plans for vacation. The conversation that followed was very surprising. We talked for about ten minutes. She is a very proud parent, and told me all about her children who were coming home for the holiday. She seemed pleasantly surprised that I had asked. And it was refreshing for me. It was the first conversation I'd had with her that I wasn't analyzing for my project, although the project is why I decided to go into her room in the first place. (MacSwan, 1996)

The increase in informal/social contacts, using questions, led to the improvement of relationships between coworkers in several projects. For example, Zakes (1996) also defined a social encounter as a turning point in her project:

> We both decided to take lunch at the same time. There were a number of other people present. I initiated a social exchange by asking about the welfare of another teacher, who had been home for some weeks. The conversation which

Figure 7.3 Social/Professional Interactions

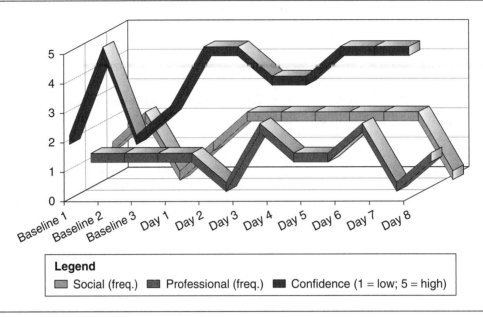

SOURCE: Cudney, 1996

resulted involved several people, but we were all speaking on a more or less equal footing. I really felt that my efforts to get to know and accept Sarah socially were reflected in my increased confidence and ability to communicate with her. On this occasion, she even asked me about my own plans and problems with my wedding. She had rarely shown any interest in my personal life prior to this point. Not only was I getting to know her, but I was allowing her to get to know me.

Friendship between coworkers was not the goal in either of these projects. Opening up lines of communication is a key step that leads to an improved professional relationship. As Zakes observed, the improved communication generalized: "As my social relationship with Sarah improved, I became more comfortable communicating on a professional level with others in the building." As Figure 7.3 (labeled as Cudney, the maiden name of Zakes) shows, during the baseline (the first three days recorded) there seemed to be little correspondence between Zakes's confidence ratings (top line) and her social or professional interactions. However, as she sustained social contacts several times a day, her confidence level reached "4" or "5" quite consistently.

Informational

In Zakes's case, the fact that she had changed the tenor and frequency of her contacts with Sarah led her to ask an informational question, another turning point in her project:

I went to work on Day 8, knowing that there was an issue I needed to investigate. I had heard that Sarah was unhappy about something that had occurred when I was working, but she had not mentioned it to me. One of the objectives I had for this project was to begin with a clean slate, disregarding past interactions and their influence. Instead of avoiding or escaping, as I used to in the past, I needed to ask questions.

This time, rather than avoiding her, I approached her, and asked her about the incident. To my surprise, she didn't blame me or tell me I had made a mistake. Instead, she explained that there had been a problem in communication, and no one had explained to me what had to be done. I left this exchange feeling extremely satisfied with the fact that I had approached her, and asked the question. (Zakes, 1996)

In this situation, Zakes used an informational question to find out her target person's perception of a problem situation. Informational questions can serve any of the following purposes:

1. Clarification: Getting additional information, necessary details, or options that might have to be explored, for example,
   - "You've told me when my lesson plans are due. How much flexibility do I have with that deadline?"
   - "I plan to contact parents to help set up the open house. Can you tell me who I need to notify, and when, to make sure the building will be open for us?"

2. Assistance: Seeking information from another person who can help you to do your own job more effectively, for example,
   - "I'm getting nervous about my first set of parent-teacher conferences. What kinds of things have you tried in advance of your conferences to make them run smoothly?"
   - "I've found that students in my classes have trouble working on their own during the afternoon. Would you describe what it is like in your class after lunch?"

3. Factual: Getting information you need, for example,
   - "What time will you be in my classroom?"
   - "How much money will the PTA give us for the field trip?"

Questions are a natural part of conversation. How often do you incorporate them into your discussions with your target person? Project Try-Out 7.5 will give you an opportunity to examine the kinds of informal/social and informational questions you and your target person ask each other.

Project Try-Out 7.5

Questioning Questions

The purpose of this activity is to assess the kinds of questions you and your target person use during a two-week period. In your collaboration notebook, draw a line down the center of the page. Label the left side "Week 1" and the right side "Week 2." Keep track of each of the items listed below for both weeks.

During the first week, keep track of what you do without trying to add or eliminate questions. During the second week, make the changes in your question pattern that you think are needed—adding or subtracting.

1. Matters of confusion
   a. How many times were you and your target person confused about what the other person wanted/expected? (Total per week)
   b. How did you resolve each point of confusion? (Each of the following should be subtotals for the total per week you recorded in 1a)
      (1) Guessed what the other person wanted.
      (2) Asked target person a question for clarification.
      (3) Asked a third person to get the question answered.
   c. How many times did you and your target person get emotional about matters of confusion? (Total for each of you per week)

2. Informal/Social
   a. How many times did you and your target person ask each other questions about informal or social matters? (Total per week)
   b. How many times did you and another person you know about as well as you know your target person ask each other questions about informal or social matters? (Total per week)

3. Comparison (Record your answers in your collaboration notebook in narrative form)
   a. As you review the information you collected, did you find the patterns you expected?
   b. Was there more or less communication than you expected?
   c. Would you like to change the pattern of communication? If yes, how?

The observations that you made during this information gathering period may be of help to you as you design the implementation of your objectives. As you work on improving your relationship with your target person, there are a number of ways to accomplish your overall goals. In the following section of this chapter, sample project activities are provided. Each one is connected to an evaluation method. Select (or adapt) methods to help you improve your relationship.

ACCOMPLISHING PRAGMATIC GOALS AND ASSOCIATED EVALUATION METHODS

In designing your collaboration project, you addressed different concerns. Here are sample activities to help you meet your goals. Some may not fit your project exactly, but you can use them as a springboard for developing activities on your own. Examples are taken from student projects. Goals (see Chapter 6) are noted in parentheses. Use a computer charting program to represent results.

Expand the Range of Discussion

1. Initiate casual discussion of professional topics relevant to our working relationships or to the events of the day, based on review of relevant current journal articles or conference sessions attended (Walsh, 1995). (Communication, Assertiveness, Getting to Know You)

Evaluation: Track number of times appropriate conversation is initiated; chart using bar graph. Track number of times self-serving conversation unrelated to the situation is initiated ("in other words, how many times I 'fall off the wagon,' so to speak, as I try to break old habits"; Walsh, 1995); chart on bar graph. Use a stacked bar graph each week to show comfort level with conversations (blue = uncomfortable, red = comfortable) (Riggi, 1995).

2. Research relevant topics by visiting the library or using the Internet to gather resource materials. Present results during weekly meetings with target person. (Communication, Values Clash, Getting to Know You)

Evaluation: Document number of resources contributed at each meeting; create a pie chart at end of project to illustrate patterns of change from meeting to meeting (Walsh, 1995). Evaluate response of target person by documenting whether the resources were actually used in the following two weeks; chart (on line graph) the number of ideas used per week (Hernandez, 1995).

3. Identify areas of expertise of your target person upon which you can build. Do this by asking questions about student projects, interests related to schoolwide projects, or other topics that connect to curricular areas of expertise of your target person. (Assertiveness, Values Clash, Clean Slate, Getting to Know You)

Evaluation: Document number of questions asked and answered; create line graph at end of project to show pattern of questions asked. Evaluate comfort level with questions asked, if desired, using the Adjective Card Strategy after each contact. On a 3 x 5 card, list five adjectives describing your feelings or the event itself after each contact. Date the card, and put it in an envelope along with all the other adjective cards you have been maintaining for the project. At the end of the project, create categories for adjectives generated, and chart (using line graph) the number of adjectives for each category used over the course of the project.

Change the Tone of Your Interactions

1. Work on having a more positive outlook on work with target person whether or not the target person is present (Plarr, 1995). (Communication, Work Styles, Clean Slate)

Evaluation: Document number of positive and negative comments made about work together while speaking to target person alone or when speaking to someone else about your target person; chart on a line graph, using different colors for positive and negative.

As Plarr describes, changing the tone can have unanticipated benefits:

As I looked at my work with my target person, I found that my frustrations and problems with her were beginning to spill over into my classroom. I was becoming more easily irritated with my students, and they were also beginning to sense that things were tense between the two of us. This seemed to foster negative comments and hostility toward her from the students. Once things eased up between the two of us, so did the students' conversations. My students are now more productive because they're not wasting time complaining. I'm more effective because I can concentrate better on my students. I've found myself more relaxed around her, and in my everyday life also. Little did I know that just simply relaxing with one individual would help others to do the same, but everyone seems to be much happier now. (Plarr, 1995)

Alternate evaluation method: Document each time a positive quality is noticed about the target person by recording the quality in the collaboration notebook; create a line graph at the end of the project, documenting number of positive qualities noticed per week (Pyszczynski, 1995).

2. Select topics and situations that will help to increase own comfort level during the conversations with target person (Riggi, 1995). Brainstorming with collaboration resource network members to figure out what to talk about and where, to increase confidence and comfort levels during both informal and informational conversations.

Evaluation: Keep track of topics using anecdotal records; rate discussion of each topic in terms of own comfort level (1 = very uncomfortable; 3 = moderately comfortable; 5 = totally at ease); create a line graph that shows the number of topics and different levels of comfort each week.

3. Develop an appropriate "self-talk" sentence for each week, which can help to refocus on the need for a positive, more constructive tone (Tendorf, 1996). Samples: "If a problem is about to happen, approach him privately." "Find ways to enable her to get invested in the class." "Remind myself that his motives are positive and that he really wants to help students." (Different Work Styles, Values Clash, Clean Slate)

Evaluation:

Baseline: In your collaboration notebook, record self-talk sentence for the week.

Strategy: Report on whether a sentence was developed or used each week. Keep a counter in your pocket or at your desk; track the number of times self-talk sentence of the week was used in work with target person to shift from a negative frame of mind to a more positive one. (Optional: Determine whether self-talk sentence was more sophisticated than in previous week.)

Change the Way You Work

1. Set up new guidelines for working together, which increase equity. Jointly generate a list of the tasks on which you need to collaborate and decide how to divide up the work. (Assertiveness, Different Work Styles, Getting to Know You)

Evaluation: Keep track of the number of tasks completed by each person on three out of five days of the week. Create a stacked bar graph showing how 100% of the tasks were accomplished (Pyszczynski, 1995).

2. Establish a personal goal that will improve the effort you put into the work you do, for example, increased patience (Pyszczynski, 1995); replacing frustration with tolerance (Partsch, 1996); setting more realistic limits and expectations. Brainstorm with members of your collaboration resource network how the goal could be achieved, and carry out a new strategy each week. Evaluate how well the strategies work. Recycle the successful ones, with necessary modifications, into routine contacts with your target person. (Different Work Styles, Values Clash, Clean Slate)

Evaluation: Keep track of the number of successes and failures each week; create a line graph to show patterns over the course of the project.

All these activities illustrate how a shift in your behavior can lead to a new interaction pattern with your target person. Even though your target person is unaware of the project, you can develop some internal accountability through self-monitoring that will give you a new perspective on your relationship. It is difficult, however, to accomplish this kind of change alone. That is why, as you begin, you need to develop a collaboration resource network.

MAKING USE OF YOUR COLLABORATION RESOURCE NETWORK

You are getting close to actually embarking on this project. You may find that you have some doubts and concerns. Although you have a plan, you may still feel uneasy.

A successful feature of many collaboration projects has been the collaboration resource network. In Chapter 6 (Idea Try-Out 6.3), you identified potential members of your network. Now you are ready to decide who to select. Your goal in assembling your network is to invite three or four people who you feel know you (or know the situation in which you will be carrying out your project). They can be people in the setting in which your project is taking place, family members, or friends who meet one or more of the following descriptions.

Members of your collaboration resource network should be

- People with whom you can comfortably share your project plan at the outset.
- People who you are confident will maintain your confidentiality. (Note: In over 1,000 projects supervised as the basis for this book, confidentiality was never violated by a member of a collaboration network.)
- People who have earned your respect and whose feedback you would value.
- People who know you well enough to give you useful feedback on your project's progress.
- People who have known you long enough to help you compare your behavior in this relationship with other situations in your life (optional).

Your involvement will have the following features:

- Your network will provide a helping hand.
- Your network will have unique perspectives on your project as people who know you well or are familiar with the situation.

- If they are in the situation, members of your network will be able to give you independent information about the changes in your interaction with your target person.
- Your network will be able to help you to brainstorm alternatives as you develop and implement your project.

As shown in the following example, the comments of a person who knows you well and has seen you in the situation before can be invaluable.

> At the end of the second week, I didn't see much happening with my project. When I reviewed my anecdotal records, it seemed as if everything was staying the same. I was discouraged.
>
> But then Chris, a teacher I'd invited to be a member of my collaboration resource network, stopped in my room after bus duty. "I don't know exactly what you are doing these days," he said, shaking his head, "but you and Tara don't seem to be at each other's throats like you used to be. I watched you at the faculty meeting this week, and you were really listening to her. I was impressed!"
>
> I took his words to heart. He made me realize that—even though I hadn't achieved my goal of improved problem solving—we were making progress. I don't think I would have ended the week on an up note if it hadn't been for Chris.

Getting input from a person familiar with the particular characteristics that you bring to the situation, as well as those of your target person, can help you to see things that you might otherwise miss. It is feasible to include people who are a distance from you as members of your resource network, as you can use e-mail or phone calls to share information. Ertmer (2003) describes several different technological formats teachers can use for sharing information and interviewing each other for multiple purposes. "These interviews were described as being *generative* (inspiring new ideas and strategies) and *cathartic* (enabling . . . [participants] to express frustrations, reflect on past successes, and anticipate future needs)" (p. 127). The immediacy of instant messaging and the opportunity to post information can reduce isolation.

CONCLUSION

If you could look into a crystal ball to see the next few decades of your work with students in schools, you would probably see many smiles. There will be students who will reach you in unexpected ways—either through the attempts they make under your guidance or their accomplishments. One of your best means of enabling those students to accomplish all they can is to effectively work with their teachers.

As a special educator, your role is inevitably that of an ombudsman—you are a listener, a problem solver, and a facilitator. This means that sometimes you must overcome the reservations you have about working with a co-teacher or administrator because your students' progress may be impeded by your reluctance.

At the completion of her project, Marzullo made this commitment to generalizing what she'd learned in her project to other work situations—to continue to collect data in her classroom via an anecdotal journal:

> The many varied and unusual ways of analyzing data from a journal will be a start, moving toward improving personal relationships by finding out about myself. By focusing on myself, examining how I am feeling, and assessing whether or not I am communicating my feelings more effectively, I will reach my personal and professional goals. Just letting the thoughts spin around in my head is like having a CD stuck in one spot—one never hears the whole disc.
>
> Collaboration skills are ones that should enhance all aspects of my life: (1) Listen and ask for evidence; (2) Assemble and identify successes and problems; (3) Identify goals that can be achieved; (4) Facilitate and monitor. Adjust but do not take over others' authority or responsibility; (5) Celebrate—continue monitoring, and when appropriate, ask, "What will I tackle next?" (Marzullo, 1996)

The outcome of the project rests largely on the data you collect and your decisions about how to use it. In the following chapter, you will learn how to set up your evaluation models and, in Chapter 10, how to analyze the results you obtain.

8

Evaluating the Success of Your Plan

How Can You Tell?

A *benefit of being a special educator is the chance to facilitate progress in situations that others view as difficult to change. Being in special education is like wearing bifocals when everyone around you is looking at the world through distance glasses. That same ability—to see clearly and uniquely— can vanish when you are trying to look at yourself collaborating. It is hard to know whether progress is taking place when the object of change is* you. *This chapter illustrates how to measure your progress toward your collaboration goals.*

Learning both *what* and *how* to evaluate is a challenge faced by all educators. When I was learning how to teach, one of the lessons most often repeated was that I had to learn how to observe—my students, myself, my school environment. Bolster (1983), one of my professors, taught me what I needed to be able to do to be effective as both a classroom teacher and as a researcher. He summarized his thoughts as follows:

> As I reflect on my work over the past two decades, I recognize that there are two critical differences between how teachers and academic researchers understand the activity of teaching. The first difference lies in how teaching is formulated: how knowledge about teaching is perceived, discovered, and structured. This involves how pieces of information and principles of action are logically and conceptually related to one another so that they may be applied to an understanding of practice. The second lies in how knowledge about teaching is determined: how it is verified or proved. . . . Events do not

become significant merely because they occur but only when they are noted and organized into a coherent pattern. (pp. 295–296)

Bolster recommends that we become researchers with regard to our own behavior, that we must learn how to behave scientifically. To detect the extent to which our behavior is changing, we must correctly select what and how to evaluate. This chapter provides a variety of ways to evaluate your collaboration, a practice that is closely related to overall assessment strategies (e.g., Angelo, 1991; McLoughlin & Lewis, 2005; Spinelli, 2006). The evaluation method must be linked to the central goal of your collaborative effort to have real value. Changes that are externally observable may also have private dimensions. For example, keeping track of an increase in the number of suggestions made or a decrease in the number of confusing questions asked are good, clear objective measures. However, using those measures alone would be insufficient if you are also trying to become more confident.

In a study by Martin (1988), changes involved both behavior and outlook. She describes the culmination of a collaborative problem-solving effort involving a group of teachers. Linda, the collaborating special education teacher, not only increased the number of suggestions accumulated but also changed her attitude:

> As the day's notekeeper, I was recording all the suggestions, along with the whole proceedings . . . but Linda was also writing down the suggestions. As she responded to each one and realized that there were possibilities that had not been tried and might make life easier in the classroom and more productive for Mario, Linda's mood visibly changed. Instead of the pained, hopeless expression she had started with, there was now energy, enthusiasm, and liveliness. (p. 498)

In this situation the teacher was visibly optimistic in her classroom. If another person had been recording evidence of change, documenting nonverbal evidence of mood change would have shown the differences described above. Evidence might have included her appropriate, animated facial cues and open body language. All might have been used as evidence to show increased investment in the collaborative process. Lawler (2003) describes principles of adult learning that can be incorporated into the context for problem solving: "Create a climate of respect, encourage active participation, build on experience, employ collaborative inquiry, learn for action, and empower the participants" (pp. 17–19). In setting the stage for the collaborative problem-solving activity, teachers in the school could have made use of these principles to support each other and share ideas.

However, in the project you are developing, you may not always be able to rely on another person to collect data. Self-monitoring has been used to document change in the consultation process (Tindal, Parker, & Hasbrouck, 1992). When in collaborative settings, you often have to creatively expand typical assessment approaches (Cramer, 1994). In this chapter, you will learn many different ways to keep track of changes. This chapter provides strategies for evaluating your own behavior that do not require an unrealistic amount of time or paperwork.

Paperwork is disliked not just by special educators but by general educators as well. Greathouse, Moyer, and Rhodes-Offutt (1992) asked 42 elementary school teachers to list the factors that contributed to job dissatisfaction. They ranked "too much paperwork" as their second choice, after "problems with administrators" (p. 44). Both of these problems can be overcome in your collaboration project. When thinking about how to overcome problems you may face with your administrators, try to consider the challenges administrators face. McGhee and Nelson (2005) provide three powerful descriptions of the challenges administrators faced in relation to the challenges of "the culture of accountability" (p. 367). Using materials provided in Chapters 6 and 7, you designed a plan with objectives and activities to help you improve your collaboration with your target person. In this chapter, you will learn how to evaluate your activities.

OBJECTIVE MEASURES OF CHANGE

How can you determine whether change has taken place? Project planners must train themselves to look at familiar situations in new ways, as the teacher in the following example did.

> *I never thought about how to look at my own behavior because I was convinced the problems were all hers. As far as I was concerned, I could just "grin and bear it." But when I started my collaboration project, I analyzed my baseline data. I had to be honest and admit that not everything I did was appropriate. I had to come to terms with the fact that I wasn't the good role model I thought I was.*
>
> *But I was sure that I could clean up my act. I was motivated to get started and see what kinds of changes I could make. As I implemented my plan and the data showed that I was becoming more consistently appropriate, I knew for sure I was improving. This data collection process helped me to identify behaviors I never thought I exhibited and helped me change my ways. Unless I'd seen it in black and white, I never would have believed it.*

The targets of observation can include both of the following: (1) independent efforts in which you change your preparation habits or attitude before or following your interactions with your target person, and (2) behaviors occurring when you interact directly with your target person.

Baseline data. As with all data collection, make sure that you collect baseline data (lasting three or four days) before carrying out any of the activities of your collaboration project. Data collection should be directly linked to each of your project objectives and should assess the effectiveness of each of your activities.

Focus your evaluation on yourself. The focus of your collaboration effort (and your data gathering) is on yourself. As discussed in Chapter 3, the opportunity to reflect on your own behavior, both productive and counterproductive, can give you much insight into the problems that other people (e.g., the target person in your plan) may be facing when trying to change behaviors. Keeping the focus on yourself is not always easy. The following comments may sound familiar.

> I knew that this project was to change my behavior and I had to keep focused on myself. I realized I had to do such things as analyze and critique my own skills, identify the behavior I was trying to change, and formulate plans to

measure change in my behavior. The primary problem I faced was keeping the focus on me. Finally, with that idea embedded in my mind, I was able to construct plans and observation criteria with an eye toward making this plan as positive as possible. (Falkowski, 1992)

The mental switch, moving from focusing on the other person as the problem source to yourself as the potential problem solver, is one that continues to be a challenge throughout the collaboration project. But, as in the following description by a new teacher who completed a collaboration project, a changed mindset can lead to increased possibilities and satisfaction:

A major turning point for me was when I began to understand how much control I had over the situation. I was right in the sense that the teachers would come to respect me as a peer if I gave them enough time. What I hadn't realized was that my own insecurities were building the walls that made the process slow and unsatisfying. As I implemented my project activities, I "found" my sense of humor again, actively implemented my objectives, and let my actions speak for themselves while being myself. (Harter, 1994)

Like Harter, you may find new ways to more confidently share parts of yourself as you implement your project goals and objectives. However, you want to make sure that you collect evidence to determine whether change is taking place. A wide range of evaluation strategies used to measure change are provided below.

Modified Communication Strategies and Initiation Patterns

The ability to communicate effectively is an important component of successful collaboration. West and Cannon (1988) identified it as a competency area receiving one of the highest ratings for collaborators. Other researchers have made similar observations (Bosworth, 1994; Darling-Hammond, 1999; Dettmer, Thurston & Dyck, 2002; Friend & Cook, 2002; Pugach & Johnson, 2002). If you want to focus on improving communication, you can use the following statements as potential targets of evaluation:

1. Communicate clearly and effectively in oral and written form.

2. Utilize active listening and responding skills to facilitate the process.

3. Interview effectively to elicit information, share information, explore problems, set goals and objectives.

4. Give and solicit continuous feedback that is specific, immediate, and objective.

5. Give credit to others for their ideas and accomplishments.

6. Manage conflict and confrontation skillfully throughout the process to maintain collaborative relationships (West & Cannon, 1988, pp. 59–60).

Each of these competencies can be used as the focus for improved communication in your collaboration project. For example, to achieve the first objective many project planners find that they have to switch their strategy away from making statements and move to asking questions, as shown in Figure 8.1.

This switch to asking questions, although difficult, has great potential rewards. As one project planner explained, weekly meetings changed from a superficial exercise to a meaningful exchange of information.

> In the beginning, our meetings were extremely brief. The relationship between the two of us was relatively new and still uncomfortable. The collaborating was done at a surface level. We discussed goals for the following week, focused on the students' IEPs. As time went on, our meetings became longer and more beneficial. The feeling of comradeship was strengthening. We started to use the meetings to develop individual plans for students that covered more than the basic needs of the IEP. I started to become more open and accepting of other ideas she brought up. (Piwowarczyk, 1994)

This project planner changed both the frequency and type of comments made while working with the co-teacher who was the target of her collaboration project. She was pleased to get the following unexpected corroboration of her efforts from a colleague who was unaware of her project.

> In the fourth week of my project, I was having lunch with a colleague who was also on my list of consults. She chose this particular time to share with me how delighted she was with my new style of consulting. She felt that I was more open to ideas and that my consulting efforts were greater than during the previous year. I was delighted with her perception. It gave me greater confidence that the changes were effective because they were noticeable to others. (Piwowarczyk, 1994)

In addition to the results she was charting, Piwowarczyk reported on feedback from another teacher. The unsolicited comments served to confirm the results she obtained from her other evaluation methods. Both assured her that she was successfully accomplishing West and Cannon's competencies 2 and 3.

Keeping Track

In Figure 8.1, the project planner was keeping track of the different types of interactions she and her target person had during their weekly meetings. Here are some different ways that you can keep track of information patterns you are trying to change:

1. *During a meeting.* Choose a particular mark or word that will represent each type of communication that you are monitoring. In your meeting notes, use one corner of your note-taking page to record the mark or word. While this may be difficult at the outset, you will become more proficient over time.

2. *In your classroom or in your building.* Focus on a single type of data to collect at a given time (e.g., to increase the number of positive comments made to your target person). Wear clothing with two pockets. Count out a specific number of paper clips and place them in one of your pockets. As you make the intended comments, move a paper clip from the full pocket to the empty one. At the end of the encounter, record the number of moved paper clips. (When you get familiar with

Figure 8.1 Communication Patterns

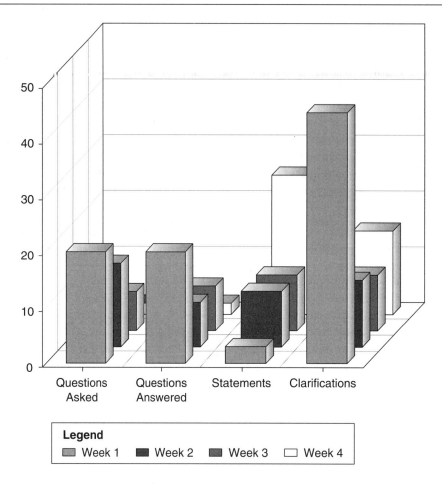

this strategy, you can use different kinds of paper clips to represent particular communication strategies you are trying to increase.)

3. *In a social setting or in the lunchroom.* Place a number of food items (e.g., pretzels, pieces of popcorn, pieces of candy, M&Ms) in front of you, and count how many you have. Eat one each time you accomplish the behavior you are trying to increase, as shown in the following situation.

I was having a very hard time contributing at faculty meetings. Whenever I got myself to say something, I was much more tentative than I meant to be. I decided to concentrate on decreasing my tentative comments and increasing my confident suggestions. I put 20 green M&Ms in my left pocket to represent the tentative comments and 20 red ones in my right pocket to stand for the kind of suggestions I wanted to make. I ate the appropriate one after each comment I made. That way, I kept track of what I was doing by the M&Ms left in my pocket at the end of the meeting. By the end of the project, I both felt and sounded more confident.

Learn to collect data. When you compare what you *think* is happening with what is *actually* happening, you can see how effective your strategies are. Idea Try-Out 8.1 will help you to get started.

Idea Try-Out 8.1

M&Ms

This Idea Try-Out will give you a way to find a data collection approach that works for you.

1. Look over the three suggestions described above for recording changes in communication patterns.

2. Think about a recent situation in which you tried to change your communication patterns. In your collaboration notebook, list three or four advantages and disadvantages of each strategy used in the situation you selected.

3. Select the strategy that you think would be most successful for you to use in a similar situation in the future.

Each situation you want to evaluate will have unique features. A quick review of options for data collection, as Try-Out 8.1 enables you to do, helps you match your situational requirements to the most appropriate evaluation technique. The more experience you have matching techniques to situations, the more automatic the whole process will become. Harter (1994) was a beginning teacher when she did her project. She wanted to initiate more often as well as feel more comfortable in the school lunchroom, a place she avoided. The lunchroom was a convenient place to use the "edible" data gathering approach. She monitored herself on Thursdays for nine weeks. She limited her self-monitoring to one day per week to look for improvement and yet not feel too self-conscious every day of the week. She went from an average of three initiations to an average of eight. At the outset her total number of interactions was much higher than the interactions about which she had positive feelings. For example, on the third Thursday she had a total of ten initiations, but she only gave positive ratings to two. By the end of the project, all initiations were rated as positive.

Many project planners are very nervous when starting any kind of collaboration effort. The start of the project is very similar to the stages Moir describes for first-year teachers: anticipation, survival, disillusionment, rejuvenation, reflection (Moir, 1996, pp. 25–26). At the start of a project, or during the first year of teaching, you will need to learn how to relax and stay focused. Relaxation strategies (such as deep breaths required before interacting with the target person) can be used as one of your strategies and monitored objectively. One project planner describes how she paid attention to her physical tension and the strategies she used to become calmer:

In the beginning, I had to spend a few moments preparing myself to approach her. I remember driving to work in the mornings and reminding myself to pay attention to my body language. I would take deep breaths before entering the room in which we were meeting. The first couple of times that I did it, it seemed to take a lot of energy. I would sit down if she was sitting down, stand if she was standing, relax my facial muscles, relax my shoulders, keep my arms from folding by holding on to something, keep my feet flat on the floor and smile often as we spoke. As I got further into the project, I began doing these things instantly without thinking about it. By the end of the project I found that I was not feeling nervous or anxious about our meetings. (Paul-Saladino, 1994)

Each of these strategies could be monitored. Figure 8.2 illustrates a simple tabulation of deep breaths used to prepare for meetings.

A different approach to self-assessment can be accomplished using an existing instrument that focuses on communication skills you want to change. Generalized queries can help you observe problems and problem solving. For example, Rutkowski, Vogel, van Genuchten, Bemelmans, and Favier (2002) report on multiple projects from different national cultures working in virtual teams. They incorporated technology to overcome social challenges. Their observation regarding technological challenges was that "continuous communication can usually avoid confrontation and resolve conflicts" (p. 225).

A more focused approach was used by Ludlow, Faieta, and Wienke (1989) in their pilot practicum project to train teachers to supervise other teachers. The researchers identified behaviors that were to be included in supervisory conferences. Their survey instrument included very specific items in the "Observation," "Feedback," and "Evaluation" categories that might be the basis of your self-assessment. Use of an

Figure 8.2   Deep Breaths to Stay Calm

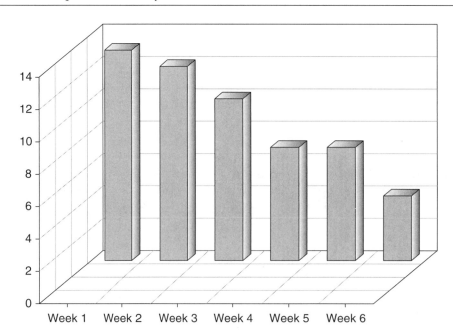

instrument designed for another purpose could highlight communication items you want to include in your own situation, such as the survey developed by Richards, Hunley, Weaver, and Landers (2003). The survey designed by Ludlow et al. (1989) could provide you with a format to use during conferencing. The focus in this type of approach is not on the interaction between the collaborators but on the types of communication items that you choose to assess.

Sheridan (1992) developed a survey to measure change in the perceived effectiveness and benefits of consultation services by subjects (student teachers and inservice teachers) in her study. The following sample of items that Sheridan incorporated into her survey might give you ideas for your self-assessment: "easy to work with; good listener; offered useful information; respected different values; provided moral support; able to see complexities of problem situation; able to see other alternatives" (p. 264).

The use of tracking systems may fit some or all of the objectives in your project. However, in other cases, you may want to monitor increasing some behaviors while decreasing others simultaneously. The following section may help you to achieve this goal.

Modified Ratio of Positive to Negative Efforts

When they look at their situations, some project planners realize that they are not approaching their colleagues as they imagined. Like the vision analogy presented at the start of this chapter, their perceptions of themselves are out of focus. As one project planner who was also a veteran teacher explains, his view of his work with his paraprofessional changed dramatically because of the project:

> Prior to this project, I was unaware that my actions and behaviors caused conflict between my target person and me. At the start of this project, I was very firm and tough-minded. I believed that if my target person could not comply with my requests, he should hear from me. Developing a better understanding of myself through self-assessment activities made it easier for me to modify my approach, decreasing the number of confrontations between us. I forced myself to be optimistic and this change proved beneficial. (Barberio, 1995)

This project planner specifically focused on increasing the number of positive comments while decreasing the number of negative comments. He was very satisfied with the results.

The self-study process is one that teachers can use to rely on themselves. Carter and Doyle (1995) recommend that teachers use personal narrative as a way to vividly describe their experiences. As Carter and Doyle explain,

> It is quite useful . . . to encourage novices to create metaphors that they feel capture their understandings of teaching. Typical examples of metaphors that novices devise include Circus Master, Air Traffic Controller, Trail Boss, [and] Talk-Show Host. As these examples suggest, novices' metaphors often express concerns for the managerial aspects of teaching. (p. 191)

Observe people you believe to be effective communicators, or talk with people you think are comfortable with communication. Mullinix (2002) described the use of "ongoing dialogue groups ... [that] serve as excellent support mechanisms for collaborative reflection and shared learning" (p. 4) as a strategy used by mentors—it is one that you can adapt for your own purposes with this project.

The objective method—documenting the objective ratio of positive to negative efforts—can document more complex descriptions of behaviors that teachers want to increase or decrease. For example, a project planner might begin by operationally defining "Trail Boss" in terms of sharing opinions assertively but appropriately. The evaluation format could consist of a chart that shows increased "Trail Boss" behaviors and decreases in the demanding, no-nonsense behaviors of the "Air Traffic Controller." You may decide to use a published survey like the one in White and White's 1992 article. They incorporated a Collaborative Teaching Survey developed by the Cobb County School District in Cobb County, Georgia to select teachers to participate in their study. A survey like this might be modified for your project.

Another way to approach a change in focus (e.g., from negative to positive) is to do a frequency count of negative and positive comments made to the target person. In some situations, it is possible to get help doing this count. For example, a teacher or paraprofessional who is aware of your collaboration project might be able to keep track along with you of how much of a change you are making. An example of this kind of comparison is shown in Figure 8.3.

When you select a behavior to monitor, target a specific time of day for data collection. It is recommended that you select a time of the day when interactions are generally more positive (e.g., during a team meeting, at a faculty meeting, or a casual conversation during lunch). You can later generalize to times that are more difficult (e.g., at a controversial CSE meeting or when trying to resolve a difference of opinion regarding a student). Give yourself a running start to help accomplish your objective more quickly by picking an easier time during which to collect data.

Figure 8.3   Negative Comments at the Start of the Day

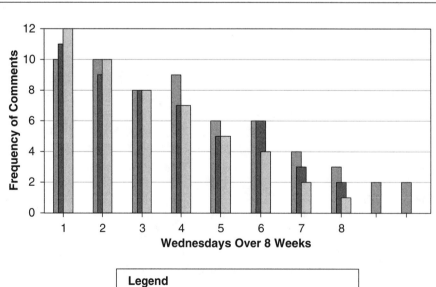

Figure 8.4   Frustrating vs. Successful Interactions

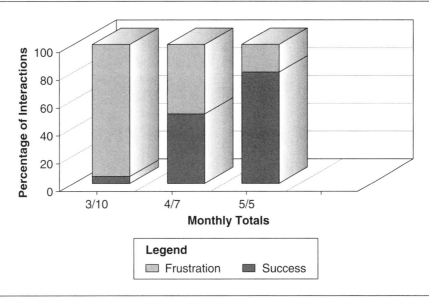

SOURCE: Griffo, 1995

Some project planners find that classifying episodes (e.g., those that have outcomes that are frustrating versus those that are successful) is a useful way of detecting change. They are able to tell whether there has been a shift away from negative and toward more positive communication. Griffo (1995) illustrates how this classification can be reported by focusing on her own subjective assessment, as shown in Figure 8.4.

Griffo rated each interaction to achieve the following objective: "I will keep track of my own feelings toward Taylor and note changes as they occur."

Smith (1994) used a more objective approach. She counted her actual comments and reported on the total number of positive and negative comments over six meetings. Her recording is shown in Figure 8.5.

You may decide to use a recording method to track changes in the ratio of your comments. You will have to decide which of the approaches described in this section is right for you.

These strategies can enable project planners to evaluate themselves systematically. None of the methods takes an inordinate amount of time, and all lead to objective evidence of change. Some projects may need to move away from exclusively self-oriented change and broaden the focus to include other communication patterns. This type of approach is discussed in the next section on sharing information about job goals and professional roles.

Professional Information Sharing

Professionals in school settings often take a great deal for granted when developing effective working relationships. For example, many teachers and their paraprofessionals never formally discuss the expectations each has for the other. Sorsby (2004) made the following observations:

Figure 8.5   Positive and Negative Comments

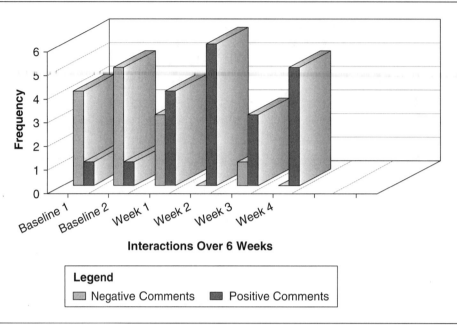

SOURCE: Smith, 1994

Over the course of my career it has concerned me that teams of workers in mainstream schools, frequently referred to as the "non-teaching staff" or the "child care assistants," are routinely undersupported. Some have . . . qualifications whereas others possess few formal academic qualifications. Nonetheless, these colleagues often have obvious talents in child care, psychology, behavior management or developing communication skills which they demonstrate daily by getting straight to the heart of any problem and coming up with practical solutions. (pp. 48–49)

Sorsby, when she became a supervisor, did much to examine the needs of these individuals and also to change the opportunities available to them in her setting. Sorsby's observations would be relevant in many other settings. Sometimes, job descriptions do not exist for paraprofessionals. Lindeman and Beegle (1988) reported on the differences between actual and expected job roles of paraprofessionals. Lack of agreement between actual and expected roles would lead inevitably to failure to meet expectations. McKenzie and Houk (1986) provided a method for selecting, training, and placing paraprofessionals that included a way to evaluate teacher and paraprofessional skills. Fletcher-Campbell (1992) describes elements of good practice for classroom assistants. Using guidelines in articles such as these can help teachers and paraprofessionals make their expectations explicit. (See discussion of developing role descriptions in Chapter 5.) Doyle (2002) published a workbook containing forms for teachers and paraprofessionals to use together to clarify roles and plan classroom routines.

A comparison of actual and expected job roles might be part of your collaboration project. It could be evaluated in several different ways:

- whether the discussion of role expectations takes place as planned;
- a letter grade given by you and the other person for the process you used to evaluate your roles;
- a letter grade for whether follow-up activities take place as planned.

Evaluation does not have to be complicated. Be sure to evaluate both objective and subjective aspects of the discussion.

Another area of concern for professionals seeking to improve their working relationship is that often they are missing information about the students with whom they are working. For example, teachers find that they are not always told about students who have histories of abuse. The needs and fears of these students make them particularly hard to reach. It is possible for colleagues to improve their working relationships by sharing articles on topics about the students they serve (e.g., Crozier & Sileo, 2005 on encouraging positive behavior through social stories; Montgomery, 2005 on involving families more actively in their children's education; Ulrich & Bauer, 2003 on creating better communication between professionals and family members; Mulack, Cohen, & Teets-Grimm, 1992 on providing help to children and youth at risk; Parette & McMahan, 2002 on assistive technology; Curwin, 1995 on reducing violence in schools; Willett & Singer, 1991 on student dropouts; and Wheldall, 1991 on classroom management). In some cases, entire issues of popular journals can be devoted to the topic of collaboration (e.g., Vol. 36, Issue 5 of *Teaching Exceptional Children*. See Peck & Scarpati, 2004 for an overview of the articles included). Information sharing on topics of professional concern can be evaluated using a slightly modified version of the structure presented above:

- whether the discussion of the professional topic takes place as planned;
- a letter grade given by people involved for the process you used to look at the topic;
- a letter-grade rating of the articles or materials you used to supplement your discussion;
- a letter grade for whether follow-up activities take place as planned.

You can prepare yourself for a professional discussion like this using Project Try-Out 8.2.

Project Try-Out 8.2

Professional Information Sharing

This Project Try-Out will give you an opportunity to investigate a topic of interest that might help you to expand your expertise in relation to your target person.

1. If you are currently involved with students, select a topic that you and your target person have mentioned regarding one of your students. If you are not currently involved with students, select a topic that follows up on something you and your target person have discussed.

2. Use your library to find two articles on the topic. You can use one of the articles in the References section of this book or conduct your own search. Key words that you may want to use are collaboration, teachers—training of, interprofessional relations, education—social aspects, multicultural education, special education, teamwork.

3. Make two copies of each article.

4. Plan a time to meet with your target person to discuss them.

5. Get together in a comfortable location and share your reactions to the articles. Identify one idea that is triggered by your sharing and agree to take action on it in your school or community.

6. At the end of your discussion, jointly evaluate your entire effort, using one of the evaluation methods provided in this chapter.

The approach used in Project Try-Out 8.2 gave you a chance to look at how professional information sharing can help you objectively consider your efforts. However, sometimes discussion alone is not enough.

In some cases, mentoring or peer coaching can be incorporated into your collaboration project. Mentoring has the oldest origins, as described by Cummins (2004):

> The first concept of a *mentor* may have come from ancient Greece, when Odysseus was planning for a long journey away from his family. Odysseus felt great concern for his family, especially for his son Telemachus, for it was traditional to provide young males with daily guidance in the virtues of strength and wisdom. Odysseus therefore asked his friend Mentor to provide Telemachus with guidance, teaching him about the world and how to be courageous, strong, and compassionate towards others. (p. 255)

Today, mentoring takes many forms. In Minnesota, an e-mentoring program connects new teachers with National Board Certified teachers—a type of assistance that Odysseus never could have imagined. An excellent overview of mentoring is provided by Mertz (2004) in his article "What's a mentor, anyway?" He distinguishes, via a hierarchy, the difference between a "peer pal" and a mentor (p. 551, Figure 1). Young, Alvermann, Kaste, Henderson, and Many (2004), in their pooled case comparison of mentoring relationships, found that friendship did appear to be a feature of the mentoring relationships studied, in that "both the mentor and mentee are aware of what the other has to offer and both are changed and shaped due to the other's contribution" (p. 34).

Mentoring and peer coaching are distinguished from each other in that mentoring is generally viewed as an asymmetrical relationship: one person (the mentor) has more experience than the other (the mentee). Donegan and Ostrosky (2000) distinguish between two peer coaching models, the expert and reciprocal. An example of the expert model would be asking an individual with in-depth knowledge to serve as a resource for you as you work on improving your collaborative relationship. In a reciprocal peer coaching relationship, a teacher who has knowledge about technology but limited understanding of behavior management techniques might spend time with a teacher whose behavior management strategies are varied and creative. Technology skills might be shared along with behavior management techniques. Characteristics of the mentor relationship were outlined by Jacobi (1991) in Clark, Harden, and Johnson (2000) as follows:

> First, mentor relationships are helping relationships designed to assist the protégé in achieving long-term, broad goals. Second, mentoring contains components related both to career and professional development and to psychological and emotional support. Third, mentor relationships are reciprocal in that the mentor as well as the protégé benefit from the interaction. Fourth, mentor relationships are personal. Fifth, within the mentoring dyad, it is the mentor who has the greater professional experience, influence, and achievement. (p. 263)

Studies have examined mentoring relationships to determine the extent to which the perception that they are of value is borne out. Clark et al. (2000) examined mentoring relationships of 787 recent graduates of doctoral programs, 521 (66%) of whom had a faculty mentor during their training. Mentoring provided acceptance, support, and encouragement for the mentees, and they observed that "students who initiate mentor relationships are most likely to be mentored" (p. 267). Cummins (2004) paired 10 teacher education adults enrolled in early childhood programs at a community college with beginning professionals in school settings. She observed significant improvements in mentoring skills, conversation strategies relevant to mentoring, and in understanding the role of the mentor, of adult learning styles, and of the developmental stages of first-year teachers (p. 256). The participation in the mentoring process can benefit the mentors as well as those who are being mentored.

The type of training the mentors receive can directly influence what they say and do in their mentoring exchanges. In their study of 16 veteran teachers paired with beginning teachers who had been taught to use the Cognitive Coaching model (Costa & Garmston, 1993, 1994), Strong and Baron (2004) found that there were very few direct suggestions (10 instances in 30 hours of recorded mentor conversations). They interpreted these results to reflect the power of the coaching model:

> Above all cognitive coaching emphasizes the development of trust between mentor and teacher, the engagement of the teachers' higher cognitive functions, and the development of teachers' cognitive autonomy. The mentors are trained to promote thinking and elicit ideas from the teachers . . . These features of the mentors' training may go a long way toward explaining our findings. (p. 53)

They conclude that "further study with mentors and teachers from other programs is called for in order to determine whether these patters are typical" (p. 55), supporting further research activities focusing on mentoring.

Lease (2004) found that neither race nor academic institution influenced the relationship of mentoring to career-making difficulties experienced by 433 (180 African American and 253 white; 294 women and 139 men) students from eight different colleges and universities (p. 243). If you are able to establish a relationship with a mentor, you may approach this project with more confidence (e.g., Prince, 2004). Mentoring can continue beyond the timeframe or setting for which it was originally established. For example, in Milner and Bossers' study (2004), follow-up with 14 of the original 124 students in the study who had been mentored in college revealed that contact with mentors continued for 8 of the students after graduation. Use of the collaboration resource network (discussed in Chapters 5 and 6) can also assist you.

If your focus is professional information sharing, you and your target person might be able to exchange ideas on areas of mutual interest via peer coaching. Peer coaching has appeared in the special education literature since the early 1980s (Joyce & Showers, 1980, 1982) and is also referred to as *reciprocal team coaching* (Ackland, 1991; Lambert, 1995). Recent publications (e.g., Allen & LeBlanc, 2004) continue to refer to this strategy as "peer coaching." Peer coaching consists of two distinct phases. The first is a training period during which the peers learn how to provide coaching. This period is followed by a coaching cycle in which teachers participate in a "mutual examination of appropriate use of a new teaching strategy" (Showers, 1985, p. 44). Reciprocal team coaching is further defined as

> an interactive process, one in which two or more teams of educational colleagues coach each other. Unlike some other forms of coaching, the relationships entailed in this approach . . . are truly reciprocal—systematic exchanges between co-equal partners that are designed to result in powerful learning for all participants. (Lambert, 1995, p. 20)

Both forms of coaching use a structured format to foster constructive dialogue about teaching.

Coaching has the benefit of overcoming some of the isolation that teachers often experience (and which Little, 1990 describes in detail). Su (1990) traces this isolation back to the training of teachers:

> Teacher candidates are not encouraged by their programs to develop a strong peer culture. By design and by default, great numbers of future teachers are being socialized into the belief and practice that teaching is largely an isolated and individualistic activity, rather than a shared enterprise. (p. 727)

Coaching is a way to overcome the isolation and also to share professional ideas. In their review of the history of peer coaching, Showers and Joyce (1996) identify a principle of peer coaching relevant to your project: "The collaborative work of peer coaching teams is much broader than observations and conferences" (p. 15). Peer coaching can be a vehicle by which you put your strategies for collaboration into practice. Donegan and Ostrosky (2000) provide five guidelines for establishing a peer coaching program:

1. Select the right model of peer coaching to fit the staff.

2. Develop a positive, trusting relationship between the participants.

3. Adapt peer coaching programs to teachers' needs, interests, desires, and abilities.

4. Help teachers select times to implement interventions.

5. Expect day-to-day variations when change is occurring. (pp. 14–15)

These guidelines can assist you as you establish a successful peer coaching relationship.

"What will we talk about?" you may wonder. Use the articles selected in Project Try-Out 8.2 as a basis for your coaching. Mello (1984) used "instructional methods" as the basis of discussions that "peer observation teams" (three or four teachers) had; these teachers provided information and support to each other. Discussing controversial articles (e.g., Shanker, 1995) can spark debate and allow you to participate in energized conversations.

Other studies describe the benefits of different types of coaching; there are many different ways to use the strategy. Showers (1985) reports on how peer coaching helps to increase teacher skills and use of new strategies. In his review of studies of peer coaching, Ackland (1991) looks at the benefits of reciprocal coaching overall, listing 18 studies that had different areas of focus for the coaching process. Garvey and Alred (2000) review mentoring as either an approach or a topic of study in higher education and outlines a program that can be incorporated into a school setting for teachers.

The opportunity to learn from a mentor while in your teacher preparation program may enable you to incorporate coaching into your own school setting. Zelaieta (2004) described the benefits that "mutual partnership" provided for teachers in her study and recommended that future partnerships include "collaborative approaches to curriculum planning and teaching" as well as "good liaison between all parties involved" (p. 46).

You may be able to set up a team that includes both your target person and members of your collaboration resource network. In so doing, you may be able to see your target person interact in new ways with different people. This may give you some new insights about the individual. In some cases, you can make use of existing structures to give/get coaching. For example, the group of student teachers examined by Beck and Kosnick (2002) valued the feedback and emotional support provided by their mentors (supervising teachers). You can evaluate the success of your coaching using the objective methods described previously or the subjective methods described in the following section.

SUBJECTIVE MEASURES OF CHANGE

Why can't you limit your evaluation to the objective evidence of change? There are several reasons:

1. Without examining subjective measures, you may be missing evidence of improvement. Even though your external behaviors may look very similar at the beginning and end of your project, you may have developed a new attitude toward your target person.

2. Unless you incorporate subjective methods into the beginning of your project, at the end you may be too close to the project to be able to tell whether things are really different. One of the most difficult things about the collaboration project is trying to determine whether you have *really* made any changes. The only way you can measure change is by setting up various evaluation strategies at the outset. These strategies would have to include objective behavioral changes. In addition, be sure to measure attitude changes that are (from your

point of view) the ultimate measure of successful collaboration with your target person.

3. Success may consist of new but subtle acceptance of your target person. It is important in constructing your total evaluation plan to make sure that you include ways to keep track of the subtle, subjective observations you make—about yourself, your work situation, and your target person. You can review them at the end of your project and discover your progress.

Many different techniques can be used to document your impressions of what has taken place. Standard data analysis procedures can be incorporated into your evaluation approach to find out whether change has occurred. Several different methods are provided below.

Content Analysis and Journal Entries

Many project planners find it extremely useful to maintain a daily journal or set of anecdotal records during their collaboration project. Even when entries are brief, they help project planners to reconstruct events that might otherwise be forgotten or distorted by memory. Look at the following entry from a student teacher's journal while taking baseline data before actually starting her project.

This was an especially chaotic day. Two of our students returned to our classroom unexpectedly. Their lessons in a regular fifth-grade classroom had been canceled, and the teacher forgot to notify us ahead of time. The time for our Science lesson with a regular fourth-grade class was changed at the last minute. Mrs. S., the teacher, needed me to make copies for a lesson she was about to teach. Then she was called out of the room by the school psychologist so she asked me to take over the lesson. I was very frustrated because we had no work planned for the two students who arrived unexpectedly, and we did not have copies for the lesson I was supposed to take over. I like organization and structure—this was a mess!

The journal entry gave the project planner a way to do several things: (1) practice promptly recording her perceptions, (2) get rid of her frustration, and (3) identify a very specific problem. Her journal entry showed that she needed to develop emergency materials and be prepared to use them. Contrast the above experience with her recording near the end of the project.

Another chaotic day! Events just like the ones that took place when I began my project were taking place, but this time I felt prepared. When our two boys arrived back from the fifth grade, I had a list of activities for them to work on. I also had a list of activities to use with the other students, so when Carol asked me to take over the class for a few minutes, I didn't have to wonder what I should do with the students. Instead of feeling frustrated, I felt very confident about having everything under control.

Although an objective assessment of "preparedness" would have illustrated some change, the vividness of the two episodes would not have been included. The change in referencing the target person, from last name to first, also would have been missing.

Another project planner reported on the benefits of the journal over other data collection techniques. Instead of waiting until the end of the project, the journal was used as an interim evaluation tool.

> The most helpful evaluation tool I used during my project was my journal. It enabled me to reflect back on my reactions and responses and also to take a look at my target person's negative behavior. One thing I wanted to keep track of was how my target person's behaviors affected me. I tried keeping track of this on a graph, but it was just too difficult. So, I kept track of it all in my journal.
>
> I divided my journal into two parts. One part was used as a diary. This is where I reflected back on the day, and rated how I felt the day went. The second part of the journal was where I wrote down my target person's negative behavior and the reactions it evoked in me. I also recorded the day of the week and the time of the day it occurred. I was very specific at the beginning of the project. This information was later used as a tool to see if I could change my behavior to avoid these situations in the future. Specifically, I wanted to see if I could reduce the number of times I got angry. (Lovejoy, 1994)

The project planner used the journal as the basis of a formative evaluation to categorize the types of episodes that were presenting problems (see Figure 8.6).

If the project planner was not sure which problem had the highest priority, or which occurred most frequently, a chart like Figure 8.6 might have been difficult to develop. Through the journal analysis, the project planner was able to target "minimizing anger" as her primary focus for the remainder of the project. Figure 8.6

Figure 8.6   Number of Angry Episodes

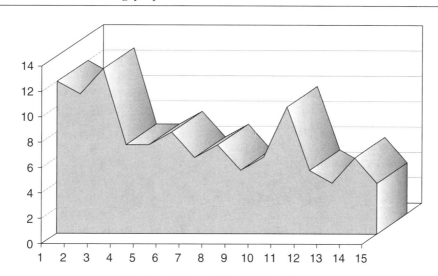

SOURCE: Lovejoy, 1994

shows her results after starting her project activities with that focus in mind. She describes how her outlook changed over the course of the project:

> This project was really a learning experience for me. I started off with very negative feelings about doing the whole thing. Then, as I started seeing some positive results, I began to realize that by changing my behavior I was capable of inspiring a change from someone else. (Lovejoy, 1994)

A different way to use a journal or anecdotal records is content analysis. This approach was defined by Berelson (1952) as a process by which the meaning of communication (written or oral) can be objectively and systematically depicted. The advantage of this approach is that it enables the project planner to benefit from insights gained throughout the course of the project. Content analysis can either be done through a patient analysis of themes or using computer tools such as SPSS Text Analysis for Surveys (2005). Johnson and LaMontagne (1993) describe the steps that can be used to address research questions. These research questions are generated after the implementation period has concluded to avoid biasing the effort. Ask questions such as the following:
Over the course of the project, did I

- become more tolerant of my target person?
- become more insightful about my own behavior?
- move the focus away from my target person and onto myself?

In a project like this one, journal entries are treated like a database. The project planner decides on the size of the unit of analysis (e.g., a single word, a sentence, or the description of an episode). As Johnson and LaMontagne (1993) recommend, the planner then "defines tentative categories for coding the responses . . . to combine thoughts that seem to address the same issue" (p. 75). You may, for example, count the number of sentences that are evidence of positive answers to the three research questions above. Most likely, you will need to refine your categories further. Then, convert your narrative into a chart; an example is Figure 8.7.

Make sure your questions are about the most important aspects of your project. One project planner, focusing on improving her working relationship with her paraprofessional, used two questions to form the basis for content analysis of her journal: "Did I set a more positive tone upon entering the classroom each morning?" and "Did I become less angry about his behavior as I learned more about him?" In both cases, there was evidence of improvement.

Another project planner used a combination of self-reminder and journal follow-up to keep track of her reactions to meetings with her target person.

> Another evaluative tool I used was a checklist of verbal and nonverbal reminders to fully prepare myself to begin an interaction with my target person. I documented each time I used the checklist with the date at the top of the list. Following each interaction, I wrote a brief narrative description of my perceptions and feelings before, during, and after the interaction. Through this subjective narration I was able to track specific feelings, reactions, and any changes I noticed in my behavior, along with observations of my target person's behaviors. I never really imagined that my relationship

Figure 8.7   References to Anger in Journal

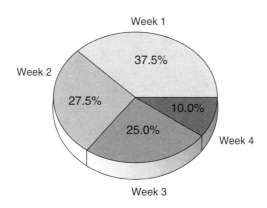

with my target person would have developed to the degree it has. I am so pleased with the changes that have occurred. (Paul-Saladino, 1994)

The journal, in combination with a strategy for becoming better prepared for meetings, enabled this project planner to make unexpected, welcomed changes in her collaboration with a difficult coworker.

Adjective Checklists: Taking Your "Emotional Temperature"

The adjective checklist, another method of gathering subjective data regularly, is quicker than the journal approach. While it does not yield as much data for review and analysis as the journal, it can help you to keep track of your subjective response to daily encounters with your target person. Here are several different ways to use this strategy:

1. *Daily Adjective/Adverb Generation.* Have a package of 3 × 5 index cards ready. If you'd like to make the cards distinctive, you can use a package with cards of different colors. You can match the card chosen each day to your mood. At the end of each day, select a card and do the following:
   a. List the first five adjectives or adverbs that come to mind to answer the question, "How was your day with (your target person)?"
   b. Circle the adjective or adverb to which you most strongly respond.
   c. Draw a box on your card. Inside it write or draw a brief description of your target person.
   d. Date the card. Put it in an envelope with all the other cards for your project.

At the end of the project, analyze the adjectives using questions generated by content analysis. Or, get a raw count of adjectives using categories (e.g., optimistic, pessimistic, open-minded, sarcastic) that are appropriate to your situation. Then, graph totals for each category on a weekly basis.

2. *Thesaurus-Generated Adjective Checklists.* Several times during the project, use a thesaurus program in a computer or a volume from your library to generate a "possibilities" adjective checklist. You can use this to describe your collaboration project. Be sure to include up to 20 words that represent a variety of adjectives and adverbs that appeal to you. For example, instead of limiting yourself to the word "friendly," you can include other words that are in the thesaurus: "generous," "helpful," "cooperative," and "supportive." Organize the page so that the synonyms for words are not next to each other but rather appear randomly around the page. Make five or six copies of your list.

At the end of each day, take out your checklist. Circle five to seven words that you think describe the way things went between you and your target person that day. Feel free to add words as you go along. Put a star beside the word to which you respond the most strongly. Date the sheet and put it in an envelope with the other checklists. When you get to the last sheet, you can either make a few more copies or develop a new one. Over the course of the project, you should try to develop three or four different adjective checklists—at least half of the words should be new. Your analysis of the adjective checklists can follow the same format as suggested for the daily adjective/adverb generation.

3. *Daily Subjective Rating.* There may be one aspect of your collaboration project that you want to use to sum up how you think things are going. This form of "emotional temperature taking" should not be the only subjective measure you use because it is so limited. However, it can be a quick, easy way for you to look back over each day to see how you felt. As shown in Figure 8.8, a single numerical rating selected daily can show a trend.

Figure 8.8   Daily Frustration Level
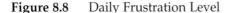
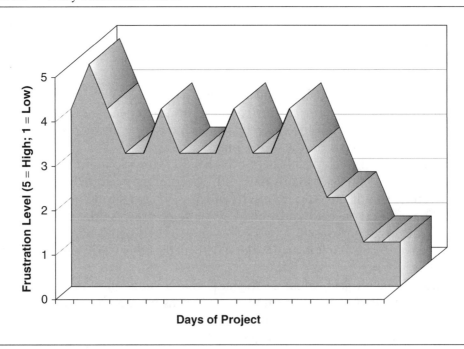

Together with your objective data, each of these personally developed subjective rating systems can enable you to get a thorough picture of the changes you achieved during your collaboration project.

4. *Collaboration Project Rating Scale.* An article by Richards et al. (2003) shares a 26-item rating scale developed by the faculty "based on a review of literature, course content, project guidelines/steps, and project goals" (p. 248). This scale is a useful example of the kinds of questions you might want to ask yourself during your collaboration project. You could adapt Richards et al.'s scale for your own use.

The difficulties experienced in interpersonal situations are often very elusive. Without the kinds of data collection described in this chapter, it is hard to know for sure whether changes have taken place. Richards et al. (2003) conclude their article with this advice: "Candidates needed a clearly outlined procedure around which to frame their collaboration and problem-solving efforts. . . . Another recommendation would be to more systematically collect data" (p. 248). Their suggestions are in line with the collaboration project on which you are currently working.

Looking to the Future

As you consider the kinds of collaboration activities you are involved in during this project, you may feel drained, as if the energy you are expending is extensive. Consider an alternative approach for use in the future: You can use critical incidents to examine an interpersonal relationship. Use your analysis of one or two incidents as the basis for a plan to modify your behavior. Griffin (2003) developed a Critical Incident form, based on David Tripp's work (Tripp, 1993), and pilot tested it over two semesters with 48 preservice teachers, collecting a total of 135 Critical Incidents. Analysis of these incidents by a two-person panel indicated that

> the use of Critical Incidents and related instructional activities increased one reflective ability of preservice teachers. Specifically, the data indicate an increase in the degree of orientation toward growth and inquiry, from concrete thinker to alert thinker. The Critical Incidents appeared to assist concrete thinkers to look beyond themselves and the immediate situation to larger, contextual issues. (p. 218)

Griffin's approach is an example of the kind of approach you can use in the future to scrutinize your experiences in an intense, focused way and to continue to be reflective. Idea Try-Out 8.3 was written by Professor Griffin for the second edition of this book.

Idea Try Out 8.3

Taking Reflection to the Next Level

This Idea Try-Out will give you the opportunity to link one of your collaborative experiences to professional standards, theory, and future professional activities. Record these steps in your collaboration notebook.

1. Select a collaborative experience that was amusing, confusing, an "aha," an "ouch," or a "hmmm." In your notebook, write up this incident in concrete terms (who, what, when, where, etc.). Avoid inferences or judgments. Ask yourself, "Would everyone involved in this experience be comfortable reading this?"

2. List the emotions you experienced as the incident unfolded (e.g., joy, confusion, sadness, anger). Did the level and type of emotion(s) change? If so, why do you think the change took place?

3. Describe why this incident happened from the perspective of each participant and how this incident affected each of its participants, including you, by using the word "I." Label each participant. For example: General Education teacher: "I. . . ." Me: "I . . ."

4. Generate a list of topics related to collaboration that this incident fits (e.g., professionalism, time management, technology, negotiation, problem solving). List as many as you can think of, then pick one that is most compelling to you.

5. Now, write a mini-paper of two or three paragraphs about the general meaning of that topic, using educational literature as resources. Your writing will have an explicit connection to theory and be related to the broad field of education, with citations. You will "bump up" your thinking from the particulars of the incident to reflection about its meaning in a broader context.

6. Determine which CEC knowledge, skills, and dispositions fit your incident and general meaning.

7. Develop a position statement about the general collaboration topic (step 5). Identifying what you, as an educator, hold to be true about its general meaning/significance; this statement will contain one or two personally held beliefs related to the topic. You can start this position statement with phrases such as "I believe" or " I think."

8. Now, based on the position you have taken, which is backed up by your scholarly description of its general meaning, describe two actions related to collaboration you will carry out in the future. These actions need to be measurable actions that can be seen or heard by an observer of your collaborative efforts.

CONCLUSION

Reid and Harris (1993) discuss characteristics of self-monitoring for special education students. Their recommendations apply to collaborating teachers who are attempting to do the kind of self-monitoring described in this chapter.

1. *Parsimonious.* Which teachers would not agree with the idea that they want to be "stingy" with the time devoted to self-monitoring? This recommendation supports that idea, recognizing that teachers want to design self-monitoring procedures that can be completed efficiently.

2. *Minimally obtrusive.* Typically, the project planner will be recording data in the presence of others. The approach may also have to be used while the planner

is involved in other activities. The suggestions provided in this chapter give a range of options for teachers to use without drawing attention to themselves or the data collection procedure.

3. *Appropriate to the target behavior.* As suggested throughout this chapter, evaluation methods need to be directly linked to objectives that are part of your collaboration project.

4. *Enjoyable.* Teachers would agree that this characteristic of self-monitoring is crucial for their students. It should not be dismissed for project planners. Some planners focus on the outcome of self-monitoring (e.g., positively reinforcing themselves for improvement via a preselected "reward" of a favorite food or a special activity). Others make the self-monitoring process itself pleasing. They may use a special pen, keep their self-monitoring logs in notebooks that have favorite pictures included, or use a time of the day that they reserve for themselves to review data trends. Suggestions for developing your own reinforcement program will be further discussed in Chapter 9.

5. *Relevant.* In designing self-monitoring, collaborating teachers need to make sure that they have been attentive to their own needs. For example, one project planner's self-monitoring of meeting behavior (on an index card) included the following features: number of times conversations were initiated, number of suggestions made, initiated successful closure, and an overall confidence rating (using a five-point scale). All these features were not needed by another project planner, who used stickers to self-monitor only the number of negative and positive comments made to the target person, along with a total rating for the week. For this second project planner, a three-point rating system ("bad," "just OK," "very good week") was sufficient.

In the end, you can design an evaluation model that works effectively for you. Be sure to keep your data charts in a protected place so they will not be accidentally discovered. Pick out both objective and subjective methods to use for evaluation and follow these guidelines:

- Be specific
- Link your evaluation methods to key collaboration project objectives
- Be realistic

Evaluation, unlike any other approach, can help you to determine how successful your project has been.

9

Self-Encouragement

Keeping Yourself Going

We've all had the same, unsettling experience. It can happen when we wake up in the middle of the night or get up in the morning. Our mind replays a recent event, and we see again, in vivid detail, something we did that we wish we could undo. The event could be trivial or significant. Either way, it is like a cartoon, in color, making us remember the episode in detail.

This chapter has been designed to help you put those moments into perspective. It will also enable you to savor times when you have been effective. When you are involved in a project like this one, inevitably there will be times to reconsider your behavior for many reasons. In this chapter, strategies are described that will enable you to be as proactive as possible throughout your project. You will learn several realistic, self-supportive strategies to use while putting your collaboration skills into practice.

The premise of this book is to maximize your sense of ownership when building an effective working relationship with another person. Your relationship exists in an environment filled with simultaneous demands. Honig and Hatch (2004), after examining the inundation of external demands individuals in schools face, conclude that "the best stewards of crafting coherence at the school and district levels may be those who can tolerate and navigate . . . highly collaborative and interdependent terrain" (p. 28). Those working in collaborative school environments come to develop their collaborative work styles in ways that foster joint effort and shared outcomes. As Idol and West (1991) suggest when looking at collaborative schools, "each . . . exudes a sense of individuality and uniqueness. This seems to create a sense of ownership and pride among faculty members that is essential to the collaborative spirit, and that is a powerful catalyst for effective schooling" (p. 78). Schools that promote collaboration rely on individuals to be personally motivated. It is only through this intrinsic, deeply felt motivation that the school can be a collaborative site.

211

Pugach and Johnson (2002) describe four roles for schoolwide collaboration, based on their earlier work (Johnson & Pugach, 1992)—"(1) Supportive role, (2) Facilitative role, (3) Informative role, (4) Prescriptive role" (p. 36)—and go on to describe how each of these roles plays a part in the school (pp. 36–40). Their descriptions imply an intrinsic foundation for collaboration.

Farnsworth and Morris (1995) provide recommendations for mentors, one of which is to be proactive. In Allen and Eby's (2004) study of mentoring using Noe's (1988) Mentor Functions Scales, there were no reported differences between formal and informal relationships: support and career advice were provided in both.

In Fowler and O'Gorman's 2003 study of 500 mentors and mentees, career development was one of the eight mentoring functions identified, along with personal and emotional guidance, coaching, advocacy, role modeling, strategies and systems advice, learning facilitation, and friendship. Duffy and Forgan's 2005 resource book, *Mentoring New Special Education Teachers*, provides a wealth of suggestions and resources for use in schools.

Campbell and Campbell (2000) examined mentoring relationships that were established on college campuses between faculty members and undergraduate students. Expectations for the benefits to mentors, although clear to the mentors, were not identified by 31% of the mentees. There were no differences related to gender or ethnic group of the mentors or mentees. Ehrich, Hansford, and Tennent (2004), in their analysis of over 300 research-based articles on mentoring in education, business, and medicine, found that "despite the shortcomings of mentoring, our findings suggest that mentoring appears to offer far-reaching benefits for mentors and mentees. Many of the reviewed studies indicated that mentoring provided both personal and emotional support as well as career development and satisfaction" (p. 531). In Minnesota, electronic mentoring was successfully used (NEA Today, 2004):

> With budget cuts, many districts have hired fewer new teachers and eliminated mentor programs, so many beginners no longer have access to an experienced teacher for help, says Sara Gjerdrum, manager of field services for Education Minnesota. E-mentoring provides the support to fill that gap. (p. 15)

You may not be fortunate enough to have either an in-person or electronic mentor available to you. How can you become your own mentor and incorporate "self-encouragement" throughout your collaboration project? It is not always easy to be proactive. This chapter presents three different approaches to provide you with necessary supports: self-talk, positive reinforcement for yourself, and self-observation. These strategies give you tools for use at different points in your collaboration project and throughout your teaching career.

SELF-TALK: THE CORNERSTONE FOR SELF-ENCOURAGEMENT OR SELF-DISCOURAGEMENT

How would a tape recording of conversations you have with yourself sound? According to Butler (1981) and Neck and Barnard (1996), inner conversations reflect our self-perceptions. We all "replay" events in our mind and try to imagine what will happen in the future. If we imagine negative rather than positive outcomes, we can impede our progress. Farnsworth and Morris (1995) suggest that one way to be proactive is to manage the thoughts that float into our heads. We can make choices about the inner reflections that are part of our inner stream of consciousness.

Voltz, Sims, Nelson, and Bivens (2005) raise questions about exchanging student information, collaborative problem solving, and collaborative teaching in an inclusive standards-based classroom. Questions concerning these issues might be going through your mind with answers like "She'll never do it" or "It's too late in the year" or "I don't have it in me." Neck and Barnard (1996) more directly address this problem. They suggest that "educators who bring their self-defeating self-talk to a level of awareness, and who rethink and reverbalize these inner dialogues, stand a good chance of improving their performance" (p. 25). Let's look at how this process might work.

Imagine the following. You are an experienced special educator working in a high school. It is Friday, and you have just completed a difficult Committee on Special Education (CSE) meeting. You, Jason (your student), Jason's family members, and the members of the multidisciplinary team spent two hours designing a complex program for the following academic year. For the most part, the meeting went well. Jason and Jason's family members asked and answered questions throughout the meeting. However, it was not perfect. There were a few points during the meeting when you, Jason's teacher, could have done a better job of drawing Jason out.

During your ride home, which of the following conversations would you most likely have with yourself?

Conversation 1

"I am such an idiot! Why did I stop Jason when he was just starting to talk about his post-graduation plans? I was too worried about getting the wording for next year's objectives just right and didn't want to listen to him talk about two years from now. That was a really important moment for him. When will I ever learn?"

Conversation 2

"I have to remember to help Jason work on his self-monitoring skills between now and the end of the school year. Otherwise, he may not make it next year. Then he would feel so defeated. It would be hard on everyone if he didn't get the most out of the next year."

Conversation 3

"I'm really proud of the way I handled that parent conference. There were a few times when I got stuck, but I relied on others to keep the ideas flowing. It was a good meeting. I'll have to review it with my team to see what we can improve next time."

These three conversations are very different responses to the same meeting. One way to compare them is to use Manz's (2003) distinctions for self-talk—*obstacle thinking* and *opportunity thinking*. Obstacle thinking reveals how individuals put problems or difficulties in the way of solutions, while opportunity thinking shows how individuals create options that might lead to solutions.

Conversation 1 is an example of obstacle thinking. It can be further defined using a category system of 10 types of dysfunctional thinking that Burns (1980) developed for self-talk. This conversation has two of these categories: "overgeneralization" and "labeling and mislabeling." When overgeneralizing, a person

> see[s] a single negative event [the failure to redirect the student] as a never-ending pattern of defeat [and concludes that the whole meeting was a failure]. Labeling and mislabeling is an extreme form of overgeneralization. Instead of describing your error, you attach a negative label to yourself. (p. 40)

The conclusion "I'm an idiot" falls into this category. During the drive home, the teacher is likely to become more defeated if this kind of self-talk continues.

Conversation 2 shows both obstacle and opportunity thinking. The obstacles that the teacher creates correspond to two more of Burns's dysfunctional categories, "magnifying and minimizing" and "personalization." The teacher exaggerates the potential importance of some things (Jason may not make the most of next year) while "inappropriately shrinking" (p. 40) the positive events that took place (a plan was developed that reflected input from all parties). When personalization takes place, "you see yourself as the cause of some negative external event which in fact you were not primarily responsible for" (p. 40). In this situation, the teacher takes the blame for what might happen (Jason might not develop the self-monitoring skills needed for next year) when the outcome could have many other causes (the plan may be overly ambitious, or Jason may not apply himself as much as he needs to).

On the other hand, the teacher identified some positive outcomes. Opportunity thinking is translated into constructive action. By developing a plan for action, the teacher is translating the meeting into outcomes.

Conversation 3 is undoubtedly rare. It shows opportunity thinking, in which the teacher feels unconditionally proud of a job well done. Though it makes sense to find ways to train ourselves to use opportunity thinking more often, it can be hard to do. However, the benefits of it are self-evident. In some collaboration projects, it can dramatically influence the outcome.

As shown in Figure 9.1, Tendorf's (1996) student project incorporated positive self-talk into his activities after completing the baseline period. He rated his job performance, allocating quality points for each two-week period. Tendorf found that the following strategy helped him to improve: "Before the work day begins, I will spend five minutes on positive thoughts relating to the day." These five minutes, combined with positive self-talk in his journal, enabled him to reframe his view of his work setting. Throughout his project, his overall quality rating was far above the baseline period, as shown in Figure 9.1.

Idea Try-Out 9.1 gives you a chance to examine your self-talk habits in the abstract. You may also find it useful to go to resources like the Voltz et al. (2005) article, which lists very specific strategies for collaboration, as they might assist you in developing ideas for countering some of your obstacle thinking with opportunity thinking. The following steps, adapted from those presented by Neck and Barnard (1996, p. 26), can help you strategically plan how to behave differently.

1. Observe and record your self-talk

2. Reflect on your observations
   a. Analyze the thoughts on which your self-talk is based by looking at how functional and constructive your thoughts are.

Figure 9.1   Interaction Patterns Using Self Talk

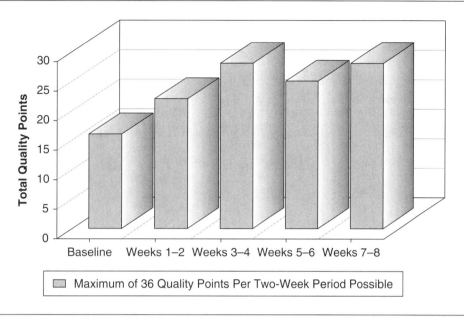

SOURCE: Tendorf, 1996

    b. For each self-talk sentence (or underlying thought) that is defeating, substitute a self-talk sentence or thought that is more functional or constructive.

  3. Change your actions
    a. Substitute your new, more constructive thoughts in difficult situations.
    b. Continue to monitor your self-talk and the accompanying, underlying thoughts.

Idea Try-Out 9.1 can help you get started. Although it is involved, it can help you analyze what to do to develop the strategies you need for more constructive inner dialogues. This exercise can enable you to get new, positive messages to yourself.

Idea Try-Out 9.1

Self-Talk Habits

This Idea Try-Out will help you review your self-talk habits and then modify them for your collaboration project.

    1. Adapt the following description to a situation in which you might find yourself at school, at work, or at home: You have nearly completed a major project on which you've worked long and hard. You realize that it could be even better if you had more time and more resources. It is due tomorrow. What would you

tell yourself as you worked on the final details? Record your answer in your collaboration notebook.

2. Adapt the following description to a situation in which you might find yourself at school, at work, or at home: You thought that you were making a friendly phone call to check up on something that had been promised to you two weeks ago. Instead, the person on the other end of the phone blames you for not calling back sooner to check up on everything. After you hang up, what would you tell yourself? Record your answer in your collaboration notebook.

3. Adapt the following description to a situation in which you might find yourself at school, at work, or at home: You are ready to apply for something big. You know that you meet the qualifications for the situation and you are ready for the challenges that the new situation would provide. Before you sit down to begin the application process, what messages would you give yourself? Record your answer in your collaboration notebook.

4. Review your answers and do the following:
   a. Underline the words or phrases that show examples of opportunity thinking.
   b. Draw a circle around the words or phrases that show examples of obstacle thinking.
   c. Comment on the pattern you observe in your collaboration notebook.

5. In the coming week, consider points in the collaboration project when you could try to shift your thinking toward opportunities and away from obstacles. Use Project Try-Out 9.2 to set up specific guidelines for yourself.

This reflection may have given you some insights into your mental discussions, which may lead to better approaches to challenging situations in the future. Working on automatically developing effective inner messages can help you approach challenging situations more constructively.

Overall, the habits you develop for self-talk may give you the messages you need to develop a more optimistic, pragmatic approach to the challenges of collaboration. However, constructive self-talk alone is not sufficient. In some cases, to maintain your momentum you may also need an explicit plan for positive reinforcement.

Project Try-Out 9.2

Self-Talk in Action

This Project Try-Out will give you an opportunity to think ahead to the coming week in your collaboration project and target one type of behavior for your revised self-talk habit using the three-step approach of Neck and Barnard (1996).

1. Pick a circumstance in the coming week when you will be interacting with your target person and you are likely to engage in defeating self-talk. Select "before," "during," or "after" the episode as the focus of this exercise.

2. Think about the circumstance you've selected and recent times that have been similar. From memory, complete Step 1 from Neck and Barnard's recommendations, "Observe and record self-talk," corresponding to this circumstance. Record the results in your collaboration notebook.

3. Complete Steps 2(a), 2(b), and 3(a) from Neck and Barnard's recommendations when interacting with your target person. Record the results in your collaboration notebook.

4. Before reviewing your records, create a believable self-talk sentence for yourself to use at the end of the review of your results.

5. Summarize your results and review what you need to do to address this issue between now and the end of your collaboration project. Record your ideas in your collaboration notebook. Then, review the sentence you just created.

6. Select a member of your collaboration resource network to discuss the results of this Project Try-Out and put your findings in perspective. Call the person to set up a time to meet, or talk on the phone to discuss the results.

7. At the end of your meeting/phone call, decide how to best accomplish Neck and Barnard's Step 3(b).

LOOKING FOR THE POSITIVES: POSITIVE REINFORCEMENT FOR YOURSELF

When designing an effective reinforcement program for their students, special education teachers automatically take into account the target behaviors to increase or decrease. In the case of your collaboration project, you should be able to identify the behavior that you want to change when working with your target person. Sometimes you will change your interaction pattern by increasing certain behaviors (e.g., in a collaboration project that focuses on assertiveness, you would increase the number of actual contacts you initiate with your target person), while other times you may decrease behaviors (e.g., you would, at the same time, want to decrease the number of times you avoid your target person). Some behaviors you select could be thought of either way—if you are trying to feel more at ease, you may plan to increase your comfort level or decrease your discomfort level.

Once you have selected the target behaviors you need to address, you can design an effective reinforcement program for yourself. Below is an example of a project that illustrates how self-reinforcement works.

SAMPLE PROJECTS INCORPORATING REINFORCEMENT

In Riggi's (1995) student project, she wanted to develop more communication (by initiating more interactions) with her agency's director. She also wanted to be able to feel more comfortable around the director. As she looked ahead, she realized that she would be struggling throughout the entire project. "I admit that whenever I have to change something, I first sit down and think of a million ways I could use that information before I change it." She decided to include some reinforcers in her project to keep herself going.

Riggi made sure that one of the members of her collaboration resource network gave her frequent verbal feedback: "I needed praise on how hard I was working on my project. Kathy, a member of my project resource team, gave that to me" (Riggi, 1995). That social reinforcer was very effective for her. It kept her going when she felt frustrated or discouraged.

As shown in Figure 9.2, Riggi increased the number of times she initiated conversation or questions with her director after the baseline period. Figure 9.3 illustrates her comfort level throughout the project, showing that overall her comfort level was greater than her discomfort level.

Figure 9.2 Contacts Initiated During Project

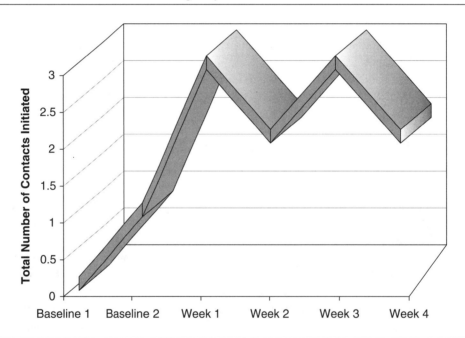

SOURCE: Riggi, 1995

Riggi selected a target behavior to increase—she wanted to increase her effort on the project. She also could have looked at a reinforcement program that focused on any of the following target behaviors:

1. Individual Progress
   a. Internal changes (e.g., changes in comfort level)
   b. External changes (e.g., changes in initiation levels)

2. Situational Changes
   a. Monitoring changes in other people in the situation (e.g., nonverbal and verbal responses from target person). Note: as long as you are not trying

Figure 9.3   Comfort Level During Contacts (Contact Analysis Technique)

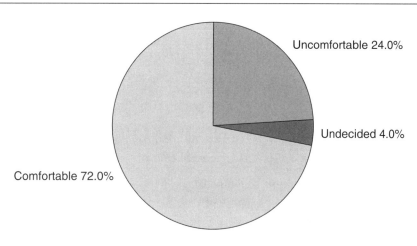

Uncomfortable 24.0%

Undecided 4.0%

Comfortable 72.0%

SOURCE: Riggi, 1995

to change the other person, it is acceptable to see what differences, if any, are taking place as you implement your project

b. Monitoring overall changes in the situation

Depending on the changes that she needed to highlight for herself and continue to keep herself going, any of these could be target behaviors for the reinforcement program.

Setting Up a Reinforcement Program

The reinforcement program you create for yourself should follow many of the guidelines that Sugai and Tindal (1993) set out for use with special education students. Effective reinforcers have the following characteristics: they should be easy to obtain and store, inexpensive, under your control, administrable in small amounts, and bridge the gap between the target behavior and a later reinforcing event (p. 177). In other words, don't plan to take a trip to Europe in the middle of your collaboration project if you reach your goal for consistently initiating interactions with your target person. It would be neither inexpensive nor administrable in small amounts. You also want to avoid a reinforcer that is not going to help you bridge the gap between reinforcement events in your project.

Identify useful, natural reinforcers to use during your project. Choose from one or more of the following types of reinforcers: (1) social (e.g., verbal praise or feedback from a member of your project resource network, phone conversation with a friend, going to a sporting event with a friend, getting together with others to do something long-desired but not accomplished), (2) token (e.g., keeping track of your progress using a token system in your data collection process and turning your tokens in for a self-reward at the end of the project), (3) tangible (e.g., a favorite food or item for a hobby that you had intended to purchase, dinner out), or (4) activity (e.g., uninterrupted time to surf the Internet, taking a bubble bath, making time for a bike ride, renting a video or DVD).

Select a target behavior that is part of your collaboration project and that you think will be difficult for you to change. Use Project Try-Out 9.3 to design and carry out a reinforcement program.

Project Try-Out 9.3

This One's for You!

This Project Try-Out is an opportunity for you to capitalize on all the times you designed reinforcement programs for your students—this one is for you. Select a target behavior on which to focus and then go through the following steps:

1. Select one or two reinforcers you think would be effective for you. Pick from among the following options, or generate one of your own.

2. Decide on a reinforcement schedule that will work best for you as you proceed with your project. You can select from among the following options:

Social	Token	Tangible	Activity
Walk with a friend in a favorite place	Keep data counters near you; when you reach a certain number, give yourself a redeemable token	Buy a favorite food you don't often eat	Surf the Internet Rent a DVD Dance
Make a phone call to a friend with whom you haven't spoken in a long time	With a member of your collaboration resource network, exchange each completed data chart for a token	Buy a set of inexpensive "surprises" for yourself and wrap them up. Pick one when you reach your goal	Take quiet time for reading or a favorite hobby
Pick a new place to meet a friend		Use stickers or stars on your project materials	Pack a special lunch to eat in a new and different place
Attend a sporting event with a friend		Roast marshmallows	Learn a new computer game or hobby
Work out with a friend		Eat out	Create a notebook for storing ideas

    a. Interval: fixed (e.g., at the end of every week, you will select a social reinforcer if you are demonstrating the target behavior regardless of the overall progress you've made).

    b. Interval: variable (e.g., you and a member of your collaboration resource network will decide on a reasonable frequency for reinforcement. On the average, after a certain number of days, you will get your reinforcer if the target behavior is being demonstrated).

Token Interval: Variable

I enjoy biking but rarely found time to fit it into my schedule. Part of the problem was that my bike needed some repairs for which I never seemed to have the money. My collaboration network member knew my situation and came up with a plan. We agreed on an interval-variable plan of every two days. He would show up in my class during math (when I was implementing my project with my student teacher) and check to see whether I was giving clear instructions. If I was, he'd put a check on a card I left on my desk. It was up to him to keep track of the times he stopped in, so I never really knew when it would happen. For each check he gave me, I put $2.00 into my bike savings account. The $2.00 is like a token for me because the amount by itself wouldn't cover the repair costs. But at this rate, it looks like I'll have the repairs paid for before the project is over. I like the unpredictability of this approach because it keeps me honest!

Social Ratio: Fixed

A teacher from my school, with whom I'd been friends, moved away at the end of last year. Even though we had promised that we would write, neither of us did. So I decided that I would use long distance as a reinforcement for sticking with my project. After I participated in 10 meetings with my paraprofessional and used my new agenda for each one, I called my friend. What a surprise! We planned another call after I finish another 10 meetings. Knowing what is coming has made me feel motivated!

The advantages of the interval reinforcement approach is that you can continue to get reinforced even if you are not accumulating a large number of target behaviors. This approach can be very helpful at the start of a project.

    c. Ratio: fixed (e.g., you plan after the 25th time you and your target person reach a mutually satisfactory decision that you get a reinforcement).

    d. Ratio: variable (e.g., on the average after you and your target person meet three times as scheduled, you will get a reinforcement). This ratio approach can be used very effectively if you are working on a target behavior that you know you can accomplish but know you need help to stay motivated and keep going.

3. Set up a system in your collaboration notebook for monitoring your reinforcement program. This will include setting it up and changing it when it loses its effectiveness.

Project Try-Out 9.3 is a way for you to motivate yourself as you work on your project. Use the following set of questions, adapted from Sugai and Tindal's procedural checklist (1993, p. 184). This way you can be sure that everything is covered.

1. Have you operationally defined your target behavior?

2. Have you sufficiently described the situation in which the target behavior must be occurring if it is to be reinforced?

3. Have you identified an effective, natural reinforcer?

4. Did you decide on the amount of the reinforcer to use?

5. Did you determine when the reinforcer should be presented (will it be immediate, or will it be delayed)?

6. Did you develop a reinforcement schedule?

7. Have you decided how to tell whether the reinforcer is effective (e.g., if the level of progress being made is at or above expectations)?

As you work on your collaboration project, you are designing ways to make sure that you have both the internal and external supports needed to keep you on track. The reinforcement that has been discussed here has all been positive—ways you can motivate yourself. For some people, the negative reinforcement approach can be more effective.

Negative Reinforcement

Another type of reinforcement is implicitly present in your project—negative reinforcement. Negative reinforcement "strengthens behaviors that function to terminate or postpone certain undesirable events" (Cipani, 1995, p. 37). In many projects, actions that you initiate will be negative reinforcers—behavior that will limit or end things that you find problematic. Masseo (1995) conducted her collaboration project when she was working as a paraprofessional. The classroom was less structured than Masseo would have liked. To eliminate her discomfort, she initiated more purposeful planning activities and, as a result, ended an unpleasant, unplanned situation. Here are "typical" events that occurred at the start and at the end of the project:

At the start, it was typical for me to sit around idle, unsure of what was expected of me, and not feeling comfortable enough to initiate anything. I would often sit in the classroom for long periods of time, not having any specific duties and waiting for instructions that came in fragmented pieces. I even was unsure if I was overstepping my bounds when I left the room. Specific communication was absent from our routine.

Near the end, prior to the start of each day, I sit down with Melissa, the teacher. Together, we review the class schedule. We note which activities will involve me, and what I should do during each one. It is not uncommon for me to now ask specific questions about the day, and offer suggestions. Knowing what is expected of me makes it comfortable for me to leave the room, when I need to, without feeling like I am "slacking off." I feel now that it is ok for me to pursue activities on my own, which I will share with Melissa and the students. Melissa is supportive of my initiative and encourages it often. (Masseo, 1995)

One of Masseo's strategies involved a review of the role of the paraprofessional with her teacher, leading to a frank discussion about how to improve their communication pattern. She made copies of the article by McKenzie and Houk (1986) for her teacher and for herself. The discussion of the article gave them a basis for structuring her role much more clearly. Two resources you might discuss with colleagues in your school are Wilmshurst and Brue's (2005) *A Parent's Guide to Special Education*, to consider the role she was taking in relation to the families of students in the class, or an article from *CEC Today* (Winter, 2005), "New IDEA delivers for students with disabilities." Both of these might serve to clarify roles beyond specific classroom responsibilities.

The new behaviors Masseo was able to initiate (increased communication) have increased value because they serve to terminate or postpone certain undesirable events (ineffective use of time by Masseo). In your project situation, you may find that use of negative reinforcement is even more effective than the positive, contingent reinforcements described above. Try Idea Try-Out 9.4 to see whether this method works for you.

Idea Try-Out 9.4

Stop It!

This Idea Try-Out can help you consider applying the concept of negative reinforcement to your project.

1. Identify three things that bother you about your project situation. Record them in your collaboration notebook.

2. Pick the one that is the most upsetting. Spend three minutes writing without stopping (free writing) in your collaboration notebook about your associations with that aspect of your situation.

3. Imagine that this problem was magically resolved. Spend three minutes imagining what this situation would be like if the problem were to be solved.

4. You've described a negative reinforcement situation. Work with members of your collaboration resource network to incorporate what you've learned from this tryout into your project.

Idea Try-Out 9.4 can help you to think about your project in a new way—not only what to start, but what to stop. The strategies outlined thus far in this chapter have given you several different ways to keep yourself going. However, they still may not be sufficient. Now that you have gotten some new perspectives on yourself, you can approach self-monitoring in some new ways. Self-monitoring is described in the next section of the chapter.

TEACHING YOURSELF TO LOOK: OBSERVING YOURSELF

In Chapter 3, you looked at things you did that made a difference in your ability to assess accurately your own behavior. What you did before you began the project, however, may have inadvertently missed some aspects of your working life that you need to include. In this section of the chapter, you will have an opportunity to reconsider self-efficacy from a more seasoned point of view.

Efficacy as a Goal

By now, you have probably developed a number of new routines that have helped you to approach your target person with new confidence and new skills such as those described in the examples below.

My worry used to be that the general education teacher would ask me a question that I couldn't answer. We seemed to get along most days. I don't think he suspected that anything was out of the ordinary, but—inside—I was on edge, always waiting for that pop question. Finally, when I had to do this project, it was time to put this whole thing to rest. I set up a new meeting schedule with him and included a section at the end of the meeting for questions called, "Between now and next time . . ." That was all I needed. Our new routine is to start each meeting with answers from last time. Now, I wonder what I was so worried about.

I can hardly believe I'm working in the same school as when I began this project. Ever since I decided that I would force myself to say hello to one new person a day and eat in the faculty lunch room twice a week, things have changed. I used to count the hours between getting here and getting home, only feeling at ease when I was with my students. Now, things are really different. Hard to believe it is really me.

In some cases, your new routines may be clearly observable to all who work with you (behavior changes). In other cases, you may have some aspects of your project that are private but have made a difference for you (attitude changes). In all that you've done, however, you want to find ways to determine whether progress has been made. McGregor (2002) describes skills that are "essential" for college students at Inver Hills Community College—those included in the categories of Appreciation Skills, Collaboration Skills, and Implementation are all pertinent to the types of routines you may be trying to establish through your collaboration project. In fact, working with area universities can give you opportunities to explore professional development on future projects or action research within your classroom (e.g., Wiseman & Knight, 2003, on collaboration between universities and K–12 schools or Armstrong & Moore's 2004 book on action research).

The direct observation of your own interaction style is discussed in Crawford's (1995) article. She identifies positive interactions with personality-challenged individuals as a goal for school and home:

Learning to interact positively with personality-challenged individuals (PCIs) will result in a more productive work and home life. It will reduce the stress you experience daily. And it will alert you to your own tendencies to be a PCI. . . . Take your first step by looking in that mirror. (p. 4)

Ongoing self-examination was identified by Howey (1985) as a preliminary part of a cycle of progress.

> More attention should be given to self-understanding because of the highly interpersonal nature of teaching. . . . The degree of understanding teachers have of their own behavior and how they have changed over time is directly related to the nature and quality of interactions they have had with others, certainly including the myriad daily interactions in schools. (p. 59)

A further discussion of the power of those self-reflective skills is presented in the next section of this chapter.

Teacher Efficacy as a Tool for Self-Reflection

In Chapter 3, teacher efficacy was presented as an abstract construct for you to use in doing preliminary self-assessment. Kaff (2003) underscores the importance of efficacy:

> Efficacy is a characteristic that is highly valued in all educators. . . . In the field, it is imperative that school administrators and staff establish a school climate that fosters and supports collaboration and empowers teachers to share in the decision-making regarding the educational practices of the school. (p. 18)

Efficacy, along with collaborative relationships, mentoring/advocacy, and community building are the "four essential components" for an effective inclusive classroom. Gibson and Dembo (1984) define teacher efficacy as teachers' beliefs that they could influence their students' learning. Use the construct to look at yourself and the efforts you are making on your project.

Scanlon, Gallego, Zamora Duran, and Reyes (2005) incorporated issues related to efficacy into interactive staff development activities aimed at improving instructional practices and providing supports for collaboration. "The interactive features of our staff development enabled teachers to learn the technical aspects of a new practice by engaging in practice, reflecting and experimenting in collaboration, and being supported in fitting the new practice into their classroom routines (Gersten et al., 2000; Gore, 2001)" (pp. 49–50). The encouragement enabled teachers to be "learners in staff development" and thus gain skills and confidence in a safe setting.

Efficacy is particularly an issue for beginning teachers. Eison (1990) had 10 recommendations for new teachers to develop confidence in the classroom. His first suggestion was "to feel confident, act confident" (p. 21), which he agreed is "easier said than done." His recommendations included suggestions for analyzing effective teaching and putting them into practice.

Agne et al. (1994) examined the relationship between efficacy (along with several other concepts) and teacher excellence. Their study compared two groups of teachers— 88 Teachers of the Year and 92 inservice teachers.

[There was] considerable interrelatedness . . . among three of the four teacher belief systems, pupil control ideology, teacher locus of control and teacher efficacy. . . . [This] suggests that . . . teacher-education majors should have knowledge of the research on teacher-belief patterns and opportunity to be exposed to those teacher beliefs which make a difference in teacher effectiveness. . . . Procedures could be developed for allowing teacher-education majors to (a) examine their own belief systems, (b) have opportunities to compare their beliefs with those cited as effective in the literature and (c) examine actual teaching experiences in light of the belief systems of the teachers involved. (pp. 148–149)

The self-examination process can begin with the activities you are developing for your project. As you observe your behavior in the project, through the data collection procedures you have implemented, look for ways to answer the following questions, based on the study by Agne et al. (1994):

1. To what extent does what you think will happen influence your actions?

2. What books or articles have you reviewed lately that help you to look at your beliefs as they influence your actions?

3. How typical do you think your ideas are in comparison to those of other teachers?

The answers you develop to these questions can help you to complete Project Try-Out 9.5.

Project Try-Out 9.5

Yes and No

This Project Try-Out is designed to help you find articles relevant to issues you are addressing in your project.

1. Identify two or three beliefs that are essential to the progress you are making on your project, for example,
   - Teachers should be role models for their students.
   - Focusing on positives rather than negatives has long-term benefits.
   - Defying authority only gets you into trouble.

2. Work with a reference librarian to develop a search strategy and collect articles on each of the beliefs you identified in Step 1. Look for a combination of research-based and theoretical articles. You can use the References in this book as a springboard for your search.

3. Use one page in your collaboration notebook for each belief. Divide each page in half—use the top half to record support for your beliefs and bottom half for contradictions to your beliefs. Keep track of the sources of these ideas and citations of referenced articles to research in the future.

4. Develop ways to incorporate some of the research conclusions into your project. This could include one or more or the following:
   a. Reflect on what you've read in your journal or anecdotal record.
   b. Share one or more of the articles you discovered with your target person and discuss what you found to be interesting.
   c. Share one or more of the articles with a member of your collaboration resource network and brainstorm ways to incorporate issues from the article(s) into your project.

Your research can help you to develop a new perspective on the underlying beliefs that are guiding you throughout your project, such as in the following example.

I used to worry a lot about how I got along with my principal, and I felt very much alone in my thinking. Until I got involved with this project, I didn't say too much to anyone. Then, after reading several articles that described other people in the same boat as I was, I finally relaxed. That was when I really got my project into gear and things began to change for me in my building.

You can also use the underlying beliefs to target areas in which you are making less progress than you would like.

Systematically Addressing Deficit Areas

As your project moves along, you are probably becoming aware of behaviors you did not address in your original plan, behaviors that you did not think of in advance, or those that you have not succeeded in changing as thoroughly as you would have liked. That is ok! Working on too many things simultaneously can undermine progress on all of them. List the behaviors you want to address. With the help of the members of your collaboration resource network, you can make decisions about these deficit areas, categorizing them in one of the following ways:

1. Behavior is key to the success of the project. A new or modified activity must be developed to address this behavior.

2. Behavior is linked to a major, but different, direction than the current project is headed. You may be able to modify an existing activity to address the newly identified behavior, or you may have to decide to address this behavior in the future.

3. Behavior is interesting but is probably not related to the outcome of the project. You can reflect on your insight in your journal/anecdotal records.

Your decision to modify your approach, or limit the scope of your project to exclude this particular behavior, is one that you will have to make. In making this decision, consider the following example.

Rogers (maiden name of Putnam, which is the name on Figures 9.4 and 9.5) and a fellow agency worker had different points of view on how to carry out their teaching roles. These different points of view came out clearly at meetings. Rather than confront her colleague directly, Rogers incorporated "use of new meeting guidelines" into her project. Figures 9.4 and 9.5 show her progress. On March 27, she observed the following:

> A Turning Point took place. I realized that I was allowing the problems between us to take over and many times ruin my day. I realized that I could not allow the situation to affect my outlook any longer. It was as if a light bulb suddenly went on in my head. I was suddenly able to accept the situation with a new attitude. (Rogers, 1996)

Her observations are shown in two ways—in Figure 9.4, showing increased ownership on the job and in Figure 9.5, showing improved meetings. When Rogers began her project, she thought that she had covered all potential areas of improvement. However, her realization that she was feeling defeated and that she could change those feelings enabled her to see improvement in several aspects of her project. In this case, the new behavior of "not letting her get to me" was central to the success of the project. She was able to benefit from her improved attitude by increasing her investment in her work.

Figure 9.4   Ownership on the Job

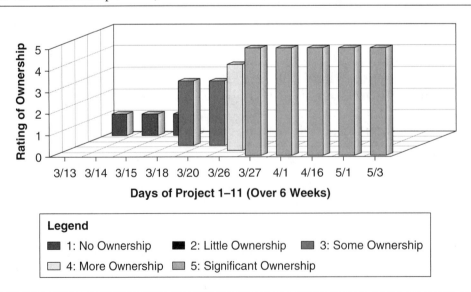

SOURCE: Putnam, 1996

Figure 9.5   How Did Meeting Rules Improve Meetings?

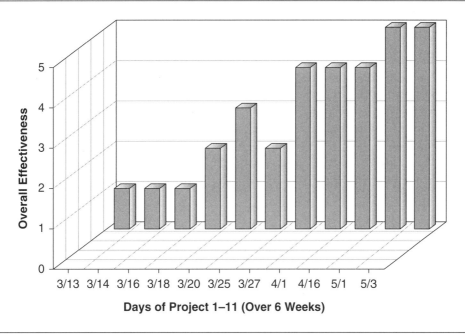

SOURCE: Putnam, 1996

NOTE: Legend = 1: Low, Ineffective; 5: High, Very Effective

CONCLUSION

The process of developing your project and maintaining it is one that can incorporate the guidelines Bozzone (1995) recommends for "de-stressing."

- Recognize that stress is unavoidable
- Realize that you have a choice about how to react to a stressful situation
- Listen to what your body is telling you
- Listen to how you talk to yourself
- Make a habit of relaxing regularly

In this chapter, self-talk, reinforcement, and self-observation have been presented as options to keep you going. In the long run, after this project is completed you want to be able to put yourself in gear to fix other problematic situations. Bozzone's guidelines for coping with stress can be generalized to many other aspects of your work and your life. Make use of de-stressing activities to keep yourself moving along in a successful direction.

The need for collaboration will continue to be a part of the world of the special educator. Whitten and Rodriguez-Campos (2003) reviewed trends in four waves of surveys collected by the National Council on Educational Statistics (NCES) from 1988 through to 2000. The actual/weighted sample size for special educators ranged from 4,307/239,786 in 1987–1988 to 4,753/329,167 in 1999–2000. There has been a sharp decline in the perception of collaboration among personnel, on the part of special educators who "strongly agree" that there is a collaborative effort among personnel in their school (from 30.0% in 1987–1988 to 4.3% in 1999–2000). The percentage of those who "strongly agree" that there are "shared beliefs and values among colleagues" also went down (from 28.3% in 1987–1988 to 3.0% in 1999–2000) (p. 144). The authors conclude that "[there is] increased need to engage in continuous collaboration with general education teachers. Educators should not be satisfied with the current state of special education until they have established a climate that seamlessly supports inclusive teaching, multiculturalism, and collaboration among staff" (p. 145). We have more to do in order to be satisfied with what we have accomplished in our classrooms and in our schools. Your collaboration project can help to turn this trend around. In the next chapter, read about how the project concludes.

10

Summing Up the Outcomes

What Have You Accomplished?

As you near the end of your project, you may be experiencing pressure. This pressure may be similar to the kind you would feel on moving day or on the last day of the school year. You have been focusing on implementing new behaviors and monitoring your progress. However, an effort of this intensity was not intended to go on forever. Just as you do at the end of every school year, take satisfaction in what has been done and distinguish it from what is left to do in the future.

Another challenge you face is what to do with all the information you have assembled. How can you put it all together to show what happened? This chapter will give you examples of ways to present the data you've collected to show what really took place in your project.

After reviewing this chapter, you will be better able to develop your talents as an organizer, redefiner, and consolidator. These skills will enable you to present your results in the clearest way possible. By the end of the chapter, you should have good ideas about what to do in future with your target person. You can decide how to change the relationship on which you've expended a lot of time and energy into one that is more realistic in terms of type and number of contacts.

Have you developed new habits based on the work you did on this project? You may have found that your collaborative efforts have influenced both your work with your target person and your general thoughts about teaching. In the following example, the effects of the project generalized far beyond the specific relationship that was its focus. This may have been true in your case as well.

After working in schools for over 20 years as a paraprofessional, I finally decided to go back to college and earn my degree. I was very nervous, especially about student teaching. I was terrified of making mistakes. What I found out, now that I am at the end of this project, is that a lot of my biggest worries were in my imagination. People were much more willing to give me a break than I thought. As soon as I lightened up, so did they. I'm ready to go out on a job interview and sell myself because now I really believe in my product—me!

When you actually collaborate, your views about collaboration change. O'Shea, Williams, and Sattler (1999) involved 103 preservice general (*n* = 54) and special education (*n* = 49) teachers in collaboration activities during an academic year. Some of the assignments involved collaboration activities in person, as well as through electronic computer exchanges.

> Preservice teachers' collaboration opportunities can be beneficial and require hard work, planning and commitment . . . More than two thirds of those reporting indicated that the completion of their course project changed their existing collaboration views . . . Many preservice teachers reported that they recognize how problem-solving practice allows them to understand why collaboration decisions are made. Individual control to empower others (rather than *others doing for or making it easier on me*) can evolve when new teachers begin to reflect on intrinsic rewards of helping. (pp. 155–156)

Their projects, much like the one you just completed, provided new insights for further work with other teachers. As Chrispeels (2004), Murphy (2002), and Fullan (1991, 2001) suggest, teacher leadership emerges from change initiatives that become the impetus for new habits. Your experience with the collaboration project can enable you to consider other new opportunities for improvement.

Your self-reflective, collaborative work style may have given you new perspectives on your accomplishments and new ways to communicate with others. These insights relate directly to some of our most fundamental teaching activities. In their use of collaborative teaming in two schools, Hunt, Soto, Maier, and Doering (2003) found that collaborative teaming gave teachers opportunities to work together on student improvement.

> The team members suggested that the collaborative process allowed participants to share their expertise and experience to support student progress. A classroom teacher commented, "With these meetings you make sure it's a collaborative effort and that everybody is informed. It's not saying 'the child is not performing'; instead, it's about what we can all do to contribute to get this child's needs met." (pp. 327–328)

Collaboration expands the resource circle for teachers and for students, providing methods to address IDEA (e.g., Jones, Apling, & Smole, 2004) and the No Child Left Behind (NCLB) regulations (e.g., Council for Exceptional Children, 2005). You may also be able to discuss your concerns for general and special education students with regard to the implementation of NCLB (e.g., "No Child Left Behind and the Political Safeguards of Federalism," 2006).

As special educators, we train ourselves to look at our students critically and creatively. We are always searching for a positive moment or behavior. We generally use positive approaches to encourage our students. In this project, you've been doing the same thing for yourself. You've also used your collaboration resource network to extend your boundaries, seeking and using assistance from others to modify your own behavior. Involving others in consideration of how you were doing and what you could do differently is similar to the approach A. Turnbull and H. R. Turnbull (2000) used to incorporate a collaboration to improve the quality of life of individuals with cognitive disabilities or autism. Villa and Thousand (2000) and Villa, Thousand, Nevin, and Malgeri (1996) encourage educators to create environments that support and educate individuals with disabilities by seeking input directly from the individuals, both about their areas of concern and about possible solutions. In so doing, strategies can be designed to make changes in key areas. Ruef and Turnbull (2002) point out that this approach is not frequently used in day-to-day activities or in research:

> Their statements suggested how infrequently their input regarding what they valued and considered important was either solicited or acted upon. A collaborative approach to supporting persons with disabilities and problem behaviors must be founded on the fact that they are people first and have disabilities second. . . . Consistent with the PBS [Positive Behavior Support] approach (Carr et al., 2002), persons with disabilities, together with other relevant stakeholders (e.g., parents, siblings, neighbors, teachers, job coaches, friends, roommates, and other persons with disabilities) should play active roles in reciprocal research processes whenever possible. (p. 138)

Your experiences with the collaboration project have given you an opportunity to experience assistance from your collaboration resource network and gain insights you might not otherwise have developed.

Your behavior throughout this project differs quite sharply from the behavior of the 52 teacher volunteers Zahorik (1987) interviewed to explore teacher interactions and assistance patterns. Zahorik compared teachers in six different schools and found that these teachers spent (on average) 40 minutes a day talking with other teachers about classroom teaching. The most frequently exchanged information (sought and offered) was the following: exchange of materials, suggestions about discipline and learning activities, and recommendations about individualization. These four topics represented 70% of the help given or received (pp. 389–390).

Zahorik made the following observation:

> These four topics seem to have a common feature: they focus on a group of students or a particular student. It is students who use materials and engage in learning activities, and it is students who have discipline or learning problems and are in need of help. (p. 390)

Why isn't help sought or offered concerning teacher behavior? When Zahorik asked his teacher volunteers that question, he received four responses most frequently: (1) teacher behavior is less important than student behavior, (2) teacher behavior is personal and private, (3) teacher behavior is too idiosyncratic, or (4) teacher behavior is too well established (pp. 390–391). As two teachers explained, "teaching methods are 'much too personal' to share with another [teacher]. . . . ' Teaching is sacred ground. It's his classroom. It's like you don't talk about politics and religion'" (p. 391). Zahorik concluded that if teachers expected to collaborate with each other, they

> must come not to fear exposing their classroom practices. They must see that knowledge of their classroom behavior by others as well as themselves is essential to improvement . . . an unavoidable first step to developing collegiality, improving instruction, and making teaching satisfying work. (p. 395)

The challenges described by the teachers interviewed by Zahorik were also implied in the work done by DiPardo (1999) in her descriptions of teachers' experiences as they moved from a traditional model to one that focused on interdisciplinary work, which "moved to the next level of collaboration" beyond surface cooperation. She asked these questions:

> How to honor these teachers' needs as learners? How to ease their transition into this bold new way of doing business? The teachers' first answer is always the same: *time,* lots more time. Time to talk about every kid, time to plan interdisciplinary units, time to explore a problem or issue until they all feel satisfied, time, even, to have a conversation in which they finish all their sentences. But how much time would it take to build the sort of trust that would allow them to address their fundamental differences? (DiPardo, 1999, p. 115)

In the model of the Demonstration Classroom described by Kabot (2004), a one-week intensive intervention by external consultants gave teachers in the classroom an opportunity to experience in-depth child study, use of curricular and behavioral strategies, as well as a model of debriefing and troubleshooting. "Any discomfort on the part of the classroom teacher or staff is discussed" (p. 8). Enabling teachers to talk with external consultants changed the dynamics of the classroom and (with follow-up support over a five-month period) facilitated change. In her more extended discussion of this project (Kabot, 2005), she explains that "Modeling, coaching, and providing feedback to classroom staff were used to build teaching skills. Collaborative problem solving was modeled and used to make adjustments to the classroom and to students' instructional programs" (p. 49), resulting in improvement in use of strategies by all five of the classroom teachers observed (though the changes observed did not reach significance in all cases) as well as improved development of IEPs and IFSPs (pp. 51–53). Trust takes time to develop.

The process that you used in this project was a step toward improved collegiality and away from a private, self-centered view of life in a school building. In the following section, you will see how to report on what you've achieved.

ASSESSING SUCCESS: HOW DID YOUR PLAN WORK OUT?

When reporting on your project, you want to be able to clearly document your progress, drawing conclusions based on the data you collected. In the following section, different approaches are used to show how to report on documented changes.

Organizing and Reviewing Data: Pre-Planned Data Analysis

Higgins's (1995) student project focused on diversifying and expanding her professional contacts with her target person. Like the teacher volunteers in Zahorik's study, her patterns of interaction with her target person were limited. She decided to illustrate changes in her interaction patterns by reporting on three sample weeks. Her results are shown in Figures 10.1, 10.2, and 10.3.

Figure 10.1   Week 1: Interaction Patterns

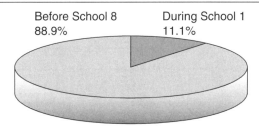

SOURCE: Higgins, 1995

Figure 10.2   Week 5: Interaction Patterns

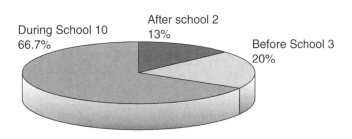

SOURCE: Higgins, 1995

Figure 10.3   Week 9: Interaction Patterns

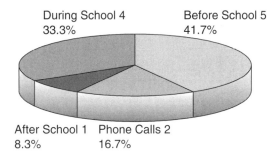

SOURCE: Higgins, 1995

As Figures 10.1 to 10.3 show, the timing as well as her methods of contact became more diversified. There was an increase in the total contacts over baseline (nine contacts in Week 1) in both subsequent weeks (15 and 12 contacts, respectively). As shown in Figures 10.4 and 10.5, Higgins also documented other patterns in the interactions that took place.

She drew the following conclusion about her work on her student project, based on her data analysis:

> I found a sense of accomplishment and confidence. While my target person and I may still disagree on how some things should be done, we have

Figure 10.4   Self-Evaluation of Journal Entries

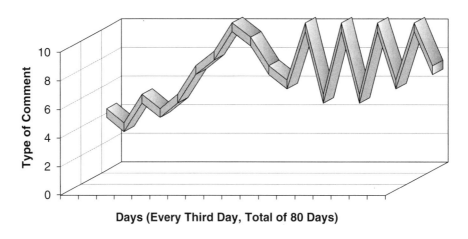

SOURCE: Higgins, 1995

Figure 10.5   Increased Involvement in Classroom

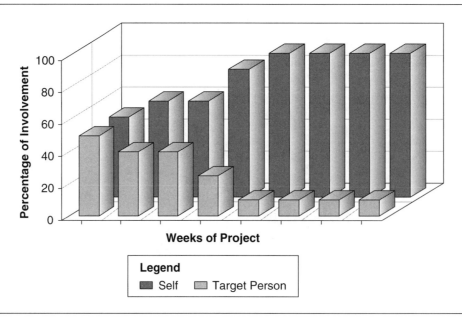

SOURCE: Higgins, 1995

established a good, professional relationship. I realized that I was much more successful communicating with my target person when I caught her alone and uninterrupted. Initially, I was trying to speak to her at inopportune times, like between classes or when students and other staff members were around. I modified my behavior by speaking to her when no one else was present. This worked out best when I came in early or stayed after school. (Higgins, 1995)

Higgins used her data collection to effectively modify her behavior as her student project went on. She summarized her reflections in this way:

In looking back at my project, I am struck by the changes I've undergone. When I retrieve my attitude from the beginning of this semester, I almost cringe at how I expected others around me to change. I, on the other hand, felt I knew what I was doing and could teach others more than they could teach me. It's been a humbling experience, but in a positive way. I feel I really benefited from this project. (Higgins, 1995)

Higgins's experiences illustrate how a project can help you to see the effects of expanding your patterns of behavior.

Mrugala's (1996) student project documented a pattern of her own frustrations, using a scale she developed:

1 = Not tolerant enough (actions based on residual effects of another incident, or own personal life)

3 = Acceptable level of tolerance (actions are objective and unemotional)

5 = Too tolerant (own actions are emotional and unobjective)

She evaluated her behavior over the course of her student project, as shown in Figure 10.6.

While her data charting reveals that she never completely stabilized at level 3, her optimal level, she was at her unacceptable levels (1 and 5) less often near the end of her student project than she was at the start. This gave her a basis for analyzing what worked, what didn't, and then planning for the future.

Mrugala documented changes in her frustration level from Baseline (Days 1–4) through to the end of her student project (Day 24), and found consistent improvement. She recommends the following to others:

Data collection assists in visually examining what you are doing in the relationship. When you change one aspect of the interaction, you can see if improvements are being made. By communicating with others based on data collected (facts), and not just impressions or feelings, you can better monitor your progress. (Mrugala, 1996)

In her student project, Tierney-Luthart (1995) kept track of the number of times she involved her target person in decision making or made decisions at meetings with him (rather than in private or without him). In Figure 10.7 improvement is shown. Tierney-Luthart reported that "involving my target person in the decision making process became easier for me as the project progressed. As our working relationship

Figure 10.6 Patterns of Frustration Tolerance

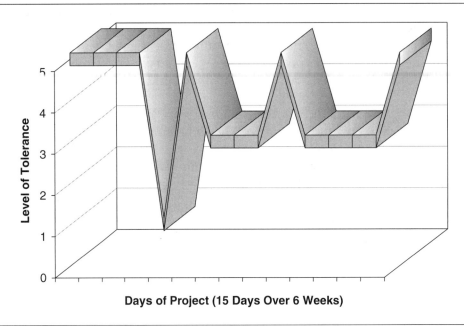

SOURCE: Mrugala, 1996

Figure 10.7 Involving Partner in Decision Making

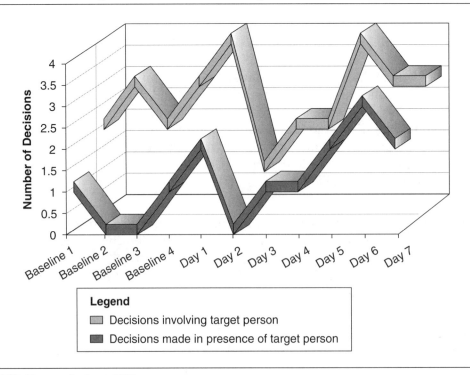

SOURCE: Tierney-Luthart, 1995

Figure 10.8 Response to Partner's Sarcasm

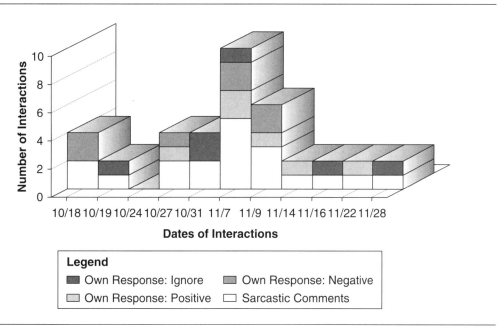

SOURCE: Tierney-Luthart, 1995

improved, I was more willing to involve him in making decisions." She attributed the change in her relationship to her modified decision-making habits.

She suspected that the change in their pattern of interaction was also related to her response to his sarcastic comments, shown in Figure 10.8. As the project progressed, she reacted less negatively to her target person's comments. Her target person also made the comments less frequently. When her project concluded, she compared both these concerns. She could see the correspondence between the two patterns.

A different approach to a similar concern took place in Pyszczynski's (1995) student project, shown in Figure 10.9. She documented her ability to notice more positive characteristics in her target person. Simultaneously, she noticed that she was reacting less negatively to the sarcastic remarks her target person made about her or about other people. By reporting on these two patterns together using an objective approach (frequency count), Pyszczynski illustrated the correspondence between seemingly separate reactions.

At the end of his student project, Barberio (1995) reported on trends in confrontational behavior, shown in Figure 10.10. He saw a decrease in problem interactions while productive interactions increased. He reported

a few noticeable trends. The confrontational interactions were more prevalent on Mondays, and decreased as the week progressed. There were times when I became confrontational with my target person for exhibiting habitual behaviors. The very same behaviors did not affect me the same way later in the week. I noticed that I continued to experience negative feelings for my target person even during non-confrontational interactions.

The second pattern, related to the positive or negative nature of the interactions, is shown in Figure 10.11 on page 241. Positive interactions increased as negative interactions decreased.

Figure 10.9   Patterns of Improvement

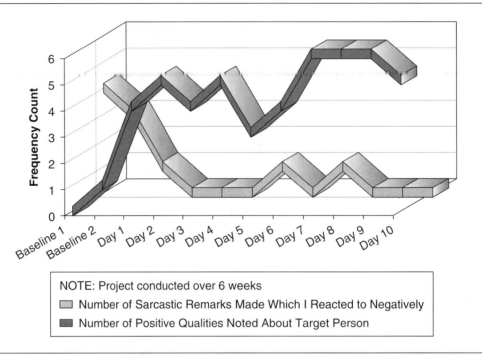

NOTE: Project conducted over 6 weeks

▨ Number of Sarcastic Remarks Made Which I Reacted to Negatively

▨ Number of Positive Qualities Noted About Target Person

SOURCE: Pyszczynski, 1995

Figure 10.10   Interaction Pattern With Target Person

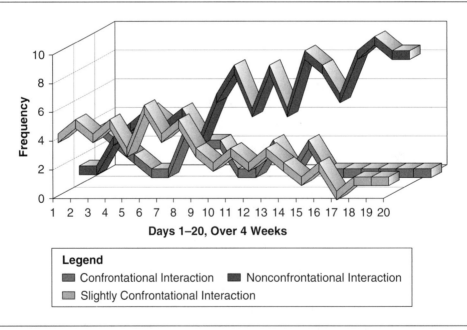

Legend

▨ Confrontational Interaction   ▨ Nonconfrontational Interaction

▨ Slightly Confrontational Interaction

SOURCE: Barberio, 1995

Smith (1994) also contrasted positive and negative behaviors: in her case, she decided at the outset of her student project that she would look for positive and negative attributes in her target person. This approach was very effective for her, as she reported at the end of her student project. Her results are shown in Figure 10.12.

Figure 10.11 Pattern of Interactions

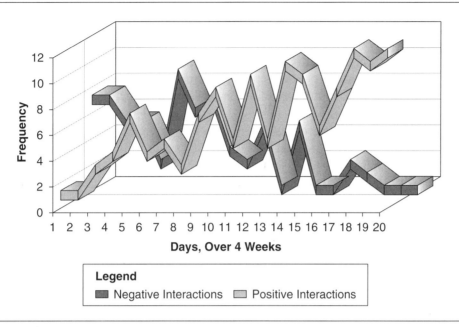

SOURCE: Barberio, 1995

Figure 10.12 Summary of Contents in Journal

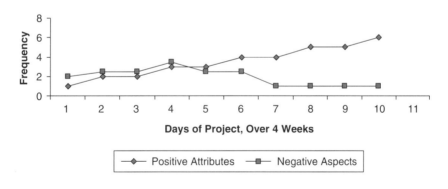

SOURCE: Smith, 1994

Before the project, I would never have believed that an evaluation process would make that much difference. The daily journal I kept was an invaluable tool that gave me insight into my behavior and my target person's reaction to it. The more positive attributes I recognized during my project, the more my positive attitude (and positive list) grew overall. The trend I observed was that once I began searching for positive attributes, they were much easier to find. The negatives became less obvious as the number of positives grew. This project has really made me more aware of the power of a self-fulfilling prophecy like mine. Before I began the project, I was looking for negatives, but then I switched to looking for positives. And I always found what I was looking for. (Smith, 1994)

Smith knew what she was planning to do at the outset of her student project. The data she collected helped her to see whether her approach was successful. Much like Carol Gilligan's (1982) seminal work, *In a Different Voice*, Smith found that investigating her own perceptions revealed patterns that surprised her and which were totally under her control. As Gilligan observed, change can come from within. Although sometimes such change is prompted in teacher education programs (e.g., Goodlad, 1990b, Griffin, 1999), it can also be initiated as part of a professional development program in schools.

All the above figures were based on frequency records maintained throughout each student project. In other words, students accurately anticipated what they wanted to monitor in their own behavior prior to implementation. However, that kind of foresight is not always possible. To make full use of the anecdotal and journal records kept, other approaches can be used. The use of post hoc analysis procedures are discussed in the next section of the chapter.

Organizing and Reviewing Data: Post Hoc Analysis

Research allows you to analyze data from many perspectives while keeping in mind that you cannot change the data you have collected. Hypothesis testing is one approach that corresponds to the first part of this chapter. This technique is used to determine whether the data you've collected corresponds to what you expected. However, you may also have developed some hunches as you conducted your research. You can test these ideas using an approach known as post hoc analysis—analysis that is done "after the fact." Several examples of post hoc analysis are presented.

After O'Sullivan (1996) completed her student project, she reviewed the journal that she had maintained for eight weeks. She was able to develop categories for her entries, which corresponded to the moods she'd been in when interacting with her target person (Figure 10.13). It would not have been possible for her to develop them before she began her project because she did not know what patterns would emerge. When she reviewed her results at the conclusion of her student project, she could tell that she was making some progress, but she had not fully stabilized her relationship.

Steinwachs (1995) planned a project to monitor her daily comfort level with her target person. At the outset of her student project, she did not know what different types of interactions she would be using. Her post hoc analysis included a detailed analysis of events, including the following:

> At the start of the project, when I was collecting my baseline data, I avoided my target person. One day, I was walking down the hall toward my classroom. The hall has a bend so I could not see him, but I heard his voice. I very quickly got out my keys and went into the ladies' room. I did not have to use the restroom, I was just attempting to avoid him. I stood in the bathroom, waiting for him to pass by. There I was, wasting my time and feeling really stupid. He soon passed by and I quickly walked to my room.
>
> A typical event at the end of the project takes place every morning before school starts. I now make it a point to go over and at least say hello to my target person. The other teacher who stands with him is a longtime friend of my target person. During the project I've become good friends with this other teacher. It has made my approach to my target person more comfortable and more natural. I am brief and polite. I say good morning, and make a positive

Figure 10.13 Personal Reactions/Feelings

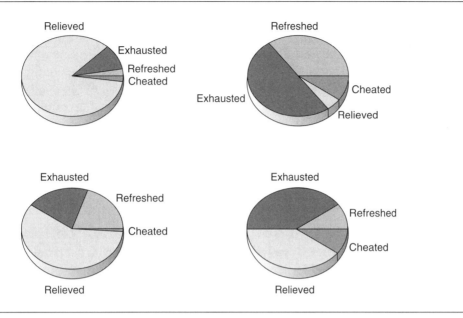

SOURCE: O'Sullivan, 1996

comment about the day. After he responds, I direct my attention to the other teacher. My target person is very attentive to our conversation. I know that this is not perfect, but it's much better than hiding in the restroom. (Steinwachs, 1995)

The data analysis of your project should point to some new patterns of behavior for you to incorporate into work with your target person. These patterns are addressed in the following section of the chapter.

Post-Project Interactions: Creating a Natural Transition to Your Next Steps Project

As you complete your project, you will terminate the intense scrutiny of (and monitoring the interactions with) your target person. You will no longer need to maintain records or extend yourself toward your target person because of your project. Now, your responsibility is to find ways to translate what you've learned in your project into practical ways to improve your working relationship, one that will be referred to as your *Next Steps project*. Sets of questions are presented in three categories: communication habits, problem-solving habits, and cooperative work efforts. You can use them to decide where to go from here.

COMMUNICATION HABITS

Observing your communication with your target person over the past few weeks has probably produced some new insights. One of the conclusions that you have drawn may parallel one developed by the five collaborating teachers who participated in a study conducted by Nowacek (1992): "The experiences of these teachers suggest that collaboration is contextual—dependent upon the educational philosophy and teaching style of each teacher, and the expectations of their individual schools and educational levels" (p. 275). The teachers in this study found that

> they learned a great deal by observing and consulting with one another over the course of the school year. To an outsider, the knowledge exchange seemed to occur by osmosis rather than by injection. In fact, the evolution of the *relationships* [italics added] among these professionals is perhaps the most striking shared feature of their experience. (p. 275)

The teachers made time for their collaborative efforts and created new contexts within which to communicate. This led to their habits of reciprocal sharing. Their experiences leads to the first question posed here.

1. What Contexts Can You Select for Communication With Your Target Person That Will Have the Best Chances of Continuing/Further Improving Your Communication Habits?

Your decision about *where* and *when* to interact with your target person could be as important as *what* you are discussing. During this project, you have probably generated both optimism and pessimism regarding your working relationship. As you review the circumstances in which you were successful as well as those in which you achieved less than you expected, develop a model to guide your communication habits in your Next Steps project.

The development of new contexts can help you in many project goals. For example, communication may have been a major focus for you. If you expand or, more specifically, focus certain aspects of your communication with your target person, you may develop new communication patterns. Assertiveness may have been one of the things you addressed in your project. Some of the ideas you generate in Idea Try-Out 10.1 may give you ways to build on what you have already done.

> I find myself in a funny place, now that this project is wrapping up. I knew when I began that I was just opening up the lines of communication with my principal, and I've been able to do that very well. What I didn't tackle was to disagree with her—and the thought of that still scares me. Where do I go from here?

In setting new goals for your Next Steps project, be specific and realistic.

Next Steps Idea Try-Out 10.1

Mapping It Out

This Idea Try-Out is designed to help you think about future communication with your target person after the conclusion of your project. It will also assist you in the review of your project's successes.

1. In your collaboration notebook, draw a rough sketch of the location(s) in which you and your target person interacted. Your drawing(s) need not be precise.

2. Think back to the very beginning of your project. Put "X"s on your diagram representing the places where you and your target person communicated.

3. Now, consider the past few weeks. Circle all the places (including those you've already marked with an "X") where you've communicated lately.

4. Beside each mark on the diagram, include a few words to remind you of some of the things you discussed.

5. Brainstorm ways to expand your communication by doing one or more of the following:
   a. add new places to communicate
   b. add new discussion topics
   c. add new people to be part of your discussion
   d. add new goals for yourself

6. Select one or two of the items you brainstormed in Step 5 to incorporate into your Next Steps project.

If you tried a Clean Slate project, you may have been able to eliminate or minimize past feelings or concerns. You may have realized that you were burdened by issues that no longer had to be part of your day-to-day life. Ideally, you were able to achieve a fresh start. The same thing may apply to a project that had little prior history, a Getting to Know You project. In both these cases, you may find that new topics or a new mix of people could lead to a continuation of the momentum developed in your project.

The conclusions drawn at the end of some projects, unfortunately, are less optimistic. In some cases, students are forced to realize that little can be done to improve a difficult situation. This does not mean that your project is a failure. You may have succeeded in changing *your* attitude. In addition, you may have developed a new goal—in the future you will have as little to do with your target person as possible. If this is the situation, you still want to consider your answers to the previous idea try-out. Your answers are important because the occasional contacts you have with your target person are still likely to be stressful.

As you try to decide how to continue a more realistic approach to collaboration, you may find it useful to incorporate the description of the "ideal collaborative enterprise" by Pugach and Allen-Meares (1985): "The existence of a unitary goal, mutuality of effort, overcoming the protection of professional 'territory,' trust between professionals to solve problems jointly, and understanding of and mutual respect for the different contributions of every school-based professional" (p. 4). This definition leads naturally to the second question.

2. How Can You Demonstrate Professional Respect When You Work Together on Common Goals?

The development of communication habits that convey respect may require a review of your nonverbal and verbal communication patterns. There may be some concerns that you didn't have time to address during your project on which you could concentrate as you move forward, as in the following example. If your focus was on an area of conflict (e.g., you had a Values Clash or Different Work Styles project), you may have had to overcome some natural resistance toward your target person. Addressing these remaining concerns can be a vital part of your future success in working with this individual. Consider Idea Try Out 10.2 as a way to answer this question.

Next Steps Idea Try-Out 10.2

Sugar, Spice, Puppy Dog Tails

This Idea Try-Out will give you an opportunity to consider how to honestly communicate with your target person. This will involve demonstrating genuine respect for at least one thing your target person does well.

1. Get out your collaboration notebook and spend three minutes writing down as many things as you can about your target person's professional style. Include whatever comes to mind—positive characteristics as well as negative ones.

2. Review what you have written and circle positive traits that could be used to develop a healthy respect for your target person.

3. Select one positive trait. Use it as the basis for building your respect for your target person in the future.

Your decision about how to incorporate mutual respect into your future working relationship with your target person presumes that your target person will do the same thing. While this is not always going to be the case, the likelihood is much greater if you begin the process than if you do not.

Communication alone, however, cannot resolve all differences. Some must be addressed by more structured dialogue. Select a circumstance for communication that maximizes your own accountability and serves a necessary purpose. The following section on problem solving may provide the circumstance you need.

PROBLEM-SOLVING HABITS

Writings about collaboration dovetail with literature on changes in school leadership. York-Barr & Duke's excellent 2004 review of teacher leadership illustrates that the results to date have not been rigorous or consistent. One of the substantive findings from their review of literature on teacher leadership was that *"developing trusting and collaborative relationships is the primary means by which teacher leaders influence their colleagues"* (p. 288). This idea was embedded in Goodlad's work (1990b). Trust is especially relevant if your project focused on value clashes or different work styles. You may have found that you had to look at your own goals within a broader context—you had to learn what was expected schoolwide. In Chapter 4, you examined a current situation in which you find yourself—for example, schoolwide norms influencing all the teachers in your school. Bolman and Deal (2003), in their classic analysis of organizations, describe four "frames" used to clarify organizational priorities. These four (structural, human resources, political, and symbolic) highlight the rationale behind choices made by leaders. Their 2002 book, *Reframing the Path to School Leadership: A Guide for Teachers and Principals,* is a resource that can enable you to gain a new perspective on your school as a result of your project. You may also find Lorna Idol's 15 questions very helpful to assist you in getting perspective. Her 1997 article, "Key Questions Related to Building Collaborative and Inclusive Schools," raises excellent points that you may now be in a position to consider.

Now that you have completed your project, review your earlier observations about your school and reconsider them from a schoolwide perspective. Leithwood's (1992) description of two different sets of buildingwide norms could assist you. He contrasts a school in which the principal is involved with "first order changes" (e.g., "improving the technical, instructional activities of the school through the close monitoring of teachers' and students' classroom work") to those that focus on "second order changes" (e.g., "building a shared vision, improving communication, and developing collaborative decision-making processes") (p. 9). Which of these descriptions fits your school? The following is an example of second order changes.

I really admire my principal because he is so connected to our community. He makes sure that our building is always involved with community centers. He does this in big and little ways. Not only do we regularly have food drives at holidays, but we do more. We get the people who go to those centers to come in and talk with us about what they'd like to see us do differently next year. He keeps on showing us that our work is never done. We have to keep on listening, thinking, problem solving, to keep our connections to the community alive.

Contrast that with this example of first order changes:

We got a new principal this year. She sends us a lot of e-mails, but they are just things she forwards to us from our superintendent, parent group, or Listservs to which she subscribes. Her focus is very specific—reminding us of upcoming deadlines, things to remember to tell our students at the end of each week, how many weeks it is until the end of the grading period. But six months into the school year, I have no better idea than I had at the start of what she really thinks is important. Still, we do get things done.

Roberts (1985) describes two kinds of leadership. One is transactional leadership, based on an exchange of services for rewards (e.g., money, status, or intrinsic rewards). The other is transformational leadership, in which the leader facilitates the outlook of others. Kouzes and Posner (2002) describe different types of transformational leaders. Transformational leadership can include "the redefinition of a people's mission and vision, a renewal of their commitment, and the restructuring of their systems for goal accomplishment" (p. 124). Think about leaders with whom you have worked and how you saw each type of leadership in action. Sometimes, temporary administrators are able to serve as interesting role models because they are able to take risks that permanent administrators cannot, as described by Morris (2004).

Leithwood and Steinbach (1991) observed staff meetings and found that schools that had transformational principals used different kinds of group problem solving than those with more traditional leaders. The transformational principals "ensured a broader range of perspectives from which to interpret the problem by actively seeking different interpretations, being explicit about their own interpretations, and placing individual problems in the larger perspective of the whole school and its overall directions" (Leithwood, 1992, pp. 10–11). The transformational principals had a different set of expectations for participation by staff members, one in which individual accountability was critical. This point is important because some assume that a collaborative environment is one in which no one is accountable. Instead, as shown in Mohr and Dichter's 2001 article, teachers working together in a learning community model are more responsible than they are when working in a directive, top-down school setting.

In Smith's (1987) article about collaborative schools, he outlines three things that collaborative schools are not. First, leaders do not seek discussion for its own sake; instead, they involve people in purposeful dialogues. Second, school administrators do not abdicate their authority in such schools. Third, such schools do not reduce teachers' accountability (pp. 47–48). In summary, collaborative schools maintain lines of authority and personal responsibility. Mohr and Dichter (2001) describe the transformation of separate individuals into a learning organization, which goes through the evolutionary change process described in Chapter 12.

Kumpulainen and Kaartinen (2003) carefully examined the interpersonal dynamics between peers who were problem solving together. Their in-depth qualitative study of twenty 12-year-old students illustrated that use of a variety of communication and social strategies enabled the students to solve problems. In one example case, collaboration and joint reasoning led to shared problem solving, use of each other's ideas, and even sharing wording. When collaboration broke down, as in another example case, confusion emerged, with comments like "I don't want to" or "I don't know" characterizing their work (p. 356). The students experienced the "social and emotional challenges of collaborative reasoning" (p. 357), such that their end products included only fragmented ideas with no evidence of joint reasoning. Kumpulainen and Kaartinen illustrated that collaboration occurs only when both participants are engaged:

> successful peer collaboration appears to be characterized by symmetric interaction, during which conceptualizing the situation is a joint effort constructed with coherent problem-solving strategies and . . . language. The lack of a shared understanding, however, appears to be reflected in incoherent strategies . . . turning easily toward conflict and domination between peers. (p. 367)

Learning to work together requires engagement in the task and understanding the thinking of one's partner.

The notion of personal responsibility, inherent in the writing of these researchers, leads to the third question.

3. How Can You Make Sure Your Accountability to the Problem-Solving Process Does Not Depend on the Behavior of Your Target Person?

Your answer to this question may depend as much on an appraisal of your school's process for promoting problem solving as it does on your own interaction style. Consider reviewing some of the systemwide analysis you did in Chapter 4 as a resource for your planned approach.

Lloyd (2002) spent one year working with teachers in an inclusive setting, with a goal of helping the teachers to incorporate problem solving and reflective practice into their work. Her model was very similar to the collaboration project. While recognizing the limitations of her small-scale, qualitative study, she makes the following summary statements:

> The action research based program . . . has clearly enabled their development as critically reflective practitioners, actively engaging in the process of understanding, developing and transforming their practice, and in the process, enabling them to empower themselves and, in some cases, their pupils. . . . [This approach] can be a valuable tool for developing and changing practice in education and can certainly be seen as crucially important in the move towards inclusion. (p. 126)

Your new way of working, reflecting, and thinking can be independent of how your target person behaves.

Elliott and Sheridan (1992) discuss ways to enhance problem solving among educators, parents, and support personnel. Their observations can be applied to your upcoming work with your target person. Questions that apply to planning, curriculum implementation, and evaluation served as guidelines. A parallel approach might be useful to you and introduces the fourth question.

4. How Can You and Your Target Person Best Solve Problems That Come Up in the Future?

By referring to your answer to the first question in this section and modifying it to focus on problem solving, you may have a way to address both Question 1 and Question 4 simultaneously. The problem-solving material in Chapter 3 might help you develop your approach. Consider building on your collaboration project to address research questions directly related to your students. Denton, Vaughn, and Fletcher (2003) contrast work in schools with and without collaboration:

> Real change will require the combined efforts of researchers, educational practitioners, teacher educators, and policymakers. Those of us who care deeply about the education of students for whom learning is difficult have a clear choice. We can continue to implement programs in which large numbers of students are allowed to fail, or we can collaborate in initiatives that have the potential to result in the widespread implementation of effective instructional practices. (p. 209)

Once you have laid the groundwork—via improved communication and problem solving—you can answer the set of questions focusing on cooperative work efforts.

COOPERATIVE WORK EFFORTS

Collins, Hall, and Branson (2002) describe the highly successful collaborative team used to involve students with disabilities in general education classroom activities in a rural setting. Thirteen guidelines illustrate the kinds of initiatives special educators took to involve individuals in the school and a university faculty member in research activities that resulted in benefits for all students. They conclude that "working on applied collaborative research projects can be beneficial for rural teachers who may feel isolated . . . Teachers who participate in research build self-confidence in their ability to problem solve and make decisions based on data" (p. 5). Cooperative work efforts in this case resulted in increased collaboration as well as five published articles.

Another effective approach used for cooperative work efforts is the Teacher Work Group model. Ferguson (1994) explains that the model originated in 1986 at the University of Oregon and consisted of "two or more teachers who get together on a regular basis to help each other understand and solve the problems they encounter as they try to improve educational outcomes for their students" (p. 43). It has since become more complexly defined. Ferguson more completely documented the original approach elsewhere (Ferguson, 1992; Ferguson, Jeanchild, & Todd, 1991), including the heuristic device used to help teachers make decisions about changes. The Teacher Work Group model could be incorporated into your Next Steps project in the coming year.

If, for example, you were working on assertiveness as the focus of your project, you could use the Teacher Work Group model to give yourself opportunities to address this concern further. This might be done directly, if your target person is a member of your group, or indirectly, if the group functions without your target person. As the following example indicates, this approach might meet your needs.

Seven of us have been getting together on Tuesday mornings, before school, for about three years now. I never imagined, when we got started, how valuable a resource this group of teachers would be for me. We've taught ourselves to ask tough questions and avoid easy answers. Each week, I leave the group feeling more focused on my teaching, on making it better. It fortifies me for the rest of the week.

According to Ferguson (1994), the Teacher Work Groups have several key features that you could adapt to meet the needs of your situation.

1. Teacher Work Groups are teacher directed. This means that teachers develop and maintain these groups. "As a consequence of teacher control, the work groups build collegiality and networks that can reduce the isolation so often felt by teachers" (p. 43). The teacher-directed nature of the groups can help you. For example, if you are continuing a Getting to Know You project, this approach could help you build on the working relationship you have established thus far.

2. Teacher Work Groups are outcome based. Teachers take opportunities to look at the concerns they have and discuss options that might be explored. All the strategies included throughout this book suggesting ways for you to actively participate with others can be used to achieve the directed outcomes you want to accomplish.

3. Teacher Work Groups focus on continuing evaluation and improvement. Similar to the evaluation system you set up for your project, the work groups emphasize accountability. The result can be an increased sense of connectedness to others. As Ferguson (1994) reports, "we are finding that getting a little help from your friends is one good way to feel in charge of your professional life, even when you find yourself in a less than ideal work situation" (p. 47). The benefits can outweigh the costs of time and energy you have to invest.

Borko's 2004 description of research on professional development for teachers highlights the cyclical nature of research and its tendency to return to the same question in different settings. Projects like the collaboration project you just completed fit into her view of ongoing scrutiny. Smith (2002) describes several mentoring models that involve technology paired with face-to-face inservice programs.

Smith and Ingersoll (2004) analyzed the pervasiveness of induction/mentoring programs and learned that "induction and mentoring have expanded from a common to a widespread practice for newcomers in the teaching occupation" (p. 691), based on their analysis of Schools and Staffing Survey (SASS) administered by the National Center for Education Statistics (NCES) data from 1999–2000. They also found that

> about two-thirds of beginning teachers said that they worked closely with a mentor, about 70% in public schools and 42% and 46% in charter and private schools respectively. In about 7 in 10 of these cases, new teachers were matched with mentors in the same field. The vast majority of mentees (nearly 9 in 10) found their mentors helpful. (p. 692)

The presence of a mentor alone was not sufficient to reduce turnover.

> The most salient factors [for reducing turnover] were having a mentor from the same field, having common planning time with other teachers in the same subject or collaboration with other teachers on instruction, and being part of an external network of teachers. . . . Teachers participating in combinations or packages of mentoring and group induction activities were less likely to migrate to other schools or to leave teaching at the end of their first year. (Smith & Ingersoll, 2004, p. 706)

Using your collaboration experience to involve others in your building in broader-based collaboration activities has the potential to assist new teachers who are acclimating to teaching and to special education.

Weiss and Lloyd (2002, 2003) analyzed how to create effective conditions for co-teaching, using a qualitative research design involving six special education teachers who were observed a total of 31 times and interviewed three times over the course of five months. They found that special educators took a number of different roles in the co-taught classroom, for example, "(a) providing support to students, (b) teaching the same content in a different classroom, (c) teaching a separate part of the content in the same classroom, or (d) teaching as a team" (2002, p. 32). Only one of the teachers developed the "teaching as a team" model, and she had this explanation for approaching co-teaching in this way: "she defined co teaching as team teaching, and her colleagues accepted her teaching style, initiative and competence in this area. Altogether, this teacher felt she was an equal partner with the general education teachers with whom she worked" (2002, p. 36). The teachers "who did not feel they knew the content well . . . consistently acted as aides to the general education teacher, not as equals" (2002, p. 38). The diversity of approaches is an issue of concern:

> Every teacher in this study stated that they were co-teaching in some form and that they were following guidelines for integration developed by the district. Yet, with six different teachers, there were four very different models of co-teaching in the classroom. How could administrators evaluate the implementation or effectiveness of co-teaching? (2002, p. 39)

In their 2003 article about a different aspect of their research, Weiss and Lloyd conclude that the heterogeneity of approaches to co-teaching needs to be further studied and that

> researchers should evaluate the outcomes of students with disabilities in these classrooms under the various role and action conditions and delineate specifically how the needs of students are met. In addition, once successful roles and actions are described, the resources and supports to put them into place must also be defined. (p. 68)

Use this time when you are alert to what you have been doing via your collaboration project to more carefully define your approach to collaboration. Commit to studying the effect of co-teaching and collaboration on the achievement and task engagement of students in your classes.

As you consider future collaborative efforts, you have some decisions to make regarding how to best work with others. This can serve as the basis for the fifth question.

5. How Can You Cooperate With Your Target Person in a Way That Promotes Teacher-Directed Cooperation and Fits Within the Norms of Your Work Setting?

Sometimes, you may use a very content-focused agenda or checklist, such as the one by Nolet and Tindal (1994) shown in Table 10.1. In other cases, you can informally brainstorm, thereby clarifying what each of you is expected to do. In her article about classroom assistants, Fletcher-Campbell (1992) makes several suggestions to "clarify the complementary roles of the teacher and classroom assistant" (p. 141) and identifies "the particular skills, expertise and interests which classroom assistants bring with them into the school" (p. 142). Her suggestions may be helpful if you work with a classroom assistant or co-teacher. York-Barr and Kronberg (2002) comment on the complexities that often prevent true collaboration from taking place: "Making the transition to new ways of thinking, doing, and being is difficult . . . The process of transition is personal and involves loss as well as opportunity" (p. 164). The story the authors share about a middle school program that examined its own practices and moved from separate to a collaborative model illustrates the types of transition issues of Bridges (2003), whom the authors cite. They conclude that "collaborative partnerships can provide an invaluable energy source for effective teaching and learning. The collaborative partnerships and instructional practices evidenced in [their chapter] provide examples of movement toward a more generative approach to inclusive schooling" (p. 180).

Table 10.1   Planning Meeting Checklist

Date of Meeting _____

Teachers _____

Task	Yes/No		Comment
Topic Identified	Yes	No	
Schedule Outlined	Yes	No	
Knowledge Forms Identified	Yes	No	
Attributes/Examples Identified	Yes	No	
Reading Tasks	Yes	No	
Problem-Solving Tasks	Yes	No	
Assignments Specified	Yes	No	
Final Test Discussed	Yes	No	
Grading Negotiated	Yes	No	
Pull-Away Schedule Discussed	Yes	No	
Student Reminders	Yes	No	
Notes			

SOURCE: "Curriculum–Based Collaboration," by Victor Nolet and Gerald Tindal, in *Focus on Exceptional Children*, 1994, Vol. 27, No. 3, (page 9). Denver: Love Publishing Company. Reprinted by permission.

Your description of classroom cooperation can serve as a fulcrum, helping you maintain your balance as a teacher. Look to the future: find other teachers and begin using a collaborative format that feels right for you. As shown in the following example, the start of the school year may be the time to initiate something new.

After the summer break, I was ready to think about school again. I wanted to figure out what to do so I wouldn't feel so by myself. The idea of the Teacher Work Groups made sense to a couple of us. We thought we'd try it and see how it goes.

CONCLUSION

As you translate what you've learned from your project into further action, you may be considering continued contact with your target person. You might change from a Getting to Know You project to a Different Work Style project now that you are more familiar with your target person.

But, you may also be ready to move on. After completing one collaboration project, a second is much easier to inaugurate. In the next two chapters, you will see how to apply what you have learned to a different target person or setting.

11

Generalizing Your Plan to Others

Improved Collaboration With Parents and Family Members of Your Students

Think back to your decision to become a teacher. Did you picture yourself making a difference in the lives of your students? Were the parents, brothers, sisters, and extended family members of your students also included in your vision? As you visualized the school year progressing, you may have imagined involving family members in classroom activities, schoolwide events, and holidays. Getting to know the students would be a two-way street, in which the family members learned from you as you were able to better understand them. And students would benefit from your involvement with their families.

Many beginning teachers imagine this hopeful scenario only to be sharply disappointed when family members they meet are reserved or distrustful. Unfortunately, the optimistic commitment to develop opportunities involving families can disappear early in the careers of teachers. This chapter will focus on adapting what you've learned in your collaboration project and applying your learning to your contacts with the family members of your students. By the end of the chapter, you will have new keys to use to unlock the challenges of working with family members.

Developing your unique connections with family members is similar to being able to teach effectively. Both take place slowly. As Cole (1992) explains, becoming a teacher takes time:

Becoming a teacher, like becoming a person, is a complex and ongoing process of personal and social interaction and interpretation. All teachers, new and experienced, have been engaged for a lifetime in a natural human growth process directly and indirectly interacting with people, places, and things, their development consequently influenced in a variety of ways. The work place, or professional context, is yet another venue for human growth and development. (p. 365)

Cole reminds us that the content we teach our students is influenced by all of our experiences. In a similar way, your work with the family members of your students will be influenced by many events such as the one described in the following example.

Even though it was 20 years ago, I can still remember that October Open House the year I was student teaching. Lana, my supervising teacher, and I spent a whole week getting everything ready, making sure we had lots for the parents to see and do. Lana baked gingerbread people, and the students decorated them. Each parent would get the cookie his or her child decorated. We were so ready, but only two parents showed up! While we were cleaning up, I asked Lana if she was discouraged. She said, "Sure. But I never want to give up hope." Her honest words stayed with me. They've helped me through bad times over the years.

Investigating how teachers can work effectively with family members continues to be central in the teacher education literature (e.g., Mandell & Murray, 2005). If you think back, you'll realize that you've already had a wide range of complex experiences with families throughout your life. Reflect on your own family and families with whom you have come into contact in schools and through friendships. All serve as a bedrock for your work with families in your career as a teacher.

Sussell, Carr, and Hartman (1996) summarize professionals' perceptions of parents historically, from the nineteenth-century view of "parents as problems" to the 1970s view of "parents as teachers" who could extend the teaching day beyond 3:00 P.M., and finally, to the current view that "parents as partners" have much to give to professionals. In commenting on the current point of view, they state that "the goal of this [current view] is to empower parents to act as advocates for themselves and for their children" (pp. 53–54). Hammond (2001) describes her involvement of family members, teacher-educators, preservice teachers, students, and community members in a collaborative effort to involve family members in urban science education. Her in-depth description of her year-long project concludes with the following observation:

Using parents as 'experts' is a strength of the project . . . The focus of this article has been on teachers and parents as learners . . . If adults can build the bridges [between two worlds], it will be much easier for the children involved to cross. (pp. 995–996)

Family involvement can transform the educational experience of all involved in the collaboration—family members, educators, and students.

The same point was made by Ann and Rudd Turnbull (their outstanding textbook about families of individuals with disabilities is now in its fifth edition; Turnbull et al., 2006). They expanded the roles of families working with professionals to include the role of collaborators. They discuss parent and family involvement in this way: "The Individuals with Disabilities Education Act (IDEA) (20 U.S.C. Sec. 1414[b][4][A]) provides that a student's parents have a right to be on the team; moreover, best practice recognizes that parents (and other individuals, including family members . . .) are essential members of the team" (Turnbull et al., 2006, p. 186). Their description, and that of Dinnebeil and Hale (1999) and Frankland (2001), highlight the incorporation of families into the team serving individuals with disabilities, via a collaborative model.

Collaboration with families is the foundation of the effective education of students. Learning how to involve family members in the education process could be the subject of a series of books. This single chapter cannot cover the topic completely. Instead, this chapter is intended to provide ways for you to build on what you have learned about yourself in the rest of this book, to enhance your family-teacher partnerships.

Idea Try-Out 11.1 is adapted from "Famous Faces," an exercise developed by Satir (1995). You can use the ideas generated in this try-out whether currently you are a full time college student (with no access to family members of your students) or are teaching. Your responses in the try-out can be based on the actual experiences you've had, or on what you imagine as you think about working with families.

Idea Try-Out 11.1

What If?

This Idea Try-Out is designed to help you to record some ideas that are important to you as you work on enhancing your contacts with the family members of your students.

1. In your collaboration notebook, jot down as many words or phrases as you can that describe the "ideal" relationship that you could develop with the family members of your students. Take about three minutes. Use the following list as a springboard.

Honest	Enlightening	Candid	Thriving
Relevant	Genuine	Caring	Full of questions
Timely	Unapologetic	Frequent	Informative

2. In your collaboration notebook, jot down as many words or phrases as you can that describe the "worst nightmare" of relationships that you could develop with your students' family members. Take about three minutes. Use the following list as a springboard.

Sarcastic	Embittered	Questioning	Nonexistent
Painful	Blaming	Resentful	Distrustful
Dishonest	Unpredictable	Hurtful	Angry

3. Review your lists. Pick the five or ten words that are most powerful for you. They can come from either list. Record them, double spaced, one below the other in the center of a new page in your collaboration notebook. At the top of the page on the right, write "Best-Case Scenario." On the left, write "Worst-Case Scenario." For each of the five or ten words you have chosen, describe what the best and worst outcome would be if you were to incorporate that word into your working relationship with family members. Look for a positive and negative in each.

    For example, if you selected the word "Timely," a best-case scenario would be that you and the family members would keep each other informed about changes or problems. This could open up your lines of communication and also minimize the possibility of ongoing problems that are never addressed. A worst-case scenario might be the constant pressure you would feel to stay in touch with the family. If you tend to be overly responsible, this could be a fatal trap.

4. Now that you have the best- and worst-case scenarios for each word, you know that the process of defining your working relationship with your students' family members is not going to be simple. Keep these words and ideas in mind as you read this chapter. We will be returning to them before the end of the chapter to put them in perspective.

You may find yourself imagining some circumstances that please you and some that discourage you. The spectrum of words you select in the Idea Try-Out represents the wide range of contacts you will have with family members throughout your teaching career. Establishing child and family teams (O'Meara, Fidler, & Parrish, 2004) can enable you to work with people who can work together to "develop wraparound plans, plan for crisis, support the implementation of the plan, assess informal and formal supports/resources, monitor services, inspire unconditional care, and provide long-term support of the family after the formal supports are gone" (p. 4).

In addition to helping each other, family members will be sources of strength and information for you. Additionally, they will present challenges. Where do you begin? One place to start is to become more aware of the diversity of families with whom you will be working. This is the first key to improving your ability to successfully involve families that are different from your own.

KEY 1: UNDERSTANDING FAMILY DIVERSITY

Educators need to be proactive to understand the complex families of today's students. While graduates of some institutions of higher education feel well-prepared to teach diverse populations (Bratlien & McGuire, 2002), others are less confident: "Teachers report that they need better preparation in how to teach diverse learners" (Brabeck & Shirley, 2003, p. 370). As Townsend (1994) cautions, increasingly, educators are calling for parents and family members to participate in their children's educational process. . . . As schools reflect society and become increasingly diverse, many differences may exist between teachers and students (Gay, 1993). They may vary in individual and cultural experiences, communication, and interaction styles. (p. 32)

Teachers' success in involving families is a combination of self-inquiry and outreach. Callicott (2003) makes the following observation: "Working with families requires objectivity. Working with families who are culturally diverse requires not only objectivity but also a willingness to examine myths and stereotypes" (p. 60). To effectively reach out to families, we have to go beyond what we think we know and learn about the cultures, customs, and communication styles important to our students, as shown in the following situation.

When I moved from the Midwest to the West Coast, I realized right away that I had a lot to learn. There were many holidays my students celebrated that were unfamiliar to me. I decided to spend my Thursday nights and Sunday afternoons visiting local community centers and houses of worship. My visits gave me an amazing feeling as I learned about new beliefs and cultures.

I asked my students questions about their experiences, to better understand them. Family members joined us, shared favorite recipes, and told us about customs that were special to their families. By the end of the school year, my class had celebrated the holidays of 23 different cultures. We've all expanded our ways to learn from each other.

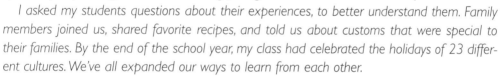

Warger (2001) made the following recommendations for addressing cultural issues when collaborating with families of students with disabilities:

- Step 1: Identify the cultural values in your interpretation of a student's difficulties or in the recommendation for service.
- Step 2: Find out whether the family members being served recognize and value your assumptions, and if not, how their views differ from yours.
- Step 3. Acknowledge and give explicit respect to any cultural differences identified, and fully explain the cultural basis of your assumptions.
- Step 4. Through discussion and collaboration, set about determining the most effective way of adapting your professional interpretations or recommendations to the value system of this family. (pp. 3–4)

Her recommendations encourage self-reflection and communication to facilitate improved collaboration with family members.

As Banks (1993) explains, diversity is a feature observable in both classrooms and the community:

Student diversity mirrors parent and community diversity. Just as teachers are expected to work with students from both genders and from different ethnic groups and social classes, parent involvement challenges teachers to work with a diverse group of parents . . . Diversity in parent and community groups can be a tremendous asset to the school. (p. 337)

Harry (1996) provides guidelines for teachers to use while attending to diversity in order to welcome family members as partners into the special education process. Ford (2004) describes how the development of effective school-community partnerships can serve as the basis for preparing special educators who are prepared to work with a diverse student body.

> This current 'linking of [school-community] resources' paradigm encompasses two interrelated premises. First, . . . schools alone cannot adequately address the multitude of problems confronting today's youth. This reality is more pronounced for districts in urban, low socioeconomic locales . . . The second premise focuses on the need to secure the involvement of significant others (e.g., parents and community leaders) who have a *direct stake* in what happens to youth. Effective school-community partnerships are beneficial to *all* students; and they are especially critical in maximizing educational opportunities for students from multicultural and/or bilingual backgrounds. (p. 226)

General and special education students can benefit from such partnerships.

If diversity is not present in the schools in which you are working, use other options to raise diversity awareness and develop comfort levels with people whose backgrounds are different from the majority culture in your school. Mbugua, Wadas, Casey, and Finnerty (2004) incorporated an intercultural, international, and intergenerational approach by bringing together two schools that had different student compositions—one was homogeneous, one was diverse. Involving family members, preservice teachers, university faculty, and experienced teachers in a series of multicultural activities enabled all to benefit. "The collaborative partnership allowed young children and their families to interact with persons from a different country and a different culture" (p. 241). The researchers involved drew the following conclusion:

> The partnership offers an effective low-cost approach to preservice and inservice teacher education; mentoring opportunities for preservice and inservice teachers; relevant, meaningful, contextual, and integrated technological experiences for preservice and inservice teachers and their students; a meaningful home-school connection; and collaborative opportunities between university faculty and K–4 school teachers for the mutual benefit of their students. (p. 243)

Collaboration was at the heart of the better understanding of diversity that occurred in this effort. Learning about schools with different majorities (e.g., Reyes, Scribner, & Scribner's 1999 description of high-performing Hispanic schools) as well as people with backgrounds different from your own (e.g., Cartledge, 1996, describing customs and values of families from many different cultural backgrounds) can assist you to be better prepared to welcome all families into your classroom.

Teachers' sensitivity to the diversity of their community can increase the likelihood of outreach to families in appropriate ways. The George Mason Project Kaleidoscope (1996–2000), funded by OSERS, included development of nine modules to include diversity training in preservice preparation programs for early childhood general and special educators. Such modules as "The Power of Stories" helped participants to gain insights such as this one: "The role of family and culture in child development is complex, and we as project staff continued to gain insights into the intricate ways that culture, family, and community influence the development of diverse children" (George Mason University, 2001, p. 4). However, understanding alone does not guarantee parent involvement. Parents have many reasons for not becoming active in school activities, as Banks explains:

> [Parents] resist becoming involved for several reasons. [1] Stress is an impor-
> tant reason for their lack of involvement. The pressure to earn a living and
> take care of a home and children can put a great deal of stress on parents. At
> the end of the day, some parents just want to rest. [2] Other parents do not
> believe they have the necessary educational background to be involved in
> their children's education. They feel intimidated by educators and believe
> that education should be left to the schools. [3] Others feel alienated from the
> school because of negative experiences they have had there or because they
> believe the school does not support their values. (p. 337)

Banks's comments underscore the need to better understand the experiences of parents and other family members you are trying to involve in school activities. Zetlin, Padron, and Wilson (1996) suggest additional reasons for lack of parent involvement, based on their extensive interviews of five Latin American families. The families "felt intimidated and confused when attending IEP meetings. . . . Four of the five parents also expressed feelings of mistrust for the teachers and other school personnel but were unable to voice their complaints regarding classroom curriculum and teaching methodology" (p. 27). The primary language in the homes of four of the five parents was Spanish. The authors conclude:

> All five mothers showed tremendous concern for their child's education and
> well being, and worried about indifferent teachers, Spanish/English con-
> fusion, functioning potential, and optimal placements. Testimonies such as
> these, which attest to high degrees of parental commitment and involvement,
> sit juxtaposed to Hispanic parents' deference to the system that inhibits overt
> criticism and advocacy. It seems logical that until schools are willing "to
> negotiate with parents from a posture of cultural reciprocity" (Harry, 1992),
> groups with the most incongruence from what is considered "typical" will
> have a difficult time fully participating in their child's education, however
> they view that role. (Zetlin et al., 1996, p. 28)

Language confusion originates both from problems understanding English and educators' use of jargon. Both of these problems left parents outside of a decision-making process in which they wanted to participate. As teachers, it is crucial for us to learn as much as we can about the perceptions of family members from diverse backgrounds. We can then adapt our outreach methods to dovetail with some of their needs and concerns. We should learn to ask questions and not to presume that we already have answers.

Armstrong and Moore (2004), analyzing how to incorporate a variety of viewpoints into their action research (focusing on inclusive practices), underscored the importance of involving others at the very start of the design of their research, so as to make sure that ideas of all were included:

> Understanding how these others are positioned in relation to proposed research
> can help to shape the enquiry and dramatically influence the relevance and

power of any project. For this reason we have changed our own perspectives on the importance of collaboration with others as part of creating inclusive practices through the research process itself. We now position consultation as the critical starting point. If possible, we want our research to be perceived as valuable, relevant, and useful by those on the receiving end of, or affected by, research outcomes, and we want our concerns and purposes to be ones they prioritize themselves. (p. 7)

Exploring the perspectives of those who will be part of research activities, and incorporating those ideas into the research plan, maximizes the likelihood that the effort will be of value. Armstrong and Moore (2004) use collaboration as a corner-stone of their work: "Our overarching intention is to encourage the development of a dynamic reciprocity between research and applied settings in order to advance the project of inclusion . . . through consultation and collaborative action and reflection" (p. 14). Collaboration serves to define the boundaries of the research activities.

Cooper (1990) warns researchers to avoid the overly simplistic approach of a single predictive model and, instead, encourages researchers to look at, and beyond, ethnicity for answers. Harry (1996) provides a comprehensive view of cultural diver-sity as it influences families involved in the special education system. She incorpo-rates consideration of economic status, ethnicity, race, culture, and proximity (both psychological and geographical) to the native culture as a framework for the analy-sis of how cultural diversity influences individuals.

Sensitivity to ethnicity should be one part of your thinking as you plan to involve family members in schools. The challenge is to find ways to move beyond lip service to action. Westling (1996), in his review of 25 studies surveying parents of children with moderate to severe mental disabilities, recommends that professionals "pro-vide parents with various ways to participate in school activities, especially ways to take part more meaningfully in the planning process. Focus especially on including minority parents and those with culturally different backgrounds" (p. 111).

Deciding how best to involve families from diverse backgrounds poses a chal-lenge. The Person Centered Planning approach, described by Callicott (2003) as of multiple names and origins, can serve as a model for collaboration among individu-als with different cultural or linguistic backgrounds. The following are a summary of the six principles used to involve students whose language, cultural background, or disabilities would differentiate them from others at their school:

1. Know your . . . individual

2. Encourage interactions

3. Provide effective feedback

4. Encourage parent participation

5. Appreciate and incorporate cultural diversity

6. Reduce prejudice (p. 66)

The school administrator is often expected to be the lead in this initiative. However, as Ford (1992) found out in her pilot study, not all administrators are qualified to meet this responsibility. Ford surveyed 21 special education administrators in Ohio and reported the following results: "Most of the special education administrators perceived that special education teachers who work with African American students should participate in multicultural education inservice training that focuses directly on issues relevant to African American youth and their families" (p. 112). Twenty of the 21 administrators had conducted a workshop or seminar in multicultural education, but only four had received any formal training on this topic. She concludes that "three essentials of high-quality programming (both preservice and inservice) are positive perceptions and attitudes of trainers concerning multicultural training, adequate qualifications of trainers, and the provision of ongoing multicultural education training" (p. 113).

To provide knowledgeable information, trainers have to be familiar with the content area. This means familiarity not only with ethnic diversity but also with the effects of family experiences on students in school. Special educators teaming together with English for speakers of other languages (ESOL) teachers can identify learning problems more effectively than either could do alone. Abrams, Ferguson, and Laud (2001) recommend

> a team approach . . . Many researchers recommend greater collaboration between ESOL teachers and special educators (Rosa-Lugo & Fradd, 2000; Brice & Roseberry-McKibbin, 1999; Board of Education of the City of New York, 1994). Working as a team, we have . . . made leaps in our professional knowledge and understanding of one another's fields. (p. 65)

Families with whom teachers will be interacting in the approaching decades will look different from those of previous generations, as shown in the following example.

When our high school Planning Committee began working on this year's graduation celebrations, we had a rude awakening. The school had always sponsored Father/Daughter and Mother/Son lunches the day of graduation. We looked at our graduating class and realized that it was time to rethink our approach. Many of our students had complicated family situations. The lunch format we had used for years had to be changed.

We brainstormed with members of our Parent/Teacher Association, and came up with a "Special Thanks" lunch. We decided to encourage our students to invite all the people who'd helped them succeed. Grandparents, elementary school teachers, and stepparents joined us and made our lunch the best one we'd ever had.

"Census data tell us that 59% of the children born in 1983 will live with only one parent before reaching 18—this is now the *normal* [italics added] childhood experience" (Williams, 1992, p. 159). The constellation of adults in the lives of students may change in the course of the students' pre-college education through divorce, separation, or death. Some students may have always lived in a single-parent household. The pressures described by Banks (1993) could easily proliferate if one parent rather than two is attempting to meet all the family's needs. It is easy to understand why help with homework or follow-through on a behavior management plan might not take the highest priority. Paterson (2001) urges us to rethink our stereotypes about single-parent households, and realize that some one-parent families are improvements over bickering or abusive family situations.

One way to address challenges faced in the single-parent households may be to increase the understanding of the underpinning of diverse family structures. The connection with the family can be usefully extended beyond the single adult in charge of the family. As Briscoe (1991) suggests, it is possible to involve members of the extended family as well:

> The concept of *family* is an integral part of the lives of both African American and Hispanic learners and serves a very essential source of external motivation for them. African American culture uses an extended family network. Defining *family* for this group in terms of a strict nuclear unit may overlook many sources of assistance in the educational process. (p. 16)

The following gives one poignant example of how to translate Briscoe's descriptions into a plan of action.

> *I decided to have Grandparents Day in my class after reading about it in one of my courses. I couldn't believe the responses I got. We had over 20 grandparents come to my preschool class, and they spent the whole morning! They told us about their lives, and we showed them the things we did. At the end of the morning, one of the grandfathers came over to me and said that this was the very first time he felt at ease with his grandson's disability. He said that whenever he spent time with his grandson (who is in a wheelchair), he was always thinking about the chair. That morning was the first time he forgot about the chair, and just thought about the boy.*

The participation of brothers, sisters, aunts, uncles, and grandparents in classroom activities can enrich the experiences for all—students in the class, family members, and the educators. Turnbull and Turnbull (1997) discuss the need for schools to become the context for family-professional collaboration and emphasize the need for a developmental approach. The content and style of interaction would have different goals for preschool children, elementary students, and secondary students (who are concerned about their lives after graduation). For example, Bouck (2004a) describes her study of six secondary students with mild mental retardation, in which she observed the peer-oriented social interactions of secondary students with mild disabilities. Friendships are the focus for students in general and special education settings. In her more extended paper (Bouck, 2004b), she identifies the following implication:

> [W]e must continue to examine students' needs, both academically and socially, when making decisions regarding instructional environments. As a field, we cannot remain 'hung up' on the endless debate of inclusion (see Kavale & Forness, 2000) but must focus on the outcomes students want and need, as well as what they, their parents, and teachers feel is best both academically and socially. As one student stated, 'the best part of the school day is seeing my friends.' (p. 18)

School activities to prepare students for experiences outside school are needed.

Turnbull, Turnbull, Bronicki, Summers, and Roeder-Gordon (1989) provide family members with strategies for transition planning for sons or daughters with disabilities. Teachers can become part of this planning process. For example, in Section 3, "Planning for Life in the Community," the Turnbulls ask and answer a series of questions (pp. 157–292). Together, teachers and parents can work toward activities that will lead to students' maximum self-sufficiency.

The potential positive impact of actively involving family members in all aspects of the education of their children is encouraged by Carter, Clark, Cushing, and Kennedy (2005). The authors, who focus on the transition from elementary to middle school for students with severe disabilities, have recommendations which include the following: "(1) Start planning early; (2) Collaborate across schools, (3) Prepare students early, (4) Encourage and support family involvement" (pp. 10–11). As an example of family involvement, consider the support and commitment to parent follow-through that was a vital part of the program developed by Townsend (1994). Family members actively participated in social skill instruction of 15 at-risk students in fourth, fifth, and sixth grade. The students were compared to nine normally achieving students (whose family members did not participate in the program). Pre- and posttest data were obtained before and after a 14-week social skills program. Both groups of students included a diverse ethnic mix.

Although there were significant differences between the two groups of students (those with and without disabilities) at the outset of the program, after the training no significant differences remained. This program resulted in benefits for both family members and teachers: "Family-involved social skill instruction can enhance relationships between school personnel and family members. Partnerships developed among home, school, and community settings increase the likelihood that the social skills taught will be used in other settings" (p. 36). Structured family involvement in school activities can lead to direct benefits for students. This kind of involvement can also serve as a basis for improved communication between home and school. Callicott (2003) cautions against oversimplification:

> Culture is easily defined on paper but not so easily identified in the flesh. As such, it must be considered for the kaleidoscope that it is. It may be fluid rather than static and is even more individually defined and applied than the educational diagnosis we give the students we work with in schools. One Hispanic student's experience and values do not define all students from Spanish-speaking countries or those with Spanish-sounding surnames. Differences related to regions, generations, religions, family structures or sizes, and economic classes exist within every culture. (p. 66)

Callicott's advice can be incorporated into all our work, whether we are considering individuals with disabilities or people from different cultures. Ideally, a program like the one implemented by Townsend (1994) can treat each person with individual attention and not run the risk of stereotyping. However, such an intense approach is not always possible. Instead, teachers must find ways to design practical linkages to family members that are realistic and meaningful. As Briscoe (1991) suggests,

> the intergenerational link between adults and youngsters is especially strong as it relates to issues surrounding culture and school success. Learners do not operate in a vacuum. Young people return home to adult caregivers at the conclusion of the school day. To overlook the context in which the youngster operates is to overlook a very vital connection required for educational success. (p. 13)

To find out more about the home environments, you can develop a collaboration project that addresses the issue of diversity. Briscoe (1991) urges educators to participate in self-reflective activities: "All currently held personal assumptions must be examined and challenged to assess the extent to which personal beliefs encompass cultural bias" (p. 17). Use the goals and activities provided in the next section to begin this examination process. Briscoe also suggests that "educators must become familiar with divergent cultures. . . . Familiarity with diverse cultural values allows an understanding of divergent behavior and an interpretation that does not automatically stereotype it" (p. 17). Increased familiarity is a first step toward reducing stereotypes.

Ford (2004) outlined a three-phase teacher education program model for special educators involving attitude and behavior changes that are designed to "prepare preservice level special education teachers to productively collaborate with SMCR [Significant Multicultural Communities Resource]" (pp. 228–229). Specific ways to incorporate collaboration related to diversity into your work are described in the next section of the chapter.

Sample Goals and Activities Addressing Family Diversity

Consider the following as potential goals for a collaboration project focused on working more effectively with family members from diverse backgrounds. The goals are based on the multicultural competencies identified in Christensen's (1992) study of training areas that 90 professionals in California and 10 national presenters deemed the most critical training areas to enable them to "work effectively with families from diverse cultures . . . [and] have the awareness, knowledge, and skill relative to a multitude of cultural issues" (p. 53).

Goal 1: Gain general understanding of specific cultures.

Sample Activity 1.1 Informally interview people from different cultural backgrounds about three or four topics of interest to you. Record your results in your collaboration notebook.

Sample Activity 1.2 Read about practices of different cultures in articles in popular magazines, newspapers, novels, anthropology studies, and on Web sites. Record your findings in your collaboration notebook.

Sample Activity 1.3 Listen to music or study artistic products of several cultures.

Sample Activity 1.4 Set up opportunities through your school to highlight holidays of different cultures, including beliefs, traditions, and special foods. Involve extended family members of students of these cultures in the learning experiences.

Sample Activity 1.5 Participate locally in cultural events sponsored by ethnic groups with which you are unfamiliar.

Sample Activity 1.6 "Establish a resource network composed of individuals or organizations that have been successful" in working with different cultures (Briscoe, 1991, p. 17).

Goal 2: Learn about the child-rearing practices, gender roles, and family patterns of specific cultures.

Sample Activity 2.1 Develop four or five questions about child-rearing practices, gender roles, and family patterns. Record both your questions and answers you collect in your collaboration notebook. Use at least three of the following sources to develop your questions: books, online search, review of articles in journals or news magazines, biographies, popular films, or personal interviews.

Sample Activity 2.2 Talk with people you know whose family background differs from yours about the questions developed in Activity 2.1. Record their answers in your collaboration notebook.

Sample Activity 2.3 Keeping this goal in mind, observe families in a recreational setting. After you get home, record what you see and hear in your collaboration notebook.

Sample Activity 2.4 Identify three friends or people you know from work whose cultural backgrounds are different from yours. Spend some time interviewing them and reviewing some of their family mementos that illustrate important events in their family experiences as you share the same reflections about your own family. If possible, work with them to create "memory pages" for your family and theirs. Use copies of pictures (e.g., scanning the originals so that you can return the originals to the people you are interviewing), narrative descriptions, and digital pictures of mementos of times that were important to each of you in your personal acculturation process. Discuss issues related to this goal as you work together on your "pages." If possible, involve members of your own family in your preliminary review of these pages. Collect these pages and put them into a notebook; continue to add to this notebook throughout your work on these goals.

Goal 3: Find out about the value people of different cultures attach to disability and their beliefs about professionals who work with people with disabilities.

Sample Activity 3.1 Develop four or five questions about disability in general, as well as a few questions about one or more specific disabilities. Collect answers using at least three of the following sources: books, online search, review of articles in journals or news magazines, biographies, popular films, Web sites, or personal interviews. Record your questions and answers in your collaboration notebook.

Sample Activity 3.2 In your collaboration notebook, record four or five assumptions you have about disabilities and the roles professionals take in relation to people with disabilities. Talk with people you know whose cultural background differs from yours. Record their answers in your collaboration notebook.

Sample Activity 3.3 Interview three or four professionals to obtain their experiences related to providing assistance to people from different cultural backgrounds.

Goal 4: Acknowledge your own cultural heritage, beliefs, values, and biases.

Sample Activity 4.1 Talk with members of your nuclear and extended family about what activities, ideas, or things were most important in communicating their own cultural experiences and values from one generation to another. Select a friend or two whose cultural background is similar to yours and have a similar discussion.

Sample Activity 4.2 Review your own experiences with people of different cultures while you were growing up and while in college. Include your friends and acquaintances and also impressions formed from books and movies. Record three or four biases you have developed that should be addressed during your professional career to help you work with families from these cultures more effectively.

Sample Activity 4.3 Together with a few members of your family (ideally from different generations), create a "family book." Include scanned photographs, narrative descriptions, and digital pictures of mementos representing times that were important to you in your acculturation process. Highlight issues related to the items in this goal.

Sample Activity 4.4 Select a role model who exemplifies the ideas and behaviors toward people of other cultures that you would like to emulate. Pick the person from your circle of friends or acquaintances, or select a public person. Develop three or four ideas about your own cultural background or stereotypes about other cultural backgrounds to monitor over the next month. Record your progress in your collaboration notebook.

These goals and activities can prepare you to collaborate with family members of students from different cultural backgrounds.

Project Try-Out 11.2

Best and Worst

This exercise is designed to help you consolidate ideas you have developed about working with families from different cultural backgrounds into a workable plan.

1. Return to Project Try-Out 11.1 in your collaboration notebook. Review your list of words and phrases as well as the best-case and worst-case scenario for each word.

2. Highlight the words on the page that could, in some way, reflect issues associated with the diversity of the families with whom you are currently working or anticipate working in the future.

3. Select one goal from the previous section of this chapter that appeals to you. Pick two or three activities listed in the chapter that you can commit to accomplishing within the next three months. Select activities from those listed under the goal you picked or from other goals, or feel free to develop your own activities.

Project Try-Out 11.2 can be a cornerstone for your future work with families whose backgrounds differ from your own. You may want to come back to it in the future when you have time to try out additional activities. However, this type of preparation alone is not enough. If we are to follow Briscoe's (1991) recommendation, we have to take responsibility for successful communication with family members. In the following section the second key is provided, highlighting ways to enhance your communication with family members.

KEY 2: DEVELOPING PRACTICAL COMMUNICATION HABITS

Communicating with family members effectively is a habit that effective teachers develop. Teachers need to both give information to and get information from family members; this dialogue becomes the basis for educating students. As Turnbull et al. (2006) explain, "Strong professional-professional partnerships have the same seven principles as strong family-professional partnerships. All partnerships must be grounded in trust and adhere to the principles that sustain it, including respect, commitment, advocacy, equality, competence, and communication" (Turnbull et al., 2006, p. 186).

The results of the study conducted by Mundschenk and Foley (1994) pertain to this communication key. The researchers interviewed 34 secondary (general and special education) teachers and 92 parents from a diverse urban environment. The parents were selected to represent, in approximately equal groups, viewpoints of students who were high achieving, average achieving, low achieving, or had a disability. The ethnicity of the subjects was not reported. Based on the interviews, which were presented in aggregate, teachers and parents had different priorities for "successful teacher-parent partnerships." They didn't see things the same way, as illustrated in the following example.

When I sit in the teachers' lounge and listen to teachers talk about parents, I cringe. As a parent of a child with a disability and a special educator, I understand things from both perspectives.

I can empathize with the parents being criticized. No matter what I do, I never have time for everything I'd like to do for and with my son. I wish I could bring some of the teachers home

> *with me. They could see the daily "assignments" I have from occupational therapists, physical therapists, and teachers!*
>
> *I struggle to explain my experience to them. I try to figure out how to help teachers understand how it is on the parents' side. Maybe some day I'll learn their language.*

While teachers rated "frequent verbal communication, written notes/mail, and parent's involvement/concern" as the top three items, parents rated "parental involvement" as last. Parents viewed "communication/parents informed, more contact and follow-up from teachers, and cooperation/working together" as their top three choices (Mundschenk & Foley, 1994, p. 18). As the example shows, parents' views can differ from those of teachers.

> Both teachers and parents felt that communication was the most critical factor in establishing positive relationships. It is interesting to note that both groups identified approaches that involved the other party in facilitating these relationships. Approximately 25% of the teachers reported that increased parental involvement or concern would be helpful, and 22% of the parents identified additional contact and follow-up from teachers as being critical for effective partnerships. . . .
>
> We need to investigate the barriers to parent participation and remove any misconceptions about who should be the initiator of home-school contacts. This is critical because many parents interviewed reported that increased teacher initiation of contacts would facilitate the establishment of effective partnerships. Schools need to engage parents, students, and teachers in active discussion and problem-solving procedures. (Mundschenk & Foley, 1994, p. 18)

The difficulties may be influenced by the format of communication or the topics chosen. Ulrich and Bauer (2003) provide an overview of "levels of awareness" of parents and family members that illustrates that there can be benefits to self-reflection: "In working with families, we must also look at our own levels of awareness and our own transformational experiences" (p. 21) so that we connect with the parents' outlook:

> The professionals and the parents may not be a match in the following types of awareness:
>
> - Their feelings about the issues of disabilities
> - Their personal histories
> - Their transformational experiences, knowledge, and learning about the issues
> - The contextual and systemic framework of their cultures and worlds
>
> These linguistic and pragmatic differences may create tension and miscommunications. (p. 21)

The suggestions that Ulrich and Bauer (2003) provide include developing a better understanding of your own outlook, which will enable you to assist parents and family members. This may enable you to avoid the problem that White, Taylor, and Moss observed.

White, Taylor, and Moss (1992) analyzed 172 studies that addressed parent involvement in early intervention with young children with disabilities. They reported differences between the assistance that parents provided to their children and the kinds of help provided to the parents/family. These differences illustrate how the needs that family members actually experienced were not always the focus of training provided to them.

Salend and Duhaney (2002) recommend interviewing family members to learn how satisfied they are with the services they are receiving. They also provide a sample survey (p. 63) and a set of sample interview questions (p. 64). As they caution, "[An] important step in collecting information from families . . . is to determine whether to use an *interview* or a *survey*" (p. 63). Ease of use, language barriers, time, and the ability to establish rapport are all considerations. "Educators must establish reciprocal family-school partnerships" (p. 65), which can facilitate improved "practices and policies that address the needs of students and their families" (p. 65). These kinds of initiatives require the commitment of school building and district administrators.

Superintendents and principals have heard from their school boards, encouraging outreach to families and other community groups. "The process of building such partnerships, called *public engagement*, is ongoing, two-way communication between a school district and the community it serves (Resnick, 2000)" (Cunningham, 2002, p. 3). As school boards develop strategies for public engagement, they look to principals to create meaningful, workable relationships with families:

> Principals play a key role in promoting community partnerships. Facilitating ongoing involvement with families, with a clear focus on improving student achievement, is perhaps the most critical step schools can take to engage the community . . . Creating stronger ties with families is accomplished by keeping parents informed about their children's progress and what they are learning. (pp. 3–4)

The strategies described in this chapter can be used to achieve these goals.

However, language barriers and jargon can pose problems. Zetlin et al. (1996) reported that

> Hispanic parents were further alienated by the school's reliance on written communication (Harry, 1992). They viewed letters sent home as a 'nuisance' since much time and energy had to be spent translating and understanding the information. Also the fact that documents were full of incomprehensible terminology and required a 6th grade readability level made the information even less accessible. (p. 23)

Callicott (2003) shares another example of a problem situation:

> Bianca's family was notified by telephone and letter that their high school-age daughter was unable to read Spanish. Bianca, however, was a

third-generation native [English] speaker who was assessed in Spanish only because of her Hispanic last name. The chaos that resulted in the home and later in school offices could have been avoided. (p. 66)

Westling (1996) advises teachers to "make parent education programs and information available to parents in different formats" (p. 111). In designing effective outreach to parents, use formats suited to the needs of parents with different amounts of available time. If your class includes family members who use a language other than English as their primary language, incorporate more than one language into your communications, using the following suggestions. Work with your building principal, fellow teachers, parents of students who were formerly in your class, or with students in your building (in your class or in another class). What you learn about communication can also assist you in working more effectively with students who have other problems with communication. Downing (2001) describes an effective approach for addressing the communication skills of students with moderate to severe disabilities:

> Because communication opportunities exist throughout the day and can occur at any time and place and involve many people, the need for a collaborative team effort is apparent. Teaching effective communication skills is a challenging endeavor and requires the input and effort of everyone involved. Certainly, family members and friends need to be actively involved in the identification of communication needs and the demands of different environments. (pp. 153–154)

Gaston (2001) reported on a peer consultation program (involving chief state school officers in analysis of interagency partnerships). This conclusion was reached by the group:

> The final barrier to collaboration that still seems most real and difficult to overcome is that of fear, on the part of parents, students, and staff. This fear emerges from a concern that collaboration will lead to a loss of services for some populations. Multiple and ongoing strategies will be needed to overcome this fear. Trust must be built over time. (p. 13)

To overcome fear, intentional planning is needed, such as the approach recommended by Salend and Sylvestre (2005), in which the focus is on developing "good collaboration and communication with students' families [which] can strengthen the connection between school and home and create a shared commitment to learning (Salend, 2005)" (p. 33). This collaboration includes involving family members in information sharing and use of a "home-school contract in which teachers communicate with the student's family regarding behavior in school and families reinforce the child's improved behavior. Before implementing a home-school contract, all parties should discuss and agree on the specifics of the contract" (p. 33). This approach can enable family members to partner effectively with educators.

What strategies might you try? Based on ideas used by teachers across the country, here are five approaches that you can adapt to meet the needs in your situation. In all of the following recommendations, take into account the primary language of the family members with whom you will be communicating.

Daily Classroom Hotline

Many teachers have found a school phone system (with voice mail or an answering machine) to be a very successful way to provide family members with daily updates on classroom activities. This method, although less thorough than a class-based Web site, depends on a resource that nearly every family will have—a telephone.

Cost does not have to prevent this strategy from being used. In one school district, the local PTA supported the development costs to put in the system so each classroom could have its own phone line and answering machine. The PTA made this investment based on feedback from parents in a pilot classroom. In another district, a business consortium sponsored the hotline as part of a citywide program to create linkages between schools and businesses. Development of effective hotlines can also involve communications faculty at area colleges and universities. College students might be involved in internships to set up and evaluate the effectiveness of the hotlines. The advantage of this approach over a classroom Web site is two-fold: ease of access for family members and ease of updating by teachers.

The maintenance of the hotline is relatively simple. Each day the teacher records a new message. The message, suited to the personality of the teacher, includes information about what took place in school during the day, homework assignments due the next day, and information about future events (e.g., an upcoming field trip, a long-term assignment, schoolwide events). The following is an example of an approach used to set up a schoolwide hotline.

When we set up help hotlines for each class, we made sure that the parents in our whole school got involved from the very beginning. We thought that the idea couldn't really work unless we included what parents wanted to hear, so we conducted a survey at Open House and of parents picking up/dropping off their children

We were surprised at a few of the requests. For example, parents wanted to know when their children would be involved in the hotline itself. As a result of this question, each class made up a monthly calendar showing who would be "DJ of the Day." We sent the calendar home along with other "features" we'd include. On Fridays, we recapped assignments due in a month or more along with top award winners in each class for the week.

Every few months, we call each parent to see how well the help hotline is working. We keep making adjustments, and we all feel like we're in this together.

Parents find it beneficial to be able to call the school at their own convenience and quickly find out what they need to know. Older brothers and sisters who help with homework assignments were also able to assist better, using hotline information about upcoming assignments. Questions or comments can be left on the phone system, or the hotline can be set for "outgoing message only," depending upon the needs of the teacher for the particular day.

Home/School Technology Connections

When Chen and Dym (2003) analyzed the use of technology in schools at Trujillo School in Chicago, they found that technology outreach to parents had a powerful impact on families as well as students and the community. A computer course for parents (offered in Spanish and in English) was designed and delivered by Jose Sanchez, a newly hired technology coordinator, who decided to reach students through the parents as well as through a community-based computer club. This motivated teachers to do more: "the teachers had said they couldn't deal with computer technology . . . but the parents' questions and concerns encouraged them to find the time" (p. 234). Technology served a purpose that connected people inside and outside of schools.

Macklem, Kruger, and Struzziero (2001) examined collaboration and how computer networks can overcome barriers such as time and space. Computer networks were very useful, facilitating contacts between teachers and parents. Previously, both teachers and parents had been frustrated by the challenges of trying to find time to meet that suited multiple schedules.

> Computer networks have introduced a new means of asynchronous communication, electronic mail (e-mail). A major advantage of asynchronous communication is that people can collaborate without coordinating when and where they communicate. A major advantage of e-mail in contrast to older means of asynchronous communication (e.g., writing letters) are speed and convenience (Johnson, 1998). (p. 81)

However, e-mail can only work as a communication mechanism if parents have easy access to computers at home or at work.

Because 80% of homes have computers (Sherman, 2004), technology is considered to be a feasible means of communication between home and school. Note that in the first edition of this book, 50% computer ownership was seen as the outside possibility: "We are running out of households that can afford to buy new computers. . . . [It is predicted that] household penetration will reach 32.6 percent by the end of 1996, and 38 percent by the end of the decade, but may never reach 50 percent" (Thomson Corporation, 1991, p. 1). Currently,

> According to an IBD [Investor's Business Daily]/TIPP poll survey, 21% of American households have skipped out on the home PC phenomenon. As expected, the number of non-PC households is larger in the lowest income brackets. Also, the percentage of homes without PCs is greatest among blacks and Native Americans . . . Native American households report the lowest level of computer ownership, as 31% don't own a computer. Next are black households, at 30%. . . . About 20% of white households don't own a computer vs. 18% of Hispanic households, and 13% of Asian households saying they didn't own a computer. (Sherman, 2004)

Macklem et al. (2001) state a major benefit of e-mail: "E-mail might have a role in making home-school collaboration more of a reality because a traditional barrier to collaboration has been the difficulty in finding a mutually convenient meeting time" (p. 87). This has been a challenge that all teachers faced, but it has been especially difficult for special educators because of the required IEP meetings. Macklem et al. (2001) go on to caution about relying exclusively on electronic communication and to examine ethical issues, including security, that teachers need to consider when communicating with family members. Harm could be done should students read messages that were intended for parents only, for example.

Parette and McMahan (2002) examine ways to enable family members to participate in assistive technology assessments of young children. When assistive technology is needed to enable a child to better communicate or participate in both school and family activities, the input of family members is a crucial component. In some cases, teachers can be instrumental in connecting family members to the appropriate professionals, who can access the most up-to-date and appropriate equipment.

It is a common frustration of teachers and administrators who plan events to involve family members that turn-out is often low. Even when free childcare is provided, it can be difficult for family members to coordinate travel to school. Interest in the topic does not overcome logistical challenges. Knapczyk et al. (2005) describe the effectiveness of Web conferencing for 54 preservice teachers in an online teacher preparation course, which is consistent with other research activities examining the benefits of a Web component. Their discussion about the development of a community opens up some exciting options for family involvement by individuals who have access to the Internet at home:

> Ninety-six percent of [the students] agreed or strongly agreed that they felt like part of a learning community in the course . . . Almost half of them reported feeling a greater level of 'connectedness' with classmates during Web discussions than during a conventional course, while only three said they felt less connected to their classmates. (p. 122)

Authors like Wentworth, Earle, and Connell (2004) discuss using technology in teacher preparation programs, and Edyburn (2000) and Parette, Jr. and Brotherson (1996) discuss use of assistive technology as a resource for students with disabilities. Teachers and families are more and more likely to have experiences with technology that they can draw upon in developing communication strategies that work for everyone.

The opportunities to involve family members can extend beyond the face-to-face format, thanks to technology, and may engage family members more than such meetings would, in the long run.

Newsletters

In the study conducted by Mundschenk and Foley (1994), several communication strategies were mentioned as useful in secondary schools. Informational letters, soliciting input prior to a curricular change or schoolwide decision, newsletters, or coverage in a local newspaper (p. 19) were methods used to communicate with parents. If the newsletters are distributed in several different languages, their potential benefits are increased.

A newsletter can enable students to analyze classroom activities while serving as reporters, editors, and illustrators. With publishing software available for a modest cost, the experience of putting a newsletter together can be educational without being expensive.

A newsletter is an excellent, focused project for student teachers to begin. A newsletter developed by the student teacher is an excellent artifact for career search portfolios. They can interview individuals in the school building and also students in the class. Their results can be incorporated into language arts. The dangers of relying totally on a student teacher for the newsletter are twofold: (1) the newsletter might not be completed during a demanding semester, and (2) the newsletter might not be continued after the student teacher leaves. If both issues are discussed and planned for, these problems can be overcome.

Resource Sharing

Sometimes, the teacher/family connection can be a less classroom-centered one. Teachers often get information about local service providers, upcoming events, and charity activities of interest to families. These resources can be made available through a bulletin board in the school, a resource book available to parents who come to school to pick up their children, or occasional mailings to parents.

It is often difficult to remain current regarding contact people or agency addresses and phone numbers. Involving student teachers in a project verifying that the resource information is current can benefit everyone. The end result is a relevant, up-to-date database that can be shared by all. A letter from the principal to the student teacher about the project is a welcome addition to the career search portfolio. If student teachers are not able to complete the task, it might be something that a volunteer (a retired teacher, a parent, or a college student looking to fulfill a service requirement) can complete—it is not something that has to be done at school, and it has a clear beginning and end.

Another resource group to whom you can turn is the family members of students who graduated from your class. Think of how many different ways they can be helpful to you.

- They can be a sounding board for you when you want to explore new options.
- They might help orient parents of students new to your class.
- They could help at Open Houses and at times when you need an extra hand.
- They may also be familiar with agencies in the community and can help you update your classroom resource database or Web site.
- They could help you to remain involved in the lives of their children and continue to support their children's academic and life goals. News about the progress of your former students can even be an inspiring addition to your class Web site or newsletter.

If former students' family members are included in classroom activities, be sure to discuss the need for confidentiality regarding all information shared in the classroom. Personal facts about, and names of, current students should not be shared with others. Former students' family members are familiar with your classroom routines, so you should not have to spend a lot of time explaining to them what you do. Overall, they are likely to be sensitive to the feelings and concerns of the families new to your classroom. Many schools have utilized former students' family members successfully, with no breach of confidentiality.

Meetings

If you need to bring the family members of students in your class together for a meeting to discuss a topic of interest to all, make sure to consider the following:

Location

Select locations for meetings that help make family members feel relaxed. For example, a get-together may have different connotations if held in the classroom, the teachers' lounge, or the cafeteria. Some families might prefer an occasional meeting in a place they suggest—getting together in a community center or public library may provide them with a comfort level they may not feel in the school. Be sure to take access to public transportation or parking into consideration when choosing a location away from your school. If necessary, provide directions for parents or extended family members who may not be familiar with the new location.

Meeting Participants

Take time to decide who should be invited to the meeting. How about striving to include different points of view?

- As discussed above, extended family members may make constructive contributions at brainstorming meetings.
- An older brother or grandmother may give teachers recommendations that would occur to no one else.
- Parents of students who have already graduated from your school may have insights to share that could improve the initiation of new classroom efforts.
- Teachers from other schools could provide a different perspective.
- To make family members more comfortable, give them the option of inviting parent advocates, community leaders, or friends.

Instead of being concerned about too few people attending, you might, instead, have to cope with the opposite problem!

Enhancing Comfort Levels

Consider a variety of ideas to make your meeting one at which people will feel free to share their ideas. One strategy to consider is to adjust your meeting starting and stopping time to the meeting holders' sense of time. Be sure to make your plans regarding time clear when you send out meeting announcements. For example, if traffic or other delays interfere with getting to meetings promptly, you can let the meeting attendees know when you actually plan to start and stop. If family members must let babysitters know when they will be home, ending the meeting on time is considerate. However, some meeting members may feel that they are rushed if you stick too closely to the clock. You need to check this out with some members of your group beforehand.

You may also find that refreshments help you make the start of the meeting more comfortable. Be sure to consider the food concerns of people attending the meeting (e.g., people concerned about eating messy food when trying to talk, health-conscious individuals, diabetics) when planning your refreshments. Incorporating ethnic options can help people feel more comfortable as well.

Stating a Purpose

A clearly stated purpose, using an agenda or schedule, can help people attending your meeting to know what they are there to do.

Which of the many ideas presented in this section of the chapter would encourage you to attend and participate in a school-sponsored meeting? Talk to parents and friends and see whether their reactions are similar to yours. The ideas you pick, along with your own understanding of families, can lead to very successful meetings.

The way you communicate may be influenced by many factors, including gender. Tannen (1995, 2001) has identified aspects of communication between men and women that are highly influenced by tone of voice, body language, phrasing, and vocabulary. Consider to whom you are presenting your ideas. Look to see whether your listeners are engaged (e.g., watching you, leaning forward, or with relaxed body language). If you see that you are losing some of the people at the meeting as you state your meeting's purpose, ask the participants what they would like to accomplish during the meeting. This can help you keep all members of the meeting focused on shared goals.

These approaches can be adapted to meet the needs of family members with limited time who still want to get involved with schools. At the start of the year, your process for introducing yourself to the family members of your students can include a question about the ways in which they would like to receive information to become involved in decision making. Use Project Try-Out 11.3 to explore how to communicate with family members.

Project Try-Out 11.3

Outreach

This Project Try-Out was developed to help you to generate ideas for use when contacting family members. You may find that more than one idea appeals to you. If so, you can put several ideas together.

1. In your collaboration notebook, write a brief description of a family member whom you would like to try to reach. This could be a real person with whom you are working now or someone you imagine working with in the future.

2. Review the different strategies included in this section of the chapter, and select a way to communicate that you think would be effective. In your collaboration notebook, record the name of your strategy and why you think it is a good choice.

3. Next to each strategy, list three or four concerns you have about its effectiveness.
   a. If you have chosen a real situation in which to use it, think of ways to modify the strategy to address each concern.
   b. If you have chosen an imaginary situation, write down questions next to each concern that you would want to try to answer before using the strategy.

This Project Try-Out gave you a way to analyze several strategies so that eventually you can select the one that fits your needs best. Realize that you may not always be able to use the strategies that feel most comfortable for you. Sometimes cost, time, or energy will preclude you from picking the "best" one. However, your goal is to make choices that take into account all you've learned in this book about communication and apply it to your work with family members. Communication can sometimes be a form of information sharing, but at other times you may need to involve family members in decisions that will influence them. You are now ready to use the third key, the generalization from your original collaboration project.

KEY 3: BUILD ON WHAT YOU'VE ALREADY LEARNED

In your collaboration project, you identified ways to change your interaction style. You may have looked at your preferences for approaching another person—in writing, by phone, or in person. You may have looked at your comfort level for handling different types of conversational topics—informal/social, informational, or problem solving. You could have examined benefits you received when involving collaboration resource network members in your project. You may have found that your negative preconceptions were holding you back and learned how to reduce their influence on you. You may have discovered that you had more control over your behavior and your attitude than you believed before. In the Next Steps Project Try-Out 11.4, reflect on what you learned in your project and translate it into your personal key for success.

Next Steps Project Try-Out 11.4

Thinking Back, Thinking Ahead

The collaboration project you completed gave you strategies and ideas to improve the relationship you selected. This Project Try-Out will help you to identify how to generalize from that project to a project involving family members.

1. Review the results of your collaboration project. Look over both your anecdotal records and the results of your evaluation model (as described in Chapter 10). Record your answers to the following questions in your collaboration notebook:
   a. How would you summarize the biggest changes you saw in your attitude as a result of the project?
   b. How would you describe the biggest changes you saw in your behavior as a result of the project?
   c. Looking back on the project, what do you think was most successful?
   d. If you had one recommendation to make to someone about to begin a collaboration project, what would it be?

2. Think about family members with whom you will work in the future and adapt your answer to Question 1. Record your responses in your collaboration notebook.

3. Think about a working relationship that, together with others in your school, you would like to develop with the family members of your students. Take three minutes and record in your collaboration notebook as many schoolwide initiatives as you can that involve family members. Remember the following:
   a. Extend your thinking beyond parents to include sisters, brothers, cousins, aunts, uncles, and grandparents.

> b. Incorporate communitywide activities such as walks for charity, community gardens, food drives, and social events.
> c. Generate lists of names of people with whom you could connect, including professional interest groups such as the Council for Exceptional Children, Phi Delta Kappa, Kappa Delta Phi.
> d. Pick areas of interest in which you could genuinely motivate others to become involved.
>
> 4. After you have completed your brainstorming activity, put a star beside the ideas that are the most appealing. If you are able to put them into effect during the coming school year, consider doing so. If not, keep your list for a time when you are ready to commit some time and energy toward implementing them.

Use the possibilities generated through this Project Try-Out as a springboard for your future work with families.

CONCLUSION

The invitation to work with family members contains both a request and a challenge. As has been described throughout this chapter, even if you are an experienced teacher you have much to learn to succeed in your work with families. The three keys in this chapter can help you begin your efforts in an organized, efficient way. Involving family members has many rich rewards that can help you to meet the needs of your students more effectively. In the following chapter, you will have an opportunity to explore ways to involve other people in your school—members of the interdisciplinary team.

12

Generalizing Your Plan to Others

Improved Collaboration With Members of Your Interdisciplinary Team

The opportunity to work with members of an interdisciplinary team can be *extraordinary—in both positive and negative ways. On the positive side, you can acquire information about your students from perspectives unfamiliar to you. You can also learn new strategies and techniques. On the negative side, you may discover how stubborn and vicious professionals can be when they disagree. Ideally, you will have more of the former experiences than the latter.*

This chapter illustrates how you can apply what you have learned in this book to working with members of your interdisciplinary team. In this chapter, specific consideration of building and working on teams will be addressed.

Teachers get stuck when trying to help students. Sometimes they get to a point where everything they've tried seems to yield little or no results. If they meet with their interdisciplinary team to explore options to use in their situation, effective new approaches can be identified—ones they might never have developed on their own. The "cross-functional team" described by Parker (2002) "uses the expertise of many different people . . . coupled with the task of *enlisting* support for the work of the team" (p. 37). Puccio (1999) defines the team as "a group of individuals who meet to perform some specific task" (p. 639), and goes on to consider both impediments and catalysts for team creativity: "It is effective leadership that enables individuals and teams to achieve extraordinary results at work. Individuals who work with effective leaders report feeling more committed, energized, and powerful at work" (p. 649). The development of effective team activities will be discussed in this chapter.

Graham and Wright (1999) report on the challenges of interprofessional collaboration. Their findings, a result of surveying 263 individuals serving in different roles in relation to students with disabilities (e.g., teachers, educational psychologists, speech therapists), led to categorization of collaboration into three categories: planning activities, sharing activities, and goal achieving activities. Working together, team members can produce some surprising results. Hanks and Velaski (2003) describe the benefits of a collaborative model for summer service delivery for students with hearing impairments:

> Everyone wins when students are the focus in education, as has been experienced through this collaborative program. . . . We hope that individuals and programs consider similar collaborative efforts with contributing entities from their areas. The more groups work together for the benefit of students, the more meaningful and functional student education will become. (pp. 62–63)

Horton et al. (2003) make the same observation regarding collaboration yielding effective results for students with physical disabilities: "The process of collaboration may initially involve uncertainty and ambiguity, but if all disciplines utilize their best practices, maximal outcomes for the students with disabilities will be obtained" (p. 17). Snell (2005) endorses collaborative teaming in inclusive schools. For Justice (2004), the team model was essential for creating language-rich preschool environments. Phillips, Prue, Hasazi, and Morgan (2000) describe the team-based approach to personal learning plans and conclude that use of these plans has

> expanded the professional conversation around educational opportunities for all students, including those with disabilities. It has challenged the faculty to continually seek more personalized ways to teach and interact with their students and collaborate with colleagues within the school. Relationships with parents and the community at large have improved, making it more comfortable for the faculty and administration to propose additional reform efforts and continue to invent engaging and effective ways to help each student achieve their dreams. (p. 34)

The value of a team approach is illustrated in the following example.

When we started meeting in November to discuss Marianne, all of us were frustrated. As a seventh grader, she was expected to follow school rules much better than she did. Her hormones were changing, and her odors kept all the other students away from her. We didn't know where to start.

It wasn't until the school nurse got involved that we started seeing some of the cause and effect. Marianne seemed to be getting into trouble on a regular basis right before gym. With Marianne's complicated school schedule, and so many people involved in providing her with services, we'd never put the pieces together before.

We invited her mother to our next team meeting. Together, we considered how to discuss hygiene with Marianne and eliminate some of the problems we were seeing. Since then, we've seen some changes. Everything isn't perfect, but we have a much better handle on the problem than we did before.

The team not only brings people with different viewpoints together, it is also responsible for ensuring that solutions generated by the team materialize. Cohen, Thomas, Sattler, and Morsink (1997) describe the interactive team as adhering to five principles: participation and leadership, development of goals, communication, decision making, and conflict resolution. Use of these principles will lead to the cohesion and effectiveness of the team (p. 430). This type of team uses a leadership approach that involves team members in the process of identifying and achieving goals.

An interdisciplinary team model can include interactions between people (e.g., collaborating on speech and language services for learning disabled students, as described by Elksnin, 1997) as well as between people and technology (e.g., Dillon, 2001, describing the MIT Media Laboratory, which is founded on an interdisciplinary model based on the work of Nicholas Negroponte). Lacey (2001) describes a variety of "collaboration in support partnerships" in pairings of teachers with physical therapists, others in school settings, and with family members. She explains that "the term 'support partnerships' is deliberately non-specific and is meant to convey that this book relates to anyone who is trying to work with at least one other person in a supportive way in the field of disabilities and difficulties" (p. 14). She illustrates a range of approaches that people working together (in pairs, teams, or networks) can use.

As Anderson (2004) movingly explains, the broader the interdisciplinary team membership, the more powerful its effects. Her description of the role of the media specialist as an indispensable team member concludes with this description of what the specialist brings to the collaboration process: "daily and practical side of collaboration and part of successful programs, successful students and successful schools" (p. 27).

Strategies such as "the circle of collaboration" (used by Burnham, Discher, & Ingle, 2003), bringing adults from different disciplines together to maximize the inclusive atmosphere in their school, can have benefits for the adults as well as the students. The authors report that "a sense of ownership has been built among our faculty" (p. 3) and use of "early out" to increase time for collaboration among teachers.

When supported by school administrators, even simple approaches can be very effective, such as the one described by Salyer, Thyfault, and Curran (2002). The results of their efforts were reported as "not hard to make and the effects are dramatic":

> A small rural school in southern Texas was plagued by truancy, vandalism, violence, etc. The school counselor gave each teacher three index cards and asked that they write the names of their three "most" troubled students on the cards. At the next faculty meeting the cards were collected and thrown into a hopper. All school personnel (teachers, counselor, administration, secretaries, janitors, cooks, bus drivers, etc.) were then asked to randomly draw two cards. The faculty and staff were asked to make a concerted effort to connect with the two students they drew on a daily basis. Students were invited to have lunch with the faculty or staff member. Some students were given special seats on the bus so the bus driver could get to know them better. Some students were given passes to sporting events as special guests of the faculty or staff member. Each day 136 of the highest risk children were recognized by an adult. Over the course of four months the number of disciplinary referrals dropped over 40%. Parents, teachers, staff members, and students noticed the difference in their school. (p. 8)

Collaboration among the adult members of this school was an essential prerequisite to this initiative. Its success was dependent upon the credibility of the counselor, the willingness of the entire school adult population to extend themselves beyond their regular work responsibilities, and a collaborative ethic. They also believed in their students and wanted to change their school climate. They succeeded, and the work they did is congruent with the descriptions provided by Phillips and McCullough below.

Phillips and McCullough (1990) identified "the central tenets of the collaborative ethic." Several pertain to the workings of interdisciplinary teams.

> Belief that pooling talents and resources is mutually advantageous, with the following benefits: (a) Increased range of solutions generated; (b) Diversity of expertise and resources available to engage problem; (c) Superiority and originality of solutions generated. Belief that teacher or student problem resolution merits expenditure of time, energy, and resources. Belief that correlates of collaboration are important and desirable (i.e., group morale, group cohesion, increased knowledge of problem-solving processes and specific alternative classroom interventions). (p. 295)

These tenets form the foundation of an effective interdisciplinary team model such as the examples about Marianne and the rural school in Texas. They illustrate the interconnected nature of interpersonal and task problems that are central to the challenges every team must face (Bales & Cohen, 1979; Napier & Gershenfeld, 2003; Smylie, Conley, & Marks, 2002; Snell & Janney, 2000). In schools, the creation of "teaming structures for collective responsibility" (Reitzug & Burrello, 1995, p. 49) can help to do many things:

> Teaming leads to a sense of collective responsibility for one another and for students and instructional support network. One teacher observed that when she had tried everything she could think of with a student, simply having team members with whom she could share these frustrations helped. (p. 49)

In the study conducted by Morocco and Aguilar (2002), the success of co-teaching pairs, or dyads, was supported by team participation:

> The parity . . . is present in the dyads observed in this study. . . . Several features of the model in this school may help to explain the mutual respect and equality present in these dyads and the high level of coordination in their teaching. First, the special education teachers were full members of their interdisciplinary teams. Their primary reference group was the team, not the special education staff, and all members had common time for planning. One of the special education teachers was elected team leader by her content teacher peers. Second, school policy dictated that teams had decision-making power in areas of curriculum, student assessment, and instructional accommodations, and the special education teacher was a part of those decisions. (p. 342)

The involvement of the special educator in the team, combined with "organizational structures to provide consistent support for teacher collaboration across the teams" (p. 342), enabled energy and time to be devoted to successful instructional and team-based models.

The development of effective teams is the foundation of effective service delivery. Kilgore et al. (2002) describe the interconnected nature of teaming and student improvement. As Allen-Meares and Pugach (1982) pointed out when P.L. 94–142 was first implemented, "Collaboration is essential for providing coordinated instruction of the highest quality to exceptional children and youth. Collaboration is one of the most problematic areas to implement because it requires redefining how professional adults work together" (p. 35). In a subsequent work, Pugach and Johnson (1989) illustrated the validity of their earlier prediction, citing an example of the need for reciprocal exchange of ideas. Listeners' responses to a team of presenters (who consisted of two general education teachers and one special education teacher) included the following:

> Other participants said it was wonderful that the classroom teachers on the team had the opportunity to learn so much from the special education teacher as a result of their co-teaching arrangement. The special education teacher said that what she was thinking was "Why doesn't anyone ask about all the things I have learned from them?" (p. 234)

With the increased use of technology, some educators are excited about the use of virtual teams as a way around the challenges of planning time and meetings. Kochan, Bredeson, and Riehl (2002) describe how rural administrators can make use of technology:

> E-mail-based discussion groups can provide a wide network of colleagues to answer questions and/or discuss general issues facing school leaders. Chat rooms on the Web sites of professional associations provide another avenue for growth, as do the variety of materials and resources that are available through education-related Web sites and full-text journals. (pp. 294–295)

Kirschner and Van Bruggen (2004) caution that overuse of virtual resources or virtual teams, while tempting, can neglect some of the fundamentals people need to work together, such as "an affective structure. Building an affective structure entails a process of affiliation, impression formation, and interpersonal attraction to induce and promote social relationships and group cohesion" (p. 137).

Teaming was introduced in P.L. 94–142 and continues to be at the core of IDEA 2004. The members of the Individual Educational Program (IEP) team include the following people:

- The parents of a child with a disability
- Not less than one regular education teacher (if the child is, or may be, participating in the regular education environment)
- Not less than one special education teacher, or when appropriate, not less than one special education provider
- A representative of the local educational agency (LEA) who is qualified to provide, or supervise the provision of, specially designed instruction
- An individual who can interpret the instructional implications of evaluation results, who may not be a member of the team described above
- Other individuals, at the discretion of the parent or the agency, who have knowledge or special expertise regarding the child
- Whenever appropriate, the child with the disability (§ 614(d)(1)(B))

In order for these individuals to meet and have efficient and effective discussions and resolution of outstanding topics, the adults in the school district or agency must work together well.

Adult working relationships on interdisciplinary teams are complex. Fleming and Monda-Amaya (2001), in a Delphi study of wraparound teams, identified critical variables for team efforts and team effectiveness, with team goals (and clarity of purpose) receiving the rating of "most important" of all items. Other categories (team membership and roles, team communication, team cohesion, team logistics, and team outcomes) contain clearly stated items (e.g., "Members feel safe sharing ideas") that could be usefully incorporated into team development in schools (e.g., Fleming & Monda-Amaya, 2001, p. 168). In many cases, assumptions about what people are learning from and giving to each other need to be questioned. In the example above cited by Pugach and Johnson (1989), assumptions might need to be challenged.

The strategies provided throughout this book addressing issues such as communication and problem solving can be used to increase your personal responsibility on your interdisciplinary team. Establishing a relationship with a mentor in your school can also help you to sort through the challenges you will face. Baugh and Scandura (1999), in their study of 250 managers and executives, report that "having one or more mentoring relationships in the workplace may result in greater commitment to the organization, greater job satisfaction, enhanced career expectations, increased perceptions of alternative employment, and lower ambiguity about one's work role" (p. 514). Smylie et al. (2002) identify teams as a new form of teacher leadership in schools, and caution that

> the development of school leadership should not be aimed primarily at individual leaders but at the leaders collectively. . . . The capacity to lead is a function of knowledge relevant to the task, knowledge of the content and process knowledge and skills (Little, 1988). (p. 182)

The development of the school-based team does not take place in a vacuum. Under the guidance of the school principal, the school-based teams can flourish.

> Principals need to know how to develop, support, and manage [teacher teams]. Their unique position in the school organization gives them the resources, the ability, and the authority to do this leadership management work well. It is the principal who may best be able to direct the work of the self-managed teams toward broader organizational objectives. (Smylie et al., 2002, p. 182)

The use of teams in schools can facilitate advancement of the schools' strategic agendas.

Strategies provided throughout this book—such as obtaining a mentor or higher self-efficacy—alone are insufficient. In order for your interdisciplinary team to function effectively, you also have to address concerns that are specific to teams.

The remainder of this chapter will focus on issues pertinent to teams. While the topic of this chapter is the basis of many texts, the scope of this chapter is focused, but narrow. Highlights relevant to interdisciplinary teams are provided here, which you can put into practice in your current professional setting.

THE LIFE CYCLE OF YOUR INTERDISCIPLINARY TEAM

In the literature on group development, there is consensus about the stages of team development. As illustrated in the following example, members of interdisciplinary teams come together at the start of every year.

> *The principal calls us together every September and gives us a pep talk. "You are my brain trust. I know I can count on you to help us with our most complex students." It is corny, but it always makes us feel like he notices what we do. It starts things off on a positive note.*

Usually, there are a few new members. The newly established team has to set up all the necessary mechanisms to facilitate their work. Routines are needed, whether the team meets regularly or only when it has a problem to solve.

In books and articles on teams in general (Napier & Gershenfeld, 2003), teams in business (Forsyth, 1990; Kouzes & Posner, 2002), and teams in schools (Abelson & Woodman, 1983), Tuckman and Jensen's (1977) description of stages is cited. After an extensive review of literature on teams and groups, Tuckman and Jensen depicted a series of stages that all teams pass through: forming, storming, norming, performing, and adjourning. Each stage has its own unique characteristics.

The Forming Stage

During the forming stage, members are oriented to the team. The following take place:

Teams in General	Interdisciplinary Teams
1. Exchange of information; polite discourse	1. Discussion of specific cases, timeframes, potential sources of information
2. Increased interdependency	2. Sharing resources
3. Task exploration; tentativeinteractions	3. Exploring options for how to proceed
4. Identification of commonalities	4. Review of members' backgrounds and perspectives

The initial responsibilities of all interdisciplinary teams must be thrashed out during a period of orientation. While these explorations usually take place during an initial meeting or two, they can also be done in other ways. The "Intervention Assistance Teams" developed by Korinek and Williams (1996) experimented with a written team orientation. The collaborative team effort began with a written description of the situation for which a teacher needed assistance. This was followed by a one-on-one meeting: the teacher making the request met with a member of the team. Together, the two of them discussed the request and expanded the written draft. The revised written description was shared with Intervention Assistance team members before their problem-solving meeting. This approach enabled team members to move more quickly to action when the meeting took place.

During the orientation meeting(s), questions can be asked about the logistics that will govern the team's operation. In schools, scheduling is an inevitable problem. Identifying times when the team can meet must be part of the orientation discussion. Prior experiences on interdisciplinary teams are usually shared by team members. Content sharing can also take place at this point. Koppang (2004) describes how general educators and special educators can incorporate "curriculum mapping" into their classroom collaboration. They begin their collaboration by sharing content, skills, and assessment information and gradually get to more in-depth joint work.

As Forsyth (1990) explains,

> [an] initial period of orientation is very typical in groups. When groups form, the members must deal with people they hardly know, and this initial unfamiliarity leaves them feeling uncomfortable and constrained. Often all the members of a new group are on their guard, carefully monitoring their behavior to make certain that they avoid any embarrassing lapses of social poise. . . . This ambiguous situation is further complicated by the absence of any specific norms regarding the regulation of interaction and goal attainment as well as uncertainty about their role in the group. (p. 78)

Idol et al. (1988) describe the initial orientation as a time for "gaining mutual acceptance among the collaborators and establishing team ownership of the problem(s). . . . Unstructured time is needed to establish a working relationship and to generate a common commitment of responsibility" (p. 58). The tone and trust established during the start-up period can influence further collaborative work done by the team. It is also a time for the clarification of roles of each team member (Falck, 1977; Friend & Cook, 2002). In this way, rapport can be established.

The Storming Stage

The second stage, storming, is one that is inevitable for most teams or groups. It is a period in which the team struggles to resolve differences of opinion about how to proceed. Snell and Janney (2000) make the following comment: "Some team conflict is to be expected; unfortunately most conflict is poorly managed and actively avoided due to the fear and anxiety it provokes in most team members" (p. 131). Examples of the kinds of conflicts that teams experience in the early stages of their development are provided below:

Teams in General	Interdisciplinary Teams
1. Disagreement over procedures; polarization and coalition formation	1. Conflicting viewpoints about legal or school-based procedures; issues of parity
2. Expression of dissatisfaction; criticism of ideas	2. Nonverbal or verbal complaints; critical questions, arguments
3. Emotional responding	3. Emotional presentation of information

Rather than avoid these kinds of challenges, interdisciplinary teams should seek them out. The members will find that not only can they learn to surface and resolve differences of opinion, but they can become stronger overall. Snell and Janney (2000) make the following observations: "Well-managed controversy within teams can stimulate interest, thinking, problem-solving, new ideas, and decision making. . . . When controversy is well-managed, it involves a process that stimulates inquiry and leads to synthesis of information and ideas" (p. 131).

What is productive group disharmony? Bales and Cohen (1979) report that group disharmony is as common as coordinated group effort. One common area of concern to all interdisciplinary teams is that of parity, or equity among team members. As Pugach and Johnson (1989) describe this potential area of disagreement, the need for two-way information exchange becomes clear:

> In our estimation, although the issue parity is raised repeatedly, very little direction is offered concerning the specific kinds of assistance classroom teachers can bring to specialists, exemplifying the reciprocal nature of collaborative consultation. What conceptions of collaboration can prospective special education teachers or school psychologists develop if the only instances of collaboration they read about or hear about are those in which classroom teachers receive assistance from specialists? (p. 234)

The authors recommend that some reconsideration of the problem take place in the following way:

> Empowerment of teachers seems to be a tricky issue relative to collaborative consultation. The question should not be whether empowered teachers will cease to need special educators or school psychologists; schools are incredibly complex places, and demographic changes in our society have increased the need for support services in the schools. These services, however, need reconceptualization to fit the current context of schooling. Special educators or school psychologists certainly are able to engage successfully in collaboration. . . . What remains to be seen is whether we can challenge ourselves to advance to the next level, that is, recognizing that collaboration can occur only when all participants have a common understanding of their strengths and weaknesses and demonstrate a willingness to learn from each other. (Pugach & Johnson, 1989, p. 235)

In the following example, the interdisciplinary team is at a standstill.

When we get close to making a decision, we wind up arguing. Things fall apart whenever that resource room teacher opens his mouth. Everyone stops listening and starts shouting. I have noticed that it happens every time our team meets. I know that he comes across as if he is very impressed with himself, but he has good insights sometimes, too. I'm afraid to take his side because then they'll think badly of me. Everyone is getting frustrated, and I'm afraid that pretty soon we'll stop meeting altogether.

In this situation, the team members have not heeded the cautions of Pugach and Johnson and, as a result, are stuck at the "storming" stage.

Friend and Cook (1990) warn that the issue of parity is critical: "Collaboration is not possible if professionals do not sense the existence of parity, the equal value given to each person's input" (p. 73). The resolution of the parity issue is unique to each interdisciplinary team. Some resolve it through division of tasks—information is collected by those professionals on the team who are likely to know the most about the topic. Another approach is to ask team members to make suggestions about how to proceed based on their professional experiences. Ideas and suggestions provided in Chapter 7 and elsewhere in the book are intended to help you to prepare for differences of opinion. Your method for working with others should fit both the requirements of the situation and your own comfort level. Use the following Idea Try-Out as a basis for sorting through your own ideas.

Idea Try-Out 12.1

Inside and Outside

This Idea Try-Out is an opportunity for you to generate options for resolving conflicts when working with members of an interdisciplinary team. In your collaboration notebook, record your ideas about how you would behave in each of the following situations. If you find it easier, role-play the situation with another person and then summarize the role play in your collaboration notebook.

Situation: The school psychologist has just made suggestions to the teachers on your interdisciplinary team to conduct observations over the next three weeks. His ideas are good ones but will take a lot of time to implement. You think he is being unreasonable.

- How would you feel in response to his suggestions?
- What would you say or do *during* the meeting to express yourself?
- What would you say or do *after* the meeting to express yourself? With whom would you have these conversations?

Situation: The parent member of your interdisciplinary team has outlined 10 team meeting problems. You concur with some of her observations, but you consider some of her points to be "too picky."

- How would you feel in response to her suggestions?
- What would you say or do *during* the meeting to express yourself?
- What would you say or do *after* the meeting to express yourself?

Situation: You have been responsible for taking notes at the meetings of your interdisciplinary team. The principal makes a correction to the minutes of the last meeting. You feel that she is correct but are embarrassed that you made a mistake.

- How would you feel in response to her suggestions?
- What would you say or do *during* the meeting to express yourself?
- What would you say or do *after* the meeting to express yourself?

As you responded to this Idea Try-Out, you may have found disagreement between your inner and outer responses. In the long run, you want to find a way to thoroughly resolve any conflicts you have so your functioning (and that of the group) is not impaired. As Forsyth (1990) suggests, "the dynamic nature of the group ensures continual change, but along with change come stresses and strains that surface in the form of conflict" (p. 79). Ideally, you can make use of all you've learned about yourself throughout this book to handle these situations professionally. You and your team members may find it useful to look up Fleming and Monda-Amaya's 2001 article and follow their advice about using their work: "This final list of critical variables is a tool for members and supervisors to use in establishing norms for teaming and in monitoring team performance" (p. 170).

The Norming Stage

The third stage, norming, is one that grows out of the difference of opinions described previously. It is a period in which the team comes together to negotiate, then establishes ground rules with which it can live.

Teams in General	Interdisciplinary Teams
1. Growth of cohesiveness and unity	1. Use jargon-free communication; include all team members in decision-making process
2. Establishment of roles, reduction in role ambiguity	2. Designate roles during meetings and in data collection; encourage participation beyond narrowly defined school-based roles
3. Agreement on procedures, standards	3. Set up ground rules for meetings; agree on outcomes
4. Increased "we" feeling	4. Refer to group history; spontaneously share pertinent information

Teams normally develop a way to work together after going through the initial start-up activities (the "nice" and the "nasty"). After the team has learned how to be candid but not hurtful or defensive, true collaboration can take place. This is a time of both emotional and logistical cohesion for members of a team. In Idol, West, and Lloyd's (1988) model, this would correspond to a time when the following would take place: "the teachers collaboratively establish specific goals for each program objective and decide who is going to provide which part of the educational program for each student" (p. 58). The team members have a reciprocal working arrangement in which they can develop a comfortable level of give-and-take. Lambert, Abbott-Shim, and Oxford-Wright (2001) surveyed 268 teachers and teacher aides in three Head Start programs that were involved in a research partnership geared toward implementation of specific strategies for collaboration with the research members. They found overall support for the collaboration:

> Collaborative efforts that involve multiple agencies coming together to share goals, objectives, and complex coordination of resources can be difficult to sustain. Communication, logistics, agreement, and even finding time to meet

and discuss important issues all represent significant challenges. . . . Future partnerships that attempt to transcend that all too frequent "shotgun marriage" approach may benefit from outlining an explicit strategic plan for sustaining the trust and involvement of the program administrators throughout all the stages of the research process. (p. 32)

The development of norms to address the topics for teams that are described above match Lambert's recommendation for effective collaboration within and among agencies. Changing the norms for meetings is suggested by Lietzow and Jackson (2004), going from a "deficit model" for IEP meetings to a "transitional model," so that transition planning enables a focus on the accomplishment of the student's vision for the future. This shift in norms for a team could only take place after the team had learned to work together effectively and agreed upon a transition-oriented approach.

The following example highlights how exchanges between team members are never totally predictable. This example shows how a team discovered their ability to work well together in the face of a crisis.

All year long, our interdisciplinary team meetings were full of squabbles. We argued about everything. That all changed in March. We saw how we could work together when we had to. Barbara, our speech pathologist, came into the meeting room, looked around at all of us, and started to cry. "I just talked with Keisha's mother. She just found out that he has to go into the hospital—he has cancer." We were all so stunned. He was a child we'd been talking about all year. We knew we had to help him and his family.

In no time at all, we'd figured out how we could help his mother and his two brothers who are in third and fourth grade. I never thought we could all agree on things so quickly, but in this case, we put all our differences aside and just got to work.

From that point on, we were able to work together amazingly well.

The Performing Stage

The fourth stage, performing, is one in which the team is able to accomplish what it set out to do. It is a period when the team is able to use its strengths to solve problems efficiently.

Teams in General	*Interdisciplinary Teams*
1. Achievement of goal	1. Routinely meet responsibilities assigned—case review, student evaluation
2. Highly focused on task	2. Team meetings start and end on time; members come to meetings prepared, with tasks accomplished
3. Make decisions and solve problems	3. Discussions freely incorporate opinions from all members; solutions generated reflect input from all members
4. Mutual cooperation	4. Team members listen to each other, piggyback on each others' ideas, work together

How do interdisciplinary teams function in your building? You may find that the performing stage involves many different tasks. For example, the team members may agree that certain data should be collected to more fully discuss a student's needs in a pre-referral conference. During this stage, teams would most likely be able to take advantage of Phillips and McCullough's (1990) recommended approaches for collaborative effort:

- Pooling of staff talents/resources
- Interdisciplinary involvement in "think tank" environment
- Evolution of problem-solving and effective intervention skills (p. 296)

These all are implied in the performing stage. Normally, the interdisciplinary team must repeat the cycle of tasks many times during each school year. As you examine the role you take on the interdisciplinary team, consider the following ways to become more capable in each approach described by Phillips and McCullough.

1. *Pooling of Staff Talents/Resources.* You and other members of your interdisciplinary team should increase the number of different tasks for which you volunteer. As shown in the following situation, you may volunteer to meet unusual needs of the team as your team becomes more capable during the performing stage. It is unlikely that the situation described here would have occurred when the team was in the forming stage.

> *We were sitting around trying to come up with an authentic way to assess Tasha's addition automaticity. She'd lost interest in everything we'd tried. We were brainstorming interest areas on which we might build, and someone said that she liked to shoot baskets. It had been a while since I played any basketball, but I thought that we might be able to see how well she could add in a one-on-one game against me. The team liked the idea—and it worked!*

2. *Interdisciplinary Involvement in "Think Tank" Environment.* Watching the exchange of ideas among members of a interdisciplinary team can be a bit like sitting at the counter of a restaurant that serves breakfast. Seeing the short-order cook, servers, and customers interact, you feel as if you are in the middle of something that has been rehearsed, yet each breakfast is happening for the first time. Being part of an effective interdisciplinary team meeting gives one that same feeling. Although each problem to be solved is unique, team members build on prior experience to explore ideas and make decisions.

Teachers who have worked with the student for some time may have a different perspective from a teacher who has just begun. The parent representative may raise questions about the home environment. Speech pathologists may help to look at communication styles that otherwise might be overlooked. Your team may find itself full of ideas. A team that is at the "productive" stage has learned how to maximize information taken in and then to go beyond information gathering to action. Members know that although the team is generating many ideas, its work has only begun.

After your team members have found ways to generate alternative explanations (brainstorming), you need to build on each others' ideas (piggybacking). Both brainstorming and piggybacking are central to the creative problem-solving approach. As Isaksen and Treffinger (1985) describe creative problem solving, these ideas would be part of "divergent" thinking. Divergent thinking is a concept originated by J. P. Guilford. When using a strategy like brainstorming, team members participate in divergent thinking, considering many unique or unusual ideas. After generating as many options as possible, the team then converges on a solution. The creative problem-solving process takes place in a prescribed way, including activities that extend over a series of stages. Each stage gets closer to the solution to the problem. While seeking solutions, the following kinds of data would be sought: information, impressions, observations, feelings, and questions (Isaksen & Treffinger, 1985).

Members of your interdisciplinary team can help you to generate different sources of data (divergent thinking). Then they can help you to converge and to categorize your data, distinguishing different types of knowledge. You can separate the "musts" (information you *need to know*) from the "wants" (information or ideas you would *like to know*) (Isaksen & Treffinger, 1985). The following example shows how generating a list of "wants" can be made into a relatively easy step and included in your team meetings.

When our team meeting is almost over and we're near the end of our information gathering time, we spend five minutes on "If Only." We found that five minutes got us to reconsider things and raise new questions to answer before our next meeting. We try to see whether other conclusions can be drawn, based on what we learned so far. Those five minutes helped us to slow ourselves down. We've come up with a surprising number of questions and ideas that way.

The creative problem-solving model encourages you to continue to search, as a true "think tank" would, until you can make use of the different perspectives of your teammates.

Welch, Judge, Anderson, Bray, Child, and Franke (1990) incorporated the following questions into the "Collaborative Options—Outcome Planner" (COOP) team process.

- What options for intervention have been identified through brainstorming?
- How and when will progress be measured and recorded?
- What roles and responsibilities will each participant have for implementing the option? (p. 31)

These questions fit naturally into the activities that an interdisciplinary team would pursue during the performing stage.

3. *Evolution of Problem-Solving and Effective Intervention Skills.* You and the members of your team can usefully develop a "success strategies" filing system. You may find, for example, that meeting early in the morning is more productive than a meeting later in the day. You may decide to set ground rules for yourselves. For example, you may need to specify the amount of time spent brainstorming before establishing a course of action. Some teams may want to come to closure too quickly, while others might spend too long generating alternatives and never get to the

decision stage. As illustrated in Chapter 10, it helps to keep track of the results of your ground rules. You can look at both the quality of your outcome and the level of satisfaction you experience. A review of your results can assist your team in deciding what works best for all of you.

Linder (1993) developed a team approach to the transdisciplinary play-based assessment in which a minimum of three professionals (a speech-language pathologist, occupational or physical therapist, and a teacher or psychologist) participate. The interdisciplinary team members are involved both with the child being assessed and the parents of the child. The outcome of the assessment is based on input from all members of the team. Each team member not directly involved in the assessment is an observer. The observation procedure takes place as follows:

> Worksheets are provided [to each team member] for each developmental area. The worksheets are structured to allow team members to take notes relating to categories of the guidelines. The worksheets provide cues to remind observers of the content of the guidelines being used. Behavioral examples are noted on the worksheets to enable team members to document specific aspects of the child's performance. These notes will serve as a basis for team discussion. . . . Team members are primarily responsible for observing "their" areas of expertise, but all team members observe all developmental areas and contribute to cross-disciplinary discussion after the session. (p. 45)

Linder's approach actively involves team members in both the collection and analysis of observations. This approach enables professionals to participate in the team activities in several different ways. Welch et al. (1990) incorporate training workshops and evaluation forms into their team process. Fleming and Fleming (1983) recommend the use of pre- and post-questionnaires, used by members of a interdisciplinary team to evaluate the utility of suggestions provided and goals developed. The use of "self ratings" was also incorporated (pp. 372–373).

Evaluation at the end of the school year can address several concerns simultaneously. Results of the evaluation can assist the team to evaluate progress, reach closure on a particular topic, and can also provide specific ways to improve in the following year. The team members can use any of the approaches identified in the above paragraph to look at satisfaction with both the process used and the outcome of the process. Changes can be tentatively identified at the end of the school year, with final decisions made when the team reconvenes the following school year. This gives all on the team a chance to think things over.

Another approach is to incorporate others outside your team, either from another school or from a nearby college or university, in brainstorming how to approach some of the topics you are discussing. Cheney's (2000) use of a Web-based "Teachers Lounge" was developed to maximize participation by individuals whose geographic distance from her teacher education course would limit their options for collaboration partners. When a group is at the performing stage, they might welcome input from people whose experiences are complementary to theirs. She observes that the Web site outgrew its original goal:

> The original goal for the Web site was for it to negate the barrier of distance among the members of the class. Soon it became clear that the site had much more potential. . . . Students from other regions of the country could also be

involved. This would enable students to hear voices that reflect diversity not represented in the local community. . . . In conclusion, as we experiment with this powerful new technology, many of us will need considerable support to be able to realize our visions. The creation of the Teachers Lounge Web site was a collaborative effort and it would not exist without the work of several persons. . . . The most effective and rewarding components of the development of this Web site came as a result of the collaboration, brainstorming and speculating that came from working with other professionals. (p. 6)

As you think about your work with members of a interdisciplinary team, use Idea Try-Out 12.2 to consider how you might improve your experiences with a member of your interdisciplinary team.

Idea Try-Out 12.2

Surprise Thank-You Letter

This Idea Try-Out is designed to help you to look at the features of teaming suggested by Phillips and McCullough (1990) and apply them to your situation:

- Pooling of staff talents/resources
- Interdisciplinary involvement in "think tank" environment
- Evolution of problem-solving and effective intervention skills (p. 296)

1. Select the feature that you think had the most benefit for your team and record it in your collaboration notebook.
2. Select a member of your collaboration resource network who you think is particularly skilled in assisting the team accomplish this feature. Even if your team is experiencing problems, focus on what this person has helped the team to do that has helped all make progress.
3. Reflect for two minutes about what your team member does well. In your collaboration notebook, write a short "thank you" letter to the person you selected in Step 2. In the letter, describe some of the things your team member does that makes the team work well. You can think of things that have happened or those that have the potential to occur.
4. At the end of the letter, include a summary statement of what your team member has given to you—new thought, insights, or feelings.
5. After you have finished the letter, you can decide whether or not to share it with the person to whom it was written.

The Idea Try-Out is intended to show you what you could learn from working with a person you know well on a interdisciplinary team. When you translate Phillips and McCullough's (1990) abstract benefits into the behaviors of a real person with whom you are familiar, you can achieve a great deal with your team members.

The Adjourning Stage

The fifth stage is one in which the team finishes what it set out to accomplish. This adjourning stage is a time for reflection and can focus on accomplishments, as shown in the following example.

> *We always breath a sigh of relief when we turn to June on the calendar. We even have a celebration party, which we call "June is busting out all over." We take time to think about all the good things that happened during the year. That gets us through the last month of school!*

With most interdisciplinary teams, this type of individual reflection (as well as the actions listed below) would normally take place at the end of each school year.

Teams in General	Interdisciplinary Teams
1. Completion of tasks	1. Case reviews completed; reports forwarded to CSEs; pre-referral strategies developed
2. Reduction of dependency	2. Team members are able to do problem solving alone or in subgroups; team members have increased autonomy
3. Regret	3. Team members talk about plans for the team for the next school year; team members express ambivalence over the ending of the school year

School-based teams experience a unique benefit. When the school year ends, members of a interdisciplinary team know that they are likely to work with their colleagues the next year. Unlike most groups or teams, there is the possibility of building on success and improving what has taken place.

ADDITIONAL USE OF TEAMS

The experiences that you have had as a member of an interdisciplinary team can offer you a base for other kinds of activities, such as research-based practices. Snell (2003), reporting on the work of Klingner et al. (2003), stated that "Teachers reported several things that facilitated their use of research-based practices: getting support from research team member and administrators" (p. 143). Learning to seek out and use a collaborative structure within your school, or a virtual network, can help you stay on the cutting edge with your practices. In discussing such a partnership, Snell reported on Abbott et al. (1999) whose study "revealed . . . that research must be in a usable form, which takes extensive collaboration time between teachers and researchers" (p. 143). In other words, incorporating research-based practices into your school activities is rarely done in isolation. Your administrator must provide support to this network in order for it to be successful.

Integrating collaboration as a practice into teacher preparation helps to illustrate, more powerfully than any article or textbook can, that teaming works. LaMontagne et al. (2002) analyzed data from early childhood and early childhood special education programs in which collaborative problem solving among the teacher educators was used to offer unified programs for young children. Their interesting article illustrates the ways those committed to unified programs evolved to achieve their goals.

> Interviews with university faculty members who have been involved in providing a unified vision of early childhood education indicate that program development has been a process, complete with barriers and successes. Preliminary data analysis suggests that the vision for unified programs is preparing students to work with all children and their families. While barriers related to attitudes, philosophical differences, and time constraints were encountered, communication and commitment to collaborative problem solving enabled people to overcome these barriers. Clearly, respondents felt that the benefits were overwhelmingly positive. (pp. 245–246)

The programs that LaMontagne et al. (2002) reported on are not the norm. Much work remains to integrate collaboration skills into both preservice preparation for all educators and specialists and into the practice within the schools. As Forbes (2003) recommends, "grappling with collaboration will require acceptance of research diversity and plurality and an expansion and opening up of research to include analyses that question and challenge assumptions in policy and practice" (p. 154). In the next decade, we can expect to see more and more studies of how collaboration is used, like the work of Dickson and Bursuck.

Dickson and Bursuck (2003), reporting on the use of collaboration in a three-tier model (at-risk students, teachers, and university partners), found collaboration to be an essential feature of the progress made:

> While collaboration was a guiding factor in the school-university partnership, it added to the demands on time and instructional opportunities. However, time given to the partnership and related instructional changes overlapped and contributed to a goal-oriented effort. Collaboration and implementing new instructional strategies requires time and effort. But as a result of the efforts, the school, university, and (most important) the students gained something from the partnership. (p. 144)

Dickson and Bursuck sum up what this book, and your collaboration project, have illustrated: collaboration is not something that happens in a vacuum. Effort and time must be invested. Results emerge that make that investment worthwhile.

Howells (2000) provides a detailed account of her collaboration experiences as a special educator and concludes with the following reflections:

> Collaboration is a process that requires continued intervention and revision, tenacity, and dedication, and most of all—time. Even at that, collaboration is far from perfect. So why do we do it? . . . We do it because together, through collaboration, we can solve problems that alone, we cannot solve. Through collaboration, we can improve situations that alone, we cannot improve. . . . Through collaboration, we can provide support for ourselves and set an example for our

students. We demonstrate, by example, that each of us is unique but important, and together we are much greater than the sum of us all. (p. 160)

Howells' consideration of the potential for our collaboration to demonstrate shared decision making and problem solving to our students helps to underscore the impact that our collaboration can have on others. Collaboration can assist us and our students at the same time.

Friend (2000) cautions that we still have our work cut out for us in terms of meaningful collaboration:

> The question is how to raise the standard for collaborative practice in schools to a new, higher level. Unfortunately, some professionals today are weary of the challenge of developing collaborative practices at the very time we are just ready in education to begin a second generation of attention to the topic. As education professionals, we must renew our commitment to being students of collaboration in order to prepare ourselves to face the complexities and uncertainties of the future of our field. No single one of us can do it alone. (p. 160)

The collaboration project you have completed will enable you to meet this challenge with intelligence, experience, and insights, as well as the "call to arms" from Dr. Jennifer Reeves, the Area Superintendent of the Orlando, FL public schools (2002):

> Although the originator of the ancient curse "May you live in interesting times" couldn't have envisioned public education in the 21st century, a more fitting axiom would be hard to find. Never in the history of mankind has so much been expected from so many with so little support . . . If all of our children are to have an opportunity to participate fully in our society under the increased demands of accountability in our public schools, we have a moral obligation to investigate our own practices. We cannot be afraid to break the mold of traditional special education practices, but, most importantly, general educators and special educators must make the commitment to work collaboratively on behalf of all children. (pp. 74–75)

Dr. Reeves' discussion of collaboration between general educators and special educators, as well as with families and administrators, explains that this service is essential to meet the needs of all students. "We have to stop looking at special education programs and begin focusing on the special needs of individual children" (Reeves, 2002, p. 74). Collaboration in preparation as well as within the schools will help make this type of education delivery possible. Your experience investigating a collaborative endeavor will help you in your work in many different ways.

CONCLUSION

Working with members of your interdisciplinary team can give you opportunities to practice the collaboration skills you have worked on throughout this book. You can review your collaboration notebook to select the try-outs that sparked new insights or provided helpful encouragement. Members of your interdisciplinary team can be people with whom you can share information, solve problems, and communicate effectively. The outcome of your successful work with them leads directly to benefits for your students.

At several points in this book, a comparison was made between professional collaboration and cooking. By now, you have many examples of how the collaboration between you and another person requires attention and skill. This expanded metaphor should have even more resonance for you now than it did at the beginning of the book. You have

- Looked around your own kitchen (situational assessment)
- Seen what is available (assembled resources and developed your collaboration resource network)
- Thought about what you feel like cooking (self assessment)
- Chosen your menu (goal selection)
- Assembled your ingredients (developed your objectives)
- Begun to cook (implementation)
- Decided what you need to add (plan modification) as you go along

When your cooking (collaboration project) is completed, you can sit down to enjoy the results of your labors. Then you can decide what to make next (next steps project with family members or members of your interdisciplinary team).

Along the way, your self-reinforcement strategies have helped you to maintain your sense of humor and your perspective. You can feel good about what you've done. Now you can to use your newly acquired skills on your *next* project.

References

Abelson, M. A., & Woodman, R. W. (1983). Review of research on team effectiveness: Implications for teams in schools. *School Psychology Review, 12,* 125–136.

Abernathy, T. V., & Cheney, C. O. (2005). TREK to student independence. *Teaching Exceptional Children, 37*(3), 52–57.

Able-Boone, H., Crais, E. R., & Downing, K. (2003). Preparation of early intervention practitioners for working with young children with low incidence disabilities. *Teacher Education and Special Education, 26*(1), 79–82.

Abrams, J., Ferguson, J., & Laud, L. (2001). Assessing ESOL students. *Educational Leadership, 59*(3), 62–65.

Ackland, R. (1991). A review of the peer coaching literature. *Journal of Staff Development, 12*(1), 22–27.

Ackoff, R. L., & Vergara, E. (1988). Creativity in problem solving and planning. In R.L. Kuhn (Ed.), *Handbook for creative and innovative managers* (pp. 77–89). New York: McGraw Hill.

Adamson, D. R., Cox, J., & Schuller, J. (1989). Collaboration/consultation: Bridging the gap from resource room to regular classroom. *Teacher Education and Special Education, 12*(1–2), 52–55.

Adamson, D. R., Matthews, P., & Schuller, J. (1990). Five ways to bridge the resource room-to-regular classroom gap. *Teaching Exceptional Children, 22*(2), 74–77.

Agne, K. J., Greenwood, G. E., & Miller, L. D. (1994). Relationships between teacher belief systems and teacher effectiveness. *The Journal of Research and Development in Education, 27*(3), 141–152.

Agness, J., Sharpe, V., Sebald, L., Turner, E., Simon, A., & Vaughan, A. (2004). *Co-planning makes the difference for facilitating student success in the least restrictive environment.* Presentation at the 9th International Conference of the Division on Developmental Disabilities, Las Vegas, NV.

Allen, D. W., & LeBlanc, A. C. (2004). *Collaborative peer coaching that improves instruction: The 2 + 2 performance appraisal model.* Thousand Oaks, CA: Corwin Press.

Allen, T. D., & Eby, L. T. (2004). Factors related to mentor reports of mentoring functions provided: Gender and relational characteristics. *Sex Roles, 50*(1/2), 129–139.

Allen-Meares, P., & Pugach, M. (1982). Facilitating interdisciplinary collaboration on behalf of handicapped children and youth. *Teacher Education and Special Education, 5*(1), 30–36.

Allinder, R. M. (1994). The relationship between efficacy and the instructional practices of special education teachers and consultants. *Teacher Education and Special Education, 17*(2), 86–95.

Anderson, L. W., & Walberg, H. J. (Eds.). (1974). Learning environments. In H. J. Walberg (Ed.), *Evaluating educational performance: A sourcebook of methods, instruments and examples* (pp. 81–98). Berkeley, CA: McCutchan.

Anderson, M. A. (2004). The many faces of collaboration. *MultiMedia & Internet @ Schools, 11*(2), 27–28.

Anderson, R. N., Greene, M. L., & Loewen, P. S. (1988). Relationships among teachers' and students' thinking skills, sense of efficacy, and student achievement. *Alberta Journal of Educational Research, 34*(2), 148–165.

Andrews, L. (2002). Preparing general education pre-service teachers for inclusion: Web-enhanced case-based instruction. *Journal of Special Education Technology, 17*(3), 27–35.

Angelo, C. (1994). *Analysis of collaboration project.* Unpublished manuscript, Buffalo State College.

Angelo, T. A. (1991, Summer). Introduction and overview: From classroom assessment to classroom research. In T. A. Angelo (Ed.), *Classroom research: Early lessons from success* (pp. 7–31). New Directions for Teaching and Learning, No. 46. San Francisco: Jossey-Bass.

Angle, B. (1996). 5 steps to collaborative teaching and enrichment remediation. *Teaching Exceptional Children, 29*(1), 8–10.

Archer, A. L., & Isaacson, S. L. (1990). Teaching others how to teach strategies. *Teacher Education and Special Education, 13*(2), 63–72.

Armstrong, F., & Moore, M. (2004). Action research: Developing inclusive practice and transforming cultures. In F. Armstrong & M. Moore, (Eds.), *Action research for inclusive education: Changing places, changing practice, changing minds* (pp. 1–16). New York: RoutledgeFalmer.

Ashton, P., & Webb, R. (1986). *Making a difference: Teachers' sense of efficacy.* Research on Teaching Monograph Series. New York: Longman.

Austin, V. L. (2001). Teachers' beliefs about co-teaching. *Remedial and Special Education, 22*(4), 245–255.

Axtell, R. E. (1991). *Gestures: The do's and taboos of body language around the world.* New York: John Wiley & Sons.

Babad, E. (1991). Calling on students: How a teacher's behavior can acquire disparate meanings in students' minds. *Journal of Classroom Interaction, 25*(1), 1–4.

Babcock, N. L., & Pryzwansky, W. B. (1983). Models of consultation: Preferences of educational professionals at five stages of service. *Journal of School Psychology, 21,* 359–366.

Bailey, D. B., Jr., Helsel-DeWert, M., Thiele, J. E., & Ware, W. B. (1983). Measuring individual participation on the interdisciplinary team. *American Journal of Mental Deficiency, 88*(3), 247–254.

Bales, R. F., & Cohen, S. P. (1979). *SYMLOG: A system for the multiple level observation of groups.* New York: The Free Press.

Banbury, M. M., & Hebert, C. R. (1992). Do you see what I mean? Body language in classroom interactions. *Teaching Exceptional Children, 24,* 34–37.

Bandura, A. (1977). Self-efficacy: Toward a unifying theory of behavioral change. *Psychological Review, 84*(2), 191–215.

Bangert, A. W. (2004). The seven principles of good practice: A framework for evaluating on-line teaching. *Internet and Higher Education, 7*(3), 217–232.

Banks, C. A. M. (1993). Parents and teachers: Partners in school reform. In J. A. Banks & C. A. M. Banks (Eds.), *Multicultural education: Issues and perspectives* (2nd ed., pp. 332–352). Boston: Allyn & Bacon.

Barberio, J. (1995). *Analysis of collaboration project.* Unpublished manuscript, Buffalo State College.

Barnes, K. L., Bullock, L. M., & Currin, H. (1997). Professional development for special educators: Foundations for collaboration. *Journal of Vocational Rehabilitation, 8*(3), 253–258.

Barr, L., & Barr, N. (1989). *The leadership equation.* Austin, TX: Eakin Press.

Barth, R. (1990). *Improving schools from within.* San Francisco: Jossey-Bass.

Bassett, P. W. (2004). Innovation, collaboration, & education. *Presidency, 7*(2), 38–39.

Bateson, M. C. (1989). *Composing a life.* New York: Grove Press.

Baugh, S. G., & Scandura, T. A. (1999). The effect of multiple mentors on protégé attitudes toward the work setting. *Journal of Social Behaviors & Personality, 14*(4), 503–522.

Bauwens, J., & Hourcade, J. J. (2003). *Cooperative teaching: Rebuilding the schoolhouse for all students* (2nd ed.). Austin, TX: Pro-Ed.

Bauwens, J., Hourcade, J. J., & Friend, M. (1989). Cooperative teaching: A model for general and special education integration. *Remedial and Special Education, 10*(2), 17–22.

Bay, M., Bryan, T., & O'Connor, R. (1994). Teachers assisting teachers: A prereferral model for urban educators. *Teacher Education and Special Education, 17*(1), 10–21.

Beale, A. V. (1990). Are you listening? Assessing and improving your listening skills. *NASSP Bulletin, 74*, 88–89, 93–94.

Beck, C., & Kosnik, C. (2001). From cohort to community in a preservice teacher education program. *Teaching and Teacher Education, 17*(8), 925–948.

Beck, C., & Kosnik, C. (2002). Components of a good practicum placement: Student teacher perceptions. *Teacher Education Quarterly, 29*(2), 81–98.

Berelson, B. (1952). *Content analysis in communication research.* Glencoe, IL: The Free Press.

Bernieri, F. J., & Rosenthal, R. (1991). Interpersonal coordination: Behavior matching and interactional synchrony. In R. S. Feldman & B. Rime (Eds.), *Fundamentals of nonverbal behavior* (pp. 401–432). Cambridge: Cambridge University Press.

Best, T. (2002). When worlds collide: Introducing information technology (IT) culture to public education. *Educational Technology, 42*(4), 19–20.

Bettencourt, E. M., Gillett, M. H., Gall, M. D., & Hull, R. E. (1983). Effects of teacher enthusiasm training on student on-task behavior and achievement. *American Educational Research Journal, 20*(3), 435–450.

Birdwhistell, R. L. (1970). *Kinesics and context: Essays on body motion communication.* New York: Ballantine Books.

Blanchard, K. H. (2001). *High five! The magic of working together.* New York: HarperCollins.

Blatt, B. (1966). *Christmas in purgatory: A photographic essay on mental retardation.* New York: Human Policy Press/Syracuse.

Board of Education of the City of New York. (1994). *English as a second language professional development manual for special education teachers.* New York: Author.

Boe, T. (1989). The next step for educators and the technology industry: Investing in teachers. *Educational Technology, 29*(3), 39–44.

Bolman, L. G., & Deal, T. E. (2002). *Reframing the path to school leadership: A guide for teachers and principals.* Thousand Oaks, CA: Corwin Press.

Bolman, L. G., & Deal, T. E. (2003). *Reframing organizations: Artistry, choice and leadership* (3rd ed.). San Francisco: Jossey-Bass.

Bolster, A. S., Jr. (1983). Toward a more effective model of research on teaching. *Harvard Educational Review, 53*(3), 294–308.

Bonk, C. (2004). I should have known this was coming: Computer-mediated discussions in teacher education. *Journal of Research on Technology in Education, 36*(2), 95–102.

Bonstingl, J. J. (1992). The quality revolution in education. *Educational Leadership, 50*(3), 4–9.

Borko, H. (2004). Professional development and teacher learning: Mapping the terrain. *Educational Researcher, 33*(8), 3–15.

Bos, C. S., & Vaughn, S. (2006). *Strategies for teaching students with learning and behavior problems* (6th ed.). Boston: Allyn & Bacon.

Bosworth, K. (1994). Developing collaborative skills in college students. In K. Bosworth & S. J. Hamilton (Eds.), *Collaborative learning: Underlying processes and effective techniques* (pp. 25–34). New Directions for Teaching and Learning, No. 59. San Francisco: Jossey-Bass.

Bouck, E. C. (2004a). *Walking in their footsteps: The daily school life of secondary students with mild mental impairment.* Presentation at the 9th International Conference of the Division on Developmental Disabilities, Las Vegas, NV.

Bouck, E. C. (2004b). *Where I am educated and with whom I interact: Experiences of six secondary students with mild mental retardation.* Unpublished manuscript.

Bouck, E. C. (2005). Secondary special educators: Perspectives of preservice preparation and satisfaction. *Teacher Education and Special Education, 28*(2), 125–139.

Bozzone, M. A. (1995). A teacher's stress survival guide. *Instructor, 104*(5), 55–59.

Braaten, S., Gable, R. A., & Stewart, S. C. (1995). Public Law 94–142: Twenty years and counting—where do we stand? *Preventing School Failure, 39*(3), 4–5.

Brabeck, M. M., & Shirley, D. (2003). Excellence in schools of education: An oxymoron? *Phi Delta Kappan, 84*(5), 368–373.

Branson, R. K. (1990). Issues in the design of schooling: Changing the paradigm. *Educational Technology, 30*(4), 7–10.

Bratlien, M. J., & McGuire, M. A. (2002). *Teachers for our nation's schools*. Paper presented at the Annual Meeting of the Phi Delta Kappa District III, Tulsa, OK. (ERIC Document Reproduction Service No. ED 471012)

Brice, A., & Roseberry-McKibbin, C. (1999). Turning frustration into success for English language learners. *Educational Leadership, 56*(7), 53–55.

Bridges, W. (2003). *Managing transitions: Making the most of change* (2nd ed.). Cambridge, MA: Da Capo Press, Perseus Books Group.

Briscoe, D. B. (1991). Designing for diversity in school success: Capitalizing on culture. *Preventing School Failure, 36*(1), 13–18.

Broer, S. M., Doyle, M. B., & Giangreco, M. F. (2005). Perspectives of students with intellectual disabilities about their experiences with paraprofessional support. *Exceptional Children, 71*(4), 415–430.

Bulgren, J. A., Lenz, B. K., McKnight, M., Davis, B., Grossen, B., Marquis, J., et al. (2002). The educational context and outcomes for high school students with disabilities: The perceptions of general education teachers. (OSERS Special Education Programs Report RR-7). Lawrence: Kansas University, Institute for Academic Access. (ERIC Document Reproduction Service No. ED 469287)

Burnett, J., & Peters-Johnson, C. (Eds.). (2004). *Thriving as a special educator: Balancing your practices and your ideals*. Alexandria, VA: Council for Exceptional Children.

Burnham, J., Discher, S., & Ingle, K. (2003). *The circle of collaboration*. Proceedings of the Annual Conference of the American Council on Rural Special Education (ACRES), Salt Lake City, UT. (ERIC Document Reproduction Service No. ED 481551)

Burns, D. D. (1980). *Feeling good: The new mood therapy*. New York: William Morrow.

Bush, G. (2003). Walking the collaborative talk. *Knowledge Quest, 32*(1), 52.

Butler, P. (1981). *Talking to yourself*. San Francisco: Harper & Row.

Buzzeo, T. (2003). Collaborating to meet standards: Teacher/librarian partnerships K–12. *Knowledge Quest, 32*(1), 29–30.

Byers, P. (1985). Communication: Cooperation or negotiation? *Theory Into Practice, 24*(1), 71–76.

Cabello, B., & Terrell, R. (1994). Making students feel like family: How teachers create warm and caring classroom environments. *Journal of Classroom Interaction, 29*(1), 17–23.

Cacioppo, J. T. (2004). Common sense, intuition, and theory in personality and social psychology. *Personality and Social Psychology Review, 8*(1), 114–122.

Callicott, K. J. (2003). Culturally sensitive collaboration within person-centered planning. *Focus on Autism and Other Developmental Disabilities, 18*(1), 60–68.

Cambone, J. (1995). Time for teachers in school restructuring. *Teachers College Record, 96*(3), 512–543.

Campbell, D. E., & Campbell, T. A. (2000). The mentoring relationship: Differing perceptions of benefits. *College Student Journal, 34*(4), 516–524.

Canning, C. (1991). What teachers say about reflection. *Educational Leadership, 48*, 18–21.

Caron, E. A., & McLaughlin, M. J. (2002). Indicators of Beacons of Excellence Schools: What do they tell us about collaborative practices? *Journal of Educational and Psychological Consultation, 13*(4), 285–313.

Carr, E. G., Dunlap, G., Horner, R. H., Koegel, R. L., Turnbull, A. P., Sailor, W., et al. (2002). Positive behavior support: Evolution of an applied science. *Journal of Positive Behavioral Interventions, 4*(1), 4–16.

Carrington, S., & Elkins, J. (2002). Comparisons of a traditional and an inclusive secondary school culture. *International Journal of Inclusive Education, 6*(1), 1–16.

Carter, E. W., Clark, N. M., Cushing, L. S., & Kennedy, C. H. (2005). Moving from elementary to middle school: Supporting a smooth transition for students with severe disabilities. *Teaching Exceptional Children, 37*(3), 8–14.

Carter, J. F. (1993). Self-management: Education's ultimate goal. *Teaching Exceptional Children, 25*(3), 28–32.

Carter, K., & Doyle, W. (1995). Preconceptions in learning to teach. *The Educational Forum, 59*, 186–195.

Cartledge, G. (1996). *Cultural diversity and social skills instruction: Understanding ethnic and gender differences*. Champaign, IL: Research Press.

Castro, J. I. (2004). Promoting leadership development and collaboration in rural schools. In J. H. Chrispeels (Ed.), *Learning to lead together: The promise and challenge of sharing leadership* (pp. 327–341). Thousand Oaks, CA: Sage.

Causton-Theoharis, J., & Malmgren, K. (2005). Building bridges: Strategies to help paraprofessionals promote peer interaction. *Teaching Exceptional Children, 37*(6), 18–24.

Chase, S., & Merryfield, M. (2000). After the honeymoon is over: What eight years of collaboration have taught us about school/university collaboration in social studies and global education. In M. Johnston, P. Brosnan, D. Cramer, & T. Dove (Eds.), *Collaborative reform and other improbable dreams: The challenges of professional development schools* (pp. 123–140). Albany: State University of New York Press.

Chen, J., & Dym, W. (2003). Using computer technology to bridge school and community. *Phi Delta Kappan, 85*(3), 232–234.

Cheney, C. O. (2000). Combining distance education and web applications for a course on collaboration in special education. In *Capitalizing on leadership in rural special education: Making a difference for children and families. Conference proceedings* (pp. 241–246). Alexandria, VA. (ERIC Document Reproduction Service No. ED 439889)

Cheney, C. O., & Demchak, M. A. (2001). Inclusion of students with disabilities in rural classrooms: Recommendations and case study. *Rural Educator, 23*(2), 40–46.

Cheng, Y. C. (1996). Relation between teachers' professionalism and job attitudes, educational outcomes, and organizational factors. *The Journal of Educational Research, 89*(3), 163–171.

Chrispeels, J. H. (Ed.). (2004). *Learning to lead together: The promise and challenge of sharing leadership.* Thousand Oaks, CA: Sage.

Christensen, C. M. (1992). Multicultural competencies in early intervention: Training professionals for a pluralistic society. *Infants and Young Children, 4*(3), 49–63.

Christiansen, H., Goulet, L., Krentz, C., & Maeers, M. (Eds.). (1997). *Recreating relationships: Collaboration and educational reform.* Albany, NY: SUNY Press.

Chrystal, C. A. (1988). Teacher management and helping style: How can we develop student self-control? *Focus on Exceptional Children, 21*(4), 9–14.

Cipani, E. C. (1995). Be aware of negative reinforcement. *Teaching Exceptional Children, 27*(4), 36–40.

Clark, R. A., Harden, S. L., & Johnson, W. B. (2000). Mentor relationships in clinical psychology doctoral training: Results of a national survey. *Teaching of Psychology, 27*(4), 262–269.

Cleese, J., & Jay, A. (1993). *Meetings bloody meetings* [Video]. Chicago: Video Arts.

Clifton, M. (2004). "We like to talk and we like someone to listen." Cultural difference and minority voices as agents of change. In F. Armstrong & M. Moore (Eds.), *Action research for inclusive education: Changing places, changing practice, changing minds* (pp. 77–91). New York: RoutledgeFalmer.

Cohen, E. G. (1994). Restructuring the classroom: Conditions for productive small groups. *Review of Educational Research, 64*(1), 1–35.

Cohen, S. S., Thomas, C C., Sattler, R. O., & Morsink, C. V. (1997). Meeting the challenge of consultation and collaboration: Developing interactive teams. *Journal of Learning Disabilities. 30*(4), 427–435.

Cole, A. L. (1992). Teacher development in the work place: Rethinking the appropriation of professional relationships. *Teachers College Record, 94*(2), 365–380.

Collins, B. C., Hall, M., & Branson, T. A. (2002). *Success with reluctant researchers: Real life experiences in a rural school setting.* Annual National Conference Proceedings of the American Council on Rural Special Education (ACRES), Reno, NV.

Conderman, G. (2001). Program evaluation: Using multiple assessment methods to promote authentic student learning and curricular change. *Teacher Education and Special Education, 24*(4), 391–394.

Conley, S. C., & Bacharach, S. B. (1990). From school-site management to participatory school-site management. *Phi Delta Kappan, 71*(7), 539–543.

Cook, L., & Friend, M. (1991a). Principles for the practice of collaboration in schools. *Preventing School Failure, 35*(4), 6–9.

Cook, L., & Friend, M. (1991b). Collaboration in special education: Coming of age in the 1990s. *Preventing School Failure, 35*(2), 24–27.

Cook, L., & Friend, M. (1996). Co-teaching: What's it all about? *CEC Today, 3*(3), 12–13.

Coombs Richardson, R., & Mead, J. (2001). Supporting general educators' inclusive practices. *Teacher Education and Special Education, 24*(1), 383–390.

Cooper, A. M. (1990). Fallacy of a single model for school achievement: Considerations for ethnicity. *Sociological Perspectives, 33*(1), 59–184.

Correa, V., & Tulbert, B. (1991). Teaching culturally diverse students. *Preventing School Failure, 35*(3), 20–25.

Costa, A. L., & Garmston, R. J. (1993). Cognitive coaching for peer reflection. *CASCD Journal, 5*(2), 15–19.

Costa, A. L., & Garmston, R. J. (1994). *Cognitive coaching: A foundation for renaissance schools.* Berkeley, CA: The Institute for Intelligent Behavior.

Council for Exceptional Children. (1995, November). The changing role of the special educator. *CEC Today, 2*(5), 1, 9.

Council for Exceptional Children. (2003). *What every special educator must know: The international standards for the preparation and certification of special education teachers* (5th ed.). Arlington, VA: Author.

Council for Exceptional Children. (2004). *The Council for Exceptional Children definition of a well-prepared special education teacher.* Arlington, VA: Author.

Council for Exceptional Children. (2005). *Public policy update.* Paper presented at Annual Convention, Baltimore, MD.

Covey, S. R. (1989). *The seven habits of highly effective people: Powerful lessons in personal change.* New York: Simon & Schuster.

Cramer, S. F. (1994). Assessing effectiveness in the collaborative classroom. In K. Bosworth & S. J. Hamilton (Eds.), *Collaborative learning: Underlying processes and effective techniques* (pp. 69–81). New Directions for Teaching and Learning, No. 59. San Francisco: Jossey-Bass.

Cramer, S. F. (2003). Challenging core assumptions: Integrating transformative leadership models into campus-wide implementation activities. *College and University Journal, 79*(1), 15–22.

Cramer, S. F. (2005). Keys to successful collaboration. In M. H. Lupi & S. M. Martin (Eds.), *Special women, special leaders: Special educators and the challenge of leadership roles* (pp. 111–123). New York: Peter Lang.

Cramer, S. F., Krasinski, S., Crutchfield, M. D., Sackmary, B., & Scalia, L. (2000). Using collaboration and the web to implement the CEC standards. *Teaching Exceptional Children, 32*(5), 12–20.

Cramer, S. F., & Puccio, G. (2004, April). *Challenging self-imposed constraints: Getting outside the box by transforming leadership through creativity.* Keynote address at Annual Conference of New York State Women Leaders in Higher Education joint presentation with the American Council on Education, Buffalo, NY.

Crawford, W. (1995). What makes people tick. *School Business Affairs, 61*(4), 3–11.

Crow, G. M., Hausman, C. S., & Scribner, J. P. (2002). Reshaping the role of the school principal. In J. Murphy (Ed.), *The educational leadership challenge: Redefining leadership for the 21st century; 101st yearbook of the National Society for the Study of Education* (pp. 189–210). Chicago: The University of Chicago Press.

Crozier, S., & Sileo, N. M. (2005). Encouraging positive behavior with social stories: An intervention for children with autism spectrum disorders. *Teaching Exceptional Children, 37*(6), 26–31.

Crutchfield, M. D. (2003). What do the CEC standards mean to me? Using the CEC standards to improve my practice. *Teaching Exceptional Children, 35*(6), 40–45.

Cudney, K. (1996). *Analysis of collaboration project.* Unpublished manuscript. Buffalo State College.

Cummins, L. (2004). The pot of gold at the end of the rainbow: Mentoring in early childhood education. *Childhood Education, 80*(5), 254–259.

Cunningham, C. (2002, April). *Engaging the community to support student achievement* (ERIC Clearinghouse on Educational Management No. 157, EDO-EA-0204). Eugene: University of Oregon. (ERIC Document Reproduction Service No. ED 464395)

Curwin, R. L. (1995). A humane approach to reducing violence in schools. *Educational Leadership, 52*, 72–75.

Dallmer, D. (2004). Collaborative relationships in teacher education: A personal narrative of conflicting roles. *Curriculum Inquiry, 34*(1), 29–46.

Daresh, J. (2004). Mentoring school leaders: Professional promise or predictable problems? *Educational Administration Quarterly, 40*(4), 495–517.

Darling-Hammond, L. (1999). Educating teachers for the next century: Rethinking practice and policy. In G. Griffin (Ed.), *The education of teachers: 98th NSSE Yearbook, Part I* (pp. 221–256). Chicago: NSSE.

Davis, G., & Thomas, M. (1989). *Effective schools & effective teachers.* Boston: Allyn & Bacon.

Dean, C. (1999). *Problem-based learning in teacher education.* Paper presented at the annual meeting of the American Educational Research Association, Montreal, Canada.

DeLuke, S. V., & Knoblock, P. (1987). Teacher behavior as preventative discipline. *Teaching Exceptional Children, 19*(4), 18–24.

Denton, C. A., Vaughn, S., & Fletcher, J. M. (2003). Bringing research-based practice in reading intervention to scale. *Learning Disabilities Research & Practice, 18*(3), 201–211.

Dettmer, P., Thurston, L. P., & Dyck, N. (2002). *Consultation, collaboration, and teamwork for students with special needs* (4th ed.). Boston: Allyn & Bacon.

Dewey, J. (1933). *How we think.* Boston: D. C. Heath.

Dickens, C. (2000). Too valuable to be rejected, too different to be embraced: A critical review of school/university collaboration. In M. Johnston, P. Brosnan, D. Cramer, & T. Dove (Eds.), *Collaborative reform and other improbable dreams* (pp. 21–42). Albany: State University of New York Press.

Dickinson, D. J., & Adcox, S. (1984). Program evaluation of a school consultation program. *Psychology in the Schools, 21*, 336–342.

Dickson, S. V., & Bursuck, W. (2003). Implementing an outcomes-based collaborative partnership for preventing reading failure. In D. L. Wiseman & S. L. Knight, (Eds.), *Linking school-university collaboration and K–12 student outcomes* (pp. 131–146). Washington, DC: AACTE.

Dieker, L. A. (2001a). Collaboration as a tool to resolve the issue of disjointed service delivery. *Journal of Educational and Psychological Consultation, 12*(3), 263–269.

Dieker, L. A. (2001b). What are the characteristics of "effective" middle and high school co-taught teams for students with disabilities? *Preventing School Failure, 46*(1), 14–23.

Dieker, L. A., & Berg, C. (2002). Collaborative program development between secondary science, mathematics and special educators. *Teacher Education and Special Education, 25*(1), 92–99.

Dieker, L. A., & Monda-Amaya, L. E. (1995). Reflective teaching: A process for analyzing journals of preservice educators. *Teacher Education and Special Education, 18*(4), 240–252.

Dietz, M. E. (1990, April). On the road to change. *Instructor, 99*, 35–37.

Dillon, D. (2001). *Interdisciplinary research and education: Preliminary perspectives from the MIT Media Laboratory.* GoodWork Project Paper 13. Cambridge, MA: Harvard University.

Dinnebeil, L. A., & Hale, L. (1999). Early intervention program practices that support collaboration. *Topics in Early Childhood Special Education, 1999, 19*(4), 225–236.

Dinnebeil, L. A., & McInerney, W. F. (2001). An innovative practicum to support early childhood inclusion through collaborative consultation. *Teacher Education and Special Education, 24*(3), 263–266.

DiPardo, A. (1999). *Teaching in common: Challenges to joint work in classrooms and schools.* New York: Teachers College Press.

Doelling, J. E., Bryde, S., Brunner, J., & Martin, B. (1998). Collaborative planning for inclusion of a student with developmental disabilities. *Middle School Journal, 29*(3), 34–39.

Donaldson, R., & Christiansen, J. (1990). Consultation and collaboration: A decision-making model. *Teaching Exceptional Children, 22,* 22–24.

Donegan, M. M., & Ostrosky, M. M. (2000). Peer coaching: Teachers supporting teachers. *Young Exceptional Children, 3*(3), 9–16.

Downing, J. E. (2001). Meeting the communication needs of students with severe and multiple disabilities in general education classrooms. *Exceptionality, 9*(3), 147–156.

Doyle, M. B. (2002). *The paraprofessionals guide to the inclusive classroom.* Baltimore, MD: Brookes.

Drucker, P. F. (1994, November). The age of social transformation. *The Atlantic Monthly,* 53–80.

Dudley-Marling, C. (1985). Perceptions of the usefulness of the IEP by teachers of learning disabled and emotionally disturbed children. *Psychology in the Schools, 22,* 65–67.

Duffy, M. L., & Forgan, J. (2005). *Mentoring new special education teachers: A guide for mentors and program developers.* Thousand Oaks, CA: Corwin Press.

Duke, T. S. (2004). Problematizing collaboration: A critical review of the empirical literature on teaching teams. *Teacher Education and Special Education, 27*(3), 307–317.

Dunlap, D. M., & Goldman, P. (1991). Rethinking power in schools. *Educational Administration Quarterly, 27*(1), 5–29.

Eanes, R. (1997). *Content area literacy: Teaching for today and tomorrow.* Albany, NY: Delmar.

Edmiaston, R. K., & Fitzgerald, L. M. (2000). How Reggio Emilia encourages inclusion. *Educational Leadership, 58*(1), 66–70.

Edwards, S. L., & Bruce, C. S. (2004). The assignment that triggered change: Assessment and the relational learning model for generic capabilities. *Assessment & Evaluation in Higher Education, 29*(2), 141–157.

Edyburn, D. L. (2000). Assistive technology and students with mild disabilities. *Focus on Exceptional Children, 32*(9), 1–24.

Ehrich, L. C., Hansford, B., & Tennent, L. (2004). Formal mentoring programs in education and other professions: A review of the literature. *Educational Administration Quarterly, 40*(4), 518–540.

Eison, J. (1990). Confidence in the classroom: Ten maxims for new teachers. *College Teaching, 38*(1), 21–25.

Elksnin, L. K. (1997). Collaborative speech and language services for students with learning disabilities. *Journal of Learning Disabilities, 30*(4), 414–426.

Elliott, S. N., & Sheridan, S. M. (1992). Consultation and teaming: Problem solving among educators, parents, and support personnel. *The Elementary School Journal, 92*(3), 315–338.

Ertmer, P. (2003). Transforming teacher education: Visions and strategies. *Educational Technology Research and Development, 51*(1), 124–128.

Falck, H. S. (1977). Interdisciplinary education and implications for social work practice. *Journal of Education for Social Work, 13*(2), 30–37.

Falkowski, J. (1992). *Analysis of collaboration project.* Unpublished manuscript, Buffalo State College.

Farmakopoulou, N. (2002). Using an integrated theoretical framework for understanding inter-agency collaboration in the special education field. *European Journal of Special Needs Education, 17*(1), 49–59.

Farnsworth, C., & Morris, D. R. (1995). The seven habits of highly effective people: The key to effective educational mentoring. *Educational Horizons, 73,* 138–140.

Fennick, E., & Liddy, D. (2001). Responsibilities and preparation for collaborative teaching: Co-teachers' perspectives. *Teacher Education and Special Education, 24*(3), 229–240.

Ferguson, D. L. (1992). *The elementary/secondary system: Supportive education for students with disabilities,* Module 5b: School Development System. Eugene: University of Oregon, Specialized Training Program.

Ferguson, D. L. (1994). Magic for teacher work groups: Tricks for colleague communication. *Teaching Exceptional Children, 27*(1), 42–47.

Ferguson, D. L., Jeanchild, L., & Todd, A. (1991). *The elementary/secondary system: Supportive education for students with severe handicaps.* Module 1a: The activity-based IEP. Eugene: University of Oregon, Specialized Training Program.

Firestone, W. A., & Pennell, J. R. (1993). Teacher commitment, working conditions, and differential incentive policies. *Review of Educational Research, 63*(4), 489–525.

Fisher, D., Frey, N., & Thousand, J. (2003). What do special educators need to know and be prepared to do for inclusive schooling to work? *Teacher Education and Special Education, 26*(1), 42–50.

Fisher, R., Ury, W., & Patton, B. (1991). *Getting to yes: Negotiating without giving in* (2nd ed.). New York: Penguin Books.

Fleming, D. C., & Fleming, E. R. (1983). Consultation with multidisciplinary teams: A program of development and improvement of team functioning. *Journal of School Psychology, 21*, 367–376.

Fleming, J., & Love, M. (2003). A systemic change model for leadership, inclusion and mentoring (SLIM). *Early Childhood Education Journal, 31*(1), 53–58.

Fleming, J. L., & Monda-Amaya, L. E. (2001). Process variables critical for team effectiveness: A Delphi study of wraparound team members. *Remedial and Special Education, 22*(3), 158–171.

Fletcher-Campbell, F. (1992). How can we use an extra pair of hands? *British Journal of Special Education, 19*(4), 141–143.

Foley, R. M., & Mundschenk, N. A. (1997). Collaboration activities and competencies of secondary school special educators: A national survey. *Teacher Education and Special Education, 20*(1), 47–60.

Forbes, A. (2004, July 16). Sent to the chopping block. *The Chronicle of Higher Education*, p. C2.

Forbes, J. (2003). Grappling with collaboration: Would opening up the research base help? *British Journal of Special Education, 30*(3), 150–155.

Ford, B. A. (1992). Multicultural education training for special educators working with African-American youth. *Exceptional Children, 59*(2), 107–114.

Ford, B. A. (2004). Preparing special educators for culturally responsive school-community partnerships. *Teacher Education and Special Education, 27*(3), 224–230.

Forsyth, D. R. (1990). *Group dynamics.* Pacific Grove, CA: Brooks/Cole.

Fowler, J., & O'Gorman, J. G. (2003). Mentoring functions: An examination of the perceptions of mentors and mentees. *Australian Journal of Psychology, 55*(Supp.), 123.

Frankland, H. C. (2001). *Professional collaboration and family-professional partnerships: A qualitative analysis of indicators and influencing factors.* Unpublished doctoral dissertation, University of Kansas.

Fraser, B. J. (1991). Validity and use of classroom environment instruments. *Journal of Classroom Interaction, 26*(2), 5–11.

Friedman, E. A. (1994). A management perspective on effective technology integration: Top ten questions for school administrators. *Technical Horizons in Education, 22*, 89–90.

Friend, M. (1984). Consultation skills for resource teachers. *Learning Disability Quarterly, 7*, 246–250.

Friend, M. (2000). Myths and misunderstandings about professional collaboration. *Remedial and Special Education, 21*(1), 130–132, 160.

Friend, M., & Cook, L. (1990). Collaboration as a predictor for success in school reform. *Journal of Educational and Psychological Consultation, 1*(1), 69–86.

Friend, M., & Cook, L. (2002). *Interactions: Collaboration skills for school professionals* (4th ed.). White Plains, NY: Longman.

Friend, M., & McNutt, G. (1987). A comparative study of resource teacher job descriptions and administrators' perceptions of resource teacher responsibilities. *Journal of Learning Disabilities, 20*(4), 224–228.

Fritz, J. J., Miller-Heyl, J., Kreutzer, J. C., & MacPhee, D. (1995). Fostering personal teaching efficacy through staff development and classroom activities. *The Journal of Educational Research, 88*(4), 200–208.

Fuchs, D., & Fuchs, L. S. (2001). One blueprint for bridging the gap: Project PROMISE (Practitioners and Researchers Orchestrating Model Innovations to Strengthen Education). *Teacher Education and Special Education, 24*(4), 304–314.

Fuchs, D., Fuchs, L. S., Dulan, J., Roberts, H., & Fernstrom, P. (1992). Where is the research on consultation effectiveness? *Journal of Educational and Psychological Consultation, 3*(2), 151–174.

Fullan, M. (1991). *The new meaning of educational change.* New York: Teachers College Press.

Fullan, M. (2001). *Leading to a culture of change.* San Francisco: Jossey-Bass.

Gable, R. A., & Manning, M. L. (1999). Interdisciplinary teaming: Solution to instructing heterogeneous groups of students. *Clearing House, 72*(3), 182–186.

Gabel, S. L. (2001). "I wash my face with dirty water": Narratives of disability and pedagogy. *Journal of Teacher Education, 52*(1), 31–47.

Gajda, R. (2004). Using collaboration theory to evalute strategic alliances. *American Journal of Evaluation, 25*(1), 65–77.

Gardner, J. W. (1990). *On leadership.* New York: The Free Press.

Garman, N. B. (1986). Reflection, the heart of clinical supervision: A modern rationale for professional practice. *Journal of Curriculum and Supervision, 2*(1), 1–24.

Gartin, B. C., Murdick, N. L., Thompson, J. R., & Dyches, T. T. (2002). Issues and challenges facing educators who advocate for students with disabilities. *Education and Training in Mental Retardation and Developmental Disabilities, 37*(1), 3–13.

Gartner, A., & Lipsky, D. K. (1987). Beyond special education: Toward a quality system for all students. *Harvard Educational Review, 57*(4), 367–395.

Garvey, B., & Alred, G. (2000). Educating mentors. *Mentoring & tutoring: Partnership in learning, 8*(2), 113–126.

Gaston, C. (2001, December). Shared successes, continuing challenges: Fostering IDEA and Title I collaboration. *Proceedings of the Council of Chief State School Officers and the Policymaker Partnership Peer Consultation, Baltimore, MD.* (ERIC Document Reproduction Service No. ED467246)

Gay, G. (1993). Ethnic minorities and educational equality. In J. A. Banks & C. A. M. Banks (Eds.), *Multicultural education: Issues and perspectives* (2nd ed., pp. 332–352). Boston: Allyn & Bacon.

Gensante, L. J., & Matgouranis, E. M. (1988). The more I see, the better I teach. *Educational Leadership, 46*(8), 28.

George Mason University. (2001). *Project Kaleidoscope, 1996–2000. Final Report, Executive Summary.* (ERIC Document Reproduction Service No. ED462779)

Gerber, M. M., English, J., & Singer, G. S. (1999). Bridging craft and academic knowledge: A computer supported problem-based learning model for professional preparation in special education. *Teacher Education and Special Education, 22,* 100–113.

Gerber, P. J., & Popp, P. A. (2000). Making collaborative teaching more effective for academically able students: Recommendations for implementation and training. *Learning Disability Quarterly, 23*(3), 229–236.

Gerber, S. (1991). Supporting the collaborative process. *Preventing School Failure, 35,* 48–52.

Gersten, R., Baker, S., & Chard, D. (2000). Factors enhancing sustained use of research-based instructional practices. *Journal of Learning Disabilities, 33,* 445–457.

Gibson, S. (1983). Teacher efficacy: A construct validation study. *Dissertation Abstracts International, 43*(11), 3573.

Gibson, S., & Dembo, M. (1984). Teacher efficacy: A construct validation. *Journal of Educational Psychology, 76*(4), 569–582.

Gijbels, D., Dochy, F., Van den Bossche, P., & Segers, M. (2005). Effects of problem-based learning: A meta-analysis from the angle of assessment. *Review of Educational Research, 75*(1), 27–61.

Gilbert, M. B. (2004). *Communicating effectively: Tools for educational leaders.* Lanham, MD: Scarecrow Education.

Gilles, C., & Wilson, J. (2004). Receiving as well as giving: Mentors' perceptions of their professional development in one teacher induction program. *Mentoring and Tutoring, 12*(1), 87–106.

Gilligan, C. (1982). *In a different voice.* Cambridge, MA: Harvard University Press.

Givens-Ogle, L., Christ, B. A., Colman, M., King-Streit, S., & Wilson, L. (1989). Data-based consultation case study: Adaptations of researched best practices. *Teacher Education and Special Education, 12*(1–2), 46–51.

Glenn, C. L. (1989). Just school for minority children. *Phi Delta Kappan, 70*(10), 777–779.

GOALS 2000: Educate America Act of 1994, Pub. L. No. 103–227, 108 Stat. 125.

Goldring, E., & Greenfield, W. (2004). Understanding the evolving concept of leadership in education: Roles, expectations, and dilemmas. In J. Murphy (Ed.), *The educational leadership challenge: Redefining leadership for the 21st century; 101st yearbook of the National Society for the Study of Education* (pp. 1–19). Chicago: University of Chicago Press.

Golightly, C. J. (1987). Transdisciplinary training: A step forward in special education teacher preparation. *Teacher Education and Special Education, 10*(3), 126–130.

Goodlad, J. (1990a). Connecting the present to the past. In J. Goodlad et al. (Eds.), *Places where teachers are taught* (pp. 3–39). San Francisco: Jossey-Bass.

Goodlad, J. (1990b). *Places where teachers are taught.* San Francisco: Jossey-Bass.

Goodlad, J. (1990c). *Teachers for our nation's schools.* San Francisco: Jossey-Bass.

Goor, M. B., & Santos, K. E. (2002). *To think like a teacher: Cases for special education interns and novice teachers.* Boston: Allyn & Bacon.

Gore, J. M. (2001). Beyond our differences: A reassembling of what matters most in teacher education. *Journal of Teacher Education, 52,* 124–136.

Graham, J., & Wright, J. A. (1999). What does 'inter-professional collaboration' mean to professionals working with pupils with physical disabilities? *British Journal of Special Education, 26*(1), 37–41.

Graseck, P. (2005). Where's the ministry in administration? Attending to the souls of our schools. *Phi Delta Kappan, 86*(5), 373–378.

Greathouse, B., Moyer, J. E., & Rhodes–Offutt, E. (1992). Increasing K–3 teachers' joy in teaching. *Young Children, 47,* 44–46.

Greer, J. V. (1989). Partnerships: What is our contribution? *Exceptional Children, 55*(5), 391–393.

Gresham, F. M., & Kendell, G. K. (1987). School consultation research. *School Psychology Review, 16*(3), 306–316.

Griffin, G. (Ed.). (1999). *The education of teachers: 98th NSSE Yearbook, Part I.* Chicago: NSSE.

Griffin, M. L. (2003). Using critical incidents to promote and assess reflective thinking in preservice teachers. *Reflective Practice, 4*(2), 207–220.

Griffo, K. (1995). *Analysis of collaboration project.* Unpublished manuscript, Buffalo State College.

Gulledge, J., & Slobe, P. (1990, September). Collaboration: A key to successful mainstreaming. *Middle School Journal, 22*(1), 34–36.

Guskey, T. R. (1988). Teacher efficacy, self-concept, and attitudes toward the implementation of instructional innovation. *Teaching & Teacher Education, 4,* 63–69.

Gwynn, J. (2004). "What about me? I live here, too!" Raising voices and changing minds through participatory research. In F. Armstrong & M. Moore (Eds.), *Action research for inclusive education: Changing places, changing practice, changing minds* (pp. 105–122). New York: RoutledgeFalmer.

Hallahan, D. P., Keller, C. E., McKinney, J. D., Lloyd, J. W., & Bryan, T. (1988). Examining the research base of the Regular Education Initiative: Efficacy studies and the adaptive learning environments model. *Journal of Learning Disabilities, 21*(1), 29–55.

Hamill, L. B., Jantzen, A. K., & Bargerhuff, M. E. (1999, Fall). Analysis of effective educator competencies in inclusive environments. *Action in Teacher Education, 21*(3), 21–37.

Hammond, L. (2001). Notes from California: An anthropological approach to urban science education for language minority families. *Journal of Research in Science Teaching, 38*(9), 983–999.

Hanks, J. A., & Velaski, A. (2003). A summertime collaboration between speech-language pathology and deaf education. *Teaching Exceptional Children, 36*(1), 58–63.

Hargreaves, A. (1990). Teachers' work and the politics of time and space. *Qualitative Studies in Education, 3*(4), 303–320.

Harms, T., & Clifford, R. M. (1980). *Early childhood environment rating scale.* New York: Teachers College Press.

Harry, B. (1992). *Cultural diversity, families and the special education system: Communication and empowerment.* New York: Teachers College Press.

Harry, B. (1996). *A teacher's handbook for cultural diversity, families, and the special education system: Communication and empowerment.* New York: Teachers College Press.

Harter, K. (1994). *Analysis of collaboration project.* Unpublished manuscript, Buffalo State College.

Haskell, D. H. (2000). Building bridges between science and special education: Inclusion in the science classroom. *Electronic Journal of Science Education, 4*(3). Retrieved January 5, 2005, from http://unr.edu/homepage/

Hayes, W. (2004). *Are we still a nation at risk two decades later?* Lanham, MD: Scarcrow Press.

Hernandez, R. (1995). *Analysis of collaboration project.* Unpublished manuscript, Buffalo State College.

Herrity, V. A., & Morales, P. (2004). Creating meaningful opportunities for collaboration. In J. H. Chrispeels (Ed.), *Learning to lead together: The promise and challenge of sharing leadership* (pp. 46–79). Thousand Oaks, CA: Sage.

Hersey, P., Blanchard, K., & Johnson, D. E. (1996). *Management of organizational behavior: Utilizing human resources* (7th ed.). Englewood Cliffs, NJ: Prentice-Hall.

Higgins, A. (1995). *Analysis of collaboration project.* Unpublished manuscript, Buffalo State College.

Holmes Group. (1986). *Tomorrow's teachers.* East Lansing, MI: The Holmes Group.

Honig, M. I., & Hatch, T. C. (2004). Crafting coherence: How schools strategically manage multiple external demands. *Educational Researcher, 33*(8), 16–30.

Hoover-Dempsey, K. V., Bassler, O. C., & Brissie, J. S. (1992). Explorations in parent-school relations. *Journal of Educational Research, 85*(5), 287–294.

Horton, M. L., Wilson, S., & Gagnon, D. (2003). Collaboration: A key component for inclusion in general physical education. *Teaching Elementary Physical Education, 14*(3), 13–17.

Hourcade, J. J., & Bauwens, J. (2003). *Cooperative teaching: Rebuilding and sharing the schoolhouse* (2nd ed.). Austin, TX: Pro-Ed.

Howells, K. D. (2000). Boldly going where angels fear to tread. *Intervention in School and Clinic, 35*(3), 157–160.

Howey, K. R. (1985). Six major functions of staff development: An expanded imperative. *Journal of Teacher Education, 36*(1), 58–64.

Hudson, P. J., Correa, V. I., Morsink, C. V., & Dykes, M. K. (1987). A new model for preservice training: Teacher as collaborator. *Teacher Education and Special Education, 10*(4), 191–193.

Hudson, P., & Glomb, N. (1997). If it takes two to tango, then why not teach both partners to dance? Collaboration instruction for all educators. *Journal of Learning Disabilities, 30*(4), 442–448.

Huefner, D. S. (1991). Judicial review of the special educational program requirements under the Education for all Handicapped Children Act: Where have we been and where should we be going? *Harvard Journal of Law and Public Policy, 14*, 483–516.

Hunt, P., Soto, G., Maier, J., & Doering, K. (2003). Collaborative teaming to support students at risk and students with severe disabilities in general education classrooms. *Exceptional Children, 6*(3), 315–332.

Idol, L. (1988). A rationale and guideline for establishing special education consulation programs. *Remedial and Special Education, 9*(6), 48–58.

Idol, L. (1997). Key questions related to building collaborative and inclusive schools. *Journal of Learning Disabilities, 30*(4), 384–394.

Idol, L., & West, J. F. (1991). Educational collaboration: A catalyst for effective schooling. *Intervention in School and Clinic, 27*(2), 70–78, 125.

Idol, L., West, J. F., & Lloyd, S. R. (1988). Organizing and implementing specialized reading programs: A collaborative approach involving classroom, remedial, and special education teachers. *Remedial and Special Education, 9*(2), 54–61.

Imada, D., Doyle, B. A., Brock, B., & Goddard, A. (2002). Developing leadership skills in students with mild disabilities. *Teaching Exceptional Children, 35*(1), 48–54.

Isaksen, S. G., & Treffinger, D. J. (1985). *Creative problem solving: The basic course.* Buffalo, NY: Bearly Limited.

Jacobi, M. (1991). Mentoring and undergraduate academic success: A literature review. *Review of Educational Research, 61*, 505–532.

Jentz, B. C., & Murphy, J. T. (2005). Embracing confusion: What leaders do when they don't know what to do. *Phi Delta Kappan, 86*(5), 358–366.

Johnson, B. J. (1998). Organizing for collaboration: A reconsideration of some basic organization principles. In D. G. Pounder (Ed.), *Restructuring schools for collaboration: Promises and pitfalls* (pp. 9–25). Albany: State University of New York Press.

Johnson, D. W., & Johnson, F. W. (1997). *Joining together: Group theory and skills.* Englewood Cliffs, NJ: Prentice-Hall.

Johnson, L. J., & LaMontagne, M. J. (1993). Research methods: Using content analysis to examine the verbal or written communication of stakeholders within early intervention. *Journal of Early Intervention, 17*(1), 73–79.

Johnson, L. J., & Pugach, M. C. (1991). Peer collaboration: Accommodating students with mild learning and behavior problems. *Exceptional Children, 57*(5), 454–461.

Johnson, L. J., & Pugach, M. C. (1992). Continuing the dialogue: Embracing a more expansive understanding of collaborative relationships. In W. Stainback & S. Stainback (Eds.), *Controversial issues confronting special education: Divergent perspectives* (pp. 215–222). Boston: Allyn & Bacon.

Johnson, L. J., Pugach, M. C., & Devlin, S. (1990). Professional collaboration. *Teaching Exceptional Children, 22*, 9–11.

Johnson, L. J., Pugach, M. C., & Hammittee, D. J. (1988). Barriers to effective special education consultation. *Remedial and Special Education, 9*(6), 41–47.

Johnston, N. S. (1990). School consultation: The training needs of teachers and school psychologists. *Psychology in the Schools, 27*, 51–56.

Jones, N.L., Apling, R.N., & Smole, D.P. (2004). Individual with disabilities education act (IDEA): Background and issues. New York: Nova Science Publishers, Inc.

Joyce, B., & Showers, B. (1980). Improving inservice training: The messages of research. *Educational Leadership, 37*(5), 379–385.

Joyce, B. R., & Showers, B. (1982). The coaching of teaching. *Educational Leadership, 40*, 4–10.

Justice, L. M. (2004). Creating language-rich preschool classroom environments. *Teaching Exceptional Children, 37*(2), 36–44.

Kabot, S. (2005). *Improving professional development for teachers of students with severe disabilities: The demonstration classroom model.* Unpublished dissertation, Nova Southeastern University.

Kabot, S. S. (2004). *The demonstration classroom.* Presentation at the 9th International Conference of the Division on Developmental Disabilities, Las Vegas, NV.

Kaff, M. S. (2003). Changing roles of rural special educators: A case study. *Rural Educator, 24*(3), 11–19.

Karge, B. D., McClure, M., & Patton, P. L. (1995). The success of collaboration resource programs for students with disabilities in grades 6 through 8. *Remedial and Special Education, 16*(2), 79–89.

Kauffman, J. M., Gerber, M. M., & Semmel, M. I. (1988). Arguable assumptions underlying the Regular Education Initiative. *Journal of Learning Disabilities, 21*(1), 6–11.

Kavale, K. A., & Forness, S. R. (2000). History, rhetoric and reality: Analysis of the inclusion debate. *Remedial & Special Education, 21*, 279–296.

Kegan, R., & Lahey, L. L. (2001). *How the way we talk can change the way we work: Seven languages for transformation.* San Francisco: Jossey-Bass.

Keller, N., & Cravedi-Cheng, L. (1995). Voice of inclusion: Developing a shared voice: Yours, mine, and ours. In R. A. Villa & J. S. Thousand. (Eds.), *Creating an inclusive school* (pp. 80–86). Alexandria, VA: Association for Supervision and Curriculum Development.

Kennedy, K. Y., Higgins, K., & Pierce, T. (2002). Collaborative partnerships among teachers of students who are gifted and have learning disabilities. *Intervention in School and Clinic, 38*(1), 36–49.

Kilgore, K., Griffin, C. C., Sindelar, P. T., & Webb, R. B. (2002). Restructuring for inclusion: Changing teaching practices (Part II). *Middle School Journal, 33*(3), 7–13.

King, M. (1994). *Analysis of collaboration project.* Unpublished manuscript, Buffalo State College.

King-Sears, M. E., Cummings, C. S., & Hullinhen, S. P. (1994). *Curriculum-based assessment in special education.* San Diego: Singular.

Kirschner, P. A., & Van Bruggen, J. (2004). Learning and understanding in virtual teams. *CyberPsychology & Behavior, 7*(2), 135–140.

Kleinert, H., McGregor, V., Durbin, M., Blandford, T., Jones, K., Owens, J., et al. (2004). Service-learning opportunities that include students with moderate and severe disabilities. *Teaching Exceptional Children, 37*(2), 28–34.

Kluth, P., & Straut, D. (2003). Do as we say *and* as we do: Teaching and modeling collaborative practice in the university classroom. *Journal of Teacher Education, 54*(3), 228–240.

Knapczyk, D. R., Frey, T. J., & Wall-Marencik, W. (2005). An evaluation of web conferencing in online teacher preparation. *Teacher Education and Special Education, 28*(2), 114–124.

Kochan, F. K., Bredeson, P., & Riehl, C. (2002). Rethinking the professional development of school leaders. In J. Murphy (Ed.), *The educational leadership challenge: Redefining leadership for the 21st century; 101st yearbook of the National Society for the Study of Education* (pp. 289–302). Chicago: The University of Chicago Press.

Koppang, A. (2004). Curriculum mapping: Building collaboration and communication. *Intervention in School and Clinic, 39*(3), 154–162.

Korinek, L., & Williams, B. (1996). *Intervention assistance teams: Collaborative support for students and teachers in inclusive programs.* Paper presented at the annual convention of the Council for Exceptional Children, Orlando, FL.

Kouzes, J. M., & Posner, B. Z. (2002). *The leadership challenge* (3rd ed.). San Francisco: Jossey-Bass.

Krutilla, J. O., & Safford, P. L. (1990). Portrait of the shared student teaching experience: Owning reflection and action. *Teacher Education and Special Education, 13,* 217–220.

Kubicek, F. C. (1994). Special education reform in light of select state and federal court decisions. *The Journal of Special Education, 28*(1), 27–42.

Kugelmass, J. (2001). Collaboration and compromise in creating and sustaining an inclusive school. *International Journal of Inclusive Education, 5*(1), 47–65.

Kugelmass, J. (2004). *The inclusive school: Sustaining equity and standards.* New York: Teachers College Press.

Kumpulainen, K., & Kaartinen, S. (2003). The interpersonal dynamics of collaborative reasoning in peer interactive dyads. *Journal of Experimental Education, 71*(4), 333–370.

Lacey, P. (2001). *Support partnerships: Collaboration in action.* London: David Fulton.

Lambert, M. (1995). Reciprocal team coaching. *Thrust for Educational Leadership, 24*(5), 20–22.

Lambert, R. G., Abbott-Shim, M., & Oxford-Wright, C. (2001). Staff percepetions of research in the context of specific strategies for collaboration with Head Start programs. *Early Childhood Research Quarterly, 16*(1), 19–34.

LaMontagne, M. J., Johnson, L. J., Kilgo, J. L., Stayton, V., Carr, V., Bauer, A., et al. (2002). Unified early childhood personnel preparation programs: Perceptions from the field. *Teacher Education and Special Education, 25*(3), 236–245.

Lasley, T. J., Matczynski, T. J., & Williams, J. A. (1992). Collaborative and noncollaborative partnership structures in teacher education. *Journal of Teacher Education, 43*(4), 257–261.

Law, J., Lindsay, G., Peacey, N., Gascoigne, M., Soloff, N., Radford, J., et al. (2001). Facilitating communication betweeen education and health services: The provision for children with speech and language needs. *British Journal of Special Education, 28*(3), 133–137.

Lawler, P. A. (2003). Teachers as adult learners: A new perspective. *New Directions for Adult and Continuing Education, 98*(3), 15–22.

Laycock, V. K., Gable, R. A., & Korinek, L. (1991). Alternative structures for collaboration in the delivery of special services. *Preventing School Failure, 35*(4), 15–18.

Lazenby, R. B., & Morton, R. C. (2003). Facilitating transformation through collaboration. *Nursing Education Perspectives, 24*(2), 91–93.

Lease, S. H. (2004). Effect of locus of control, work knowledge, and mentoring on career decision-making difficulties: Testing the role of race and academic institution. *Journal of Career Assessment, 12*(3), 239–254.

Leithwood, K. A. (1992). The move toward transformational leadership. *Educational Leadership, 49*(5), 8–12.

Leithwood, K. A., & Steinbach, R. (1991). Indicators of transformational leadership in the everyday problem solving of school administrators. *Journal of Personnel Evaluation in Education, 4*(3), 221–244.

Lenz, B. K., & Deshler, D. D. (1990). Principles of strategies instruction as the basis of effective preservice teacher education. *Teacher Education and Special Education, 13*(2), 82–95.

Levin, B. B. (2001). *Energizing teacher-education and professional development with problem-based learning.* Alexandria, VA: ASCD.

Levin, B., Hibbard, K., & Rock, T. (2002). Using problem-based learning as a tool for learning to teach students with special needs. *Teacher Education and Special Education, 25*(3), 278–290.

Lietzow, K., & Jackson, C. (2004). *Making sense of transition planning: Pulling the pieces together.* Presentation at the 9th International Conference of the Division on Developmental Disabilities, Las Vegas, NV.

Lindeman, D. P., & Beegle, G. P. (1988). Preservice teacher training and use of the classroom paraprofessional: A national survey. *Teacher Education and Special Education, 11*(4), 183–186.

Linder, T. W. (1993). *Transdisciplinary play-based assessment* (Rev. ed.). Baltimore: Paul H. Brookes.

Little, J. W. (1988). Assessing the prospects for teacher leadership. In A. Lieberman (Ed.), *Building a professional culture in schools* (pp. 78–106). New York: Teachers College Press.

Little, J. W. (1990). The persistence of privacy: Autonomy and initiative in teachers' professional relations. *Teachers College Record, 91*(4), 509–536.

Little, M. E., & Crawford, P. A. (2002). Collaboration among educators for true innovative programming. *Teacher Education and Special Education, 25*(3), 320–324.

Little, M. E., & Houston, D. (2003). Research into practice through professional development. *Remedial and Special Education, 24*(2), 75–87.

Lloyd, C. (2002). Developing and changing practice in special educational needs through critically reflective action research: A case study. *European Journal of Special Education Needs, 17*(2), 109–127.

Lopez, S. A., Torres, A., & Norwood, P. (1998). Building partnerships: A successful collaborative experience between social work and education. *Social Work in Education, 20*(3), 165–177.

Love, D., McKean, G., & Gathercoal, P. (2004). Portfolios to webfolios and beyond: Levels of maturation. *EDUCAUSE Quarterly, 27*(2), 24–37.

Lovejoy, K. (1994). *Analysis of collaboration project.* Unpublished manuscript, Buffalo State College.

Ludlow, B. L., Faieta, J. C., & Wienke, W. D. (1989). Training teachers to supervise their peers: A pilot practicum project. *Teacher Education and Special Education, 12*(1–2), 27–32.

Macklem, G., Kruger, L. J., & Struzziero, J. (2001). Using e-mail to collaborate with professionals and parents. *Special services in the schools, 17*(1–2), 77–95.

MacSwan, J. (1996). *Analysis of collaboration project.* Unpublished manuscript, Buffalo State College.

Maeroff, G. I. (1993). Building teams to rebuild schools. *Phi Delta Kappan, 74*(7), 512–519.

Magiera, K., Smith, C., Zigmond, N., & Gebauer, K. (2005). Benefits of co-teaching in secondary mathematics classes. *Teaching Exceptional Children, 37*(3), 20–24.

Mallette, B., Maheady, L., & Harper, G. F. (1999). The effects of reciprocal peer coaching on preservice general educators' instruction of students with special learning needs. *Teacher Education and Special Education, 22*(4), 201–216.

Malone, D. M., Gallagher, P. A., & Long, S. R. (2001). General education teachers' attitudes and perceptions of teamwork supporting children with developmental concerns. *Early Education & Development, 12*(4), 577–592.

Maloney, M. (1996). New technology for researching special education law. *Intervention in School and Clinic, 31*(3), 186–189.

Mandell, C. J., & Murray, M. M. (2005). Innovative family-centered practices in personnel preparation. *Teacher Education and Special Education, 28*(1), 74–77.

Manouchehri, A. (2001). Professional discourse and teacher change. *Action in Teacher Education, 1*(1), 89–115.

Manouchehri, A. (2002). Developing teaching knowledge through peer discourse. *Teaching and Teacher Education, 18*(6), 715–737.

Manz, C. C. (2003). *Mastering self leadership: Empowering yourself for personal excellence* (3rd ed). Englewood Cliffs, NJ: Prentice-Hall.

Mariage, T. V., & Garmon, M. A. (2003a). A case of educational change. *Remedial & Special Education, 24*(4), 215–234.

Mariage, T. V., & Garmon, M. A. (2003b). Expanding the potential of school-university collaboration: Special and general education as partners in improving student achievement in a rural professional development school. In D. L. Wiseman & S. L. Knight (Eds.), *Linking school-university collaboration and K–12 student outcomes* (pp. 49–69). Washington, DC: AACTE Publications.

Martin, A. (1988). Screening, early intervention and remediation: Obscuring children's potential. *Harvard Educational Review, 58*(4), 488–501.

Marzullo, G. (1996). *Analysis of collaboration project.* Unpublished manuscript, Buffalo State College.

Mason, C., Thormann, M. S., O'Connell, M., & Behrmann, J. (2004). Priority issues reflected in general and special education association journals. *Exceptional Children, 70*(2), 215–230.

Masseo, C. (1995). *Analysis of collaboration project.* Unpublished manuscript, Buffalo State College.

Mauriel, J. J., & Lindquist, K. M. (1989). School-based management: Doomed to failure. *Education and Urban Society, 21*(4), 403–416.

Mayberry, S. C., & Lazarus, B. B. (2002). *Teaching students with special needs in the 21st-century classroom.* Lanham, MD: The Scarecrow Press.

Mbugua, T., Wadas, J., Casey, M. A., & Finnerty, J. (2004). Authentic learning: Intercultural, international, and intergenerational experiences in elementary classrooms. *Childhood Education, 80*(5), 237–244.

McBreen, D., & Polis, K. (1996). Collaborative planning in West Virginia: Hanging together or being hung separately. *Adult Learning, 7*(4), 10–12.

McCormick, L., Noonan, M. J., Ogata, V., & Heck, R. (2001). Co-teacher relationship and program quality: Implications for preparing teachers for inclusive preschool settings. *Education and Training in Mental Retardation and Developmental Disabilities, 36*(2), 119–132.

McGhee, M. W., & Nelson, S. W. (2005). Sacrificing leaders, villainizing leadership: How educational accountability policies impair school leadership. *Phi Delta Kappan, 86*(5), 367–372.

McGregor, J. (2002). Getting to the heart of assessment: The liberal studies/professional skills program at Inver Hills Community College. *Community College Journal of Research and Practice, 26*(9), 723–735.

McKenzie, R. G., & Houk, C. S. (1986). The paraprofessional in special education. *Teaching Exceptional Children, 18*(4), 246–252.

McLaughlin, M. J. (2002). Special issue introduction: Examining special and general education collaborative practices in exemplary schools. *Journal of Educational and Psychological Consultation, 13*(4), 279–283.

McLeskey, J., & Waldron, N. L. (2002). Inclusion and school change: Teacher perceptions regarding curricular and instructional adaptations. *Teacher Education and Special Education, 25*(1), 41–54.

McLoughlin, J. A., & Lewis, R. A. (2005). *Assessing students with special needs* (6th ed.). Englewood Cliffs, NJ: Prentice Hall.

Mello, L. T. (1984). Peer-centered coaching: Teachers helping teachers to improve classroom performance. Idaho Springs, CO: Associates for Human Development. (ERIC Document Reproduction Service No. ED274648)

Memmott, J. L. (1993). Models of helping and coping: A field experiment with natural and professional helpers. *Social Work Research & Abstracts, 29*(13), 11–21.

Merseth, K. K. (1991). Supporting beginning teachers with computer networks. *Journal of Teacher Education, 42*(2), 140–147.

Mertz, N. T. (2004). What's a mentor, anyway? *Educational Administration Quarterly, 40*(4), 541–560.

Meyers, J., Gelzheiser, L. M., & Yelich, G. (1991). Do pull-in programs foster teacher collaboration? *Remedial and Special Education, 12*(2), 7–15.

Miller, P. W. (1986). *Nonverbal communication* (2nd ed.). Washington, DC: National Education Association.

Miller, S. L., Ray, S., Dove, T., & Kenreich, T. (2000). Perspectives on personal professional development. In M. Johnston, P. Brosnan, D. Cramer, & T. Dove (Eds.), *Collaborative reform and other improbable dreams* (pp. 141–151). Albany: State University of New York Press.

Milner, T., & Bossers, A. (2004). Evaluation of the mentor-mentee relationship in an occupational therapy mentorship programme. *Occupational Therapy International, 11*(2), 96–111.

Minnesota Department of Children, Families and Learning. (2002). *Five step process.* St. Paul, MN: Author.

Mohr, N., & Dichter, A. (2001). Building a learning organization. *Phi Delta Kappan, 82*(10), 744–747.

Moir, E. (1996). *Phases of new teacher growth: California Department of Education guide to prepare support providers for work with beginning teachers. Training Modules* (Rev. ed.). Sacramento: California Department of Education.

Montgomery, D. J. (2005). Communicating without harm: Strategies to enhance parent-teacher communication. *Teaching Exceptional Children, 37*(5), 50–55.

Morford, J. A., & Willing, D. (1993). Communication: Key to effective administration. *Adult Learning, 4*(4), 9–10, 30.

Morocco, C. C., & Aguilar, C. M. (2002). Coteaching for content understanding: A schoolwide model. *Journal of Educational and Psychological Consultation, 13*(4), 315–347.

Morocco, C. C., Walker, A., & Lewis, L. R. (2003). Access to a schoolwide thinking curriculum: Leadership challenges and solutions. *Journal of Special Education Leadership: The Journal of the Council of Administrators of Special Education, 16*(1), 5–14.

Morris, D. (1995). *Bodytalk: The meaning of human gestures.* New York: Crown Trade Paperbacks.

Morris, L. R. (2004). The case for an outside interim director. *American Libraries, 35*(6), 53–54.

Mrugala, A. (1996). *Analysis of collaboration project.* Unpublished manuscript, Buffalo State College.

Mulak, G., Cohen, S. T., & Teets-Grimm, K. (1992). Hospitals and school districts: Creating a partnership for child protection services. *Social Work in Health Care, 17,* 39–51.

Mullinix, B. B. (2002). *Selecting and retaining teacher mentors.* Washington, DC: American Association of Colleges for Teacher Education. (ERIC Document Reproduction Service No. ED477728)

Mundschenk, N. A., & Foley, R. M. (1994). Collaborative relationships between school and home: Implications for service delivery. *Preventing School Failure, 39*(1), 16–20.

Murawski, W. W., & Swanson, H. L. (2001). A meta-analysis of co-teaching research. Where are the data? *Remedial and Special Education, 22*(5), 258–267.

Murphy, J. (Ed.). (2002). *The educational leadership challenge: Redefining leadership for the 21st century; 101st yearbook of the National Society for the Study of Education.* Chicago, IL: The University of Chicago Press.

Napier, R. W., & Gershenfeld, M. K. (2003). *Groups: Theory and experience* (7th ed.). Dallas, TX: Houghton Mifflin.

National Commission on Excellence in Education. (1983). *A nation at risk: The imperative for educational reform.* Washington, DC: U.S. Government Printing Office.

National Council on Teacher Quality. (2004). *Increasing the odds: How good policies can yield better teachers.* Washington, DC: National Council on Teacher Quality.

National Governors' Association. (1986). *A time for results*. Washington, DC: Center for Policy Research and Analysis.

National Information Center for Children and Youth with Disabilities (NICHCY). (1991). The education of children and youth with special needs: What do the laws say? *NICHCY News Digest, 1*(1), 1–15.

NEA Today. (2004). Need a mentor? Check your e-mail. *NEA Today, 22*(4), 15.

New IDEA delivers for students with disabilities. (Winter, 2005). *CEC Today Online, 11*(3). Retrieved January 5, 2006, from http://www.cec.sped.org/bk/cectoday/

Neck, C. P., & Barnard, A. W. H. (1996, March). Managing your mind: What are you telling yourself? *Educational Leadership, 53*, 24–27.

No child left behind and the political safeguards of federalism. (2006). *Harvard Law Review, 119*(3), 885–906.

Noe, R. A. (1988). An investigation of the determinants of successful assigned mentoring relationships. *Personnel Psychology, 41*, 457–479.

Nolet, V., & Tindal, G. (1994). Curriculum-based collaboration. *Focus on Exceptional Children, 27*(3), 1–12.

Nowacek, E. J. (1992). Professionals talk about teaching together: Interviews with five collaborating teachers. *Intervention in School and Clinic, 27*(3), 262–276.

Ochoa, T. A., & Robinson, J. M. (2005). Revisiting group consensus: Collaborative learning dynamics during a problem-based learning activity in education. *Teacher Education and Special Education, 28*(1), 10–20.

Odell, S. (1988). Induction support of new teachers: A functional approach. *Journal of Teacher Education, 37*, 26–29.

O'Meara, L., Fidler, D., & Parrish, P. (2004). *Wraparound services for students with dual diagnosis.* 9th International CEC-Division on Developmental Disabilities Conference, Las Vegas, NV.

Osborne, S., Garland, C., & Fisher, N. (2002). Caregiver training: Changing minds, opening doors to inclusion. *Infants and Young Children, 14*(3), 43–53.

Osborne, S. C., Kniest, B. A., Garland, C. W. (2000). *SpecialCare curriculum and trainer's manual.* Norge, VA: Child Development Resources.

O'Shea, D. J., Williams, A. L., & Sattler, R. O. (1999). Collaboration across special education and general education: Preservice teachers' views. *Journal of Teacher Education, 50*(2), 147–158.

O'Sullivan, E. (1996). *Analysis of collaboration project.* Unpublished manuscript, Buffalo State College.

Ozer, J. (1996a). Internet videoconferencing. *PC Magazine, 15*(17), 137–148.

Ozer, J. (1996b). Internet collaborative tools. *PC Magazine, 15*(17), 149–155.

Packard, W. B., Walsh, L., & Seidenberg, S. (2004). Will that be one mentor or two? A cross-sectional study of women's mentoring during college. *Mentoring and Tutoring, 12*(1), 71–86.

Parette, H. P., Jr., & Brotherson, M. J. (1996). Family participation in assistive technology assessment for young children with mental retardation and developmental disabilities. *Education and Training in Mental Retardation and Developmental Disabilities, 31*(1), 29–43.

Parette, P., & McMahan, G. A. (2002). What should we expect of assistive technology? Being sensitive to family goals. *Teaching Exceptional Children, 35*(1), 56–61.

Parker, G. M. (2002). *Cross-functional teams: Working with allies, enemies, and other strangers* (2nd ed.). San Francisco: Jossey-Bass.

Partsch, K. (1996). *Analysis of collaboration project.* Unpublished manuscript, Buffalo State College.

Paterson, W. A. (2001). *Unbroken homes: Single parent mothers tell their stories.* NY: Haworth Press.

Patriarca, L. A., & Lamb, M. A. (1990). Preparing secondary special education teachers to be collaborative decision makers and reflective practitioners: A promising practicum model. *Teacher Education and Special Education, 13*, 228–234.

Patterson, S. L., & Brennan, E. M. (1983). Matching helping roles with the characteristics of older natural helpers. *Journal of Gerontological Social Work, 5*(4), 55–66.

Paul-Saladino, S. (1994). *Analysis of collaboration project.* Unpublished manuscript, Buffalo State College.

Peck, A. F., & Scarpati, S. (2004). Collaboration in the age of accountability. *Teaching Exceptional Children, 36,* 5, 7.

Peters, T., & Austin, N. (1997). *A passion for excellence: The leadership difference.* New York: Random House.

Phillips, C., Prue, J. F., Hasazi, S. B., & Morgan, P. (2000). Personal learning plans: Building collaboration among teachers, students with disabiliites and their parents. *NASSP Bulletin, 84*(613), 28–34.

Phillips, L., Sapona, R. H., & Lubic, B. L. (1995). Developing partnerships in inclusive education: One school's approach. *Intervention in School & Clinic, 30*(5), 262–272.

Phillips, V., & McCullough, L. (1990). Consultation-based programming: Instituting the collaborative ethic in school. *Exceptional Children, 5*(4), 291–304.

Phipps, J. J. (2005). E-journaling: Achieving interactive education online. *EDUCAUSE Quarterly, 28*(1), 62–65.

Pianta, R. C., Kraft-Sayre, M., Rimm-Kaufman, S., Gercke, N., & Higgins, T. (2001). Collaboration in building partnerships between families and schools: The National Center for Early Development and Learning's Kindergarten Transition Intervention. *Early Childhood Research Quarterly, 16*(1), 117–132.

Pierce, J. W. (1999). *Problem-based learning: A learner-centered tool for higher education.* Paper presented at the annual meeting of the American Educational Research Association, Montreal, Canada.

Piwowarczyk, M. (1994). *Analysis of collaboration project.* Unpublished manuscript, Buffalo State College.

Plarr, M. (1995). *Analysis of collaboration project.* Unpublished manuscript, Buffalo State College.

Polsgrove, L., & McNeil, M. (1989). The consultation process: Research and practice. *Remedial and Special Education, 10*(1), 6–13, 20.

Ponti, C. R., Zins, J. E., & Graden, J. L. (1988). Implementing a consultation-based service delivery system to decrease referrals for special education: A case study of organizational considerations. *School Psychology Review, 17*(1), 89–100.

Prawat, R. S., & Nickerson, J. R. (1985). The relationship between teacher thought and action and student affective outcomes. *The Elementary School Journal, 85*(4), 529–540.

Price, J. P. (1991). Effective communication: A key to successful collaboration. *Preventing School Failure, 35*(4), 25–28.

Prince, S. R. (2004). The magic of mentoring. *Educational Leadership, 61*(8), 84–87.

Puccio, G. (1999). Teams. In S. Pritzker (Ed.), *Encyclopedia of Creativity* (Vol. 2., pp. 639–649). San Diego, CA: Academic Press.

Pugach, M. C., & Allen-Meares, P. (1985). Collaboration at the preservice level: Instructional and evaluation activities. *Teacher Education and Special Education, 8*(1), 3–11.

Pugach, M. C., & Johnson, L. J. (1988a). Rethinking the relationship between consultation and collaborative problem solving. *Focus on Exceptional Children, 21*(4), 1–8.

Pugach, M., & Johnson, L. J. (1988b). Peer collaboration. *Teaching Exceptional Children, 20*(3), 75–77.

Pugach, M. C., & Johnson, L. J. (1989). The challenge of implementing collaboration between general and special education. *Exceptional Children, 56*(3), 232–235.

Pugach, M. C., & Johnson, L. J. (1995). Unlocking expertise among classroom teachers through structured dialogue: Extending research on peer collaboration. *Exceptional Children, 62*(2), 101–110.

Pugach, M. C., & Johnson, L. J. (2002). *Collaborative practitioners, collaborative schools* (2nd ed.). Denver, CO: Love.

Pultorak, E. G. (1993). Facilitating reflective thought in novice teachers. *Journal of Teacher Education, 44,* 288–295.

Pyszczynski, M. (1995). *Analysis of collaboration project.* Unpublished manuscript, Buffalo State College.

Raywid, M. A. (1993). Finding time for collaboration. *Educational Leadership, 51*(1), 30–34.

Reeve, P. T., & Hallahan, D. P. (1994). Practical questions about collaboration between general and special educators. *Focus on Exceptional Children, 26*(7), 1–12.

Reeves, J. E. (2002). Superintendent's commentary: "May you live in interesting times." *Journal of Special Education Leadership, 15*(2), 74–75.

Reid, R., & Harris, K. R. (1993). Self-monitoring of attention versus self-monitoring of performance: Effects on attention and academic performance. *Exceptional Children, 60*(1), 29–40.

Reif, S. F., & Heimburge, J. A. (2002). *How to reach and teach all students in the inclusive classroom.* Indianapolis, IN: Wiley/Jossey-Bass.

Reisberg, L., & Wolf, R. (1986). Developing a consulting program in special education: Implementation and interventions. *Focus on Exceptional Children, 19*(3), 1–14.

Reitzug, U. C., & Burrello, L. C. (1995). How principals can build self-renewing schools. *Educational Leadership, 52,* 48–50.

Renegar, S. L. (1993, Spring). Peer pressure among teachers: Enemy of educational excellence. *Kappa Delta Pi, 29*(3), 68–72.

Repetto, J. B., & Correa, V. I. (1996). Expanding views on transition. *Exceptional Children, 62*(6), 551–563.

Resnick, M. (2000). *Communities count: A school board guide to public engagement.* Alexandria, VA: National School Boards Association.

Reyes, P., Scribner, J. D., & Paredes Scribner, A. (Eds.). (1999). *Lessons from high-performing Hispanic schools: Creating learning communities.* Williston, VT: Teachers College Press.

Richards, S. B., Hunley, S., Weaver, R., & Landers, M. F. (2003). A proposed model for teacher collaboration skills to general and special education preservice candidates. *Teacher Education and Special Education, 26*(3), 246–250.

Riggi, P. (1995). *Analysis of collaboration project.* Unpublished manuscript, Buffalo State College.

Ripley, S. (1998). Teaching strategies: Collaboration between general and special education teachers. *Journal of Early Education and Family Review, 5*(4), 16–20.

Roache, M., Shore, J., Gouleta, E., & de Obaldia Butkevich, E. (2003). An investigation of collaboration among school professionals in serving culturally and linguistically diverse students with exceptionalities. *Bilingual Research Journal, 27*(1), 117–136.

Roberts, N. C. (1985). Transforming leadership: A process of collective action. *Human Relations, 38*(11), 1023–1046.

Robinson, E. L., & Fine, M. J. (1994). Developing collaborative home-school relationships. *Preventing School Failure, 39*(1), 9–15.

Rogers, H. (1996). *Analysis of collaboration project.* Unpublished manuscript, Buffalo State College.

Rosa-Lugo, L., & Fradd, S. (2000). Preparing professionals to serve English-language learners with communication disorders. *Communication Disorders Quarterly, 22*(1), 22–42.

Ross, D. D. (1989). First steps in developing a reflective approach. *Journal of Teacher Education, 40*(2), 22–30.

Ross, D. D., Bondy, E., & Kyle, D. W. (1993). *Reflective teaching for student empowerment: Elementary curriculum and methods.* New York: Prentice Hall.

Rubin, A. M. (1993). The effect of locus control on communication motivation, anxiety, and satisfaction. *Communication Quarterly, 41*(2), 161–171.

Ruef, M. B., & Turnbull, A. P. (2002). The perspectives of individuals with cognitive disabilities and/or autism on their lives and their problem behavior. *Research & Practice for Persons with Severe Disabilities, 27*(2), 125–140.

Rutkowski, A. F., Vogel, D. R., van Genuchten, M., Bemelmans, T. M.A., & Favier, M. (2002). E-collaboration: The reality of virtuality. *IEEE Transactions on Professional Communication, 45*(4), 219–231.

Sack, J. L. (1999, November 24). Special education conference puts emphasis on collaboration. *Education Week, 19*(13), 6–7.

Sage, S. (1999). *What does a mobile home park have to do with it anyway? Using problem-based learning to teach problem-based learning in graduate teacher education.* Paper presented at the annual meeting of the American Educational Research Association, Montreal, Canada.

Sailor, W. (Ed.). (2002). *Whole-school success and inclusive education.* New York: Teachers College Press.

Salend, S. J. (2005). *Creating inclusive classrooms: Effective and reflective practices* (5th ed.). Upper Saddle River, NJ: Merrill/Prentice Hall.

Salend, S. J., & Duhaney, L. M. G. (2002). What do families have to say about inclusion? How to pay attention and get results. *Teaching Exceptional Children, 35*(1), 62–66.

Salend, S. J., & Sylvestre, S. (2005). Understanding and addressing oppositional and defiant classroom behaviors. *Teaching Exceptional Children, 37*(6), 32–39.

Sallinen-Kuparinen, A. (1992). Teacher communication style. *Communication Education, 41*, 153–166.

Salyer, B. K., Thyfault, A., Curran, C. (2002, March). *Tools of the trade: Effective strategies to support the collaboration of educators in rural schools.* American Council on Rural Special Education (ACRES), Reno, NV. (ERIC Document Reproduction Service No. ED463122)

Sarason, S. B. (1990). *The predictable failure of school reform.* San Francisco: Jossey-Bass Publishers.

Satir, V. (1995). *Your many faces: The first step to being loved.* Millbrae, CA: Celestial Arts.

Scanlon, D., Gallego, M., Zamora Duran, G., Reyes, E. I. (2005). Interactive staff development supports collaboration when learning to teach. *Teacher Education and Special Education, 28*(1), 40–51.

Scheflen, A. E. (1972). *Body language and the social order: Communication as behavioral control.* Englewood Cliffs, NJ: Prentice-Hall.

Schmidt, R. J., Rozendal, M. S., & Greenman, G. G. (2002). Reading instruction in the inclusion classroom: Research-based practices. *Remedial and Special Education, 23*(3), 130–140.

Schmoker, M., & Wilson, R. B. (1993). Transforming schools through total quality education. *Phi Delta Kappan, 74*(1), 389–395.

Schon, D. (1983). *The reflective practitioner: How professionals think in action.* New York: Basic Books.

Scribner, A. P., & Scribner, J. D. (2001). *High-performing schools serving Mexican American students: What can they teach us.* Charleston, WV: ERIC Clearninghouse on Rural Education and Small Schools. (ERIC Document Reproduction Service No. ED459048)

Scribner, J. D., & Reyes, P. (1999). Creating learning communities for high-performing Hispanic students: A conceptual framwork. In P. Reyes, J. D. Scribner, & A. Paredes Scribner (Eds.), *Lessons from high performing Hispanic schools: Creating learning communities* (pp. 188–210). Williston, VT: Teachers College Press.

Seabrooks, J. J., Kenney, S., & LaMontagne, M. (2000). Collaboration and virtual mentoring: Building relationships between pre-service and in-service special education teachers. *Journal of Information Technology for Teacher Education, 9*(2), 219–236.

Senge, P. M. (1990). *The fifth discipline: The art & practice of the learning organization.* New York: Currency, Doubleday.

Shanker, A. (1995). Full inclusion is neither free nor appropriate. *Educational Leadership, 52*(4), 18–21.

Shapiro, D. R., & Sayers, L. K. (2003). Who does what on the interdisciplinary team regarding physical education for students with disabilities? *Teaching Exceptional Children, 35*(6), 32–38.

Sharpe, M. N., & Hawes, M. E. (2003). *Collaboration between general and special education: Making it work.* Minneapolis, MN: National Center on Secondary Education and Transition. (ERIC Document Reproduction Service No. ED481548)

Shea, C., & Babione, C. (2002. March). *Wisdom from those who do it well: Special education master teachers.* Annual National Conference Proceedings of the American Council on Rural Special Education (ACRES), Reno, NV. (ERIC Document Reproduction Service No. ED463115)

Sheridan, S. M. (1992). Consultant and client outcomes of competency-based behavioral consultation training. *School Psychology Quarterly, 7*(4), 245–270.

Sherman, K. (2004, January 9). IBD/TIPP poll finds a fifth of U.S. households still don't have PCs. *News from Investor's Business Daily.* Retrieved February 1, 2005, from www .investors.com

Shoffner, M. F., & Briggs, M. K. (2001). An interactive approach for developing interprofessional collaboration: Preparing school counselors. *Counselor Education & Supervision, 40*(3), 193–202.

Showers, B. (1985). Teachers coaching teachers. *Educational Leadership, 42*(7), 43–48.

Showers, B., & Joyce, B. (1996). The evolution of peer coaching. *Educational Leadership, 53*(6), 12–16.

Shumow, L. (1999). *Problem-based learning in undergraduate educational psychology: Contributor to student learning and motivations?* Paper presented at the annual meeting of the American Educational Research Association, Montreal, Canada.

Simpson, E. S., & Yocom, D. J. (2005). Every child: A journey toward individualized education for all. *Teaching Exceptional Children, 37*(5), 36–40.

Simpson, L. (2004). Students who challenge: Reducing barriers to inclusion. In F. Armstrong & M. Moore (Eds.), *Action research for inclusive education: Changing places, changing practice, changing minds* (pp. 63–76). New York: RoutledgeFalmer.

Simpson, R. L., & Myles, B. S. (1990). General education collaboration: A model for successful mainstreaming. *Focus on Exceptional Children, 23*(4), 1–10.

Simpson, R. L., Whelan, R. J., & Zabel, R. H. (1993). Special education personnel preparation in the 21st century: Issues and strategies. *Remedial and Special Education, 14*(2), 7–22.

Smith, D. (1994). *Analysis of collaboration project.* Unpublished manuscript, Buffalo State College.

Smith, R. (1994). *Analysis of collaboration project.* Unpublished manuscript, Buffalo State College.

Smith, S. (2002). Teacher mentoring and collaboration. *Journal of Special Education Technology, 17*(1), 47–48.

Smith, S. C. (1987). The collaborative school takes shape. *Educational Leadership, 45,* 46–48.

Smith, S. D. (1992). Professional partnerships and educational change: Effective collaboration over time. *Journal of Teacher Education, 43*(4), 243–256.

Smith, T. M., & Ingersoll, R. M. (2004). What are the effects of induction and mentoring on beginning teacher turnover? *American Educational Research Journal, 41*(3), 681–714.

Smylie, M. A., Conley, S., & Marks, H. (2002). Building leadership into the roles of teachers. In J. Murphy (Ed.), *The educational leadership challenge: Redefining leadership for the 21st century; 101st yearbook of the National Society for the Study of Education* (pp. 162–188). Chicago: The University of Chicago Press.

Snell, M. E. (2003). Applying research to practice: The more pervasive problem? *Research and Practice for Persons with Severe Disabilities, 28*(3), 143–147.

Snell, M. E. (2005). *Collaborative teaming* (2nd ed.). Baltimore, MD: Paul H. Brookes.

Snell, M. E., & Janney, R. E. (2000). Teachers' problem-solving about children with moderate and severe disabilities in elementary classrooms. *Exceptional Children, 66*(4), 472–490.

Snell, M. E., & Janney, R. (with Elliott, J., Burton, C. C., Colley, K. M., & Raynes, M.) (2000). *Teachers' guides to inclusive practices: Collaborative teaming.* Baltimore: Paul H. Brooks.

Sorsby, C. (2004). Forging and strengthening alliances: Learning support staff and the challenge of inclusion. In F. Armstrong & M. Moore (Eds.), *Action research for inclusive education: Changing places, changing practice, changing minds* (pp. 48–62). New York: RoutledgeFalmer.

Sparks, R., & Rye, D. R. (1990). Teacher self-esteem and personality: The major ingredients in teacher-student relationships. *Middle School Journal, 22,* 32–33.

Spinelli, C. G. (2006). *Assessment for the classroom: Students with special needs in inclusive settings* (2nd ed.). Englewood Cliffs, NJ: Prentice-Hall.

Sprague, D., Cooper, J., & Pixley, C. (2004). *High tech mentoring: Evaluating the impact of a PT3 project.* Paper presented at the Northeastern Educational Research Association conference, October, 2004, Kerhonkston, NY

SPSS. (2005). *SPSS text analysis for surveys 1.5.: User's guide.* Chicago: Author.

Stefani, L. A. (1998). Assessment in partnership with learners. *Assessment and Evaluation in Higher Education, 23,* 339–350.

Stefani, L. A. J., Clarke, J., & Littlejohn, A. H. (2000). Developing a student-centered approach to reflective learning. *Innovations in Education and Training International, 37*(2), 163–171.

Steinkuehler, C. A., Derry, S. J., Hmelo-Silver, C. E., & Delmarcelle, M. (2002). Cracking the resource nut with distributed problem-based learning in secondary teacher education. *Distance Education, 23*(1), 23–39.

Steinwachs, K. (1995). *Analysis of collaboration project.* Unpublished manuscript, Buffalo State College.

STEP Project Group. (2000). Promoting teachers' flexible use of the learning sciences through case-based problem solving on the WWW: A theoretical design approach. In *Proceedings of the Fourth International Conference of the Learning Sciences* (pp. 273–279). Mahwah, NJ: Lawrence Erlbaum Associates.

Stewart, R. A., & Brendefur, J. L. (2005). Fusing lesson study and authentic achievement: A model for teacher collaboration. *Phi Delta Kappan, 86*(9), 681–687.

Stough, L. M., & Palmer, D. J. (2001, April). *Teacher reflection: How effective special educators differ from novices.* Paper presented at the annual Council for Exceptional Children conference, Kansas Cit, MO. (ERIC Document Reproduction Service No. ED463279)

Stough, L. M., Palmer, D. J., & Sharp, A. N. (2001, February*). Teachers' reflections on special education students' cognition.* Paper presented at the annual meeting of the Southwest Educational Research Association, New Orleans, LA. (ERIC Document Reproduction Service No. ED452626)

Strong, M. A., & Baron, W. (2004). An analysis of mentoring conversations with beginning teachers: Suggestions and responses. *Teaching and Teacher Education, 20*(1), 47–58.

Strunk, Jr., W., & White, E. B. (2005). *The Elements of Style* (3rd ed.) New York: The Penguin Press.

Stump, C. S., & Wilson, C. (1996). Collaboration: Making it happen. *Intervention in School & Clinic, 31*(5), 310–312.

Su, Z. (1990, May). The function of the peer group in teacher socialization. *Phi Delta Kappan, 70*(9), 723–727.

Sugai, G. M., & Tindal, G. A. (1993). *Effective school consultation: An interactive approach.* Pacific Grove, CA: Brooks/Cole.

Sunderman, G. L. (2000). Implementing Title I schoolwide programs in a complex policy environment: Integrating standards and school reform in the Chicago public schools. *Journal of Negro Education, 69*(4), 361–374.

Sussell, A., Carr, S., & Hartman, A. (1996). Families R us: Building a parent/school partnership. *Teaching Exceptional Children, 28*(4), 53–57.

Tannen, D. (1995). The power of talk: Who gets heard and why. *Harvard Business Review, 36,* 138–148.

Tannen, D. (2001). *You just don't understand: Men and women in conversation.* New York: Morrow.

Tendorf, C. (1996). *Analysis of collaboration project.* Unpublished manuscript, Buffalo State College.

Thompson, V. (2004). Disability and empowerment: Personal integrity in further education research. In F. Armstrong & M. Moore (Eds.), *Action research for inclusive education: Changing places, changing practice, changing minds* (pp. 17–31). New York: RoutledgeFalmer.

Thomson, C., Brown, D., Jones, L., Walker, J., Moore, D. W., Anderson, A., et al. (2003). Resource teachers learning and behavior: Collaborative problem solving to support inclusion. *Journal of Positive Behavior Interventions, 5*(2), 101–111.

Thomson Corporation. (1991, April 16). *Computers now to be found in 13.7m US homes, the Census Bureau finds.* Cupertino, CA: Author.

Thomson, K., Bachor, D., & Thomson, G. (2002). The development of individualised educational programmes using a decision-making model. *British Journal of Special Education, 29*(1), 37–43.

Thousand, J. S., & Villa, R. A. (2000). Collaborative teaming: A powerful tool in school restructuring. In R. A. Villa & J. S. Thousand (Eds.), *Restructuring for caring and effective education: Piecing the puzzle together* (2nd ed., pp. 254–292). Baltimore: Paul H. Brooks.

Tiegerman-Farber, E., & Radziewicz, C. (1998). *Collaborative decision-making: The pathway to inclusion.* Upper Saddle River, NJ: Merrill.

Tierney-Luthart, A. (1995). *Analysis of collaboration project.* Unpublished manuscript, Buffalo State College.

Tindal, G., Parker, R., & Hasbrouck, J. E. (1992). The construct validity of stages and activities in the consultation process. *Journal of Educational and Psychological Consultation, 3*(2), 99–118.

Tindal, G., Shinn, M. R., Rodden-Nord, K. (1990). Contextually based school consultation: Influential variables. *Exceptional Children, 56*(4), 324–337.

Tindal, G., & Taylor-Pendergast, S. J. (1989). A taxonomy for objectively analyzing the consultation process. *Remedial and Special Education, 10*(2), 6–16.

Townsend, B. L. (1994). Involving families of at-risk and normally achieving children in social skill instruction. *Preventing School Failure, 39*(1), 31–36.

Trent, S. C. (1998). False starts and other dilemmas of a secondary general education collaborative teacher: A case study. *Journal of Learning Disabilities, 31*(5), 503–513.

Trent, S. C., & Dixon, D. J. (2004). "My eyes were opened": Tracing the conceptual change of pre-service teachers in a special education/multicultural education course. *Teacher Education and Special Education, 27*(2), 119–133.

Trent, S. C., Driver, B. L., Wood, M. H., Parrott, P. S., Martin, T. F., & Smith, W. G. (2003). Creating and sustaining a special education/general education partnership: A story of change and uncertainty. *Teaching and Teacher Education, 19*(2), 203–219.

Tripp, D. (1993). *Critical incidents in teaching: Developing professional judgement.* London: Routledge.

Tschantz, J. M., & Vail, C. O. (2000). Effects of peer coaching on the rate of responsive teacher statements during a child-directed period in an inclusive preschool setting. *Teacher Education and Special Education, 23*(3), 189–201.

Tuckman, B. W. (1995). The interpersonal teacher model. *The Educational Forum, 59,* 177–185.

Tuckman, B. W., & Jensen, M. A. C. (1977). Stages of small group development revisited. *Group & Organization Studies, 2*(4), 419–427.

Turnbull, A., & Turnbull, H. R., III. (2000). *Enhancing individual and family quality of life.* Presentation at the 7th International Conference of the Division on Mental Retardation and Developmental Disabilities, Baltimore, MD.

Turnbull, A. P., & Turnbull, H. R., III (1997). *Families, professionals and exceptionality: A special partnership* (3rd ed.). Upper Saddle River, NJ: Merrill.

Turnbull, A. P., Turnbull, H. R., III, Erwin, E. J., & Soodak, L. C. (2006). *Families, professionals, and exceptionality* (5th ed.). Upper Saddle River, NJ: Merrill.

Turnbull, H. R., III, & Turnbull, A. P. (2000). *Free appropriate public education: The law and children with disabilities* (6th ed.). Denver, CO: Love.

Turnbull, H. R., III, Turnbull, A. P., Bronicki, G. J., Summers, J. A., & Roeder-Gordon, C. (1989). *Disability and the family: A guide to decisions for adulthood.* Baltimore, MD: Paul H. Brookes.

Ulrich, M. E., & Bauer, A. M. (2003). Levels of awareness: A closer look at communication between parents and professionals. *Teaching Exceptional Children, 35*(6), 20–23.

Van Meter, P., & Stevens, R. J. (2000). The role of theory in the study of peer collaboration. *Journal of Experimental Education, 69*(1), 113–128.

Vaughn, S., Bos, C. S., Harrell, J. E., & Lasky, B. A. (1988). Parent participation in the initial placement/I.E.P. conference ten years after mandated involvement. *Journal of Learning Disabilities, 21,* 82–89.

Vaughn, S., Bos, C. S., & Schumm, J. S. (2005). *Teaching exceptional, diverse, and at-risk students in the general education classroom: IDEA 2004 Update edition* (3rd ed.). Boston: Allyn & Bacon.

Vaughn, S., & Coleman, M. (2004). The role of mentoring in promoting use of research-based practices in reading. *Remedial and Special Education, 25*(1), 25–38.

Villa, R. A., & Thousand, J. S. (1988). Enhancing success in heterogeneous classrooms and schools: The power of partnership. *Teacher Education and Special Education, 11*(4), 144–154.

Villa, R. A., & Thousand, J. S. (1990). Strategies for educating learners with severe disabilities within their local home schools and communities. *Focus on Exceptional Children, 23,* 1–25.

Villa, R. A., & Thousand, J. S. (1992). How one district integrated special and general education. *Educational Leadership, 50*(2), 39–41.

Villa, R. A., & Thousand, J. S. (Eds.). (2000). *Restructuring for caring and effective education: Piecing the puzzle together* (2nd ed.). Baltimore: Paul H. Brooks.

Villa, R. A., & Thousand, J. S. (2005). *Creating an inclusive school* (2nd ed.). Alexandria, VA: Association for Supervision and Curriculum Development.

Villa, R. A., Thousand, J. S., Nevin, A. I., & Malgeri, C. (1996). Instilling collaboration for inclusive schooling as a way of doing business in the public schools. *Remedial & Special Education, 17*(3), 169–182.

Voltz, D. L., Sims, M. J., Nelson, B., & Bivens, C. (2005). M2ECCA: A framework for inclusion in the context of standards-based reform. *Teaching Exceptional Children, 37*(5), 14–19.

Walsh, B. (1995). *Analysis of collaboration project.* Unpublished manuscript, Buffalo State College.

Walther-Thomas, C., Bryant, M., & Land, S. (1996). Planning for effective co-teaching: The key to successful inclusion. *Remedial and Special Education, 17*(4), 255–265.

Walther-Thomas, C., Korinek, L., & McLaughlin, V. L. (1999). Collaboration to support students' success. *Focus on Exceptional Children, 32*(3), 1–18.

Walther-Thomas, C., Korinek, L., McLaughlin, V. L., & Williams, B. T. (2000). *Collaboration for inclusive education: Developing successful programs.* Boston: Allyn & Bacon.

Warger, C. (2001). *Cultural reciprocity aids collaboration with families.* ERIC Clearinghouse on Disabilities and Gifted Education. (ERIC Document Reproduction Service No. ED457633)

Webb, B. (2004). *Social skill instructions for adolescents with autism/Asperger's disorder.* Paper presented at 9th International CEC Division on Developmental Disabilities Conference, Las Vegas, NV.

Webb, R. B., & Barnash, K. (1997). *Coral Springs Middle School: School climate and school improvement.* Gainesville, FL: University of Florida, College of Education, Research and Development Center for School Improvement.

Weisberg, D. (1995). *Analysis of collaboration project.* Unpublished manuscript, Buffalo State College.

Weiss, M. P., & Lloyd, J. (2002). Congruence between roles and actions of secondary special educators in co-taught and special education settings. *The Journal of Special Education, 36*(2), 56–68.

Weiss, M. P., & Lloyd, J. (2003). Conditions for co-teaching: Lessons from a case study. *Teacher Education and Special Education, 26*(1), 27–41.

Welch, M., & Brownell, K. (2000). The development and evaluation of a multimedia course on educational collaboration. *Journal of Educational Multimedia and Hypermedia, 9*(3), 169–194.

Welch, M., & Brownell, K. (2002). Are professionals ready for educational partnerships? The evaluation of a technology-enhanced course to prepare educators for collaboration. *Teacher Education and Special Education, 25*(2), 133–144.

Welch, M., Brownell, K., & Sheridan, S. M. (1999). What's the score and game plan on teaming in schools? A review of the literature on team teaching and school-based problem-solving teams. *Remedial and Special Education, 20*(1), 36–49.

Welch, M., Judge, T., Anderson, J., Bray, J., Child, B., & Franke, L. (1990). Collaborative options outcome planner: A tool for implementing prereferral consultation. *Teaching Exceptional Children, 22*(2), 30–31.

Welch, M., & Sheridan, S. M. (1995). *Educational partnerships: Serving students at risk.* Fort Worth, TX: Harcourt Brace.

Welch, M., & Sheridan, S. M. (2000). The tele-educational consortium project: Video-mediated staff development for establishing educational partnerships. *Teacher Education and Special Education, 23*(3), 225–240.

Wentworth, N., Earle, R., & Connell, M. L. (Eds.). (2004). *Integrating information technology into the teacher education curriculum: Process and products of change.* New York: Haworth Press.

West, J. F., & Cannon, G. S. (1988). Essential collaborative consultation competencies for regular and special educators. *Journal of Learning Disabilities, 21*(1), 56–63, 28.

West, J. F., & Idol, L. (1987). School consulation (Part 1): An interdisciplinary perspective on theory, models, and research. *Journal of Learning Disabilities, 20*(7), 388–408.

Westling, D. L. (1996). What do parents of children with moderate and severe mental disabilities want? *Education and Training in Mental Retardation and Developmental Disabilities, 31*(2), 86–114.

Westling, D. L., Cooper-Duffy, K., Prohn, K., Ray, M., & Herzog, M. J. (2005). Building a teacher support program. *Teaching Exceptional Children, 37*(5), 8–13.

Wheelan, S. A. (2005). *Faculty groups: From frustration to collaboration.* Thousand Oaks, CA: Corwin Press.

Wheldall, K. (1991). Managing troublesome classroom behaviour in regular schools: A positive teaching perspective. *International Journal of Disability, 38*(2), 99–116.

White, A. E., & White, L. L. (1992). A collaborative model for students with mild disabilities in middle schools. *Focus on Exceptional Children, 24*(9), 1–10.

White, K. R., Taylor, M. J., & Moss, V. D. (1992). Does research support claims about the benefits of involving parents in early intervention programs? *Review of Educational Research, 62*(1), 91–125.

Whitford, B. L., & Metcalf-Turner, P. (1999). Of promises and unresolved puzzles: Reforming teacher education with professional development schools. In G. A. Griffin (Ed.), *The education of teachers: 98th NSSE Yearbook, Part I.* (pp. 257–278). Chicago: NSSE.

Whitten, E., & Rodriguez-Campos, L. (2003). Trends in the special education teaching force: Do they reflect legislative mandates and legal requirements? *Educational Horizons, 81*(3), 138–145.

Wiggam, L. (1992). Expanding the sphere: The importance of effective communications in change. *Educational Technology, 32,* 54–57.

Will, M. C. (1986). Educating children with learning problems: A shared responsibility. *Exceptional Children, 52*(5), 411–415.

Willett, J. B., & Singer, J. D. (1991). From whether to when: New methods for studying student dropout and teacher attrition. *Review of Educational Research, 61*(4), 407–450.

Williams, B. F. (1992). Changing demographics: Challenges for educators. *Intervention in School and clinic, 27*(3), 157–163.

Williams, E. J., Matthews, J., & Baugh, S. (2004). Developing a mentoring internship model for school leadership: Using legitimate peripheral participation. *Mentoring and Tutoring, 12*(1), 53–70.

Wilmshurst, L., & Brue, A.W. (2005). *A parent's guide to special education.* New York: AMACOM.

Wilson, M. (1993). The search for teacher leaders. *Educational Leadership, 50*(6), 24–27.

Wiseman, D. L., & Knight, S. L. (Eds.). (2003). *Linking school-university collaboration and K–12 student outcomes.* Washington, DC: AACTE.

Woolfolk, A. E., & Hoy, W. K. (1990). Prospective teachers' sense of efficacy and beliefs about control. *Journal of Educational Psychology, 82*(1), 81–91.

Yell, M. L. (1992). School reform and special education: A legal analysis. *Preventing School Failure, 36*(4), 25–28.

York-Barr, J., & Duke, K. (2004). What do we know about teacher leadership? Findings from two decades of research. *Review of Educational Research, 74*(3), 255–316.

York-Barr, J., & Kronberg, R. (2002). From isolation to collaboration: Learning from effective partnerships between general and special educators. In W. Sailor (Ed.), *Whole-school success and inclusive education: Building partnerships for learning, achievement and accountability* (pp. 163–181). New York: Teachers College Press.

Young, J. P., Alvermann, D., Kaste, J., Henderson, S., & Many, J. (2004). Being a friend and a mentor at the same time: A pooled case comparison. *Mentoring and Tutoring, 12*(1), 23–36.

Zahorik, J. A. (1987). Teachers' collegial interaction: An exploratory study. *The Elementary School Journal, 87*(4), 385–396.

Zakes, K. (1996). *Analysis of collaboration project.* Unpublished manuscript, Buffalo State College.

Zelaieta, P. (2004). From confusion to collaboration. In F. Armstrong & M. Moore (Eds.), *Action research for inclusive education: Changing places, changing practice, changing minds* (pp. 32–47). New York: RoutledgeFalmer.

Zetlin, A. G., Padron, A., & Wilson, S. (1996). The experience of five Latin American families with the special education system. *Education and Training in Mental Retardation and Developmental Disabilities, 31*(1), 22–28.

Index

**CORWIN
PRESS**

The Corwin Press logo—a raven striding across an open book—represents the union of courage and learning. Corwin Press is committed to improving education for all learners by publishing books and other professional development resources for those serving the field of PreK–12 education. By providing practical, hands-on materials, Corwin Press continues to carry out the promise of its motto: **"Helping Educators Do Their Work Better."**